John Zinkin
The Challenge of Sustainability

The Alexandra Lajoux Corporate Governance Series

Edited by
Alexandra Reed Lajoux

John Zinkin

The Challenge of Sustainability

Corporate Governance in a Complicated World

DE GRUYTER

ISBN 978-3-11-067040-0
e-ISBN (PDF) 978-3-11-067048-6
e-ISBN (EPUB) 978-3-11-067060-8
ISSN 2629-8155

Library of Congress Control Number: 2020936594

Bibliographic information published by the Deutsche Nationalbibliothek
The Deutsche Nationalbibliothek lists this publication in the Deutsche Nationalbibliografie;
detailed bibliographic data are available on the Internet at http://dnb.dnb.de.

© 2020 Walter de Gruyter GmbH Berlin/Boston
Typesetting: Integra Software Services Pvt. Ltd.
Printing and binding: CPI books GmbH, Leck

www.degruyter.com

Praise for *The Challenge of Sustainability*

John Zinkin has written a book which will enable board members to see the big picture, and drive them toward developing a long-term sustainable model for their businesses rather than a short-term profit maximizing model. Full of useful information and arguments, this book belongs on every company director's shelf.

Edward Clayton, partner, leader of PwC Strategy&, Malaysia/Vietnam

Capitalism as we have known it for the past forty years is now failing more than ever to allocate the results of growth fairly. The demands of short-term shareholders are often clashing with the long-term needs of an increasingly diverse and vocal group of stakeholders who want risks and opportunities related to environmental, economic, and social sustainability to be taken seriously.

As we enter the third decade of the 21st century, increased levels of volatility, uncertainty, complexity and ambiguity faced by companies make the job of Boards more complex than ever before. Often, Board members are ill-equipped, unable or unwilling to recognize these complexities and may oversimplify matters in order to come to grips with the issues in the time available. This book offers a clear and analytical situation analysis focusing on accurately defining the problem at hand. Furthermore, it provides valuable and comprehensive solution models. It is definitely a book that I want to keep in my small library of selected reference readings to check if you are on the right track.

Roberto Benetello, Executive Director, BCSD Malaysia

The Challenge of Sustainability is an important and timely work. The book is a journey beginning with a well-argued case that western style capitalism is at a crossroads. The thrust of Milton Friedman's argument privileging shareholders above all other stakeholders, has driven a wedge between the interests of shareholders and managers and the rest of society. At the same time, globalization and structural changes in global society are creating challenges of uncertainty. Zinkin provides explicit guidance to members of corporate boards on how to approach their responsibilities in regard to social needs. For anyone interested in the role of corporations in thriving healthy societies, they now have a roadmap to follow.

Dr Gary Dirks, Senior Director, Global Futures Laboratory and Director,
LightWorks, Arizona State University

John Zinkin's *The Challenge of Sustainability* is a provocative and stimulating book. Directors and managers of all companies should read and consult the book on a regular basis as a standard source of reference. This is probably the

https://doi.org/10.1515/9783110670486-202

first book that deals with the subjects of CG and sustainability treating the two subjects in a comprehensive and integrated manner. The case made in the book is a compelling one – that if the returns a company generates on its investment are to be earned on a sustained basis, it has to ensure that its activities do not adversely affect the environment within which it operates and simultaneously it has to take care of the interests of all its stakeholders, namely of its customers, employees, community and not just of its stockholders.

Dr R. Thillainathan, Chairman of the Audit Committee, Allianz Malaysia Berhad; board member of The Institute for Democracy and Economic Affairs; member of the board of directors, University Malaya

Acknowledgments

I would like to thank Dr Gary Dirks for the discussions on energy alternatives to fossil fuels and their feasibility in sustaining the environment; discussions that we have had over the years since 1997 when John Browne, then CEO of BP, gave his revolutionary speech at Stanford University on the need to take climate change seriously. I would also like to thank Chris Bennett for helping me appreciate the importance of context and complexity in decision-making – a theme which runs throughout the book – and which is often overlooked in board deliberations. Dr Thillainathan, Edward Clayton, and Roberto Benetello helped me greatly in ensuring that what I proposed is both relevant and practical, based respectively on their experiences as an experienced board director of long standing, a senior management consulting partner, and an expert in sustainability. If I have misunderstood or misrepresented their views, the fault is entirely mine.

I would like to thank Jeff Pepper, my excellent editor, for challenging my assumptions robustly and constructively, giving me an invaluable insight into American attitudes and beliefs about sustainability, and how they can differ from those in Europe. I would also like to thank him for improving my writing, helping me to keep complex subjects simple, but without oversimplifying the issues involved. I am grateful to Mary Sudul, my copy editor, whose meticulous attention to detail and care in improving the text makes the book all the better. I would like to thank Jaya Dalal for her excellent coordination of production, as usual, and André Horn for final production.

Last and most important of all, I must thank my wonderful wife, Lisa, who let me work on this book when we were on holiday travelling in Europe, without whose support, this book would not have been possible.

https://doi.org/10.1515/9783110670486-203

About the Author

John Zinkin has written four books on corporate governance: *Better Governance Across the Board: Creating Value Through Reputation, People, and Processes*, published by Walter de Gruyter in 2019, *Rebuilding Trust in Banks: The Role of Leadership and Governance*, published by John Wiley & Sons in 2014; *Challenges in Implementing Corporate Governance: Whose Business Is It Anyway?*, published by John Wiley & Sons in 2010; and co-authored *Corporate Governance*, published by John Wiley & Sons in 2005. He wrote the *FIDE Good Governance Handbook* (2013), designed specifically for Malaysian banks and insurance companies, under the auspices of Bank Negara Malaysia. He is a faculty member of the Institute of Corporate Directors Malaysia and Securities Industry Development Corporation. He has contributed a chapter on "Corporate Governance in Asia Pacific" and another chapter on "Corporate Governance in an Age of Populism" for the *Handbook on Corporate Governance*, 2nd edition, edited by Professor Richard Leblanc published by John Wiley & Sons in 2020.

John was a member of the Malaysian working party in 1999 and was involved in the launch of the Malaysian Code on Corporate Governance in 2000. He was a member of the working party that drew up the Malaysian Corporate Governance Blueprint in 2011 and the revised Malaysian Code on Corporate Governance in 2012.

He speaks regularly on leadership and governance and used to write fortnightly for *The Star* newspaper on governance-related topics (2007–2013). He was voted "Writer of the Year" on CG matters in 2014 by the Minority Shareholders Watchdog Group. His other specialties are "Leading Brand-Based Change," "Reconciling Leadership and Governance" and "Ethics in Business." He has led board effectiveness evaluations in banking, insurance and government entities and has written codes of conduct and board charters for several development banks. He is a certified training professional who has done extensive training in CG, branding and leadership. Since 2007, he has trained more than 1,500 directors in CG as well as senior managers of public listed companies. He has trained securities regulators from Cambodia, Hong Kong, Laos, Malaysia, Philippines, Singapore, Thailand and Vietnam on behalf of the Securities Commission Malaysia and the Australian Government as part of their CG capacity building programs in ASEAN and APEC.

During his career, starting in 1971, John worked in the UK in fast-moving consumer goods (Unilever), insurance brokering (Hogg Robinson), management consulting (McKinsey), and office products (Rank Xerox) before moving to Hong Kong in 1985 for Inchcape Pacific. There John ran marketing and distribution companies in a variety of industries across the Asia Pacific, before joining Burson-Marsteller in 1997 as the Asia-Pacific Marketing and Change Management Practice Chair where he became interested in CG as a result of client work. John moved to Malaysia in 2001 and from 2001 to 2006, was Associate Professor of Marketing and Strategy at Nottingham University Business School, Malaysia Campus, responsible for its MBA program. In 2006 he was asked to set up the Securities Industry Development Corporation, the capital markets training arm of the Securities Commission Malaysia and in 2011 he was

https://doi.org/10.1515/9783110670486-204

appointed Managing Director, Corporate Governance of the Iclif Leadership and Governance Centre under the aegis of Bank Negara Malaysia, responsible for training directors of banks and insurance companies in CG. Since 2013, he works independently as the Managing Director of Zinkin Ettinger Sendirian Berhad, a boutique consultancy specializing in CG, brand-based change and ethical leadership.

John is married to a Malaysian. He has Malaysian permanent residency and was awarded a Federal Datukship in 2013 for services to Malaysia. John graduated from Oxford University with a BA in Politics, Philosophy and Economics (1968) and the London Business School with an MSc in Business Administration (1971).

About the Series Editor

Alexandra Reed Lajoux is Series Editor for Walter De Gruyter, Inc. The series has an emphasis on governance, corporate leadership, and sustainability. Dr. Lajoux is chief knowledge officer emeritus (CKO) at the National Association of Corporate Directors (NACD) and founding principal of Capital Expert Services, LLC (CapEx), a global consultancy providing expert witnesses for legal cases. She coauthored *Making Money: The History and Future of Society's Most Important Technology* with Peet van Biljon (Walter de Gruyter, 2020). She has served as editor of *Directors & Boards, Mergers & Acquisitions, Export Today,* and *Director's Monthly,* and has coauthored a series of books on M&A for McGraw-Hill, including *The Art of M&A* and eight spin-off titles on strategy, valuation, financing, structuring, due diligence, integration, bank M&A, and distressed M&A. For Bloomberg/Wiley, she coauthored *Corporate Valuation for Portfolio Investment* with Robert A. G. Monks. Dr. Lajoux serves on the advisory board of Campaigns and Elections, and is a Fellow of the Caux Round Table for Moral Capitalism. She holds a B.A. from Bennington College, a Ph.D. from Princeton University, and an M.B.A. from Loyola University in Maryland. She is an associate member of the American Bar Association.

https://doi.org/10.1515/9783110670486-205

Introduction

As I finished writing *Better Governance Across the Board: Creating Value Through Reputation, People and Processes*, published in May 2019, designed as a guide on how boards could fulfill their responsibilities as fiduciaries better, I realized I had not really dealt with the sustainability problems boards face. These are major challenges to environmental, economic, employment, and social sustainability and their impact on the long-term viability of organizations.

I realized if boards were to meet these four sustainability challenges, governments, academia, communities, investors, and businesses would have to work together. In particular, businesses would have to find new ways of using corporate governance to achieve environmental, economic, employment, and social sustainability. Only in this manner could businesses become part of the solution rather than denying the need for change and continuing to be part of the problem through their efforts, lobbying or otherwise, to retain the status quo.

I believe failure to achieve sustainability in any one of the four areas is likely to lead to turmoil, bringing on significant changes in capitalism as we know it. The result could be what I refer to throughout this book as a "political tragedy of the commons"[i]; as the journey to change through unrest may be difficult to navigate. This seems to me to be possible, given the already high levels of discontent with the current economic system in many developed economies caused by globalization, rising inequality, and the devastating impact on the middle class of the 2008 global financial crisis. Populist politicians have capitalized on the resulting disaffection in the US, UK and the EU. Social media has vented grievances and helped polarize political discourse so that we could face a rerun of the 1930s, if we do not find a way of averting the social and "political tragedy of the commons."

Such a social and "political tragedy of the commons" could be precipitated by the unexpected global health and economic crisis caused by the Covid-19 pandemic. This has laid bare some of the flaws of the current economic system. First, the excessive emphasis on maximizing efficiency through complex and tightly coupled global supply chains that proved extremely fragile. Companies and countries will have to move away from "just-in-time" thinking if they are to

---

i A "political tragedy of the commons" occurs when actions which are individually sensible are harmful to communities if everyone takes the same action at the same time. For example, it may make excellent sense for one company to lay off 30% of its workforce because of AI; but if all companies lay off 30%, the resulting disemployment and fall in consumption will create social and economic havoc, potentially leading to revolution.

https://doi.org/10.1515/9783110670486-206

build resilience into their supply chains. Second, the underinvestment in public health systems everywhere will need to be corrected to prevent future pandemics from overwhelming hospital frontlines and creating economic crises. Third, the pandemic has highlighted the need for government intervention and will change the role of governments and how we live and work in ways that will take time to get right. Fourth, it may help governments realize that global problems require global solutions and that global solutions can only be implemented by global institutions. Regardless of the pandemic's impact, I believe three things must change in the way businesses are governed if a rerun of the 1930s is to be averted.

First, boards need to spend much more time and energy discussing the impact of environmental, economic, employment, and social sustainability on their organizations. In a 2014 survey of 3,800 senior managers, 65% of the companies identified sustainability as a management agenda item, but only 22% of the interviewed senior executives believed their own boards were actually providing substantial oversight on sustainability issues.[1] This is in large part because insufficient time is devoted to sustainability and how it affects every part of the value chain. It is also because boards do not have the right tools to measure the impact and costs of unsustainable behavior and often do not appreciate complicated reality, relying instead on executive summaries which simplify issues that are really complicated. There is a reason why we have the saying "The devil is in the details." It is the truth and it applies to sustainability.

Second, boards must find a way to reconcile the needs of stakeholders and not just shareholders. The pendulum has begun to swing away from shareholder value maximization of the previous thirty years towards stakeholder capitalism, culminating in the August 2019 US Business Roundtable Declaration replacing shareholders with stakeholders; recognizing that profits are a result rather than the purpose of business.[2] Maybe Milton Friedman's worldview has finally been jettisoned.[3] For this momentous change in outlook to mean something quantifiable, company law will have to change and boards will have to be explicit about the priorities they attach to different stakeholders. My hope is that boards will rediscover Peter Drucker's view that

> *The customer is the foundation of a business and keeps it in existence.* He alone gives employment. And it is to supply the consumer that society entrusts wealth-producing resources to the business enterprise.[4]   [Emphasis mine]

Third, once boards take the time needed to understand the likely impacts on their organizations of imminent sustainability challenges, they will also need to appreciate the social impact of collective decisions that may make sense for their organizations individually, when undertaken simultaneously. What makes sense for one organization may be absolutely the wrong thing to do; if all companies do the same thing at the same time, as has been amply demonstrated by the impact of the Covid-19 pandemic. Yet the fiduciary duty of directors only requires boards to do what is in the best interests of shareholders, without considering the broader consequences of everybody else doing the same thing at the same time. This is the source of complication, usually ignored by boards; not surprisingly, given their duty as fiduciaries in company law is only to shareholders; and they have no way of measuring the costs of externalities and putting them on the P&L.

As the title *The Challenge of Sustainability: Corporate Governance in a Complicated World* suggests, I:

1. Explore how corporate governance has changed over the past thirty years.
2. Discuss the challenge boards face when considering environmental, economic, employment, and social sustainability.
3. Suggest a number of ways boards could use corporate governance to achieve greater sustainability.

The book is presented in three parts.

Part 1: "Expanding Corporate Governance's Remit"

Part 1 covers the development of corporate governance and its development in the Anglo-Saxon capitalist world. Anglo-Saxon capitalism's focus between 1990 and 2008 moved gradually from maximizing shareholder value to beginning to consider the needs of stakeholders, evidenced by the rise of corporate social responsibility (CSR) in the 1990s. The global financial crisis (GFC) of 2008 and the resulting economic and political dislocations that followed led to questioning the role of capitalism in twenty-first-century society.

Chapter 1, "Corporate Governance – An Evolving Idea in Challenging Times," reviews the evolution of CG over time; the challenge to CG posed by the dissatisfaction with the current economic order; and the need for CG to evolve further, if it is to reduce this discontent.

Chapter 2, "No One Single Approach to Corporate Governance," explains why there can be no one single correct approach to CG because it reflects the development histories of countries and their complicated underlying capital market structures resulting in five different CG approaches.

Part 2: "Corporate Governance's Five Sustainability Challenges"

Part 2 deals with the five sustainability challenges to CG that have arisen since 2000 as a result of increased awareness of environmental issues and climate change; the retreat from full-bore globalization as result of political change; the impending disruption of "Industry 4.0"; and the rise of the internet and social media. As a result, CG's remit has broadened to one of ensuring long-term success and sustainability of organizations – a much more complicated and challenging responsibility for boards and directors, for which they may not be well-prepared.

Chapter 3, "Environmental Sustainability," deals with three increasingly urgent challenges to environmental sustainability: climate change, moving to a circular economy, and conservation.

Chapter 4, "Economic Sustainability," deals with two social issues challenging the sustainability of neoliberal capitalism: the importance of growth being inclusive, and reducing rising inequality so that everybody can benefit, not just the few.

Chapter 5, "Employment Sustainability," deals with the challenges for boards created by the impact of disruptive technologies on employment and employability, and whether education systems provide what is needed.

Chapter 6, "Social Sustainability," explores issues and challenges for boards when considering how they can contribute by being responsible citizens, and bridging cultures.

Chapter 7, "Volatility and Uncertainty," deals with the challenges posed by volatility and uncertainty on board decision-making.

Chapter 8, "Complexity and Ambiguity," deals with the challenges posed by complexity and ambiguity on board decision-making.

Part 3: "Achieving Sustainability in a Complicated World"

Part 3 consists of four chapters with suggestions for boards on how best to meet the challenges of environmental, economic, employment and social sustainability in a complicated world.

Chapter 9, "Adopting a Proactive Approach to VUCA," combines volatility with vision, using the "Five P" framework; uncertainty with understanding; complexity with courage and commitment; and ambiguity with adaptability to suggest a new and better way of making decisions.

Chapter 10, "Adopting New Processes," introduces suggestions for additional processes boards could consider to improve their ability to meet the challenges of environmental, economic, employment and social sustainability.

Chapter 11, "Valuing People Properly," challenges the underlying assumptions boards have about how to treat people and suggests sustainable ways of investing in people.

Chapter 12, "Making Capitalism Sustainable," makes the case for an urgent need for reform of capitalism, arguing for an end to "predatory value extraction," and emphasizes the importance of companies embracing a sustainable purpose.

References

1 Kiron, D. et al. (2015), "Joining forces: Collaboration and leadership for sustainability," *MIT Sloan Management Review,* 56 (3), pp. 1–31, retrieved from https://sloanreview.mit.edu/proj ects/joining-forces/ cited in "The state of corporate governance in the era of sustainability risk and opportunities, *WBCSD,* 2019, p. 27, https://docs.wbcsd.org/2019/03/WBCSD-The_state_of_ corporate_governance_in_the_era_of_sustainability_risks_and_opportunities.pdf, accessed on January 30, 2020.

2 Business Roundtable (2019), "Business Roundtable Redefines the Purpose of a Corporation to Promote 'An Economy that Serves All Americans'," August 19, 2019, https://www.business roundtable.org/business-roundtable-redefines-the-purpose-of-a-corporation-to-promote-an-economy-that-serves-all-americans accessed on January 30, 2020.

3 Orszag, P. (2020), "Milton Friedman's World Is Dead and Gone," *Bloomberg Opinion,* January 29, 2020, https://www.bloomberg.com/opinion/articles/2020-01-29/tell-davos-that -milton-friedman-s-world-is-dead-and-gone?utm_medium=email&utm_source=n accessed on February 3, 2020.

4 Drucker, P. (1955), *The Practice of Management* (Oxford: Butterworth Heinemann), p. 35.

Contents

Part 1: Expanding Corporate Governance's Remit

Part 2: **Corporate Governance's Five Sustainability Challenges**

Part 3: **Achieving Sustainability in a Complicated World**

Part 1: **Expanding Corporate Governance's Remit**

I should begin by declaring that I am a committed capitalist and strong believer in democratic freedom, despite the flaws in both. The flaws that have surfaced in the last forty years in the capitalist system have created grievances in developed economies; grievances highlighted by populists of both the left and the right to their political advantage; but without providing effective solutions. This has created acrimony and division in public discourse, making necessary compromises on finding solutions to environmental, economic, employment and social sustainability more difficult.

I am not alone in believing that reforming the current capitalist system is necessary if these grievances are to be effectively dealt with and that failure to do so may lead to authoritarian governments of either the right or the left. However, I believe that reforming the system also requires changing corporate governance so that businesses can become part of the solution rather than being part of the problem.

Capitalism's focus between 1990 and 2008 moved gradually from maximizing only shareholder value to beginning to consider the needs of stakeholders, evidenced by the rise of corporate social responsibility (CSR) in the 1990s. The global financial crisis (GFC) of 2008 and the resulting economic and political dislocations that followed have in part led to re-evaluation of the role of capitalism in 21st century society.

Chapter 1
Corporate Governance – An Evolving Idea in Challenging Times

This chapter is presented in three parts. The first describes corporate governance's evolution over the past thirty years; the second introduces the challenge posed to corporate governance by the dissatisfaction with the current economic order and asks what more it needs to do to meet the challenges posed by populism; the third closes with a summary of the discussion.

Corporate Governance – An Evolving Idea

Corporate Governance, or CG, is a relatively recent idea,[1] though the principles on which it is based are as old as humanity's invention of organizations – people coming together to achieve a common purpose. It has only existed since the early 1990s. Its original remit was very narrow – focusing on legal and audit concerns of regulators and investors, as a result of the Polly Peck[2] and Robert Maxwell[3] corporate scandals in the UK.

The Purpose of CG

Originally CG was designed to achieve two things. The first was to provide a system of checks and balances to prevent CEOs and management from abusing the trust investors placed in them when they invested their money to build successful businesses. This was to deal with the so-called "principal-agent" problem where investors (principals) entrusted their money to managers (agents) in the hope they would build sustainable businesses with a good rate of return on their investments. The second was to create transparency through insisting on formal structure and process in board decision making, thereby allowing regulators and investors to understand why and how such decisions had been made in the event things went wrong.

This was a reaction to the behavior of managers during what Peter Drucker termed "managerial capitalism" from the late 1940s until the early 1970s. Investors came to realize management had their own agendas, abusing the trust placed in them in order to build their own empires, guaranteeing themselves status and job

https://doi.org/10.1515/9783110670486-001

security at the expense of shareholders.[4] By insisting on formal checks and balances on the authority of management through the use of audit committees, investors were able to tilt the balance of power back toward shareholders. However, the pendulum swung too far in favor of short-term satisfaction of shareholder needs, as a result of Milton Friedman's claim that the purpose of business was "to maximize shareholder value."[5]

In reaction to the resulting excesses of shareholder capitalism with its focus on short-term profit maximization, there was a gradual recognition of the need to build into the system of checks and balances the idea that long-term value creation mattered. This became the third reason for CG: to help boards and management focus on long-term sustainability, as opposed to only maximizing short-term shareholder value. This led to a change in emphasis from "shareholder capitalism," focusing almost uniquely on total shareholder returns (TSR) to "stakeholder capitalism" as the 21st century began.

The Transition Toward Stakeholder Capitalism

Seen from a purely legal perspective, shareholder primacy is defended because it is deemed capable of dealing with complexity, to be legally efficacious and efficient, though its supporters admit it may not be socially efficient, equitable, or ethical.[6] In its purest form, it places severe constraints on what boards should consider, evidenced by the following judgments in the Delaware Chancery Court:

> [A] clear-eyed look at the law of corporations in Delaware reveals that, within the limits of their discretion, *directors must make stockholder welfare their sole end, and that other interests may be taken into consideration only as a means of promoting stockholder welfare.*[7]
> [Emphasis mine]

> Having chosen a for-profit corporate form . . . directors are bound by the fiduciary duties and standards that accompany that form. Those standards include acting to promote the value of the corporation for the benefit of the stockholders. The "Inc." after the company name has to mean at least that. *Thus, I cannot accept as valid . . . a corporate policy that specifically, clearly and admittedly seeks not to maximize the economic value of a for-profit Delaware corporation for the benefit of its stockholders. . .*[8]   [Emphasis mine]

The Delaware judgments are perhaps the most restrictive in terms of their focus on benefitting shareholders. There is a less restrictive perspective which makes the case that the law does *not* require shareholder value maximization to be achieved by ignoring externalities. Rather it is the belief within boards that this is what the law demands and the resulting incentives and management remuneration that drive corporations to focus excessively on short-term profitability:

> While company law in some jurisdictions adheres to shareholder value (the legal concept, which we distinguish from the social norm of shareholder primacy), the underlying rationale for facilitating the corporate form through legislation is always that it is thought to be beneficial for society through its contribution to economic development. *No company law system insists on boards focusing only on returns for shareholders. We see shareholder value jurisdictions, like the UK, expressly stipulating that broader societal concerns, including environmental protection, should be taken into account. Generally, company law across jurisdictions allows boards to integrate environmental and social externalities beyond legal compliance, at least as far as the business case argument goes.*
>
> However, boards generally do not opt for corporate sustainability within the realm of the business case, let alone challenge the outer boundaries of the scope to pursue profit in a sustainable manner by going beyond the business case. *Shareholder primacy, supported by management remuneration incentives and other drivers, dictates that boards and senior managers are the 'agents' of the shareholders, and should maximize returns to shareholders as measured by the current share price. This leads to an extremely narrow, short-term, profit maximization focus.*
>
> The resulting general practice of companies is detrimental to those affected by climate change, environmental degradation and human rights violations today, and to the possibility for future generations to fulfil their own needs. *It is also damaging to the interests of shareholders with more than a very short-term perspective on their investment, including institutional investors such as pension funds or sovereign wealth funds, as well as companies themselves.*[9]　　　　　　　　　　　　　　　　　　　　　[Emphases mine]

There is a way of reconciling the constraints of the law with its emphasis on shareholder primacy and the need to consider the wider needs of society:

> Importantly, in addressing issues often framed as matters of corporate social responsibility, the *shareholder primacy path does not preclude a for-profit company from taking social issues into account in the conduct of its business.* What is required to stay on the path is that the company's consideration of those social issues have a sufficient nexus to shareholder welfare and value maximization.[10]　　　　　　　　　　　　　[Emphasis mine]

The beginning of this transition toward "stakeholder capitalism" can be seen in the definition of CG in the 1992 Cadbury report – the first formal attempt to codify CG best practice, with still a rather narrow area of authority that looked only at rules, procedures, and processes within the company:

> Governance is a *system of rules, procedures and processes* by which a company is directed and controlled. Specifically, *it is a framework* by which various stakeholder interests are balanced and efficiently and professionally managed.[11]　　　　　　　　　[Emphases mine]

By 2015 there was further movement toward recognizing the importance of stakeholders in the OECD's definition of CG – from CG merely being a *framework* linking decisions to stakeholder interests to a *relationship between the key players in the business and its stakeholders*:

> Corporate Governance *involves a set of relationships between a company's management, its board, its shareholders and other stakeholders.* Corporate Governance also *provides the structure through which the objectives of the company are set,* and the means of attaining those objectives and monitoring performance are determined.[12]   [Emphases mine]

By 2017, the definition of CG and its guidelines were broadened considerably, as a result of the global financial crisis (GFC); by introducing an additional responsibility for ethical behavior (as opposed to merely legal behavior) and a much more specific and wider definition of stakeholders:

> Corporate governance is defined as the *process and structure* used to direct and manage the business and affairs of the company towards promoting business prosperity and corporate accountability with the ultimate objective of realising long-term shareholder value while [considering] the interest of other stakeholders.
>
> Corporate governance provides a *framework of control mechanisms* that support the company in achieving its goals, while preventing unwanted conflicts. *The pillars of corporate governance such as ethical behaviour, accountability, transparency and sustainability are important to the governance of companies and stewardship of investors' capital.* Companies that embrace these principles are more likely to produce long-term value than those that are lacking in one or all.
>
> Proper governance identifies the distribution of rights and responsibilities among different participants in the company and outlines among others the rules and procedures for decision-making, internal control and risk management. *Corporate governance is not only concerned with shareholder interests but requires balancing the needs of other stakeholders such as employees, customers, suppliers, society and the communities in which the companies conduct their business.*[13]   [Emphases mine]

This third definition of CG broadened the areas of responsibility and accountability of directors to include long-term outcomes and the needs of other stakeholders, going further than just focusing on the needs of shareholders. It finally reflects the transition from shareholder capitalism of the 1980s and 1990s to stakeholder capitalism in the 21st century and introduces the concept of stewardship (i.e., that boards are expected to leave the company in a better state than they found it).

The common features of the three approaches are the system of rules, procedures, and processes boards are expected to adopt and the existence of a structure by which policies are set, implemented, and assessed. The third definition builds on the two earlier ones to provide increased focus on the future; on the explicit distribution of rights and responsibilities between the key players in the organization; on ethics, transparency, and sustainability; and on a much broader definition of stakeholders whose requirements need to be reconciled.

No "One Size Fits All"

The two earlier definitions were accepted worldwide and served their purpose well. After all, the Cadbury Committee Report was the foundation document for regulatory approaches to CG; and the OECD Principles of CG were the reference document for regulators in IOSCO.[i] Limited reference was made to stakeholders, reflecting the 20th century emphasis on shareholders. They also seemed to assume CG frameworks could be applied universally without too much difficulty. As jurisdictions began to take CG seriously, they discovered applying the principles of CG proved to be more challenging than expected. As a result, the OECD redefined CG in 2015, recognizing "one size does not fit all":

> Effective corporate governance requires a sound legal, regulatory and institutional framework that market participants can rely on when they establish their private contractual relations. This corporate governance framework typically comprises *elements of legislation, regulation, self-regulatory arrangements, voluntary commitments and business practices that are the result of a country's specific circumstances, history and tradition.* The desirable mix between legislation, regulation, self-regulation, voluntary standards, etc., will therefore vary from country to country. The legislative and regulatory elements of the corporate governance framework can usefully be complemented by soft law elements based on the "comply or explain" principle such as corporate governance codes in order to allow for flexibility and address specificities of individual companies. *What works well in one company, for one investor or a particular stakeholder may not necessarily be generally applicable to corporations, investors and stakeholders that operate in another context and under different circumstances.*[14]　　　　　　　　　　　　　　　　　　[Emphases mine]

The GFC highlighted the need to include ethics as an element of good CG, and other failures raised questions about what should be done about pension funds. I therefore like the following definition of CG which recognizes the diversity of jurisdictions; articulates the need to take into account ethics and long-term stakeholder expectations; and includes recognizing the rights of workers, past, present, and future:

> *Different countries have different ideas as to what constitutes good corporate governance.*[ii]
> . . . In essence we believe that good corporate governance consists of a system of structuring, operating and controlling a company such as to achieve the following:

---

i IOSCO stands for the International Organization of Securities Commissions.
ii Belinda Gibson formerly of ASIC, the Australian regulator, is reported to have said, "the role of a regulator is to match the risk appetite of the society where they regulate," in email correspondence between the author and Chris Bennett on October 6, 2018.

- a culture based on a foundation of sound business ethics fulfilling the long-term strategic goal of the owners while taking into account the expectations of all the key stakeholders, and in particular:
    - *consider and care for the interests of employees, past, present and future*
    - work to maintain excellent relations with both customers and suppliers
    - *take account of the needs of the environment and the local community*
    - maintaining proper compliance with all the applicable legal and regulatory requirements under which the company is carrying out its activities.[15]

[Emphases mine]

Partial Recognition of the Challenge

The rise of populism in the last twenty years presents a challenge to neoliberal economic orthodoxy, defined as follows:

Neoliberalism sees competition as the defining characteristic of human relations. It redefines citizens as consumers, whose democratic choices are best exercised by buying and selling, a process that rewards merit and punishes inefficiency. It maintains that "the market" delivers benefits that could never be achieved by planning.

Attempts to limit competition are treated as inimical to liberty. Tax and regulation should be minimised, public services should be privatised. The organisation of labour and collective bargaining by trade unions are portrayed as market distortions that impede the formation of a natural hierarchy of winners and losers. Inequality is recast as virtuous: a reward for utility and a generator of wealth, which trickles down to enrich everyone. Efforts to create a more equal society are both counterproductive and morally corrosive. The market ensures that everyone gets what they deserve.[16]

It may be helpful to define what I mean by populism, since the term is used by different writers to mean different things:

The distinctive trait of populism is that it claims to represent and speak for "the people," which is assumed to be unified by a common interest. This common interest, the "popular will," is in turn set against minorities and foreigners (in the case of right-wing populists) or financial elites (in the case of left-wing populists).

Since they claim to represent "the people" at large, populists abhor restraints on the political executive. They see limits on their exercise of power as necessarily undermining the popular will.

In politics this is a dangerous approach that allows a majority to ride roughshod over the rights of those in the minority. Without separation of powers, an independent judiciary, or free media – institutions which all populist autocrats detest – democracy degenerates into the tyranny of those who happen to be currently in power. Elections become a sham: in the absence of the rule of law and basic civil liberties, populist regimes can prolong their regimes by manipulating the media and judiciary at will.[17]

Perhaps the best explanation for the potential for difficult and unexpected interactions between populist agendas and directing an individual enterprise is the following:

> "*Corporate governance – the authority structure of a firm – lies at the heart of the most important issues of society*". . . such as "who has claim to the cash flow of the firm, who has a say in its strategy and its allocation of resources." The corporate governance framework shapes corporate efficiency, employment stability, retirement security, and the endowments of orphanages, hospitals, and universities. "It creates the temptations for cheating and the rewards for honesty, inside the firm and more generally in the body politic." It "*influences social mobility, stability and fluidity . . . It is no wonder then, that corporate governance provokes conflict. Anything so important will be fought over . . . like other decisions about authority, corporate governance structures are fundamentally the result of political decisions*".[18]   [Emphases mine]

This is a partial response to the changes in the political economy and the resulting populist challenge. Boards are now required to consider externalities they ignored when only considering the narrow financial and legal aspects affecting publicly listed enterprises.

Apart from climate change, pollution, congestion, corruption, and tax avoidance where we are "all in it together" whether we like or not, there is also a crisis of trust in institutions created by the failure of the neoliberal elite to appreciate the pain of "citizens of somewhere," alienated by the policies of "citizens of nowhere," articulated forcefully by Theresa May, then British Prime Minister, at the Conservative Party Conference in October 2016:

> Now don't get me wrong. We applaud success. We want people to get on. But we also value something else: the spirit of citizenship. That spirit that means you respect the bonds and obligations that make our society work. That means a commitment to the men and women who live around you, who work for you, who buy the goods and services you sell. That spirit that means recognising the social contract that says you train up local young people before you take on cheap labour from overseas. That spirit that means you do as others do and pay your fair share of tax.
>
> *But today, too many people in positions of power behave as though they have more in common with international elites than with the people down the road, the people they employ, the people they pass in the street. But if you believe you are a citizen of the world, you're a citizen of nowhere. You don't understand what the very word "citizenship" means.*
>
> So if you're a boss who earns a fortune but doesn't look after your staff . . . An international company that treats tax laws as an optional extra . . . A household name that refuses to work with the authorities even to fight terrorism . . . A director who takes out massive dividends while knowing that the company pension is about to go bust . . . I'm putting you on warning. This can't go on anymore.[19]   [Emphasis mine]

Failure to deal with this pain and resentment and its populist reaction undermine the liberty we take for granted and could put free-market capitalism and democracy at risk. In the words of Geoffrey Garrett, Dean of Wharton School of Business (University of Pennsylvania):

> I am increasingly convinced of three things:
>
> First, the populist outrage expressed toward all elite institutions (governments, corporations, universities) is not a top-down case of charismatic leaders inflaming a rudderless society. Rather, *today's populist leaders are the product of profound societal dissatisfaction with an elite-driven political economy.*
>
> Second, *the rise of populism is at its core an economic phenomenon – with enormous social and political consequences – driven above all by the deteriorating economic situation of the middle class.*
>
> Third, *there is negativity toward "the system" including democracy itself.* The deep potential support base for populist leaders who want to blow it up – not reform it through the established push and pull of democratic politics – is highest among millennials. *We used to think of young adults as being the most idealistic and committed to democracy. No longer.*[20]   [Emphases mine]

Yet dealing with this pain and resentment presents boards with a serious dilemma. On the one hand, they are expected by the tenets of Milton Friedman[21] and shareholders to do what is in the best interests of the organization on whose board they sit, with little regard for the cost of the externalities they create for society;[iii] while on the other hand, such behavior creates resentment in the general public and leads politicians like Theresa May and others to threaten them because, in her words, they do not understand what "citizenship" means.

This dilemma is made worse because the individual company decisions they take, ignoring externalities to maximize short-term profitability, when taken collectively by all enterprises, fuels this resentment and dissatisfaction with the current economic order. What may be sensible for one firm can become a recipe for disaster if all firms do the same thing at the same time.

Boards must therefore recognize the collective impact of externalities created by their focusing on short-term profit maximization means no firm is an island and we are still "all in this together." However, recognizing the fact we are still "all in this together" is made doubly difficult by the populist assertion that we are not; and by the fact that boards do not have adequate decision-making tools to reflect the true costs they impose on the environment, economy, and society of the externalities they create through their individual profit-maximizing decisions.

Leading boards recognize shareholder value reflects their effectiveness first in creating value by selecting strategies to create sustainable competitive

---

iii In the United States, directors could face class actions by activist shareholders, in particular hedge funds, if they were perceived to be making decisions deemed not to maximize short-term shareholder value.

advantage; second in extracting value by implementing such strategies efficiently; and third in sharing it with investors through dividends, share buybacks, and capital gains. However, that is no longer everything they must consider; if they are to contain the rise of populism. There are serious additional issues of distribution at stake – job security, income inequality, and social welfare which make reconciling long- and short-term time horizons more difficult and which have been largely ignored.

The failure of politicians and companies to consider these additional issues over the past thirty years has helped fuel the rise of populist politics with its volatile mix of nostalgia for imagined past greatness; resentment of elites that have rigged the economic system against those left behind by globalization and technological change; and fear of cultural change brought about by immigration.

The Challenge to Neoliberal Capitalism

There is growing recognition that the way neoliberal capitalism has been practiced in the past thirty years needs to change if populist tendencies are to be contained. Most of the focus has been on changes needed to the politics of the developed world; however, for changes in the approach to capitalism to be effective and realistic, businesses must be involved and the way publicly listed companies respond needs to reconcile previously ignored issues of the *political economy* as a whole. This will require further evolution in CG and in how issues are discussed at the board.

As a firm believer in the merits of capitalism, like Ray Dalio, I fear we may see a replay of the 1930s with different actors,[22] but the same outcome. Again, in the words of Geoffrey Garrett, Dean of the Wharton School of Business:

> My message to our students was that we must all be *realistic* optimists, not naive ones. For me, that means acknowledging that we must all do whatever we can to navigate and reverse three intersecting geo-economic and geo-political trends:
> - After four decades of ever-increasing engagement between China and the United States, the world's two leading powers seem increasingly determined to decouple their economies from each other – making a second Cold War a reality and superpower war more likely.
> - Notwithstanding that past technological revolutions have improved both the quality of life and the world of work, the combination of robots and AI threatens to destroy many more jobs than it creates – undermining the foundations of a good life based on a good job.
> - While it remains tempting to dismiss the recent rise of anti-establishment politics as an aberration, the roots of populism run much deeper and stronger – weakening the foundations of democracy and increasing the chances of international conflict.[23]

Given the level of dissatisfaction with the current political-economic order, I ask myself whether good modern corporate governance (CG) will be sufficient to prevent a "political tragedy of the commons," caused by boards doing what is in the best interests of their individual organizations without considering the collectively negative impact of their decisions on society as a whole?

I believe boards will need to consider not just the sustainability of their organizations, but also the impact on society of externalities they create and their effects on the long-term viability of capitalism. This may prove to be challenging and boards may not have the tools and skills to meet the challenge.

Dealing with Symptoms Rather than Causes

As Ray Dalio pointed out, capitalism in the past forty years failed to deliver benefits to enough people for the body politic to continue believing in its merits:

> Contrary to what populists of the left and populists of the right are saying, these unacceptable outcomes aren't due to either a) evil rich people doing bad things to poor people or b) lazy poor people and bureaucratic inefficiencies, as much as they are due to how the capitalist system is now working . . . As a result of this dynamic, *the system is producing self-reinforcing spirals up for the haves and down for the have-nots, which are leading to harmful excesses at the top and harmful deprivations at the bottom.* More specifically, I believe that:
>
> 1. *The pursuit of profit and greater efficiencies has led to the invention of new technologies that replace people,* which has made companies run more efficiently, rewarded those who invented these technologies, and hurt those who were replaced by them. *This force will accelerate over the next several years, and there is no plan to deal with it well.*
> 2. *The pursuit of greater profits and greater company efficiencies has also led companies to produce in other countries and to replace American workers with cost-effective foreign workers, which was good for these companies' profits and efficiencies but bad for the American workers' incomes.* Of course, this globalization also allowed less expensive and perhaps better quality foreign goods to come into the US, which has been good for both the foreign sellers and the American buyers of them and bad for the American companies and workers who compete with them.[24]
>
> [Emphases mine]

I believe a plan to deal with the consequences of the disemployment highlighted by Ray Dalio is essential if capitalism is to survive in its present form. This will need work by governments but it will also depend on what boards do and how they make their decisions. This is where a revised CG has a role to play and it will need to consider how the moral foundations of capitalism have been weakened over the past sixty years.

I believe sustainable capitalism is built on three pillars: deferred gratification (the reason for investing is to make the world a better place in the future rather than consuming any surplus immediately); trust (my word is my bond); and mutuality (the same rules and outcomes for everyone). As these pillars crumble, so does the moral case for global capitalism, helping explain the rise of populism.

1. Destruction of Deferred Gratification

As a child, I was taught "anything worth having was worth waiting for." With the invention of the credit card in 1964, banks destroyed the idea that deferred gratification was something we, as consumers, should value. In the UK, the National Westminster Bank launched its Access credit card in 1964 with the slogan "We take the waiting out of wanting."

I do not think any of us realized then how corrosive this would be for our values regarding the importance of saving and being responsible with our money. It endorsed our desire for instant gratification, reinforced further by a 24/7 mentality propagated by the media (with the launch of CNN in 1980 followed by its imitators) and now the internet.

We came to believe that it was our right to be satisfied materially, emotionally, and intellectually **immediately**, *without having to work hard and make sacrifices.* Securitization taught businesses the same lesson. Those who valued deferred gratification and being responsible about incurring debt were regarded as fools. Tax treatment favored debt over equity, promoting unsustainable levels of leverage causing the GFC.[iv] Quantitative easing, in its attempt to prevent another Great Depression, reinforced the destruction of the principle of deferred gratification by destroying yields and the value of savings and pensions with the introduction of *negative interest rates* in a number of countries.[v]

---

iv When I was studying economics at Oxford in 1964, UK banks had leverage of eight times. When Long Term Capital Management collapsed in 1998, Myron Scholes (one of its founders) opined that its level of leverage of twenty-five times was unsustainable. Yet when the Royal Bank of Scotland collapsed in 2009, its level of equity was only 1.97%, implying a level of leverage of more than fifty times. ("The Failure of the Royal Bank of Scotland, Financial Service Authority Report," p. 68, https://www.fca.org.uk/publication/corporate/fsa-rbs.pdf, accessed on April 2, 2020).

v The following central banks have adopted a regime of negative interest rates in an attempt to raise the level of inflation and discourage excessive savings in the hope of boosting growth: Denmark, Japan, Sweden, Switzerland. https://tradingeconomics.com/country-list/interest-rate, accessed on April 2, 2020.

2. Destruction of Trust

We can no longer rely on "my word is my bond." This is seen most particularly in financial services, where trust is more important than in almost any sector because of the complexity of products being offered in the name of innovation – products whose defects are unknown because of their long life; products which have not gone through the kind of beta-testing any physical good has to go through before it can come to market; and where caveat emptor "hides in plain sight" in legalese ordinary customers cannot understand. Deliberate mis-selling of payment protection insurance (PPI) in the UK and subprime mortgages in the US before 2008, as well as the Australian banking malpractices in 2017 made this destruction of trust more serious. In addition, there has been egregious behavior by big business (Boeing's 737 MAX, Deepwater Horizon, "Dieselgate," etc.).

The physical, emotional, intellectual, and cultural distance between metropolitan Davos elites and people firmly rooted in their rural and small town communities increased the trust gap – captured in former Prime Minister Theresa May's "citizens of nowhere" speech in October 2016 after the Brexit vote wherein she described a citizen of the world as a citizen of nowhere.

3. Destruction of Mutuality

A sense of mutuality is essential if we are to preserve the idea of "we are all in this together," so critical for democracies to prosper. For this to exist, I believe there are three minimum criteria: first, rules must apply to everyone regardless of their wealth, education, and status; second, economic benefits are distributed in a way that is perceived to be fair so that economic policy creates a win-win solution for all demographic groups of society; third, "blood and soil" cannot become the overriding definition of citizenship.

The "citizens of nowhere," living in metropolitan areas with their liberal, globalist mindsets benefitted over the past forty years, while the "citizens of somewhere," living in small towns and their supporting rural communities faced increasing hardship through de-industrialization. The result is a clear geographical as well as cultural divide between winners (the "citizens of nowhere") and losers (the "citizens of somewhere") and was reflected in their voting patterns.

Worse still, the type of investment that drove GDP growth created fewer jobs for more wealth as a result of technology and the network effects of IT. In the past, Mark Zuckerberg would have had to employ hundreds of thousands of people to create a company with the market capitalization of Facebook; the same is true of Airbnb or Uber. Instead, these companies employ a few thousand only and create jobs with little job security and or social security benefits. Add to this, former US Attorney General Eric Holder's admission in 2013 that badly behaved US banks were not just "too big to fail," but "too big to jail," and we can see why there was a populist reaction against elites who rigged the system at their expense. The GFC saw the rise of privatized profits and socialized losses. Taxpayers paid for bad behavior of banks in Switzerland, the UK, and the US, instead of the CEOs and investors who created the problems in the first place.[25]

Thomas Piketty has documented how inequality has grown in the developed world – the result of a "winner takes all" capitalism created by technology and globalization's network effects.[26] Despite neoliberals arguing the economic problems of the Great Recession are being resolved, the benefits of GDP growth are not accruing fairly. Technology makes matters worse; and if the doomsayers about AI are correct, large swathes of white-collar work will disappear with nothing really meaningful to replace them in the next twenty years. Climate change contributes to the fears of millennials that they will live less well than their elders, increasing their alienation from the current economic system.

The Wrong Neoliberal Response

The metropolitan neoliberal response to loss of jobs and status made matters worse. Priding themselves on being meritocrats, they have often argued "losers" deserved to lose because they were undereducated and unable to keep pace with the changes around them. Sometimes, this sense of meritocratic moral superiority was expressed quite openly, merely angering the "losers" further.[27] This patronizing expression of superiority by voters who supported democrats in the US or by remainers in the UK has ignited a deep sense of being disrespected in those who have done less well by the current system, triggering a "thymotic reaction" against the current system and its elites, where the emotional need to regain lost status and self-respect outweighs the economic benefits of globalization and remaining in the EU.[vi,vii]

---

vi For an excellent discussion of the conflict between the needs of "thymotic man" and "economic man," read Fukuyama, F. (2012), *The End of History and the Last Man* (London: Penguin Books), pp. 143–185.
vii Orszag, P. (2020), "Milton Friedman's World Is Dead and Gone," *Bloomberg Opinion*, January 29, 2020, https://www.bloomberg.com/opinion/articles/2020-01-29/tell-davos-that-milton-friedman-s-world-is-dead-and-gone?utm_medium=email&utm_source=n, accessed on February 3, 2020.

Neoliberals have continued to promote the concept of Ricardian free trade, with its *static comparative advantage* where capital, land, and labor were fixed geographically and disruptive technology was not a factor. It may have made sense in the 19th century, as Ricardo's examples of wine and wool proved.[28] However, in today's world, only land is fixed geographically and technology is designed to overcome even that through global supply chains, whose intricate workings politicians do not always seem to understand.[viii]

Instead of Ricardo's static comparative advantage, we have Yotaro Kobayashi's (a former chairman of Fuji Xerox) concept of *dynamic comparative advantage*. He argued, as early as 1986 at a conference I attended in Taipei, that, if Ricardo was correct, the Japanese would never have learned to make cars, leaving it to the Americans instead. He proposed a theory of dynamic comparative advantage where comparative advantages change over time, as a result of deliberate government policy choices.

Dramatic examples of this are high-speed rail and smartphones. Twenty years ago, China had no high-speed rail. Japan, France, and Germany led the world in terms of rail networks and technology. According to Ricardo, China should never have become a global competitor in high-speed rail. Yet today, China has the world's biggest network with 26,869 kilometers (16,696 miles) in 2018, and aims to reach 38,000 kilometers by 2025.[29] It is competing successfully against the Japanese, French, and Germans. The same is true of mobile phones and smartphones. Fifty years ago, China was a backward country in telephony. The US was the most advanced, with landlines managed by AT&T. Today, China has the largest mobile phone market, and in the last five years, Huawei has become a threat to Samsung and has overtaken Apple in smartphones.[ix] If Ricardo was correct, Huawei would threaten nobody. There are more Chinese examples such as Alibaba, Alipay, TenCent, Baidu, and WeChat in mobile apps. Korean industrialization and its creation of globally branded champions is yet another example of the shortcomings of Ricardian analysis.

We must accept that dynamic comparative advantage harnesses the power of disruptive technology to put entire industries at risk, with the ensuing rapid dislocation of employment depending on those industries – for example, Finland

---

viii Hence the dangerous emphasis on a "clean break" with the EU of hard Brexiteers and Donald Trump's declaration of a trade war with China that will be "easy to win."
ix Q1 2019, Samsung (S. Korea) had 23.0%, Huawei (China) 18.9%, Apple (US) 11.8%; Xiaomi (China) 8.9%; Vivo (China) 7.4%, and Oppo (China) 7.4%, *IDC* (2019), "Smartphone Market Share – Vendor, 2019 Q1," June 18, 2019, https://www.google.com/search?q=huawei+market+share+by+product&oq=huawei+market+share+by+pro&aqs=chrome, accessed on August 16, 2019.

and the rise and fall of Nokia.[x] Economists and politicians seem to forget that the decline in jobs is much more rapid and devastating than the rise of replacement jobs of *equivalent social and economic status*. An unemployed Ohio steelworker will not likely find work at Facebook – the geographical and skills barriers are too great. He may find a job in his local Walmart, but with lower pay and much lower status; becoming a target for populists.

Dynamic comparative advantage, combined with globalization, undermines the principle of economic mutuality. We are not "all in it together"; there really are zero-sum conditions. Until politicians recognize dynamic comparative advantage works differently from static comparative advantage, they will continue to promise undeliverable benefits from global free trade for those who do not have the ability to adapt quickly enough in a "winner takes all" capitalism that creates ever fewer jobs per dollar of revenue. Moreover, global network effects disproportionately benefit the few who own the networks or the stars (authors, entertainers, celebrities, and athletes) who are featured on the networks, dramatically reinforcing highly visible inequality. The internet and 24/7 media with their love of celebrities and reality shows sharpens the disconnect between "winners and losers."

The Populist Challenge

Populists everywhere have proven adept at connecting with the pain, insecurities, and resentment of the "losers" in today's capitalism. However, identifying the problem is not the same as finding a sustainable solution.

Believers in modern neoliberal capitalism are put on the defensive by its failure to distribute its benefits fairly and by the egregious behavior of the few, as well as the systemic failure of financial services to behave responsibly. It is extremely difficult to justify the dramatic jump in CEO remuneration in both the US and the UK over the past forty years. Peter Drucker argued in 1965 that CEOs should earn twenty times the average American salary. Clearly, he has been ignored.[xi] What is worse, the tenuous link between pay and individual

---

x At its peak in 2007, Nokia had 41% of the global market in mobile phones, representing 3.5% of Finland's GDP. Today Nokia is no longer in the mobile phone business, having sold it to Microsoft, who failed to revitalize it.

xi "In 1993, the US Congress amended the tax code to tie executive pay closer to performance by allowing stock options. As a result, the percentage of CEO pay in options went from 35% in 1994 to more than 85% in 2001 and *average pay went from 140 times that of average employees in 1991 to 500 times in 2003*." McRitchie, J. (2016), "The Individual's Role in Driving Corporate Governance," quoted in *The Handbook of Corporate Governance*, op. cit., p. 433.

CEO performance suggests it is rent-seeking at the expense of employees and shareholders:

> Research into CEO pay shows that total shareholder return (TSR) is, by far, the most dominant performance metric . . . Yet, increased TSR often has little to do with CEO effort or actually growing a business for the long term . . . TSR is easily gamed through cost-cutting measures . . . reducing R&D, stock buybacks, or financial engineering. In contrast, developing new products, training staff, and increasing sales take more creativity and may take years to bear fruit. *Researchers found that economic performance explains only 12 percent of variance in CEO pay, whereas more than 60 percent is explained by company size, industry, and existing company pay policy. None of those other measures are performance driven.*[30]   [Emphasis mine]

If we fail to find a compelling moral justification for capitalism and if populist solutions will only further impoverish those they are supposed to benefit, I foresee a replay of the 1930s. The script is the same; only the actors differ: Russia replacing Germany as the revanchist power in Eastern and Central Europe; China instead of Japan, as the previously humiliated, but expansionist power in the East; with possibly Turkey trying to recreate the Ottoman Empire in the Middle East. Worryingly, the Kondratieff Wave shows that since the 1780s the US has only managed to recover from serious national debt overhangs by going to war. Not a comforting thought, given the number of potential flashpoints. The alternative could be a "political tragedy of the commons" – revolution followed by repression, like the failed Arab Spring of 2011 or the Russian Revolution of 1917 with its creation of the Leninist state.

Although I believe populism is not the answer, we would do well to heed the following words of warning:

> Democracy and free markets can produce unsatisfying outcomes, after all, especially when badly regulated, or when nobody trusts the regulators, or when people are entering the contest from very different starting points. Sooner or later, the losers of the competition were always going to challenge the value of the competition itself.
>
> More to the point, *the principles of competition, even when they encourage talent and create upward mobility, don't necessarily answer deeper questions about national identity, or satisfy the human desire to belong to a moral community. The authoritarian state, or even the semi-authoritarian state – the one-party state, the illiberal state – offers that promise: that the nation will be ruled by the best people, the deserving people, the members of the party, the believers in the Medium-Size Lie. It may be that democracy has to be bent or business corrupted or court systems wrecked in order to achieve that state. But if you believe that you are one of those deserving people, you will do it.*[31]   [Emphasis mine]

Summary

CG was designed to provide checks and balances to prevent abuse of executive power and to provide transparency to shareholders. Over time the declared purpose of business changed from Drucker's "creating and maintaining satisfied customers" to Friedman's "maximizing shareholder value." This change of purpose affected how capitalism operated as it became neoliberal.

The neoliberal capitalist model of the past forty years is showing serious signs of stress caused by its failure to distribute the results of growth fairly. This has helped fuel the rise of populist political agendas, based on emotion and resentment, made worse by the wrong response by the supporters of the economic status quo; dealing with symptoms rather than causes of discontent. This will pose an increasingly severe challenge to the way boards decide how best to reconcile the demands of short-term shareholders on the one hand with the long-term needs of an increasingly diverse and vocal group of stakeholders, many of whom have ceased to trust the economic system and the elites who fashioned it.

This may have potentially profound consequences on the best ways to approach CG in the future, given that there is no single best way of implementing CG, forcing boards to consider wider issues of distribution of the fruits of economic growth, while recognizing that sustainability discussions will need to recognize the impact of decisions they make regarding externalities on the ecological, economic, and social environments in which they operate. The remit of CG will have to expand to cover these additional considerations, making decision making more complicated in a less certain world.[xii] At the same time, boards will have to think differently if they are to integrate the wider issues into their discussions and develop measurement tools that currently do not exist to internalize the externalities they create when making decisions. Boards will no longer be able to optimize outcomes for their organizations only, without considering the cumulative collective systemic impacts of what could happen when all organizations come to the same conclusions. In other words, what made excellent sense for an individual enterprise may no longer make collective sense, if all enterprises choose to make the same decision at the same time. Failure to

---

xii The reader might be forgiven for thinking CG is only relevant to publicly listed companies. In fact, CG is important to every enterprise that selects and implements strategy, manages risk, plans succession, engages stakeholders, and ensures there are proper controls on how work is done – whether or not it is listed, incorporated, or for-profit. Despite this commonality, there is no one way of implementing good CG because there are many ways to organize an efficient enterprise (discussed in Chapter 2).

recognize this and develop a way of dealing with it will contribute toward a "political tragedy of the commons" that boards may come to regret.

The conditions in which regulators and boards must make decisions have become more complicated, requiring them to take more time to think through the implications of their decisions; time they may not have, with tools they may not possess, to deal with the increased complexity they face.

References

1 Eells, R.S. (1960), "The meaning of modern business: an introduction to the philosophy of large corporate enterprise" (New York). This is the first time the concept is mentioned in academic literature. The first time the term is applied to companies is by Sir Adrian Cadbury in the "Report of the Committee on the Financial Aspects of Corporate Governance" in 1992.

2 "Timeline of Polly Peck fraud case," *The Times,* August 22, 2012, https://www.thetimes.co.uk/article/timeline-of-polly-peck-fraud-case-322sd6xdqqt, accessed on August 14, 2019.

3 Cohen, R. (1991), "Maxwell's Empire: How it Grew, How It Fell – A Special Report; Charming the Big Bankers Out of Billions," *The New York Times,* December 20, 1991, https://www.nytimes.com/1991/12/20/business/maxwell-s-empire-it-grew-it-fell-special-report-charming-big-bankers-billions.html, accessed on August 14, 2019.

4 Bogle, J. (2003),"Owners Capitalism vs Managers Capitalism," Speech given to the 2003 National Investor Relations Conference, Orlando, Florida, June 11, 2003, *Bogle Financial Center,* https://www.vanguard.com/bogle_site/sp20030611.html, accessed on August 7, 2019.

5 Friedman, M. (1970), "The Social Responsibility of Business is to Increase Profits," *New York Times Magazine,* September 13, 1970, http://umich.edu/~thecore/doc/Friedman.pdf, accessed on August 8, 2019.

6 Rhee, R. J. (2017), "A Legal Theory of Shareholder Primacy," *Harvard Law School Forum on Corporate Governance and Financial Regulation,* April 11, 2017, https://corpgov.law.harvard.edu/2017/04/11/a-legal-theory-of-shareholder-primacy/, accessed on September 26, 2019.

7 Strine, Jr., L.E. (2015), "The Dangers of Denial: The Need for a Clear-Eyed Understanding of the Power and Accountability Structure Established by the Delaware General Corporation Law," 50 *Wake Forest Law Review,* pp. 761, 768 (2015) quoted in Atkins, P. et al. (2019), "Social Responsibility and Enlightened Shareholder Primacy: Views From the Courtroom and Boardroom," *Skadden,* February 4, 2019, https://www.skadden.com/insights/publications/2019/02/social-responsibility/social-responsibility-and-enlightened-shareholder, accessed on September 27, 2019.

8 Chandler III, W. (2010), *eBay Domestic Holdings, Inc. v. Newmark,* 16 A.3d 1, 34 (Del. Ch. 2010), quoted in Atkins, P. et al. (2019), op. cit.

9 Sjafjell, B. (2016), "Regulating for Corporate Sustainability: Why the Public-Private Divide Misses the Point," *University of Oxford Faculty of Law,* May 30, 2016, https://www.law.ox.ac.uk/business-law-blog/blog/2016/05/regulating-corporate-sustainability-why-public-private-divide-misses the point, accessed on September 26, 2019.

10 Atkins, P. et al. (2019), op. cit.

11 Cadbury, A. (1992), *The Financial Aspects of Corporate Governance,* December 1, 1992, https://www.appcgg.co.uk/cadbury-committee-code-on-the-financial-aspects-of-corporate-governance-december-1992/, accessed on April 2, 2020.

12 OECD (2015), G20/OECD Principles of Corporate Governance 2015, p. 9, https://www.oecd.org/daf/ca/Corporate-Governance-Principles-ENG.pdf, accessed on August 6, 2018.

13 Securities Commission Malaysia (2017), *Malaysian Code on Corporate Governance,* p. 1.

14 OECD (2015) op. cit., p. 13, https://www.oecd.org/daf/ca/Corporate-Governance-Principles-ENG.pdf, accessed on June 8, 2018.

15 "Definition of Corporate Governance," https://www.applied-corporate-governance.com/definition-of-corporate-governance/, accessed on June 8, 2018.

16 Monbiot, G. (2016) "Neoliberalism – The Ideology at the Root of all Our Problems," *The Guardian,* April 15, 2016, https://www.theguardian.com/books/2016/apr/15/neoliberalism-ideology-problem-george-monbiot, accessed on April 2, 2020.

17 Rodrik, D. (2018), "Is Populism Necessarily Bad Economics?" *AEA Papers and Proceedings 2018,* 108, p. 196.

18 Gourevitch, P.A. and Shinn, J. (2005), *Political Power and Corporate Control: The New Global Politics of Corporate Governance* (Princeton, N.J.: Princeton University Press), quoted in James McRitchie, "Corporate Governance Defined: Not So Easily," https://www.corpgov.net/library/corporate-governance-defined/, accessed on June 8, 2018.

19 Theresa May, Prime Minister of the UK, "Full text: Theresa May's conference speech," *The Spectator,* October 5, 2016.

20 Garrett, G. (2019), "The Answer to Populism: Looking Forward, Not Back," *Knowledge@Wharton,* University of Pennsylvania, May 10, 2019, https://knowledge.wharton.upenn.edu/article/answer-populism-pessimism-looking-forward-not-back/, accessed on August 15, 2019.

21 Friedman, M. (1970), "The Social Responsibility of Business is to Increase Profits," *New York Times Magazine,* September 13, 1970, http://umich.edu/~thecore/doc/Friedman.pdf, accessed on August 8, 2019.

22 Dalio, R. (2019), "Why and How Capitalism Needs To Be Reformed," LinkedIn, April 5, 2019.

23 Garrett, G. (2019), "Why 2019 Feels Like 1929 – and What We Can Do To Change Course," https://knowledge.wharton.upenn.edu/article/2019-feels-like-1929-can-change-course/?utm_source=kw_newsletter&utm_mediu, *Knowledge@Wharton,* University of Pennsylvania, August 13, 2019.

24 Dalio, R. (2019), op. cit.

25 Zinkin, J. (2014), *Rebuilding Trust in Banks: The Role of Leadership and Governance* (Singapore: John Wiley & Sons).

26 Piketty, T. (2014), *Capital in the Twenty-First Century* (Boston, Mass.: Harvard University Press).

27 Fox, M. (2002), "Michael Young, 86, Scholar; Mocked 'Meritocracy'," *The New York Times,* January 25, 2002, https://www.nytimes.com/2002/01/25/world/michael-young-86-scholar-coined-mocked-meritocracy.html, accessed on November 5, 2019.

28 Ricardo, D. (1817), *On the Principles of Political Economy and Taxation* (London: John Murray).

29 Molitch-Hou, M. (2019), "How China's High-Speed Rail Zooms Past Other Countries," *Engineering.com*, June 14, 2019, https://www.engineering.com/BIM/ArticleID/19288/How-Chinas-High-Speed-Rail-Zooms-Past-Other-Countries.aspx, accessed on August 16, 2019.

30 McRitchie, J. (2016), "The Individual's Role in Driving Corporate Governance," quoted in *The Handbook of Corporate Governance*, edited by Richard Leblanc (Hoboken, New Jersey: John Wiley and Sons), p. 433.

31 Applebaum, A. (2018), "Warning from Europe: The Worst is Yet to Come," *The Atlantic*, October 2018. https://www.theatlantic.com/magazine/archive/2018/10/poland-polarization/568324/, accessed on June 20, 2020.

Chapter 2
No One Single Approach to Corporate Governance

This chapter is presented in three parts: the first explores the impact of different capital market structures on the development of corporate governance (CG); the second covers the shift of economic power to Asia; and the third reviews five different approaches to CG. It closes with a summary of the discussion.

In discussing what are the best approaches to CG, there are two temptations to remember. The first temptation to resist is that CG and its issues apply only to listed organizations. This is incorrect. CG is important to every enterprise that selects and implements strategy, manages risk, plans succession, engages stakeholders, and ensures there are proper controls on how work is done – whether or not it is listed, incorporated, or for-profit. Despite this commonality, there is no one way of implementing good CG because there are many ways to organize an efficient enterprise. The second temptation is to assess CG using one single frame of reference, since so much of the literature views CG from an Anglo-Saxon perspective – written in English, about Anglo-Saxon capital markets,[i] which for decades represented the *overwhelming majority of business capital raised through equity*. There are, however, three reasons why it may no longer make sense to assess CG solely through a purely Anglo-Saxon worldview. As a result, in 2015, the OECD recognized there could not be a "one size fits all" approach to CG:

> Effective corporate governance requires a sound legal, regulatory and institutional framework that market participants can rely on when they establish their private contractual relations. This corporate governance framework typically comprises elements of legislation, regulation, self-regulatory arrangements, voluntary commitments and business practices that are the result of a country's specific circumstances, history and tradition . . . *What works well in one company, for one investor or a particular stakeholder may not necessarily be generally applicable to corporations, investors and stakeholders that operate in another context and under different circumstances.*[1]   [Emphasis mine]

---

i The Cadbury Report in 1992 is regarded by many as the seminal document on CG. Much of the literature has been based on reactions to failures of CG in the UK and US, the Asian financial crisis, and the global financial crisis, and on work done by the King Committee on Corporate Governance in South Africa. There have been scandals in Germany, France, Italy, and Japan and codes of conduct have been developed there; but less has been written about them in English.

https://doi.org/10.1515/9783110670486-002

Three elements are at work in making it impossible to have a "one size fits all" approach. The first is the difference in the capital market conditions of each jurisdiction. The second is the variation in approaches that are best suited for each individual organization's unique circumstances. The third, not mentioned by the OECD, is the diminished role of Anglo-Saxon capital markets as economic power shifts east to Asia, and, in particular, China with its predominance of state-owned enterprises (SOEs).

Different Types of Capital Markets

Despite gradual convergence of views across IOSCO's[ii] emerging markets regarding the importance of good CG,[2] it is clear different jurisdictions are at different stages of development and have different solutions.[3] Assuming only one way of evaluating the effectiveness of CG will apply to all jurisdictions globally, fails to consider their political history, chosen path of industrial and economic development, and the maturity of their capital markets.[4]

Research by McKinsey in 2001[5] suggested there were two types of capital markets, with different foundations, different modus operandi, and different assumptions of how companies operate, shown in Figure 2.1. Regulatory superstructures, built on these foundations, differed between the US "black letter" law approach, the "principles-based" approach favored by the UK and the Commonwealth, Japan's combination of both, and the need for each regulatory regime to reflect the levels of maturity of their market and its participants – where developed markets were more likely to choose a "principles-based" approach and underdeveloped ones a "rules-based" approach.

As you can see from the institutional contexts (on the left side of both circles), the shareholder environments in the two models are quite different, as are the chances of activist shareholders holding boards to account because of the difference in the liquidity of the two types of markets and in the levels of ownership concentration. What about the corporate contexts (on the right side of each circle)? The boards are structured differently, including unitary boards in common law jurisdictions, as opposed to two-tier boards in others. This affects their respective levels of independence and the value placed on the importance of shareholder rights and transparency.

---

ii IOSCO stands for International Organization of Securities Commissions.

Different market structures lead to different worldviews

"Anglosphere" worldview

Market model – prevalent in the UK and US (also known as the Anglo capitalist model)

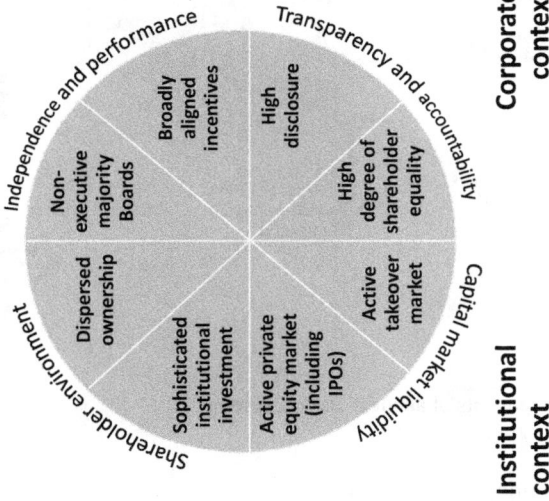

Independence and performance

- Non-executive majority Boards
- Broadly aligned incentives

Transparency and accountability

- High disclosure
- High degree of shareholder equality

Shareholder environment

- Dispersed ownership
- Sophisticated institutional investment

Capital market liquidity

- Active private equity market (including IPOs)
- Active takeover market

Institutional context
Corporate context

Alternative worldview

Control model – found in Asia, Latin America and much of Continental Europe

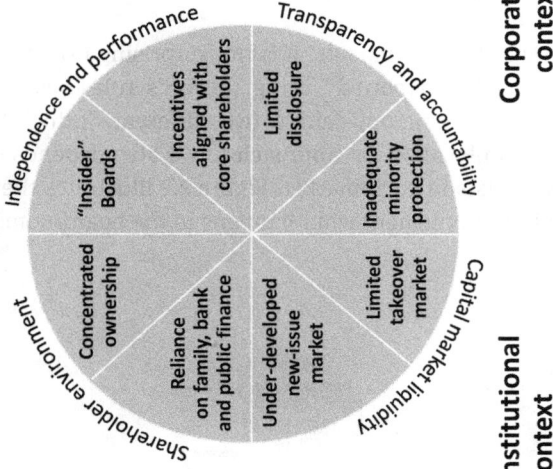

Independence and performance

- "Insider" Boards
- Incentives aligned with core shareholders

Transparency and accountability

- Limited disclosure
- Inadequate minority protection

Shareholder environment

- Concentrated ownership
- Reliance on family, bank and public finance

Capital market liquidity

- Under-developed new-issue market
- Limited takeover market

Corporate context
Institutional context

Figure 2.1: Two capital market models: worlds apart.

Importance of a Healthy CG "Ecosystem"

Given the disparity in the two models, it is not surprising CG needs to be localized and cannot just be "exported" using the US's rules-based "black letter law" or the UK's and Commonwealth's two different "principle-based" approaches. The need to localize the approach to CG also depends on what type of CG "ecosystem" exists in each market. Figure 2.2 illustrates the "ecosystem" elements required to complement what happens in the boardroom.

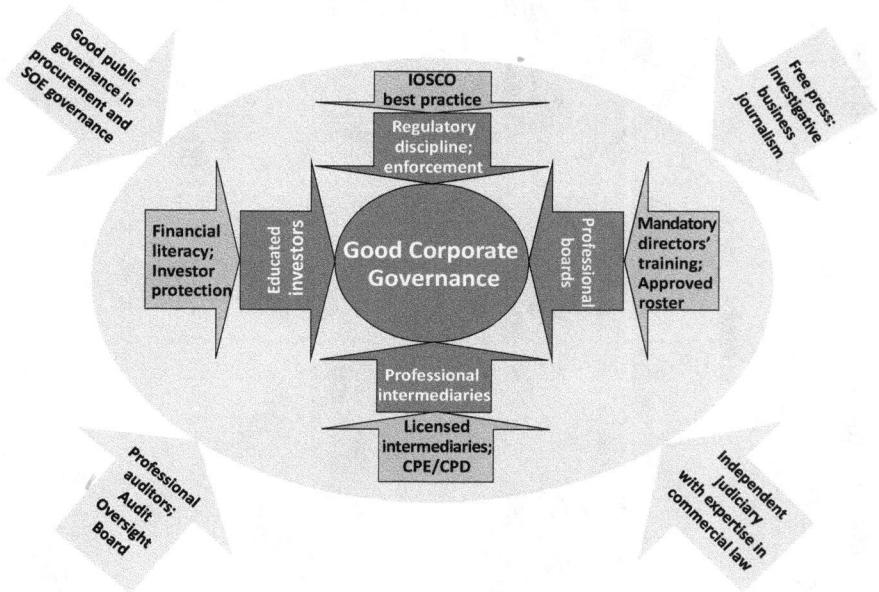

Figure 2.2: Eight components of an ideal CG "ecosystem."

Effective CG depends on eight components:[6]

1. ***Effective regulatory discipline:*** For publicly listed companies, regulatory discipline reflects IOSCO best practices, administered and *enforced* by national securities commissions and stock exchanges. Regulatory discipline, however, does not just apply to capital market rules; it applies to all relevant legislation and regulation: occupational health and safety, environmental protection, consumer protection, workplace legislation, and anti-money laundering and anti-bribery laws.

2. ***Professional boards:*** Leading practice is to "professionalize" directors, insisting on mandatory training before they join boards and on continuing professional development (CPD) once they have joined. Some jurisdictions maintain a *roster of professionally qualified directors* from which INED (independent non-executive director) candidates are drawn for listed companies (e.g., Australia, New Zealand, and Malaysia[iii]).
3. ***Professional financial intermediaries:*** Trust is the most important attribute in capital market intermediaries. As far as financial intermediaries are concerned, their professionalization is an essential regulatory response to rebuild the trust lost because of the Asian financial crisis in 1998, the GFC in 2009, and banking malpractices in Australia in 2017.[7] Regulators expect professional behavior from licensed financial intermediaries when dealing with bank, insurance, and securities customers *to whom they now owe a fiduciary duty in addition to the traditional duty of care.*[iv]
4. ***Educated investors:*** Educating retail investors regarding the inherent risks of capital markets is essential to ensure they have realistic expectations regarding investing and their own exposures to risk and the consequences of investment downsides. The more governments have financial inclusion as an ambition, the more money will need to be spent on educating and protecting investors. In developed markets, the regulatory focus is increasingly on encouraging institutional investors to use stewardship charters[v] when dealing with boards on important issues of sustainability, strategy, structure, investment policy, and remuneration.

---

iii In Malaysia, financial institutions are regarded as systemically important, following the 1998 Asian financial crisis. There is a cadre of professionally trained financial institution directors who undergo *mandatory* continuous professional development (CPD) specifically related to banking, insurance, and capital markets. These CPD programs are overseen by the Securities Commission for capital market intermediaries and by Bank Negara for banking and insurance boards. Bank Negara follows up on the training of bank and insurance company directors to ensure it has been effective, by reviewing board minute discussions and the contributions of individual directors.

iv The duty of care is defined as "a moral or legal obligation to ensure the safety or well-being of others."

v Stewardship charters are statements by investor organizations regarding how they undertake stewardship activities, which may include monitoring and engaging with companies on matters such as strategy, performance, risk, capital structure, and corporate governance, including culture and remuneration. Engagement is purposeful dialogue with companies on these matters as well as on issues that are the immediate subject of votes at general meetings.

5. ***Good public governance:*** The behavior of the government and its entities in setting the tone of public governance is even more critical if the government-related sector is a major part of the economy. When governments are corrupt, violating the basic principles of CG in their companies; turning a blind eye to malpractice by cronies; their bad example corrodes and undermines the entire CG ecosystem.

    The only forces preventing this are a diverse, robust free press and an independent judiciary. Whenever governments control the press and the judiciary, there will be an erosion of CG. Malaysia's 1MDB[8] is a tragic object lesson.

6. ***Honest free press:*** The press must have good investigative journalists who are not beholden to political parties; who understand business and how it works; and who are not afraid of "following the money" regardless of where or how high it leads.

7. ***Independent judiciary:*** The judiciary must have judges who are independent-minded, *specialists in commercial law and white-collar crime,* who can come to proper judgments and who are then not afraid of punishing malefactors, regardless of who they are.

8. ***Professional external auditors:*** Auditors' processes must be robust and reflect professional independence to ensure accurate and timely financial reporting. To achieve this requires adhering to high standards, reinforced by an independent audit oversight board (AOB) to ensure external auditors fulfill their roles competently, without fear or favor.

A healthy CG ecosystem is a critical support for good CG within companies. Regulations are necessary to protect the public from bad actors, but they often are attacked by politicians, businessmen, and commentators who believe in minimal regulation, without appreciating why such regulation may be necessary.

Different jurisdictions need different approaches to CG because of the fundamental differences in the foundations of capital markets identified by McKinsey in 2001. These differences are amplified by the extent to which individual jurisdictions are blessed or not with the eight components of an effective "CG ecosystem"; or, if they have them, it is with differing levels of development or political support.

The Shift to Asia

The shift to Asia means there has to be more than one approach to CG. Figure 2.3 shows Asia's growth in importance in public equity financing globally – a trend the OECD expects to continue:

Share of Asian non-financial companies in global public equity financing, 2000–2017

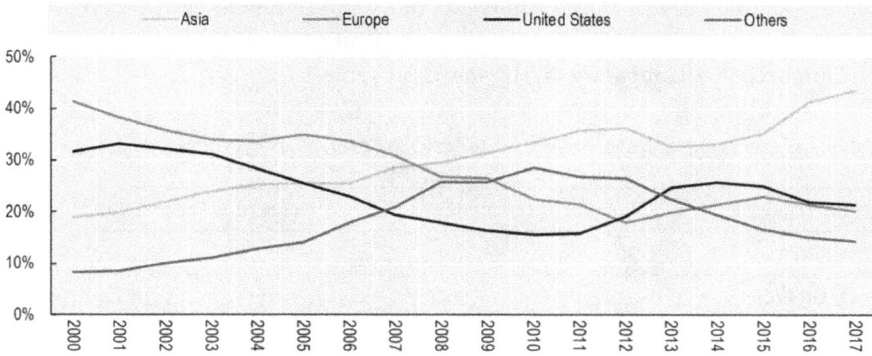

Note: The shares of regions are calculated as a three-year moving average.

Source: **OECD Capital Market Series dataset**

Figure 2.3: Asia's growing importance in global public equity financing.

Figure 2.4 shows the breakdown globally of IPOs in 2017. Key points to note are the relative unimportance now of the US, UK, Australia, and Canada – the formerly pre-eminent "Anglosphere" capital markets – compared with Asian markets and of course China.

In 2017 Asian companies accounted for 43% of all public equity capital raised worldwide

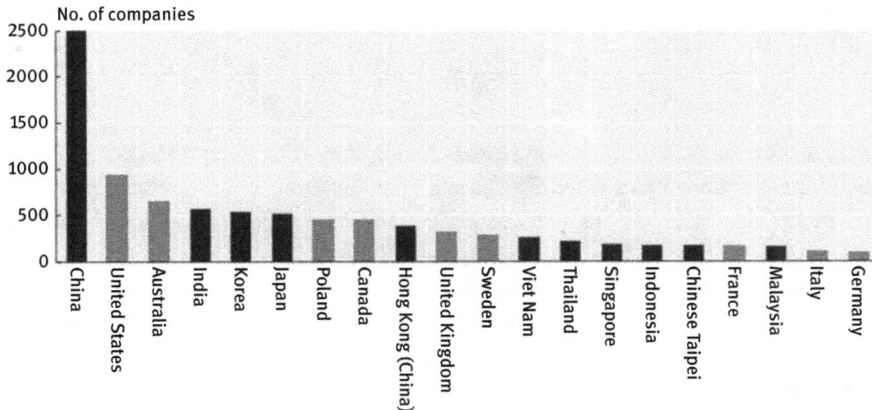

Source: **OECD Capital Market Series dataset**

Figure 2.4: Asia's dominance in IPOs in 2017.

The significance of this shift in economic power toward Asia is further highlighted by the fact that Asian companies represented 41.6% of the Fortune Global 500 in 2019; and for the first time, "Greater Chinese"[vi] companies (130), outnumbered US companies (121),[9] shown in Table 2.1.

Table 2.1: Asian companies in the Fortune Global 500 (2019).[10]

Country/Region	Number of companies	Percentage of Fortune 500
Total US	121	24.2
Total Other	164	32.6
Total Asia	208	41.6
China	119	23.8
Japan	50	10.0
South Korea	14	2.8
Taiwan	10	2.0
India	7	1.4
Saudi Arabia	2	0.4
Singapore	2	0.4
Hong Kong	1	0.2
Malaysia	1	0.2
Thailand	1	0.2
U.A.E.	1	0.2

More significant still, China's state-owned enterprises (SOEs) represented 80.2% of the Chinese organizations listed. The Saudi, Thai, Malaysian, and Emirati companies which are also SOEs, as are some of India's, must be added to the list of Chinese SOEs. As SOEs, their mandates and purpose differ from those of privately held companies and therefore the most suitable approaches to their CG will reflect this.

This shift toward Asia means the OECD and IOSCO will need to recognize even more than they already do that the "Anglosphere" approach to CG will become less relevant. There are two reasons for this. The first is that there are already different approaches to CG in the countries reviewed by the Asian Corporate

---

vi "Greater China" = PRC, Taiwan, Hong Kong, and Macao.

Governance Association (ACGA). The second is that they reflect the political and economic history of each country, their unique paths of industrial development, the role of the state in their development, and the resulting diverse ownership structures of their leading businesses:

1. ***"Anglosphere" model:*** Australia's capital market (like the US and the UK) has dispersed ownership and sophisticated institutional investors with a liquid capital market and active equity participation requiring shareholder protection. It emphasizes director independence and performance.

2. ***"Control" model:*** China's capital markets reflect Communist party controls over SOEs and their importance in the economy, representing an extreme "control" model. China is anomalous, however, in that its market participants are overwhelmingly retail punters (risk takers).[11] Japan has developed its own model with interlocking alliances of companies grouped around a bank at their center (*keiretsu*) with boards of insider directors, making it difficult for external investors to really understand what is happening.[12] South Korea's variant on the Japanese model reflects state-driven investment priorities, government-directed bank credit to a few chosen industry champions (*chaebols*) with limited historical interest in shareholder protection, but with a minimum of 25% outside directors.[13] India, Indonesia, the Philippines, Taiwan, and Thailand have reasonably developed markets that fit the "control" model and, with the exception of India and the Philippines, have legal traditions not based on Anglo-Saxon commercial common law.

3. ***"Hybrid" model:*** Although the Malaysian and Singaporean capital markets should be "control model" markets – given the dominance of government companies (GLCs) and government listed investment companies (GLICs) and family firms creating concentrated ownership and "insider" boards – they have adopted a regulatory framework typical of the "Anglosphere" model. Like Hong Kong, they compete in international capital markets with an "Anglosphere" CG ecosystem overlaid on what suits their domestic participants, who are more likely to favor the "control" model.

In some jurisdictions, companies have two-tier boards,[vii] while others have unitary boards.[viii] Their different political histories affected their choice of legal system: some have a long tradition of "Anglosphere" commercial common law,[ix]

---

vii China, Indonesia, Taiwan, and Vietnam.

viii Australia, Hong Kong, South Korea, Malaysia, and Singapore.

ix Australia, Hong Kong, India, Malaysia and Singapore share a common law tradition and judges will cite cases from each other and from the UK and US. With the exception of India, their Companies Acts, however, specify directors "manage and direct the affairs of the

some chose continental European commercial law,[x] yet others developed their own unique approaches,[xi] and some are still works-in-progress.[xii]

Differences in Ownership

These choices reflect the real differences in ownership structures and levels of ownership concentration in the various Asia-Pacific markets, shown in Tables 2.2 and 2.3. Table 2.2 shows the percentages of the 100 top-listed companies in each jurisdiction owned by other corporations, governments, institutional investors, and strategically important individuals.

Key points to note about Asia-Pacific markets on average are:

1. *Corporations owning shares in other corporations come first* (24%), unlike in the UK (7%) and US (2%).
2. *Governments owning shares in corporations come second* (21%), compared with the UK (6%) and US (2%).
3. *Institutional investors owning shares in corporations come third* (15%), unlike the UK (60%) and the US (68%).
4. *Strategic individuals owning shares in corporations come fourth* (9%), unlike the UK (2%) and the US (3%).

Ownership concentration makes a critical difference to the relevance of the principal-agent conflict at the heart of CG regulation in "Anglosphere" markets. Asia-Pacific markets have a quite different level of concentrated ownership from "Anglosphere" markets, shown in Table 2.3.

With the exceptions of Taiwan, Japan, and South Korea, Asia-Pacific markets exhibit such high levels of concentrated ownership.

Governments, in particular, play a significant role in Asian capital markets, reflecting the development trajectories of the countries in Asia-Pacific. In some cases, notably Malaysia and Singapore, the government stakes may be understated because some of their SOEs' investments might be counted under corporations holding stakes in other companies. The relative unimportance of institutional investors versus governments in Asia-Pacific markets is highlighted in Figure 2.5.

---

company," as opposed to reflecting the view of most CG codes that "boards direct and govern, management manages."

x Indonesia and Vietnam.
xi China, Japan, South Korea, Philippines, Taiwan, and Thailand.
xii Cambodia, Laos, and Myanmar.

Table 2.2: Share of 100 largest listed companies[xiii] by type of ownership (%).[14]

Jurisdiction	Corporations	Governments	Institutional Investors[xiv]	Strategic Individuals
China	12	35	9	12
Hong Kong	11	41	12	7
India	31	21	22	7
Indonesia	36	20	11	7
Japan	20	7	28	3
South Korea	23	13	21	9
Malaysia	22	42	12	6
Philippines	52	1	10	19
Singapore	29	14	14	9
Taiwan	14	7	25	5
Thailand	21	21	13	14
Vietnam	19	30	6	10
Asia average	*24*	*21*	*15*	*9*
UK	7	6	60	2
US	2	2	68	3

Figure 2.5 shows there is an inverse correlation between the importance of institutional investors and the importance of government investment and whether the capital markets are Asian, with the exception of Japan, the Philippines, and Taiwan. This difference matters because publicly listed companies, family firms,

---

xiii Foreign institutional investors are likely to be only interested in the largest listed companies, so the table shows market capitalization weighted average ownership by category of owner. Calculations are based on ownership data for the largest 100 listed companies in each market:

xiv "The increased integration of Asian capital markets with global markets has given foreign institutional investors the opportunity to increase their participation in the region. Today most of the institutional ownership in Asian countries is attributed to foreign institutional investors who on average hold 12% of the capital," OECD (2018), op. cit., p. 45.

Table 2.3: Companies (%) with controlling shareholdings greater than 50%.[15]

Jurisdiction as of end 2017	Largest shareholder	2 largest shareholders	3 largest shareholders
China	40	54	63
Hong Kong	51	56	61
India	47	56	62
Indonesia	69	84	87
Japan	8	10	10
South Korea	11	21	30
Malaysia	40	66	82
Philippines	52	71	81
Singapore	37	48	54
Taiwan	2	5	8
Thailand	23	39	50
Vietnam	28	42	47

and SOEs have different objectives by which their success is measured, affecting how they are governed, discussed next.

Government and institutional ownership in the listed corporate sector, as of end 2017

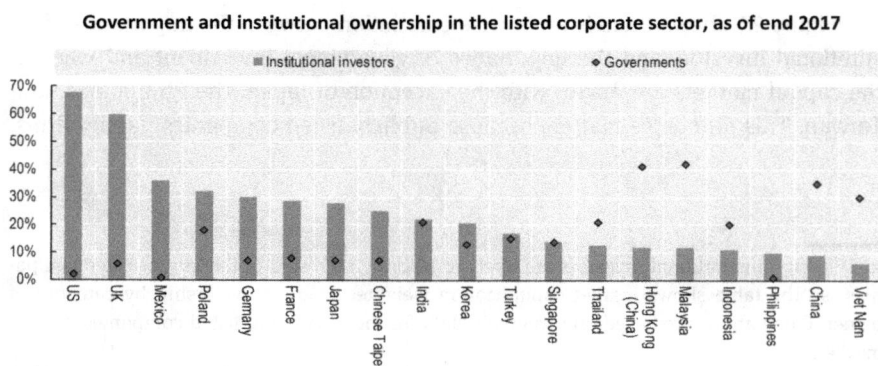

Source: OECD Capital Market Series dataset, FactSet

Figure 2.5: Relative importance of government and institutional investors.

Five CG Approaches

Each company's approach to CG will vary, reflecting five different types of capitalist organizing philosophy: family and owner, managerial, shareholder, state, or stakeholder. Each has merits and each has weaknesses and unanswered questions.

There are three types of ownership underlying these five organizing philosophies: family firms, publicly traded firms, and SOEs.[xv] They affect the purpose of each type differently, shown in Table 2.4.

Table 2.4: Differences in organizational purpose.[16]

Family firm	Publicly traded firm	State-owned firm
Level 1 "The overall aim of our company is shared family wealth and work."	*Level 1* "The ultimate aim of the company is return on shareholder equity better than the return for firms with similar risk characteristics."	*Level 1* "The ultimate purpose of state ownership of enterprises should be to maximize value for society, through an efficient allocation of resources."[17]
Level 2 "Our first priority is the family stays together, with appropriate, satisfying, and rewarding work for every adult member who chooses to work in the company. Our second priority is that the worth of the company, and the worth of each family member's shares grows at a rate comparable to indexed funds."	*Level 2* "Risk characteristics for comparison will include similar size, industry, and maturity of market. Better return will mean above the median for such firms, rather than above the average."	*Level 2* "Our first priority is to promote and create business and job opportunities in our industry and provide quality products and services at a fair price. Our second priority is to enlarge the country's industrial base and ensure a clean and safe environment."

---

xv In Malaysia and Singapore these are called GLCs and GLICs.

Family and Owner Capitalism

The ultimate purpose of the established family firm is:[18]

Level 1

"The overall aim of our company is shared family wealth and work."

Level 2

"Our first priority is the family stays together, with appropriate, satisfying, and rewarding work for every adult member who chooses to work in the company.

Our second priority is that the worth of the company, and the worth of each family member's shares grows at a rate comparable to indexed funds."

Family controlled firms do not have a principal-agent problem because they are both owners and managers:[xvi]

> Obviously, CG is not a problem for the 100 percent owner-manager of a business. Nor is it much of a problem for the majority stockholder (or group) which controls the board of directors and can fire managers at any time [e.g., venture capitalists and family firms].[19]

Family controlled firms perform better than widely held publicly listed companies for the obvious reason that the controlling shareholders are still behaving as *owners* of the stock rather than as *renters* of stock to use Jack Bogle's distinction[20] between the behavior of mutual funds in the late 1940s and early 2000s. The extent to which this is so, is shown by the following:

> The financial performance of family-owned companies provides support for their strong relative share-price performance. Revenue growth of family-owned companies has been higher than for non-family-owned peers for each of the past ten years, EBITDA margins are higher and cash flow returns are stronger too. In addition, *family-owned companies tend to focus more on future growth as below-average pay-out ratios support in-line-to-above capex intensity and above-average R&D spending. . .*
>
> These calculations show a clear "alpha" generated by the family-owned universe. We would specifically highlight the following revenue growth characteristics:
> - For each of the past ten years, family-owned companies have shown stronger revenue growth than their non-family-owned peers.
> - In 2009, when non-family-owned companies experienced a revenue decline of around 7%, family-owned companies still managed to grow their top lines, albeit by just 30 bp [basis points].

---

xvi This is also true of unlisted firms where there is a dominant controlling bloc of shareholders, e.g., venture capitalists.

- Over the past two years, the family-owned companies have managed to increase their top-line growth differential to 370 bp in 2016 from 320 bp in 2013, and 250 bp in 2014.
- *Family-owned companies generated a high risk-adjusted revenue growth (i.e., annual average revenue growth divided by the standard deviation of this growth), which might indeed be a result of taking more of a longer-term view with regard to investment decisions.*
- We have also analyzed revenue growth differentials between family and non-family owned companies on a regional basis. *Generally speaking, we find that the revenue growth "alpha" is apparent across all main regions.*[21]   [Emphases mine]

Family firms seem to have a more balanced approach to sustainability and stakeholder needs, shown in Figure 2.6.

Family companies are more long-term focused

Please signal your agreement with the following characteristics of family-owned companies relative to non-family owned companies

Source: Company data; Credit Suisse estimates

Figure 2.6: Characteristics of family firms.

There is an old saying "From rags to riches to rags in three generations." It is a British version of a Chinese saying that states a company, founded with vision and drive, gets conservative by the second generation and goes into decline by the third. While there is a great deal of truth in it because the third generation may lack talent, or are no longer interested in going into the family business, or because there are family feuds about the inheritance and priorities, family-controlled businesses that have hired professional managers to continue the vision have prospered for many generations. Notable examples are shown in Appendix 2.1 "Notable Family Firms Prospering Across the Generations." As these examples illustrate, family firms will likely continue to be a formidable force in the foreseeable future.

Managerial Capitalism

The ultimate purpose of managerial capitalism has been defined as follows:[22]

A new system developed – *managers* capitalism – in which "the corporation came to be run to profit its managers, in complicity if not conspiracy with accountants and the managers of other corporations."

Managerial capitalism developed after World War II and reached its peak in 2000, despite the rise of shareholder capitalism in the 1990s. The late Jack Bogle, founder and long-time CEO of the Vanguard Group described it as follows:

> A new system developed – *managers* capitalism – in which "the corporation came to be run to profit its managers, in complicity if not conspiracy with accountants and the managers of other corporations.". . .
>
> That transmogrification – that *grotesque transformation* – of a system of owners capitalism into a system of managers capitalism required only two ingredients: (1) the diffusion of corporate ownership among a large number of investors, none holding a controlling share of the voting power; and (2) the unwillingness of the agents of the owners – the boards of directors – to honor their responsibility to serve, above all else, the interests of their *principals* – the shareowners themselves.
>
> When most owners either don't or won't or can't stand up for their rights, and when directors lose sight of whom they represent, the resulting power vacuum quickly gets filled by corporate managers. . . *"When we have strong managers, weak directors, co-opted accountants, and passive owners, don't be surprised when the looting begins."*
>
> . . .*When we consider. . .the average CEO's compensation has risen from 42 times that of the average worker in 1980 to 121 times in 1988, and to an astonishing 531 times in 2000 (now it's "only" about 411 times) – it's certainly fair to say that there has been an extraordinary increase in the portion of corporate earnings that corporate managers have arrogated to themselves. . .*
>
> . . .Much of the compensation increase has been fueled by executive stock options. . . Options are almost universally described as "linking the interests of management to the interests of shareholders." *But the fact is that there is no such linkage.* Rather than holding onto their shares, executives typically sell them at the earliest moment the options can be exercised, too often leaving their shareholders holding the bag.[23]
>
> [Emphases mine]

CG is an issue mainly for minority stockholders, in a firm controlled by the managers where there are no significant stockholders that can easily work together.[xvii] In that situation, the stockholders potentially can still exert control to protect their interests but face formidable difficulties (in terms of transaction costs and inadequate incentives) in actually working together.[24]

Managerial capitalism has gone out of fashion because it so obviously was a rigged system allowing management to benefit at the expense of customers, suppliers, and shareholders without being held accountable for the damage they created to the physical, economic, and social environments within which they operated. It was responsible in large part for increasing the inequality that has fueled the rise of populism.

Shareholder Capitalism

The ultimate purpose of shareholder capitalism is defined as follows:[25]

Level 1
"The ultimate aim of the company is return on shareholder equity better than the return for firms of similar risk characteristics."

Level 2
"Risk characteristics for comparison will include similar size, industry, and maturity of market. Better return will mean above the median for such firms, rather than above the average."

Shareholder capitalism was based on Milton Friedman's argument:

The social responsibility of business is to increase its profits. . .*What does it mean to say that the corporate executive has a "social responsibility" in his capacity as businessman? If this statement is not pure rhetoric, it must mean that he is to act in some way that is not in the interest of his employers.* For example, that he is to refrain from increasing the price of the product in order to contribute to the social objective of preventing inflation, even though a price increase would be in the best interests of the corporation. Or that he is to make

---

xvii During discussions at the OECD Asian Roundtable on Corporate Governance held on November 7, 2018, at the Securities Commission Malaysia, one of the speakers from the OECD argued that the focus on resolving the principal-agent conflict resolves a problem that exists mainly in "Anglosphere" capital markets because of their widely dispersed shareholders; but does not exist to the same degree in Asian capital markets where dominant controlling shareholders (either family or government) are the norm who do not face the principal-agent conflict to the same extent because their control allows them to behave as owners with "skin in the game."

expenditures on reducing pollution beyond the amount that is in the best interests of the corporation or that is required by law in order to contribute to the social objective of improving the environment. Or that, at the expense of corporate profits, he is to hire "hardcore" unemployed instead of better qualified available workmen to contribute to the social objective of reducing poverty. *In each of these cases, the corporate executive would be spending someone else's money for a general social interest. Insofar as his actions in accord with his "social responsibility" reduce returns to stockholders, he is spending their money. Insofar as his actions raise the price to customers, he is spending the customers' money. Insofar as his actions lower the wages of some employees, he is spending their money.*[26]   [Emphases mine]

Milton Friedman's argument has been interpreted to mean that the purpose of business is to *maximize* shareholder value – the basis of 1990s shareholder capitalism. There are two fundamental problems with this modified definition of the original argument. The first problem is that different classes of owner do not have the same expectations regarding risk and time horizons. There are:

1. *Shareholders looking for immediate returns* (high frequency traders, day traders).
2. *Hedge funds and analysts interested in quarterly results.*
3. *Patient capital:* Buy-to-hold investors like Warren Buffett, pension funds, insurance companies, and sovereign wealth funds with a long-term view that may extend beyond the tenure of existing management and boards.

This leaves directors with the question: which shareholders should be given priority if they do not all have the same objectives, risk appetites, and time horizons?

The second problem is that it is unclear what time horizons should be applied: short-, medium-, or long-term; and what does sustainability mean? As a result, long-term issues of sustainability can be kicked further down the road to be dealt with by the next generation of directors and management, by which time it may be too late. Sustainability has, however, become a much more pressing problem, as some of its issues have now become clear and present dangers to the neoliberal capitalist economy, as opposed to a distant threat about whose imminence and seriousness there may be legitimately different points of view.

I believe the diverse sustainability challenges to shareholder capitalism's survival in the current political environment are sufficiently serious to invalidate Milton Friedman's central contention that managers who pay attention to stakeholder issues are spending someone else's money. While that may be true of philanthropic CSR (corporate social responsibility), responsible strategizing on behalf of the owners, customers, and employees requires boards and management to engage stakeholders to establish the best routes to long-term sustainability; maintaining the social and political "license to operate," without which none of their interests are well-served.

I believe a better definition of the purpose of a publicly traded company is:

The ultimate aim of the company is return on shareholder equity better than the return for firms of similar risk characteristics.[27]

By comparing the performance of the company with that of its peers, this definition avoids the problem of deciding which shareholders have priority and of needing to specify the time horizon by which shareholder value is to be maximized.

Although it is tongue-in-cheek, I think this is one of the clearest explanations of how shareholder capitalist CG is supposed to work:

> Corporate finance is a business of incentives. There are investors, who put up money, and there are entrepreneurs and managers, who do stuff with the money. The investors would like to get their money back with a profit, but the managers are the ones who control whether or not that happens. The whole theory is about aligning incentives, setting things up so that it is in the managers' own interests to make money for the investors. There are a lot, really a lot a lot a lot, of very standard and well-known tools to do this. The managers are also shareholders and participate along with the investors; the managers get incentive pay that goes up as the investors' returns go up; the managers' future career opportunities depend on their track record of making money for investors; the managers have disclosure obligations, and the shareholders have the right to vote them out if things are going badly; the managers have fiduciary duties to the shareholders; the idea that the managers' duty is to make money for shareholders is taught in business schools and endorsed in the press and generally part of the cultural air that we breathe.[28]

While this approach to capitalism seems sensible, it suffers from two problems. The first is that it assumes institutional investors are still behaving as owners, as they used to just after World War II when stock turnover was only 16% per annum, whereas in 2003 it had risen to 110% – so they no longer behaved as owners. In the words of Jack Bogle describing US mutual funds behavior:

> We are a *rent*-a-stock industry, a world away from Warren Buffett's favorite holding period. Forever.
> But while a fund that *owns* stocks has little choice but to regard proper corporate governance. One that *rents* stocks could hardly care less.[29]

The second problem is it does not deal with the potential sustainability problems caused by externalities that are not costed properly and charged back to the companies that create them. Nor does it deal with the fact that actions taken by one organization may be sensible, but when taken by all organizations at the same time can create catastrophic systemic risk.

State Capitalism

The ultimate purpose of government owned enterprises or SOEs is as follows:[30]

Level 1
"The ultimate purpose of state ownership of enterprises should be to maximize value for society, through an efficient allocation of resources."[31]

Level 2
"Our first priority is to promote and create business and job opportunities in our industry and provide quality products and services at a fair price.
Our second priority is to enlarge the country's industrial base and ensure a clean and safe environment."

In considering how this purpose is to be achieved, it is helpful to revisit the OECD guidelines for SOEs:

1. ***Justifying the existence of SOEs:*** "The state exercises the ownership of SOEs in the interests of the general public. It should carefully evaluate and disclose the objectives that justify state ownership and subject these to a recurrent review."[32]
2. ***State's role as owner:*** "The state should act as an informed and active owner, ensuring that governance of SOEs is carried out in a transparent and accountable manner, with a high degree of professionalism and effectiveness."[33]
3. ***Level playing field:*** ". . . the legal and regulatory framework for SOEs should ensure a level playing field and fair competition in the marketplace when SOEs undertake economic activities."[34]
4. ***Equitable treatment of shareholders and other investors:*** "When SOEs are listed or otherwise include non-state investors among their owners, the state and the enterprises should recognize the rights of all shareholders and ensure shareholders equitable treatment and equal access to corporate information."[35]
5. ***Disclosure and transparency:*** "[SOEs] should observe high standards of transparency and be subject to the same high quality accounting, disclosure, compliance and auditing standards as listed companies."[36]
6. ***Board responsibilities:*** "Boards of SOEs should have the necessary authority, competencies and objectivity to carry out their functions of strategic guidance and monitoring of management. They should act with integrity and be held accountable for their actions."[37]

From a CG viewpoint, SOEs are most likely to fail to meet the standards set by these OECD guidelines in the areas of transparency and accountability as informed and active owners; in disclosure and accounting/auditing standards; and in exercising their board responsibilities. The reasons for such shortfalls, should they occur, are the temptations for governments to use SOEs as a source of political patronage and economic control combined with the shortage of experienced directors who understand business and the shortage of good auditors. Succession planning, in particular, poses problems both at board and senior management levels as a result of political interference, most notably when there is a change of government or minister.

Such shortfalls were tolerated because SOEs were never meant to maximize shareholder value measured in terms of bottom-line results. They were expected to help develop "pillar industries" and help with "social engineering," as well as providing products or services to clients or customers. Clearly, important trade-offs took place to deliver social benefits, even if this meant making less money.

Maybe the impact of these shortfalls can be seen in the performance of SOEs on average, as governments seem to take higher stakes in lower performing companies, shown in Table 2.5. Is this the result of poorer governance or of the fact that governments tend to invest in utilities or companies whose primary purpose is development and social engineering, as opposed to seeking to maximize financial value creation; and which will therefore by their very nature underperform non-governmental enterprises?

Table 2.5: Average government ownership and performance as of end 2017.[38]

Jurisdiction	High performers (%)	Low performers (%)	Difference
China	20	37	−17
Hong Kong (China)	7	47	−40
India	11	26	−15
Indonesia	14	30	−16
Malaysia	21	36	−15
Thailand	8	17	−9
Vietnam	29	38	−9

Taxpaying citizens might be willing to accept lower performance as investors because of the social and economic development benefits their countries as a whole received. For overseas investors, however, there are no such advantages to compensate them for the lower profitability of SOEs.

Stakeholder Capitalism

The ultimate purpose of stakeholder capitalism is defined as:[39]

Promoting business prosperity and corporate accountability with the ultimate objective of realizing long-term shareholder value while [considering] the interest of other stakeholders.

The approach of including all appropriate stakeholders in making company decisions is what differentiates stakeholder capitalism from shareholder capitalism. However, there is still disagreement about the overall goals of stakeholder capitalism, as is clear from the following definition:

> The stakeholder approach is . . . about understanding and using the relationships between the corporation and the groups that have a stake in it so that the best possible economic result can be reached. . . [It] requires decision makers to identify the legitimate stakeholder[s] and their interests first, then weigh and balance the latter against each other and finally make their choice on that basis. How to finally make those choices is up to the decision makers. There also is no overall agreement on what the overall goal of stakeholder theory is. One idea is to make long term value maximization the goal since only by means of pursuing maximization of value created all corporate units and society as a whole can benefit. Another idea puts the balancing of stakeholder interest in the center and makes the coordination of those interests the objective of the corporation . . . a firm can and will be run more efficiently if not only the interests of its shareholders but also of other parties which have a legitimate interest in the corporation are taken into consideration. No interest is predetermined to be more important than another. The decisions are based on a complete consideration of all interests or rather stakes, what includes identification, analysis and making the necessary trade-offs.[40]   [Emphases mine]

Stakeholder capitalism is very much a work in progress and the various issues stakeholders need to consider are multiplying, making it harder than ever to agree on priorities between environmental, economic, employment, and social sustainability. However, it received critical endorsement on August 19, 2019 when the US Business Roundtable's close to 200 members, generating US$7 trillion in annual revenues, issued a new statement of business purpose that dropped the previous Friedmanite purpose that it was to maximize shareholder returns, replacing it with the new purpose placing shareholders as one of five stakeholders, alongside customers, workers, suppliers, and communities.[41]

Summary

There can be no single approach to CG. There are three reasons for this. The first is that capital markets worldwide can be divided into two models, each with key differences in both their institutional and corporate contexts. They affect the likelihood of activist shareholders holding boards to account because of the difference in the liquidity of the two types of market and in the levels of ownership concentration. The corporate contexts show boards are structured differently. This alters their respective levels of independence and the value placed on the importance of shareholder rights and transparency.

Different jurisdictions need different approaches to CG because of the fundamental differences in the foundations of capital markets, amplified by the extent to which individual jurisdictions are blessed with the eight components of an effective CG "ecosystem"; or if they have them, they have them with differing levels of development or political support.

The second reason is the growing importance of Asian capital markets, and in particular China's, which practice the "control" or "hybrid" approaches to CG, reinforcing the move away from the "Anglosphere" approach to CG with its focus on resolving the principal-agent conflict and its excessively short-term attention to bottom-line results.

The third reason is that historically, even within "Anglosphere" markets, there have been five different ways in which companies practiced CG: the family; managerial; shareholder; state; and stakeholder capitalist approaches. Each has its strengths and weaknesses and the managerial capitalist approach has fallen out of favor because it allowed managers (in the words of Jack Bogle) to "loot" their companies. Family firms do well, creating better long-term sustainable results than either the managerial or shareholder capitalist models. The shareholder model has morphed into the stakeholder model, as a result of the growing recognition neoliberal capitalism has failed to answer questions raised by issues of environmental, economic, and social sustainability. State capitalism is, in theory, well-placed to deal with these issues, but has performed less well in economic terms and is vulnerable to political interference and cronyism.

If neoliberal capitalism is to survive current populist attacks, governments, society, and companies will have to find new ways to reconcile competing claims of sustainability, working together internationally as well as nationally and locally – hence the move toward stakeholder capitalism, culminating in the US Business Roundtable's endorsement on August 19, 2019. Making this move successfully requires a fundamental change in the way government, civil society, academia, and business interact with each other; with business finding the lead, without stepping on the others' toes.[42]

Appendix 2.1: Notable Family Firms Prospering Across the Generations

Family	Generations	Comment
Rothschild (UK, France, Germany, Switzerland)	7th	"The family empire is divided among a web of descendants and a few external shareholders. The ownership structure is opaque, which makes it hard to estimate the family wealth, although it is one of the richest in the world." "The closest thing to a 'Rothschild's family' business today is the Rothschild Group, a multinational investment banking company . . . The Rothschild Group's annual revenue was approximately $500 million in 2017 . . . In April 2017, the Rothschilds' net worth was estimated by *Celebrity Net Worth* to be around $400 billion."[43]
Ayala (Philippines)	7th	"Seven siblings control more than one third of Ayala Corp., one of the Philippines' oldest companies, run by members of the seventh generation. The business started as a small Manila distillery and is now a holding company for Ayala Land, Bank of the Philippine Islands, Globe Telecom, and Manila Water. Jaime II is chairman and CEO, brother Fernando is the president and chief operating officer. The family also has stakes in San Miguel, the largest publicly listed food, beverage, and packaging company in Southeast Asia. Inigo Zobel, Jaime's cousin, sits on San Miguel's board."[44]
Wallenberg (Sweden)	5th	"Together, brothers Jacob and Peter junior and their cousin Marcus are the public face of the fifth generation of the Wallenbergs, the Swedish dynasty that can arguably be called Europe's pre-eminent business family. Others may be older or richer but none can combine the Wallenbergs' longevity with the breadth of their holdings. Their company stakes range from drugmaker AstraZeneca and white-goods manufacturer Electrolux to defense group Saab and telecoms-equipment maker Ericsson. Together, they add up to an empire that controls businesses worth €250bn."[45]

Mars (US)	4th	"Forrest Mars, Jr. died in 2016 and Mars, Inc. is now 100% owned by John and Jacqueline Mars. Victoria Mars is the current chairman of the company, a position her father Forrest Mars, Jr. and grandfather Forrest Mars, Sr. once held. She attended Yale and received her MBA from the Wharton School at the University of Pennsylvania. She has spent her entire career in the family business and has been chairman of Mars, Inc. since 2014.The Mars family is determined to keep the company in the family."[46]
Quandt (Germany)	3rd	"The Quandts hold a 46.7-percent stake in BMW, but their investments in other areas have been considered to be brilliant. One of them is SGL Carbon, manufacturer of carbon fiber, an important lightweight material used in the construction of BMW cars. Other investments include the chemicals maker Altana and wind turbine manufacturer Nordex."[47]

References

1 OECD (2015), op. cit., p. 13, https://www.oecd.org/daf/ca/Corporate-Governance-Principles-ENG.pdf, accessed on June 8, 2018.

2 G20/OECD Principles on Corporate Governance, revised in 2015.

3 OECD (2016), op. cit., p. 70.

4 OECD (2016), op. cit.

5 Coombes, P. and Watson. M. (2001), "Corporate Reform in the Developing World," cited in Zinkin, J. (2010), *Challenges in Implementing Corporate Governance: Whose Business is it Anyway?* (Singapore: John Wiley and Sons), p. 10.

6 Zinkin, J. (2019), *Better Governance Across the Board: Creating Value Through Reputation, People and Processes* (Boston, Mass: De|G PRESS).

7 Ralston, D. (2018), "The problem with Australia's banks is one of too much law and not enough enforcement," *The Conversation*, September 29, 2018, https://theconversation.com/the-problem-with-australias-banks-is-one-of-too-much-law-and-too-little-enforcement-103996, accessed on September 30, 2018.

8 Wright, T. and Hope, B. (2018), *Billion Dollar Whale: The Man Who Fooled Wall Street, Hollywood and the World* (New York: Hachette).

9 Fortune Global 500, *Fortune,* https://fortune.com/global500/2019/search/, accessed on August 6, 2019.

10 Ibid.

11 Allen, J. and Li, R. (2018), "Awakening Governance: The Evolution of Corporate Governance in China," *Asian Corporate Governance Association*, p. 22.

12 "Lectures on Corporate Governance – Three Models of Corporate Governance from Developed Capital Markets," *EWMI/PFS Program*, October 2015, p. 7, http://www.emergingmarketsesg.net/esg/wp-content/uploads/2011/01/Three-Models-of-Corporate-Governance-January-2009.pdf, accessed on October 23, 2018.

13 Jang, H. and Kim, J. (2001), "Korea Country Paper: The Role of Boards and Stakeholders in Corporate Governance," The Third OECD Asian Roundtable On Corporate Governance Singapore, 4th-6th April 2001, http://www.oecd.org/corporate/ca/corporategovernanceprinciples/1873050.pdf, accessed on October 23, 2018.

14 OECD (2018), op. cit., p. 45.

15 Ibid., p. 46.

16 Zinkin, J. (2019), op. cit., p. 49.

17 OECD (2015), *OECD Guidelines on Corporate Governance of State Owned Enterprises, 2015 Edition* (Paris: OECD Publishing), p. 17, https://www.oecd-ilibrary.org/docserver/9789264244160-en.pdf?expires=1542261379&id=id&accname=guest&checksum=29D7D3455C42A7989C3D141939B2AAC9, accessed on November 15, 2018.

18 Zinkin, J. (2019), op. cit., p. 49.

19 Scott, K. (2002), "Agency Costs and Corporate Governance" in *The New Palgrave Dictionary of Economics and the Law* (London: Palgrave Macmillan), p. 26, quoted in Wallace, P. and Zinkin, J. (2003), *Corporate Governance* (Singapore: John Wiley & Sons), p. 2.

20 Bogle, J. (2003), "Owners Capitalism vs Managers Capitalism," Speech given to the 2003 National Investor Relations Conference, Orlando, Florida, June 11, 2003, *Bogle Financial Center*, https://www.vanguard.com/bogle_site/sp20030611.html, accessed on August 7, 2019

21 Klerk, E. et al. (2017), "The CS Family 1000," *Credit Suisse Research Institute*, September 2017, pp. 18–19

22 Bogle, J. (2003), Speech given to 2003 National Investor Relations Conference, Orlando, Florida, June 11, 2003, *Bogle Financial Center*, https://www.vanguard.com/bogle_site/sp20030611.html, accessed on August 7, 2019.

23 Ibid.

24 Scott, K. (2002), op. cit., p. 3.

25 Zinkin, J. (2019), op. cit., p. 49.

26 Friedman, M. (1970), "The Social Responsibility of Business Is to Increase Profits," *New York Times Magazine*, September 13, 1970, http://umich.edu/~thecore/doc/Friedman.pdf, accessed on August 8, 2019.

27 Wallace, P. and Zinkin, J. (2005), *Corporate Governance* (Singapore: John Wiley & Sons), p. 57.

28 Levine, M. (2019), "The MoviePass Economy," *Bloomberg Opinion: Money Stuff*, August 8, 2019, https://www.bloomberg.com/opinion/articles/2019-08-07/moviepass-worked-out-great, accessed on August 8, 2019.

29 Bogle, J. (2003), op. cit.

30 Zinkin, J. (2019), op. cit., p. 49.

31 OECD (2015), *OECD Guidelines on Corporate Governance of State-Owned Enterprises, 2015 Edition* (Paris: OECD Publishing), p. 17, https://www.oecd-ilibrary.org/docserver/9789264244160-en.pdf?expires=1542261379&id=id&accname=guest&checksum=29D7D3455C42A7989C3D141939B2AAC9, accessed on November 15, 2018.

32 OECD (2015), op. cit., p. 17.

33 Ibid., p. 18.

34 Ibid., p. 20.

35 Ibid., p. 22.

36 Ibid., p. 24.

37 Ibid., p. 26.

38 OECD (2018), op. cit., p. 48.

39 Securities Commission Malaysia (2017), *Malaysian Code on Corporate Governance*, p. 1.

40 Brandt, F. and Georgiou, K. (2016), "Shareholders vs Stakeholders Capitalism," *Penn Law: Legal Scholarship Repository*, Spring 2016, University of Pennsylvania Law School https://scholarship.law.upenn.edu/cgi/viewcontent.cgi?article=1002&context=fisch_2016, accessed on August 9, 2019.

41 Henderson, R. and Temple-West, P. (2019), "Group of US corporate leaders ditches shareholder-first mantra," *Financial Times*, August 19, 2019.

42 Dirks, G. (2020), in an email reply to the author on January 26, 2020.

43 Putterman, S. (2019), "Meme Way Off in Claim that the Rothschild Family Holds 80 Percent of the World's Wealth," *Politifact*, January 9, 2019, www.politifact.com, accessed on August 12, 2019.

44 "2017 Asia's Richest Families Net Worth, # 43, Zobel Family," *Forbes*, November 14, 2017, https://www.forbes.com/profile/zobel/#72c0ddb864ba, accessed on August 11, 2019.

45 Milne, R. (2015), "Meet the Wallenbergs," *Financial Times Magazine*, June 5, 2015, https://www.ft.com/content/4f407796-0a35-11e5-a6a8-00144feabdc0, accessed on August 11, 2019.

46 Lamare, A. (2018), "How the Mars Family Became One Of The Wealthiest Families On The Planet With A Combined Net Worth of $90 Billion," *Celebrity Net Worth*, September 26, 2018, https://www.celebritynetworth.com/articles/billionaire-news/how-the-mars-family-became-one-of-the-wealthiest-families-on-the-planet-with-a-combined-net-worth-of-90-billion/, accessed on August 11, 2019.

47 Boeriu, H. (2014), "The Quandts: Germany's Wealthiest Family," *BMW Blog*, November 2, 2014, https://www.bmwblog.com/2014/11/02/quandts-germanys-wealthiest-family/, accessed on August 11, 2019.

Part 2: **Corporate Governance's Five Sustainability Challenges**

Five sustainability challenges to CG have arisen since 2000 as a result of increased awareness of environmental issues and climate change; the retreat from full-bore globalization as result of political change; the impending disruption of "Industry 4.0"; and the rise of the internet and social media. As a result, CG's remit has broadened to one of ensuring long-term success and sustainability of organizations – a much more complicated and challenging responsibility for boards and directors, for which they may not be well-prepared.

Chapter 3, "Environmental Sustainability," deals with three increasingly urgent challenges to environmental sustainability: climate change, moving to a circular economy, and conservation.

Chapter 4, "Economic Sustainability," deals with two social issues challenging the sustainability of neoliberal capitalism: the importance of growth being inclusive and reducing rising inequality so that everybody can benefit, not just the few.

Chapter 5, "Employment Sustainability," deals with the challenges for boards created by the impact of disruptive technologies on employment and employability, and whether education systems provide what is needed.

Chapter 6, "Social Sustainability," explores issues and challenges for boards when considering how they can contribute by being responsible citizens and bridging cultures.

Chapter 7, "Volatility and Uncertainty," deals with the challenges posed by volatility and uncertainty on board decision making.

Chapter 8, "Complexity and Ambiguity," deals with the challenges posed by complexity and ambiguity on board decision making.

Chapter 3
Environmental Sustainability

This chapter is presented in three parts. The first discusses the CG challenge posed by climate change; the second examines the issues raised by moving to a circular economy; the third explores the questions raised by conservation. It closes with a summary of how boards can move toward environmental sustainability.

It is tempting to focus only on climate change given the extreme weather events of the last two or three years in various parts of the globe. However, environmental sustainability requires people to recognize the broader impact we have had on the planet:

> The Anthropocene is a multidimensional challenge. . .
>
> . . .The climate has certainly changed, but so too have other aspects of the planetary system. Take the lithosphere: 193,000 human-made "inorganic crystalline compounds," or what you and I might call "rocks," now vastly outnumber Earth's ~5000 natural minerals, while *8.3 billion tons of plastics coat the land, water, and our internal organs. Due to modern agribusiness techniques, so much topsoil is washing away that England has only about 60 more harvests left.*
>
> The biosphere is equally altered. Never has the planet been so crowded with human beings. In 1900, there were around 1.5 billion of us; in the 1960s, around 3 billion; today there are upwards of 7.4 billion. *Human beings and our domesticated animals comprise an astounding 97% of the total zoomass of terrestrial mammals, meaning that wild creatures make up a miserly 3%. Humans and our companion species occupy considerably more than half of the planet's habitable land surface. . . fresh water renews itself at the rate of about 1% a year, but currently 21 out of 37 of the world's major aquifers are being drawn down faster – in some cases much faster – than they can be replenished.*
>
> . . .*Warmer oceans interfere with the production of oxygen by phytoplankton, and some scientists predict that with a rise of 6°C – which could happen as soon as 2100 – this oxygen production could cease.*[1]

Dealing with the consequences of humanity's abuse of the planet's resources requires governments, society, companies, and individuals to change their behavior in four areas with the help of academia: population control; climate change; moving to a circular economy;[i] and conservation.

The challenges posed for boards in the three environmental areas are sufficiently different that they should be treated separately, even though there is

---

i The linear economy is characterized by industrial processes and business models of "Make, Use, Waste, Dispose," whereas the circular economy is characterized by "Reduce, Make, Use, Recycle, Reuse, and Remanufacture," avoiding problems of disposal and waste.

https://doi.org/10.1515/9783110670486-003

considerable overlap between them. Unlike tackling climate change which requires global collaboration, moving to a circular economy is something every organization can do without having to wait for global agreements. Conservation is rather different in that it affects most organizations only indirectly, unless they are in the business of converting animals and plants into food, or services such as ecotourism.

The common thread that binds these three environmentally related topics is the fact we can no longer afford to take the services nature provides for granted. When people were few and the planet empty, the abundance of services provided by nature meant we could treat them as free goods. Now that humanity is expected to reach 8 billion by 2023[2] and natural resources are being depleted, economics remind us that the price of the services provided by nature must inevitably rise. In 2011, these free services were valued at US$75 trillion annually, equivalent to one year's global production.[3]

Boards therefore must stop taking nature for granted. They would do well to remember the words of Sir Crispin Tickell, former chief scientific adviser to the British government, that "the economy is a subset of the ecology, and not the other way around."[4] Perhaps we find it so hard to remember that ecology and nature define what is humanly possible, and that humanity does not have total power over nature because we believe what the book of Genesis in the Bible tells us:

> Then God said, "Let us make man in our image, after our likeness. And let them have dominion over the fish of the sea and over the birds of the heavens and over the livestock and over all the earth and over every creeping thing that creeps on the earth."[5]

Climate Change

Climate change may create existential problems for humanity and businesses and therefore must be considered when boards make decisions. However, the length of the time horizons involved and the requirement for globally coordinated solutions present serious problems for boards required by shareholders to maximize short-term objectives without recognizing the impact of externalities they create at the local level, let alone at the global level.

The first time I became aware of climate change was when BP China was my client for corporate affairs in 1997. John Browne (now Lord Browne), then CEO of BP worldwide, gave a historic speech at Stanford University where he raised the issue, explaining BP was prepared to consider climate change as a real concern, unlike all other oil companies at the time. His reasoning was as follows:

A year ago, the Second Report of the Inter-Governmental Panel on Climate Change was published. That report and the discussion which has continued since its publication, shows that there is mounting concern about two stark facts. *The concentration of carbon dioxide in the atmosphere is rising, and the temperature of the earth's surface is increasing.*

Karl Popper once described all science as being provisional. What he meant by that was that all science is open to refutation, to amendment, and to development. That view is certainly confirmed by the debate around climate change. *There's a lot of noise in the data. It is hard to isolate cause and effect. But there is now an effective consensus among the world's leading scientists and serious and well-informed people outside the scientific community that there is a discernible human influence on the climate, and a link between the concentration of carbon dioxide and the increase in temperature.*

The prediction of the IPCC is that over the next century temperatures might rise by a further 1 to 3.5 degrees centigrade, and that sea levels might rise by between 15 and 95 centimeters. Some of that impact is probably unavoidable, because it results from current emissions. Those are wide margins of error, and there remain large elements of uncertainty – about cause and effect . . . and even more importantly about the consequences. But it would be unwise and potentially dangerous to ignore the mounting concern.

The time to consider the policy dimensions of climate change is not when the link between greenhouse gases[ii] *and climate change is conclusively proven . . . but when the possibility cannot be discounted and is taken seriously by the society of which we are part.*

We in BP have reached that point. It is an important moment for us. A moment when analysis demonstrates the need for action and solutions. *To be absolutely clear – we must now focus on what can and what should be done, not because we can be certain climate change is happening, but because the possibility can't be ignored.*

If we are all to take responsibility for the future of our planet, then it falls to us to begin to take precautionary action now. . .[6]   [Emphases mine]

John Browne made three fundamental points in the speech. The first and most important was BP's adoption of the "precautionary principle." Even though there was considerable noise around the IPCC findings in 1996, he argued it was better to be safe by taking action before it was too late. The second was that dramatic action to move away from fossil fuels would crash into two realities of economic growth: first, there was no immediate practical alternative available in developed economies; second, developing countries still needed fossil fuels to continue developing. The third was that the only way forward was to adopt a step-by-step, "learning as you go" approach, and that such an approach needed to be adopted immediately.

In May 1997, such a statement by the CEO of a major oil company was revolutionary. Leading oil companies publicly denied the possibility of a link between burning fossil fuels and climate change; even though both Shell and Exxon had secret documents as early as the 1980s warning them of climate

---

ii The primary greenhouse gases (GHGs) are water vapor, carbon dioxide, methane, nitrous oxide, and ozone.

change.[7] This speech was particularly significant for two reasons: first, it was given in the United States, at the time the leading emitter of greenhouse gases (GHGs), and second because the burning of fossil fuels in transportation is so important.

Meeting the Challenge of Climate Change

Twenty-two years later, these three arguments remain just as valid as they were in 1997; only the urgency to act is much greater if we are to meet the targets set in the 2016 Paris Agreement:

> The Paris Agreement central aim is to strengthen the global response to the threat of climate change by keeping a global temperature rise this century well below 2 degrees Celsius above pre-industrial levels and to pursue efforts to limit the temperature increase even further to 1.5 degrees Celsius.[8]

The 2018 United Nations Environment Emissions Gap Report summarized the situation as follows:

> Trends in global GHG emissions:
> - Global greenhouse gases show no signs of peaking.
> - Global CO_2 emissions from energy and industry increased in 2017, following a three-year period of stabilization.
> - Total annual greenhouse gas emissions, including from land use change, reached a record high of 53.5 $GtCO_2e$[iii] in 2017, an increase of 0.7 $GtCO_2e$ compared with 2016.
> - In contrast, *global GHG emissions in 2030 need to be approximately 25 percent and 55 percent lower than in 2017 to put the world on a least-cost pathway to limiting global warming to 2°C and 1.5°C respectively.*[9]   [Emphasis mine]

The fact that 2018 saw a faster growth in emissions than 2017 is a cause for concern.[10] It reflects a number of factors: the cold winter and hot summer in the US leading to increased demand for heating and air conditioning; China's increased emissions as a result of economic stimulus aimed at the construction sector with its heavy emissions; and the growth in developing countries which created further energy demands:

> Insufficient emission reductions in developed countries and a need for increased energy use in developing countries where per capita emissions remain far below those of

---

iii $GtCO_2e$ = 1 billion metric tons of carbon dioxide equivalent. It is a simplified way to put emissions of various GHGs on a common footing by expressing them in terms of the amount of carbon dioxide that would have the same global warming effect.

wealthier nations will continue to put upward pressure on CO2 emissions. *Peak emissions will occur only when total fossil CO2 emissions finally start to decline despite growth in global energy consumption, with fossil energy production replaced by rapidly growing low- or no-carbon technologies.*[11]   [Emphasis mine]

Potential Consequences of Failure

The impact of climate change on land use varies by region. The Intergovernmental Panel on Climate Change (IPCC) estimates in its summary for policymakers that 25% of the planet's ice-free land area is already affected by human-caused degradation. Agricultural soil erosion where there is no tillage is 10 to 20 times greater than the rate at which soil is formed. Where there is conventional tillage, it is eroding 100 times faster than it is being formed. Climate change makes things worse in low-lying coastal areas, river deltas, drylands, and in permafrost areas. Over the period 1961–2013, the annual area of drylands in drought has increased, on average, by slightly more than 1% per year, with large variations in given years.

People living in already degraded or desertified areas are increasingly badly affected by climate change. In 2015, an estimated 380–620 million people lived within areas experiencing desertification between the 1980s and 2000s. The highest numbers of people affected are in South and East Asia and the regions bordering the Sahara. Other dryland regions have also experienced desertification.[12]

The other consequences of climate change are rising sea levels and melting ice. Melting ice does not just contribute to the rise in sea levels, it also puts billions of people at risk in Asia and South America who depend on glaciers to store water for them, acting as "water towers in the clouds":

1. ***Rising sea levels:*** 70.8% of the Earth's surface is covered by sea.[13] The seas are expected to rise by around a half meter in the next eighty years, though they could rise by twice as much in some places:

> While all coastal cities will be affected by sea-level rises, some will be hit much harder than others. Asian cities will be particularly badly affected. About four out of every five people impacted by sea-level rise by 2050 will live in East or South East Asia. US cities, especially those on the East and Gulf coasts, are similarly vulnerable. *More than 90 US coastal cities are already experiencing chronic flooding – a number that is expected to double by 2030. Meanwhile, about three-quarters of all European cities will be affected by rising sea levels,* especially in the Netherlands, Spain and Italy. Africa is also highly threatened, due to rapid urbanization in coastal cities and the crowding of poor populations in informal settlements along the coast. . .
>
> So-called "delta cities" are already bearing the brunt of rising seas. More than 340 million people live in deltas like Dhaka, Guangzhou, Ho Chi Minh City, Hong Kong, Manila, Melbourne, Miami, New Orleans, New York, Rotterdam, Tokyo and Venice. . . .

> The 48 major coastal deltas in the Americas, Europe and Asia formed ideal sites for cities to thrive, owing to their access to the sea and fertile farmland. . . *But coastal living is becoming a liability: the costs of sea-level rise could rise to trillions of dollars a year in damages by 2100.*[14]   [Emphases mine]

Major storm surges could make matters worse, as Hurricane Sandy did in New York in 2012.[15]

2. ***Disappearing glaciers:*** Scientists gathered on August 18, 2019, in Iceland to memorialize Okjökull, known as Ok for short, after it lost its status as a glacier in 2014. The inscription, titled "A letter to the future," in English and Icelandic, on the monument paints a bleak picture.

> Ok is the first Icelandic glacier to lose its status as a glacier. In the next 200 years, all our glaciers are expected to follow the same path. This monument is to acknowledge that we know what is happening and know what needs to be done. Only you know if we did it.[16]

If glaciers continue to melt at the current rates around the world, their disappearance will create severe problems:

a. *The resulting rise in sea levels will displace people.* The coastal climate refugees will increase competition for ever scarcer land and food, leading to greater economic hardship and maybe to unforeseen conflicts. By 2060, 1.6 billion people may have to move inland and this could rise to 2 billion by 2100:[17]

> We're going to have more people on less land and sooner than we think . . . The future rise in global mean sea level probably won't be gradual. Yet few policy makers are taking stock of the significant barriers to entry that coastal climate refugees, like other refugees, will encounter when they migrate to higher ground.[18]

b. *The disappearance of mountain glaciers will reduce available drinking water.* Millions depend on glaciers for their drinking water from the Andes in South America and the Hindu Kush and Himalayas in Asia.[19] Mountain glaciers act as "water towers in the sky," storing winter precipitation as ice and releasing it slowly in summer as water for drinking and agriculture. In their absence, the likelihood of flooding increases whenever there is serious precipitation, which will not be suitable for drinking.

c. *The disappearance of glaciers will increase the threat of disease.* The glacier runoff in Greenland and the Antarctic will raise the level of the sea, making flooding more likely in coastal areas. Without mountain glacier "water towers," winter precipitation is more likely to cause floods, increasing the threat of disease through resulting sewage pollution:

One particularly gross consequence of that flooding is the impact on sewage treatment plants, which are often built at low elevations close to the oceans.

Floods can cause massive amounts of untreated sewage to flow into rivers, streams, streets and even homes. That pollutes sources of water, harms wildlife and helps spread diseases.[20]

Reaching Agreed Targets

Perhaps the most important conclusions of the IPCC report were that to reach the targets agreed in Paris, we will have to:

1. ***Change the way we manage land*** so that it releases less CO_2. Peat lands will have to be restored by halting drainage schemes so they continue to act as long-term sinks for CO_2 sequestration. We will have to stop cutting down forests to replace them with grazing land for livestock. Felling trees accelerates climate change in two ways: first by removing trees to sequester CO_2; and second by increasing the amount of methane produced by livestock:

> As trees are felled and farms take their place, this human-managed land emits about a quarter of global greenhouse-gas pollution every year, including 13 percent of carbon dioxide and 44 percent of the super-warming but short-lived pollutant methane.[21]

Changing land use is critical, but it is far more difficult than we imagine. Every major food chain on Earth begins with a plant, somewhere, transfiguring photons into sugar. This is the net primary production the IPCC refers to. But what are the implications of this?

> The human demand for food, meat, clothes, and warmth now consumes at least 25 percent of the net product of photosynthesis on land. . . The global economy devours as many as *one out of every three sugar molecules* by dirt-bound plants. . . And we have roughly hooked one out of every four of them into our planetary system of consumption and speculative exchange. . .
>
> For the scientific community, [the IPCC] document is a milestone because it assumes that land *is* scarce and precious. Climate researchers, for decades, have sometimes talked about land as if it is a limitless global sponge capable of cleaning the worst mess in human history. *A recent high-profile study, for instance, cheerfully suggested soaking up most of the planet's carbon pollution by planting 1.2 trillion trees across 2.2 billion acres worldwide.* It was impressive research sold to the public as The Solution to Climate Change. And there's a problem with that. *Those 2.2 billion acres – an area roughly the size of the continental United States – are already in use.* They comprise, in large part, the planet's most productive farmland! And in the decades to come, that farmland is going to be very useful if we hope to feed the 9.8 billion people who will soon reside on the planet. . .
>
> *The biggest of these issues: Land can't really multitask.*[22]   [Emphases mine]

2. ***Produce and consume food less wastefully.*** The UN Food and Agriculture
   Organization estimates that one-third of the food we grow is lost or wasted
   between farm and fork. Figure 3.1 shows the losses per capita by region
   and whether they occur between farm and retail or between retail and
   consumer:[23]

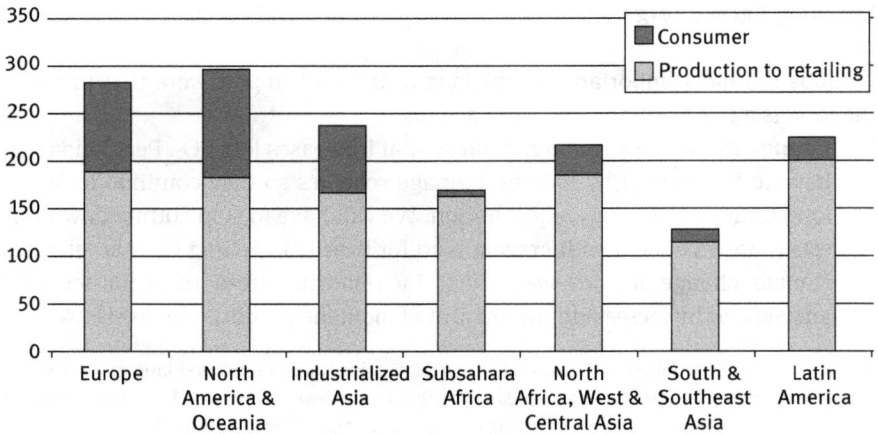

Figure 3.1: Per capita food loss and waste between farm and fork.

Rich countries produce nearly twice as much food as poor countries per capita
(900 kilos a year versus 460 kilos in the poorest regions). In the industrialized
regions, more than 40% of losses occur at retail and consumer levels, as a result of quality standards overemphasizing appearance and adherence to strict
sell-by dates. In developing countries, 40% of losses occur post-harvest and
during processing. These occur mainly at early stages of the food value chain
and can be traced back to financial, managerial, and technical constraints in
harvesting techniques as well as inadequate storage and cooling facilities.
Strengthening the supply chain through the direct support of farmers and investments in infrastructure and transportation, as well as in an expansion of
the food and packaging industry could help to reduce food loss and waste.

Food loss and waste are not just a major squandering of resources, including water, land, energy, labor, and capital; they also needlessly produce GHGs, contributing further to global warming and climate change.[24]
However, given that land cannot multitask, much greater focus should be
placed on eliminating the enormous waste in the ways we currently produce food.

3. ***Change the mix of food we eat.*** Among the measures put forward by the report is the proposal of a major shift towards vegetarian and vegan diets.

> "The consumption of healthy and sustainable diets, such as those based on coarse grains, pulses and vegetables, and nuts and seeds . . . presents major opportunities for reducing greenhouse gas emissions," the report states.[25]
>
> But unlike other sources of pollution – such as the burning of fossil fuels, which must be quickly reduced globally – land can't just be shut down. It must be made into a tool in the climate fight. . .it will require hundreds of millions of affluent people in the Northern Hemisphere to change their diet, eating many more plants and much less meat – and especially much less red meat – than they do now.[26]

This idea is not new. Agricultural engineers at Ohio State University *in 1975* compared the energy costs of producing poultry, pork, and other meats with the energy costs of producing soybeans, corn, and other plant foods. They found that even the *least* efficient plant food is *nearly ten times* as efficient as the *most* energy efficient animal food:

> Even the best of the animal enterprises examined returns only 34.5% of the investment of fossil energy to use in food energy, whereas the poorest of five crop enterprises examined returns 328%.[27]
>
> Corn or wheat provide [sic] 22 times more protein per calorie of fossil fuel expended than does feedlot beef. Soybeans are even better – **40** times more efficient than feedlot beef![28]

Changing Institutional Attitudes

If boards thought they could avoid discussing climate change because reconciling what shareholders want in the short-term was incompatible with resolving issues that might occur in ten, twenty, or thirty years, or on the grounds that climate change is a hoax, that is no longer the case.

In the UK and Australia, regulators now require boards to make public what they are doing to mitigate their climate change risks. The UK Parliament's Environmental Audit Committee (EAC) has called for the City of London to face mandatory climate reporting within the next three years to avoid jeopardizing hundreds of billions of pounds worth of pension savings. The committee urged the government to "clarify in law" that pension funds have a duty to consider long-term environmental risks to protect their savers. The UK Treasury has also outlined plans to force companies and pension funds and financial services providers to show by 2022 how the climate emergency could put their finances at risk. The EAC supported the Treasury's approach, calling for "climate risk" reporting to be mandatory on a "comply or explain" basis.[29]

Mary Creagh, who chairs the committee, said: "Climate change poses financial risks to a range of investments – from food and farming, to infrastructure, construction and insurance liability. . .

. . .We need to fix the incentives in our financial system that encourage short-term thinking. Long-term sustainability must be factored into financial decision making," Creagh said. *"We want to see mandatory climate risk reporting and a clarification in law that pension trustees have a duty to consider long term sustainability, not just short-term returns."*[30]   [Emphasis mine]

These calls for change in reporting are the result of the UK government legislating for a net zero carbon economy by 2050, following Parliament's declaration of a climate emergency on May 1, 2019.[31]

The governors of the Bank of England (Mark Carney) and of the Banque de France (Francois Villeroy de Galhau) wrote an open letter to the *Guardian* in April 2019 urging financial regulators around the world to carry out climate change stress tests to spot any systemic risks and called for a massive reallocation of capital to prevent global warming above the 2°C maximum target set in the Paris Agreement; arguing that "if some companies and industries fail to adjust to this new world, they will fail to exist."[32]

Insurers already face increased losses from more frequent extreme weather events (hurricanes, floods, droughts, and heatwaves). Banks could be hit by major asset write-offs if the assets depended on burning fossil fuels, once net zero carbon economies become the norm. The Bank of England estimates as much as US$20 trillion could be wiped out by climate change, if effective actions are not taken by boards.[33]

Even in Australia, where the current coalition government backs the coal industry, supported by parts of a press that cites anecdotes to cast doubt on the findings of scientists,[34] in opposition to Pacific islanders who fear their nations will disappear as a result of climate change,[35] there has been a major change in institutional attitudes:

This week the head of the Reserve Bank, Philip Lowe, gave a speech specifically about the risks to the economy at the 14th Annual Risk Australia conference. He devoted one section to "climate risk" in which he told the audience of risk managers to take appropriate account of one risk that plays out over a longer horizon, namely "climate risk."

He also advised that "climate is a challenging risk to assess but an increasingly necessary one. *Businesses need to take account of both the physical risks and the transition risks."*

He referenced information released this week by the Australian Securities and Investment Commission, which noted its regulatory guidance for company directors was to "to adopt a probative and proactive approach to emerging risks, including climate risk" and "disclose meaningful and useful climate risk related information to investors."

Such bodies don't do these things for laughs or to please the greenies. They do it because they know climate change is real and that companies that ignore it could be held liable in the future.

It is why reinsurers . . . very much take climate change into account. Earlier this year the world's largest reinsurer, Munich Re, warned that the cost of insurance in areas likely to be affected by the impact of climate change – whether it be flooding, bushfire, or increased hurricanes and cyclones – could cause them to have to increase their risk prices, which in turn could mean that *"some people on low and average incomes in some regions will no longer be able to buy insurance."*[36]   [Emphases mine]

Pressure on boards can only be expected to increase as politicians begin to take the threat of climate change seriously. For example, in the UK, after Parliament voted for declaring a climate emergency and the government legislated carbon neutrality by 2050, a cross-party Parliamentary report looking into actions taken so far concluded much more was needed. The MPs recommended the government should discourage personal vehicle use, ban sale of petrol (gasoline) and diesel vehicles by 2035 instead of 2040, and reward energy-efficient homebuilding with stamp duty relief to meet its legally binding target of net-zero carbon emissions by 2050.[37]

In these circumstances, boards in Britain will have to consider carefully what they need to do about climate change, even if it is only to manage their insurance costs. Those who will find reconciling the long-term impact of climate with the needs of shareholders the most difficult are boards whose organizations contribute most to creating GHGs. In 2018, the United States Environmental Protection Agency (EPA) documented US contributions to global warming by sector (see Table 3.1).

The past focus of climate activists on transportation, electricity generation and industry made sense. More recently, attention has been given to the emissions created by agriculture and land use, as people have begun to recognize belatedly that land cannot "multitask" – it cannot act as a source of food, warmth, and clothing at the same time as acting as a sink to capture CO_2.

The difficulties directors face when attempting to reconcile how best to continue with their existing business models while preparing for climate change is illustrated by BP's journey from being the earliest advocate for recognizing the threat posed by climate change back to investing unashamedly in fossil fuels.

In 1997, BP signalled it was going to lead the way away from fossil fuels. In 2000, BP changed what BP stood for from "British Petroleum" to "BP." This was interpreted as meaning "Beyond Petroleum" by stakeholders. So, at the first AGM [annual general meeting] following its name change, environmentalist shareholders demanded BP should immediately exit its fossil fuels businesses to demonstrate that it meant what the name change signified, much to the embarrassment of the

Table 3.1: United States sectoral contribution to global warming (2017). [38]

Sector	%
Transportation: The majority of GHGs are CO_2 from the combustion of petroleum-based products, like gasoline. Passenger cars and light-duty trucks, including sport utility vehicles, pickup trucks, and minivans account for over half of the emissions. The remaining greenhouse gas emissions come from freight trucks, commercial aircraft, ships, boats, and trains, as well as pipelines and lubricants. Relatively small amounts of methane (CH_4) and nitrous oxide (N_2O) are emitted during fuel combustion. In addition, a small amount of hydrofluorocarbon (HFC) emissions result from the use of mobile air conditioners and refrigerated transport.	28.9
Electricity production: Approximately 62.9 percent of US electricity comes from burning fossil fuels, mostly coal and natural gas. Given the importance of this sector, the emphasis on renewables is not a surprise.	27.5
Industry: Greenhouse gas emissions from industry primarily come from burning fossil fuels for energy, as well as greenhouse gas emissions from certain chemical reactions necessary to produce goods from raw materials.	22.2
Commercial and residential: Greenhouse gas emissions from businesses and homes arise primarily from fossil fuels burned for heat, the use of certain products that contain greenhouse gases, and the handling of waste.	11.6
Agriculture: Greenhouse gas emissions from agriculture (primarily methane) come from livestock such as cows, agricultural soils, and rice production (particularly from burning off rice stalks after harvest).	9.0
Land use and forestry: Land areas can act as a sink or a source of greenhouse gas emissions. In the United States, since 1990, managed forests and other lands have absorbed more CO_2 from the atmosphere than they emit.	(11.1)

board who argued such a move would be impossible, as fossil fuels still represented more than 90% of the business.

The board was presented with an excruciating dilemma – how to reconcile the fact that BP's long-term future was to exit fossil fuels; without destroying its existing business, potentially becoming vulnerable to a class action by shareholders who were not interested in its long-term future. This dilemma became more acute over time because BP was involved in the Alberta oil sands project and then the Deepwater Horizon disaster.[39] This uncomfortable disconnect led BP to being accused of "greenwashing" (the process of conveying a false impression or providing misleading information about how a company's products are more environmentally sound) with the company finally selling its wind assets in 2013, having exited solar in 2011.[40]

The fossil fuel industry is not the only industry faced with long-term existential threats from climate change, though it is the one most directly and obviously at risk of ending up with "stranded assets" that have no further use once economies make the transition to net-zero carbon economies.

Moving to a Circular Economy

Moving from a linear to a circular economy improves environmental sustainability, independent of tackling climate change. It aims to achieve sustainable value creation by breaking the link between growth and profitability and the need to consume ever more resources. This can be done through a rigorous application of "Reduce, Reuse, Recycle, and Remanufacture," reducing stresses on the environment caused by depletion, pollution, and waste, coincidentally helping slow down global warming.

Boards will still find themselves facing difficulties reconciling what needs to be done with the demands of shareholders, who are only interested in quarterly time horizons or annual performance. Their decisions will be more stressful because they can see some businesses have already made the transition to the circular way of doing business successfully. They will be subjected to increased investor and regulatory pressure to adopt a stakeholder capitalist approach, putting shareholders' interests alongside those of other stakeholders. The pressure to move from a linear to a circular business model is immediate.

There are a number of ways by which we can reduce the impact of capital investments on the demand for virgin raw materials, including energy inputs. Investments can be made using recycled materials – for example, electric steel rather than basic oxygen steel, recycled aluminum rather than newly smelted aluminum and so on. The savings in choosing electric steel, for example, can be impressive, even though 30% more electricity is needed. When comparing electric steel with basic oxygen steel, electric steel uses one-tenth of the fuel, one-eighth of the water, one-fifth of the air, and less than one-fortieth of other materials, compared with basic oxygen steel.[41]

Energy demands can be reduced significantly by constructing offices differently and retrofitting old ones to make them energy efficient.

This pressure is most likely to be translated into measurements of the organizational "footprint," meaning all the positive and negative environmental and social impacts throughout the organization's value chain. At its most simple, the buildings, land, and equipment owned by organizations, the resources they consume, the emissions they produce, and any resulting waste created by the energy, water, and materials used to source, manufacture, market, sell, transport, and ultimately dispose of their products and services are the basis of the "footprint." The more advanced lifecycle view of "footprint" extends this analysis to include the organization's entire supply and value chain:[42]

> *Today, like it or not, every company is responsible for its full life cycle impacts. . .*
>
> *A company's responsibility does not end at the factory gate.* Coca-Cola and Pepsi are not only responsible for the energy and water used to make their products; they are also responsible – in a growing way – for the obesity epidemic and the litter of used soda cans and bottles that end up on roadsides or in the Great Pacific garbage patch. . . Likewise, Ford and General Motors and BMW bear some responsibility for the carbon footprint of all of us driving their vehicles throughout our lifetime. And let's face it: auto companies also bear responsibility for not having been (and being) as effective as they could in minimizing the overall impact of cars and trucks on society globally. Over the past several decades, a growing number of companies have sold off their "dirty businesses" perhaps as part of their transformation to becoming more sustainable companies. *But selling off your dirty businesses, especially to owners in countries that are not strictly regulated, does not help the global ecosystem.* Responsibility for legacy businesses can have a long tail, as U.S. companies have found with their former contaminated ("Superfund") sites.[43]
>
> [Emphases mine]

If economic activity is to be sustained and increased, the stock of "manmade capital" must at a minimum be maintained. As we replace capital there is a chance that we can do this in a way that uses fewer raw materials than were used in the old capital stock. Closed loop thinking to do this was already being practiced successfully in the 1990s. Reducing the use of materials of all types can be achieved by moving away from the outright sale of products where manufacturers have no interest in making their products and services last long. This move away can be achieved as follows:

1. ***Leasing instead of selling***: Once manufacturers *offer consumers/buyers a stream of services to be enjoyed* as a result of leasing equipment, manufacturer profits are maximized by minimizing the number of times equipment needs to be serviced and replaced – provided it can continue to provide desired levels of service. This is the opposite of a policy of outright sale, where manufacturer profits are maximized by the sale of as many units as possible, with an attendant consumption of raw materials and the issues of depletion,

pollution, and disposal this consumption creates. The only drawback to this approach is that it can impede innovation.[iv]

2. *Extended product liability*: Here manufacturers have every interest in making their products long-lasting, so both manufacturer and customer are rewarded for moving away from a disposable mentality. Once again, the only drawback of this approach is that it may slow down innovation.

3. *Joint ownership or use*: This requires fewer products for the same amount of services, since customers are rewarded for sharing the capital goods and the services they provide. Car-pooling, taxi sharing, subsidizing public transport so people use common equipment more in going about their daily lives are well-known examples. The same applies in apartment buildings, where inhabitants share laundry facilities rather than investing wastefully in individual washing machines. This principle also applies to co-generation, where power stations use the waste heat they generate to heat entire neighborhoods. This principle has been adopted to great effect by Airbnb, Uber and Lyft, and other IT platforms built on the concept of sharing underutilized facilities and capital equipment.

4. *Remanufacturing:* This is achieved by preserving the stable frame of a product after use and replacing only worn-out parts combined with product design optimized for durability, remanufacturing, and recycling. Volkswagen's mainly aluminum Audi is designed to maximize the opportunity to recycle the car after it has served its purpose.[44] The same approach can be used for PVC with Belland materials:

> As is the case with aluminium, the recycled material has precisely the same properties as the virgin material, but far less energy and matter are needed to produce the recycled version. *On a lifecycle basis, a factor of four to ten is easily achieved in material efficiency when changing from, say, PVC to Belland material.*[45]   [Emphasis mine]

---

iv Originally, Xerox charged for how many copies customers made rather than selling their photocopiers outright – an early application of service selling rather than product selling. As long as there was no serious competition, this model worked well. Xerox copiers were built to last. However, once the Japanese entered the market with an outright selling business model, Xerox found itself threatened, in particular by Canon. The Japanese copiers had an expected life of around three years and were much cheaper as a result. They were able to undermine Xerox because the technological lifecycle was shorter than three years, giving their customers an opportunity to trade in their old models before they noticed they were becoming unreliable to replace them with faster, better photocopiers with more innovative features than the long-life Xerox models. Xerox was forced to meet the Japanese challenge by moving to outright sale in the 1980s, with its shorter product life cycles and more rapid innovation. Only as environmental issues came to the fore in the 1990s, was Xerox able to revert to its original business model with a new tagline: "Zero waste products from zero waste factories."

Conservation

Conservation is a different matter. It affects the long-term viability of organizations only indirectly, unless they are actively engaged in converting animals and plants into products or services from which they make money. That said, we still do not understand fully how biodiversity benefits us all; so maybe preventing the sixth mass extinction is more than an emotional and moral obligation boards must consider:

> The destruction of nature has reduced wildlife populations by 60% since 1970 and plant extinctions are running at a 'frightening' rate according to scientists. In May, the world's leading researchers warned that humanity was in jeopardy from the accelerating decline of the planet's natural life-support systems, which provide the food, clean air and water on which society ultimately depends.[46]
>
> In the past two years scores of scientific studies have suggested that trillions of murmuring, droning, susurrating honeybees, butterflies, caddisflies, damselflies and beetles are dying off. "If all mankind were to disappear," wrote E.O. Wilson, the doyen of entomologists, "the world would regenerate. . . If insects were to vanish the environment would collapse into chaos."[47]

We need those insects to pollinate the plants that create the food we eat; and to feed all the other animals that live off them. Without them, the environment would collapse.

What we do know is that:

> People currently use one quarter to one third of land's potential net primary production for food, feed, fibre, timber and energy. Land provides the basis for many other ecosystem functions and services, including cultural and regulating services, that are essential for humanity. In one economic approach, *the world's terrestrial ecosystem services have been valued on an annual basis to be approximately equivalent to the annual global Gross Domestic Product.*[48]
>
> [Emphasis mine]

The critical "natural capital" agenda divides into four parts: (1) pollution in general and the biosphere being used as a sink for the undesirable outputs of human economic activity – i.e., managing waste; (2) degradation of the environment, as a result of the desperately poor in the Third World damaging their surroundings because they have little alternative, given their distressed circumstances; (3) management of water resources; and (4) issues raised by intensive farming on land and at sea.

From a purely CG perspective, boards can only consider the issues of pollution and waste, and dealing with intensive farming on land and sea. Preventing the desperately poor from damaging the environment because they cannot wait for a better future is the role of governments, as is managing water resources better from a supply perspective. I will therefore confine the discussion to pollution and waste and to intensive farming on land and at sea. As far as water management is concerned, I will only deal with the demand side – which is up to companies to manage.

Pollution and Waste

Boards must be aware of the increasing anxiety the public feels regarding pollution and waste. The pollution caused by single use plastics in the oceans has recently been highlighted as a result of the BBC's Blue Planet II series[49] and pictures of sea life dying from ingesting these plastics.[50]

It may be helpful to illustrate the sources of waste and pollution in a typical company value chain to provide directors with a simple framework for considering what to do to minimize them. This is shown in Figure 3.2.

Once boards appreciate the possible sources of waste and pollution in their organizations' value chains, they need to agree on policies to reduce their impact. What has become more urgent in the last three years is how to deal with the threats posed by plastic and recycled waste. In the case of plastic, this is the result of a change in consumer awareness and in resulting attitudes of the big supermarkets to plastic;[51] whereas in the case of recycled waste, this is the consequence of Asian countries refusing to continue accepting waste from developed countries.

1. ***Problems with plastic:*** Plastics are versatile, inexpensive, and durable. They are also used to make single-use products[v] we value for their convenience; which we throw away without thinking about what happens after we have disposed of them. Their durability means they do not biodegrade and remain with us in one form or another for centuries. Even when they break down over time, they still remain in the environment in the form of microplastics which then enter the marine food chain,[52] fall in rain in Colorado and in polar snow.[53]

    We still do not know whether ingesting microplastics are harmful,[vi] though the evidence so far suggests it might not be.[54] The same is definitely

---

v Examples of single-use plastic products: PET bottles for beverages and mineral water; plastic straws; plastic lids for portable coffee cups from fast food and coffee shops; disposable cutlery and plates; plastic trays, wrapping, and bags in supermarkets and retail outlets; to name a few.

vi "93% of bottled water around the world and 92% of tap water is contaminated with microplastics. A recent report also concludes that the average person could be ingesting 100,000 pieces or 9 ounces (250 g) of microplastics per year." "How to filter and remove microplastics from tapwater," *TAPPWATER,* June 12, 2019, https://tappwater.co/us/how-to-filter-and-remove-microplastics-2/, accessed on August 24, 2019.

Raw materials processing	Shipping and transport	Production	Distribution	Marketing and sales	Company policies

▪ Depletion of:
  ▪ Resources
  ▪ Biodiversity
  ▪ Topsoil
 ▪ Pollution
  ▪ Spills
  ▪ GHGs
  ▪ Toxins
 ▪ Fish bycatch
 ▪ Environmental damage to:
  ▪ Forestry
  ▪ Watersheds
 ▪ Processing waste
 ▪ Tailings
	▪ Pollution
	  ▪ Spills
	  ▪ GHGs
	  ▪ Toxins
	 ▪ Waste
	  ▪ Materials
	  ▪ Energy
	  ▪ Packaging
	 ▪ Congestion
		▪ Pollution
		  ▪ Spills
		  ▪ GHGs
		  ▪ Toxins
		 ▪ Waste:
		  ▪ Materials
		  ▪ Energy
		  ▪ Water
		  ▪ Packaging
			▪ Pollution
			  ▪ Spills
			  ▪ GHGs
			  ▪ Toxins
			 ▪ Waste
			  ▪ Materials
			  ▪ Energy
			  ▪ Packaging
			 ▪ Congestion
				▪ Promoting consumerism :
				  ▪ Maximize sales
				  ▪ Promote single-use products
				  ▪ Promote fast fashion
				 ▪ Ignoring life cycle costs
				 ▪ Using excessive packaging
					▪ Shareholder focused
					 ▪ Bottom-line thinking:
					  ▪ Short-term focus
					  ▪ Ignoring externalities
					 ▪ Linear business model:
					  ▪ "Take"
					  ▪ "Make"
					  ▪ "Waste"

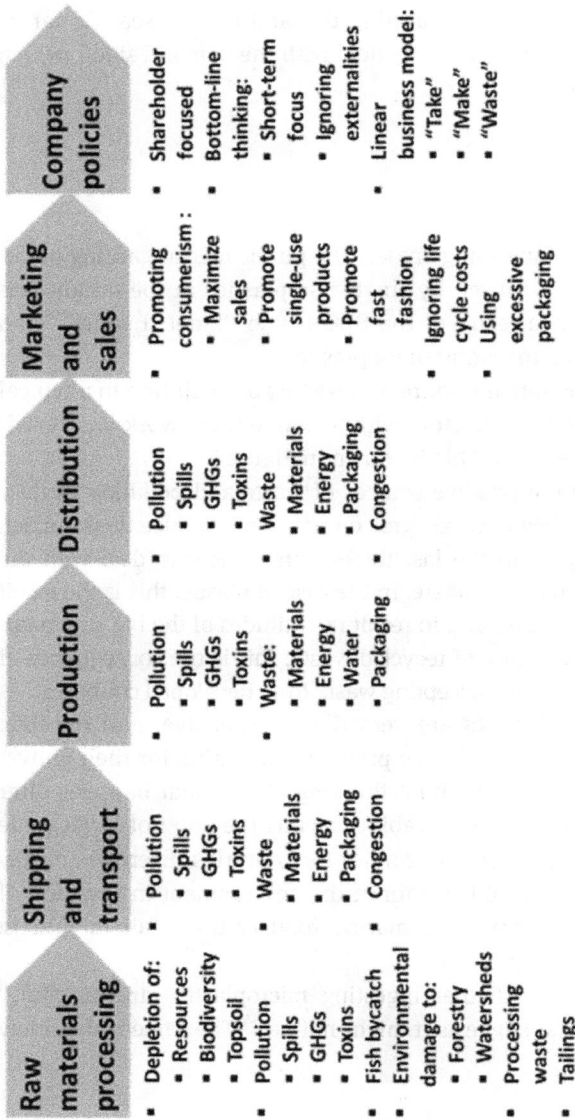

Figure 3.2: Sources of pollution and waste in the value chain.

not true of plastic waste in the seas – which kills marine animals that confuse plastic bags for jellyfish[55] or get tangled in discarded netting and lines.[56] The plastic waste washing up on previously pristine shores spoils the beauty of even the most isolated places like Aldabra atoll in the Seychelles – thousands of miles away from the sources of pollution in East and Southeast Asia[57]– and is even found in the deepest parts of the ocean.[58]

2. ***Realities of recycling:*** Recycling in practice is difficult. There is a growing shortage of landfills[59] and landfills represent health hazards if the toxins in them leach into aquifers.[60] They also are a source of GHGs.[61] Moreover, households are not good at separating waste appropriately, making it harder for recyclers to do their work.[62] Many household items we think can be easily recycled are in fact difficult, because they are made of layered materials, some of which are not suitable for recycling or because they have chemicals attached to them that must be removed before they can be recycled.[63] Finally, much of what is collected in developed countries for recycling is not recycled in countries of origin, but exported to poorer ones with lower environmental standards thus creating environmental problems and health hazards there instead.[64] These countries are increasingly unwilling to accept the trash and pollutants and this has caused serious bottlenecks in the waste management value chain.[65]

Intensive Farming

We believe we can manipulate nature to our advantage – a habit of mind humankind has assumed since the invention of settled agriculture. The industrial food chain in the developed world is beginning to provide early warning signals all is not well. The creation of drug-resistant bacteria has been in part the result of feeding animals in the human food chain too many antibiotics as part of the drive for ever-increasing productivity.[66] A BBC program[67] gave another example of potential problems: the disappearance of wild Atlantic salmon in rivers where there is salmon farming, the result of their becoming infested with sea-lice caused by the densely populated farmed fish pens.

Aquaculture promises much in terms of our ability to raise new, cheap, good sources of protein. However, to be sustainable, it must find ways of being disease free. It must also find ways of competing with poultry – it only takes six weeks to get chickens to market, but two years for salmon. This is leading to attempts to create transgenic fish that grow five times faster than natural salmon. Already there are worrying incidences of deformity, mutations, and disability (such as blindness caused by cataracts) in the stocks of farmed salmon in the lochs and fjords of Scotland and Norway.[68]

Success in fish farming highlights another source of concern if development is to prove sustainable. As with land-based farming, fish farming is about raising "livestock" that is high up the food chain. This causes two potential problems:

1. ***There is a need for concentrated inputs in the form of feed***, designed to maximize the rate of weight gain. If the source of the feed were to go directly to humans, rather than having to be processed by the salmon (or poultry, pigs, and beef) into flesh, there would be great savings in the intensity of the process. For example, one kilo of salmon requires five kilos of capelin, since salmon are carnivores. Will the capelin catches be sustainable, or are we merely moving the pressure of over-fishing down the food chain to a less valued stock?

2. ***More serious is the effect of pollutants, pesticides, and PCBs on the food chain***. The fish we prize most are high up the marine food chain. As a result, life-harming chemicals in their fatty tissues are concentrated several times over because of biological amplification, where each life form takes its turn to concentrate the chemicals already in its prey into its own fatty tissues. Consequently, the success of fish farming brings with it an increased need to ensure that harmful chemicals do not get into the food chain. On January 12, 2001, the US FDA warned pregnant and nursing women as well as small children that they should not eat swordfish, shark, king mackerel, and tilefish because of the high levels of methyl mercury in them as a result of bioaccumulation.[69]

Intensive aquaculture is likely to be as essential for increasing the stock of food as intensive agriculture. The hope however is that key players in the aquaculture industry will take to heart the lessons that need to be learned from industrial agriculture.

Industrial agriculture has been with us since the middle of the 20th century. It has achieved remarkable successes. Poultry used to be an expensive delicacy everywhere in the Western world. Now both chicken and turkey are cheap forms of meat. This has been achieved through the transformation of poultry farming from an extensive, free-range, open-air system to intensive factory farming.

Leaving the ethics of factory farming aside, there are now issues about the safety of the process concerning the long-term use of antibiotics to help poultry and pigs gain weight, as well as the issue of the contamination of much of the fish-meal[70] that is used as feed. Raising beef cattle is also an extremely wasteful process. By cycling grain through livestock, we lose 90% of the calories available to feed humans directly. For every sixteen pounds of grain and soybeans fed to beef cattle, we get back only one pound as meat – the other fifteen are waste. We lose 94% of the protein fed to beef cattle; 88% of the protein fed to pigs; 83% of the protein fed to poultry, and 78% of the protein fed to dairy cattle.[71]

The real issue with food is not whether we are able to grow enough of it to meet the needs of humanity in 2025. The issue is more one of equity and social justice. Overall, there is enough food to meet our needs; the problem may be that it is in the wrong place at the wrong time, or of the wrong type. Amartya Sen makes the point that famines are not caused by a decline in food production, but rather by the food being in the wrong place.[72] We can feed ourselves now, and in the future, even if it meant abandoning extravagant feedlot beef.

Managing Water

The irony of our planet is that 75% of the world's surface is water, but our situation is best captured in the words of *The Rhyme of the Ancient Mariner*,[73] "Water, water, everywhere, Nor any drop to drink." The following report from 2001 stated

> Of the 2.5% of the world's water that is non-saline, 65% of it is locked up in glaciers and the polar ice caps. Of the remaining 35% that is part of the continuous hydrological cycle, some 20% of it is too deep underground or too remote to be accessible to human beings, and most of the other 80% comes at the wrong time and place, namely in floods and monsoons when it is not easily captured for human use. . .
>
> Our need for water continues to rise as economic activity increases and as agricultural activity expands to meet the need for food. Agriculture represents some 70% of the world's use of water, with the remaining 30% shared between household, industrial, hydropower, navigation and leisure uses. . .

Agriculture is the largest user of water worldwide (70%),[vii][74] and so it is crucial that savings in agricultural water use are achieved. The waste involved can

---

vii "Globally we use approximately 70 percent of freshwater withdrawals for agriculture.

However, this share varies significantly by country – where there are large variations geographically and by income level. The average agricultural water use for low-income countries is 90 percent; 79 percent for middle income; and only 41 percent at high incomes. There are a number of countries across South Asia, Africa, and Latin America which use more than 90 percent of water withdrawals for agriculture. The highest is Afghanistan at 99 percent. Countries in the global north tend to use a much lower share of water for agriculture; Germany and the Netherlands use less than one percent." Better Meets Reality, https://www.bettermeetsreality.com/which-industries-use-the-most-water/, accessed on August 22, 2019.

be stopped relatively easily by pricing water appropriately – the World Water Commission believes this is the most important single issue – and making farmers pay[vii] the real costs incurred in storing, diverting, and channelling water to places where agricultural activity has no *natural* basis and using subsurface drip techniques rather than spray irrigation.

Industrial users represent 18–19% of global demand for water.[75] The amounts of water used by industrial sector are surprising, shown in Table 3.2.

Table 3.2: Water usage by industrial sector as of 2018.[76]

Industrial sector	Gallons
Power generation	
To produce 1,000 kilowatt hours of electricity:	
1. Thermo-electric	20,897
2. Coal-fired	140
3. Gas-fired	10
Textile and garments	
To produce one pair of jeans, the EPA estimates	2,900
Beverages	
To produce:	
1. Half-liter bottle of soda[viii]	175
2. Pint of beer	20
3. Cup of coffee (ingredients for a cup)	37
Automotive	
To produce average domestic car, including tires	39,000
Food	
To produce US$1.00 worth of:	
1. Sugar	270
2. Petfood	200
3. Milk	140

Boards are beginning to take water conservation seriously, though most have yet to adopt a "water stewardship" approach.

---

viii According to the *National Geographic Magazine*, a single half-liter of soda requires up to 175 liters of water. The build-up is as follows: 30 liters to grow the natural sweeteners used; 53 liters for the coffee beans required for the caffeine in the soda; 80 liters used in the processing of flavorings; 5.3 liters used in molding the plastic for the bottle; 7 liters used in manufacturing and packaging; and 0.5 liters for the fluid content. Leahy, S. (2018), "World's Water Crisis Explained," *National Geographic Magazine,* March 23, 2018, https://www.nationalgeographic.com/news/2018/03/world-water-day-water-crisis-explained/ accessed on April 2, 2020.

Summary

Achieving environmental sustainability depends on dealing with climate change, moving to a circular economy, and protecting the planet's biodiversity through effective conservation. Although these three agendas overlap, they are sufficiently dissimilar to require different types of response by boards.

Climate Change

As far as climate change is concerned, the following appears to be reasonably clear. First, the threat to humanity in general needs to be taken seriously, if only on the basis of applying the "precautionary principle," that it is better to be safe than sorry. Second, there are a number of industrial sectors where such mitigation may not just be disruptive, but could remove the basis for their continued existence, at least in their present form. This applies to all companies involved in the extraction and conversion of fossil fuels into energy for transportation and heating, when they are replaced by renewables, supported by appropriate electricity storage technologies. Third, there are the mobility providers that depend on power from fossil fuels in their current forms such as car, truck and aircraft manufacturers who could be put out of business by competitors using electricity, as long as it is competitive and easy to access. They could also be threatened by changes in society's demand for their services, as a result of better public transport and apps promoting the sharing of fixed assets rather than wasteful individual ownership, and the resulting changes in customer behavior triggered by heightened climate change awareness.

This presents boards with three serious challenges when attempting to reconcile the need to change the way business is done in the future with the demands of shareholders in the present. The first is to decide whether there is a future at all; whether it would not be better to exit the business and give all the proceeds back to shareholders to invest as they see fit. The second is to recognize the need for collaboration with other companies, governments, and nations to make any progress. In other words, their ability to make unilateral decisions in the best interests of their organizations is limited by what other companies, governments, and countries are doing. The third is that the time horizons for transformation are so long that directors may have difficulties implementing them, since they will not be there to see them coming to fruition. It is made even harder when they have to use financial tools that do not show the costs of externalities properly.

Moving to a Circular Economy

Moving to a circular economy is entirely within the hands of boards; they do not have to depend on getting agreement from other organizations and governments to go ahead. To move to a circular business model, boards need to do the following: First, they must decide to switch their business models from focusing on growth based on maximizing sales that require increased resource inputs. Second, having made that decision, they need to examine their own value chains and supply chains to identify the areas where they can introduce policies of "Reduce, Recycle, Reuse, and Remanufacture." This can be achieved by leasing equipment to provide the services customers need rather than selling it outright; extending product liability so they avoid building obsolescence into their products; encouraging joint ownership/usership models; and designing products from the start to make recycling and remanufacturing an integral part of their lifecycles rather than being an afterthought.

Conservation

The actions needed to contribute to improving the chances of conservation are entirely within the authority of boards, acting on their own. First, they should review the sources of waste and pollution in their own value chains – in their processing of raw materials, in their inbound and outbound logistics and distribution; in their manufacturing processes; in the extent to which their marketing and sales encourage wasteful and polluting behavior by their customers; and finally in their own priorities as a board.

If boards are involved in agriculture or aquaculture, they need to consider both the environmental impact of intensive rearing methods and the morality of treating animals and fish in such a way, as well as the health hazards posed to humanity by the excessive use of antibiotics to speed up weight gain.

In tackling the three issues of environmental sustainability, boards are confronted with having to choose between what appears to be best for their shareholders immediately and what matters if humanity is to survive:

> Will mankind survive? Who knows? The question I want to put is more searching: Who cares? It is clear that most of us today do not care – or at least do not care enough. How many of us would be willing to give up some minor convenience – say, the use of aerosols – in the hope that this might extend the life of man on earth by a hundred years? Suppose we also knew with a high degree of certainty that humankind could not survive a thousand years unless we gave up our wasteful diet of meat, abandoned all pleasure

driving, cut back on every use of energy that was not essential to the maintenance of a bare minimum. *Would we care enough for posterity to pay the price of its survival?*

I doubt it. A thousand years is unimaginably distant. Even a century far exceeds our powers of empathetic imagination. By the year 2075, I shall probably have been dead for three quarters of a century. My children will also likely be dead, and my grandchildren, if I have any, will be in their dotage. *What does it matter to me, then, what life will be like in 2075, much less 3075? Why should I lift a finger to affect events that will have no more meaning for me 75 years after my death than those that happened 75 years before I was born?*[77] [Emphases mine]

Our ability to achieve environmental sustainability depends on boards, governments, and nations answering this question in favor of posterity. Let us hope that in the years that have passed since 1975, their answer will have become favorable, though given the complexities involved, I remain concerned.

References

1 Adeney-Thomas, J. (2019), "Why the 'Anthropocene' is not 'Climate Change' and Why It Matters," Asiaglobalonline, January 10, 2019, https://www.asiaglobalonline.hku.hk/anthropocene-climate-change/, accessed on August 18, 2019.
2 Ibid.
3 Intergovernmental Panel on Climate Change (2019), *Climate Change and Land: Summary for Policymakers,"* p. 2, https://www.ipcc.ch/2019/08/08/land-is-a-critical-resource_srccl/,accessed on August 12, 2019.
4 Tickell, C. (2005), International Media Environment Summit, Kuching, Sarawak, November 30, 2005.
5 Genesis, chapter 1, verse 26.
6 Browne, J. (1997), *Climate Change Speech*, Stanford University, May 19, 1997, https://assets.documentcloud.org/documents/2623268/bp-john-browne-stanford-1997-climate-change-speech.pdf, accessed on August 17, 2019.
7 Franta, B. (2018), "Climate Consensus – the 97% Climate Change: Shell and Exxon's secret 1980s climate change warnings," *The Guardian*, September 19, 2018, https://www.theguardian.com/environment/climate-consensus-97-per-cent/2018/sep/19/shell-and-exxons-secret-1980s-climate-change-warnings, accessed on August 17, 2019.
8 United Nations Climate Change (2018), "The Paris Agreement," October 22, 2018, https://unfccc.int/process-and-meetings/the-paris-agreement/the-paris-agreement, accessed on August 18, 2019.
9 UNEP (2018), *Emissions Gap Report 2018*, p. 5, https://www.ipcc.ch/site/assets/uploads/2018/12/UNEP-1.pdf accessed on August 17, 2019.
10 Lindsey, R. (2020), "Climate Change: Atmospheric Carbon Dioxide," *NOAA, Climate.gov*, https://www.climate.gov/news-features/understanding-climate/climate-change-atmospheric-carbon-dioxide, accessed on March 20, 2020.
11 Hausfather, Z. (2018), "Analysis: Fossil fuel emissions increasing at fastest rate for seven years," *CarbonBrief*, December 5, 2018, https://www.carbonbrief.org/analysis-fossil-fuel-emissions-in-2018-increasing-at-fastest-rate-for-seven-years, accessed on August 18, 2019.

12 Intergovernmental Panel on Climate Change (2019), *Climate Change and Land: Summary for Policymakers,*p. 2, https://www.ipcc.ch/2019/08/08/land-is-a-critical-resource_srccl/, accessed on August 12, 2019.

13 *The Economist* (2019), "One way or another the deluge is coming: How to prepare for rising sea levels," *The Economist,* August 17, 2019, https://www.economist.com/leaders/2019/08/15/one-way-or-another-the-deluge-is-coming, accessed on August 19, 2019.

14 World Economic Forum (2019), "The world's coastal cities are going under. Here's how some are fighting back," https://www.weforum.org/agenda/2019/01/the-world-s-coastal-cities-are-going-under-here-is-how-some-are-fighting-back/, accessed on August 19, 2019.

15 Ibid.

16 Kaur, H. (2019), "Scientists bid farewell to the first Icelandic glacier lost to climate change. If more melt, it can be disastrous," *CNN Health,* August 18, 2019, https://edition.cnn.com/2019/08/18/health/glaciers-melting-climate-change-trnd/index.html, accessed on August 20, 2019.

17 Friedlander, B. (2017), "Rising seas could result in 2 billion refugees by 2100," *Cornell Chronicle,* June 19, 2017, https://news.cornell.edu/stories/2017/06/rising-seas-could-result-2-billion-refugees-2100, accessed on August 20, 2019.

18 Geisler, C. (2017), "Impediments to Inland Resettlement Under Conditions of Accelerated Sea Level Rise" *Cornell Institute for the Social Sciences' Contested Global Landscapes Project,* cited in Friedlander, B. (2017). Ibid.

19 Kaur, H. (2019), op. cit.

20 Ibid.

21 Meyer, R. (2019), "This Land Is the Only Land There Is," *The Atlantic,* August 8, 2019, https://www.theatlantic.com/science/archive/2019/08/how-think-about-dire-new-ipcc-climate-report/595705/, accessed on August 19, 2019.

22 Ibid.

23 Food and Agriculture Organization (2019), "SAVE FOOD: Global Initiative on Food Loss and Waste Reduction" http://www.fao.org/save-food/resources/keyfindings/en/, accessed on August 18, 2019.

24 Meyer, R. (2019), op. cit.

25 McKie, R. (2019), "We must change food production to save the world," *The Guardian,* August 4, 2019, https://www.theguardian.com/environment/2019/aug/03/ipcc-land-use-food-production-key-to-climate-crisis-leaked-report, accessed on August 19, 2019.

26 Meyer, R. (2019), op. cit.

27 Robbins, J. (1987), *A Diet for a New America* (Walpole, New Hampshire: Stillpoint Publishing), p. 376.

28 Robbins, J. (1987), ibid., p. 376.

29 Ambrose, J. (2019), "City urged to attach 'climate risk' reports to pensions," *The Guardian,* August 12, 2019, https://www.theguardian.com/business/2019/aug/12/city-urged-to-attach-climate-risk-reports-to-pensions, accessed on August 19, 2019.

30 Ibid.

31 BBC (2019), "UK Parliament declares climate change emergency," *BBC News,* May 1, 2019, https://www.bbc.co.uk/news/uk-politics-48126677, accessed on August 22, 2019.

32 Ibid.

33 Ibid.

34 Jericho, G. (2019), op. cit. https://www.theguardian.com/business/grogonomics/2019/aug/18/accepting-anecdotes-more-readily-than-climate-science-is-wilful-ignorance, accessed April 2, 2020.

35 Lyons, K. (2019), "Pacific Islands Forum: 'Our people are dying': Australia's climate confrontation in the Pacific," *The Guardian,* August 18, 2019, https://www.theguardian.com/world/2019/aug/18/our-people-are-dying-australias-climate-confrontation-in-the-pacific, accessed on August 18, 2019.

36 Jericho, G. (2019), op. cit.

37 Watts, J. (2019), "UK should cut back on vehicle use to hit zero-carbon target, say MPs," *The Guardian,* August 22, 2019, https://www.theguardian.com/world/2019/aug/18/our-people-are-dying-australias-climate-confrontation-in-the-pacific, accessed on August 22, 2019.

38 EPA (2018), *Sources of Greenhouse Gas Emissions,* https://www.epa.gov/ghgemissions/sources-greenhouse-gas-emissions, accessed on August 19, 2019.

39 Landman, A. (2010), "BP's 'Beyond Petroleum' Campaign Losing its Sheen," *PR Watch,* May 3, 2010, https://www.prwatch.org/news/2010/05/9038/bps-beyond-petroleum-campaign-losing-its-sheen, accessed on August 17, 2019.

40 David, J. E. (2013), "'Beyond Petroleum' No More? BP goes back to basics," April 22, 2013, https://www.cnbc.com/id/100647034, accessed on August 17, 2019.

41 Von Weizsacker, E. et al. (1998), *Factor Four: Doubling Wealth, Halving Resource Use – The New Report to the Club of Rome* (Abingdon, Oxon/New York, NY: Earthscan), p79.

42 Hedstrom, G. S. (2019), *Sustainability: What It Is and How to Measure It* (Boston/Berlin: Walter de Gruyter Inc.), p. 21.

43 Ibid., pp. 24–25.

44 Von Weizsacker, E. et al. (1998), op. cit., p. 69.

45 Ibid., p. 106.

46 Carrington, D. (2019), "World's nations gather to tackle wildlife extinction crisis" https://www.theguardian.com/environment/2019/aug/17/frog-tortoises-cites-wildlife-summit *The Guardian,* August 17, 2019, accessed on August 17, 2019.

47 *The Economist* (2019), "Plague without locusts: Is insectageddon imminent?" *The Economist,* May 21, 2019 https://www.economist.com/leaders/2019/03/21/is-insectageddon-imminent, accessed on August 24, 2019.

48 Intergovernmental Panel on Climate Change (2019), op. cit.

49 Allen, B. (2018), "Viewers react to David Attenborough's final Blue Planet II conservation rallying cry," *RadioTimes,* https://www.radiotimes.com/news/tv/2018-08-29/blue-planet-2-plastic-waste-final-episode/, accessed on August 22, 2019.

50 Binder, L. (2019), "Dead green turtle found with 183 pieces of plastic in its gut in Cyprus," *Sky News,* August 13, 2019, https://news.sky.com/story/dead-green-turtle-found-with-183-pieces-of-plastic-in-its-gut-in-cyprus-11780814, accessed on August 22, 2019.

51 Lewis, D. (2019), "I want Tesco's packaging overhaul to plug into a new national framework," *The Guardian,* August 22, 2019, https://www.theguardian.com/business/2019/aug/22/tesco-effort-packaging-national-recycling-target, accessed on August 24, 2019.

52 Thiele, C. and Hudson, M. D. (2018), "How you're eating microplastics – and don't even realise," *The Independent,* July 6, 2018, https://www.independent.co.uk/life-style/food-and-drink/food-microplastics-eating-plastic-pollution-environment-a8395556.html, accessed on August 24, 2019.

53 Wetherbee, J. et al. (2019) "It's raining plastic," *US Geological Survey,* https://pubs.usgs.gov/of/2019/1048/ofr20191048.pdf, accessed on August 24, 2019.

54 Foulkes, I. (2019), "Microplastics in water pose 'no apparent health risk,'" *BBC News, Geneva,* August 22, 2019, https://www.bbc.co.uk/news/health-49430038, accessed on August 24, 2019.
55 Smith, K. (2016), "This Image Shows Why Sea Turtles Are Confusing Plastic Bags For Jellyfish," *OneGreenPlanet,* https://www.onegreenplanet.org/news/what-a-plastic-bag-looks-like-to-a-sea-turtle/, accessed on August 24, 2019.
56 Whale and Dolphin Conservation, "Prevent deaths in nets," https://uk.whales.org/our-4-goals/prevent-deaths-in-nets/, accessed on August 24, 2019.
57 Oxford University Department of Plant Sciences (2018), "Plant Sciences students head-up a plastic pollution project on Aldabra Atoll," https://www.plants.ox.ac.uk/article/plant-sciences-students-head-plastic-pollution-project-aldabra-atoll, accessed on August 24, 2019.
58 Morelle, R. (2019), "Mariana Trench: Deepest-ever sub dive finds plastic bag," *BBC News,* May 13, 2019, https://www.bbc.co.uk/news/science-environment-48230157, accessed on August 24, 2019.
59 UIA (2019), "Shortage of waste landfill sites," *The Encyclopedia of World Problems and Human Potential,* May 8, 2019, http://encyclopedia.uia.org/en/problem/157367, accessed on August 24, 2019.
60 Newton, J. (2018), "The Effects of Landfills on the Environment," *Sciencing,* April 19, 2018, https://sciencing.com/effects-landfills-environment-8662463.html, accessed on August 24, 2019.
61 Gies, E. (2016), "Landfills Have a Huge Greenhouse Gas Problem. Here's What We Can Do About It," *Ensia,* October 25, 2016, https://ensia.com/features/methane-landfills/, accessed on August 24, 2019.
62 Whelan, L. (2015), "The 15 Everyday Items You Shouldn't Be Recycling," *Citylab,* December 15, 2015, https://www.citylab.com/life/2015/12/the-15-everyday-items-you-shouldnt-be-recycling/420618/, accessed on August 24, 2019.
63 O'Connor, M. (2019), "The 10 things you can't put in your household recycling," *BBC News,* August 19, 2019, https://www.bbc.co.uk/news/uk-49280709, accessed on August 24, 2019.
64 O'Neill, K. (2019), "As more developing countries reject plastic waste exports, wealthy nations seek solutions at home," *The Conversation,* June 9, 2019, https://www.greenbiz.com/article/more-developing-countries-reject-plastic-waste-exports-wealthy-nations-seek-solutions-home, accessed on August 24, 2019.
65 Laville, S. (2017), "China waste clampdown could create UK cardboard recycling chaos, say industry experts," *The Guardian,* December 15, 2017, https://www.theguardian.com/environment/2017/dec/15/china-waste-clampdown-could-create-uk-cardboard-recycling-chaos-say-industry-experts accessed on August 24, 2019.
66 National Health Service (2015), "Antibiotic use in farm animals 'threatens human health,'" December 9, 2015, https://www.nhs.uk/news/medication/antibiotic-use-in-farm-animals-threatens-human-health/, accessed on August 22, 2019.
67 BBC 2 (2001), "Warnings from the Wild: The Price of Salmon," January 7, 2001, https://genome.ch.bbc.co.uk/cf35abbae0bb4cb4bbe5fdc1d45438af, accessed on August 22, 2019.
68 Ibid.
69 CNN (2001), "Report: Fish-mercury risk underestimated," April 12, 2001, http://edition.cnn.com/2001/HEALTH/parenting/04/12/fish.pregnant/index.html, accessed on August 22, 2019.
70 Scientific Committee on Animal Nutrition (2000), "Dioxin Contamination of Feedingstuffs and Their Contribution to the Contamination of Food of Animal Origin," November 6, 2000,

p. 7, https://ec.europa.eu/food/sites/food/files/safety/docs/animal-feed-undes-sub-out55_en.
pdf, accessed on August 22, 2019.

71 Robbins, J. (1987), op. cit., p. 351.

72 Sen, A. (1999), *Development As Freedom* (Oxford: Oxford University Press).

73 Coleridge, S. T. (1798), *Rhyme of the Ancient Mariner.*

74 Better Meets Reality (2018), "Which Industries Use the Most Water," October 1, 2018, https://
www.bettermeetsreality.com/which-industries-use-the-most-water/, accessed on August 22, 2019.

75 Better Meets Reality (2018), op. cit.

76 Ibid.

77 Heilbroner, R. L. (1975), "What has Posterity Ever Done For Me?" *The New York Times,*
January 19, 1975, https://www.nytimes.com/1975/01/19/archives/what-has-posterity-ever-done-for-
me.html, accessed on August 26, 2019.

Chapter 4
Economic Sustainability

The chapter is presented in two parts: The first explores the drivers of globalization; and the second discusses how its success has created rising inequality. It closes with a summary of the discussions.

This chapter is based on two fundamental assumptions.

The first assumption (discussed in Chapter 1) is that the globalized neoliberal economy, in its present form, may face serious political challenges because it appears to have failed to share the benefits of growth equitably since the GFC (global financial crisis). If the majority who have not benefitted from the growth since 2009 become sufficiently discontented and vote to change the way the economy is organized, they could undermine globalization and the sustainability of the economy as it operates currently.

The second assumption (discussed in Chapter 3) is that we can no longer regard environmental sustainability as something separate from economic sustainability. The growing realization that climate change needs to be taken seriously, even if only on the basis of the "precautionary principle," will have major consequences for those industries and companies contributing to global warming on how they do business.[i] Agriculture may also be disrupted, responding to changes in how and what we eat, as consumers move away from meat and dairy to plant-based proteins.[ii] Moving to a circular economy with its emphasis on remanufacturing as well as reducing and re-using raw material inputs will affect companies that promoted conspicuous consumption and encouraged a disposable mentality. They may have to change the way they do business,[iii] if they are to prosper in

---

i Fossil-fuel-dependent companies in the energy and transportation sectors face fundamental threats to their existence as result of the growing move toward zero-carbon economies. Although economies will continue to need providers of energy and transportation, the companies that will be those providers will have to change.

ii As consumers are educated in the health benefits of eating less meat and dairy and realize how it can help with reducing the impact of climate change as well, the per capita demand for meat and dairy in developed countries will fall.

iii Although such changes will matter greatly to each organization, they will likely enhance the sustainability of the economy overall from an environmental point of view. For example, this may affect the garment and apparel industries as customers may come to appreciate the serious environmental harm caused by "fast fashion" where clothing is so cheap it is thrown away after only being worn a few times, creating inflated demand for practices that are environmentally damaging and wasteful as the clothing ends up in landfills.

https://doi.org/10.1515/9783110670486-004

an environment where consumers become more aware of the problems caused by waste and pollution, changing their purchasing habits as a result. Conservation will affect companies involved in the business of providing food and clothing as NGOs insist on companies adopting Fairtrade[iv] policies to maximize sustainability.

Consequently, this chapter focuses on what boards might need to consider regarding their exposure to globalization and the threat to their business models of inequality to help ensure the economy benefits more people than just the top 1.0% or 0.1%.

Whither Globalization?

Given the dreadful lesson of how globalization works provided by the Covid-19 virus, I would like to begin this section on globalization and how it has evolved over time with a quote from an article, "Not New and Never Costless: Globalisation," written by my late father in 2001 for *International Relations:*

> There have been many [paths] to globalisation: conquest, with the new ways and ideas conquest brought with it; the spread of religion and the change in belief, and therefore in behaviour that it brought about. Today, trade, capitalism, the idea of the free market are central. Travel, especially by air, has changed the world from the time a tribe first moved into a neighbouring territory. Missionaries, pilgrims, package holidays, all take ideas with them, even if it is only that hotel rooms should have bathrooms attached. Investment brings with it, ideas about everything from bankruptcy to laws on risk in banking. Books influence readers' values, whether explicitly, as in philosophy or by the way as in [reading] Homer or Jane Austen. Improved maps have always had to be adopted by neighbours of those who invented them; if they did not adopt them, they risked slavery or even extermination. *Most damaging of all [consequences of] globalisation has been the spread of disease; hunter-gatherers had few diseases, we have many. . .*
>
> . . .The great economic globalisation only began some ten thousand years ago. Agriculture was invented in quite small areas of the Middle East, China and Mexico and from there spread in a very few thousand years over the whole globe. Again, there were losers; in society after society the hunter-gatherers disappeared or were subdued. Societies of considerable equality, where distinction was personally earned, gave way to taxation and hierarchies. With agriculture came money, writing, armies, kings and priests. These too spread relatively quickly over the globe, though the process was not completed till firearms destroyed almost the last hunter-gatherer societies in the 19th century. . .

---

iv "Fairtrade means fairer trading conditions and opportunities for producers in developing countries to invest in their businesses and communities for a sustainable future," Sainsburys' (the UK's second largest supermarket group) explanation of Fairtrade on their own label chocolate wrapper.

Historically, the greatest globaliser has been conquest. The Romans in most of Europe, the Chinese of the Yellow River to China's modern boundaries, the Spaniards and Portuguese in Latin America, the British and French in Africa, Asia, North America, Oceania. These conquerors took with them their ideals, their inventions, their organisation of society, their knowledge. . .

Conquest was only one way in which that great globaliser, ideas, were spread. Equally important were missionaries, sometimes people who devoted their lives to proselytisation, sometimes those like Marx or Darwin, whose books were intended to revolutionize the way men thought, sometimes the result of scientific discoveries others fell over themselves to adopt.[1]   [Emphasis mine]

Globalization from an economic perspective includes:

1. *International activities* where borders are crossed involving the sale of goods and services, financial flows and some movement of people. Typically, this is where a company based in one country exports its goods and services without having its own operations established in the countries to which it exports, using third parties to distribute them.

2. *Multinational activities* where multinational companies headquartered in one country establish subsidiaries employing people and investing in fixed assets in the markets that they serve.

3. *Offshore activities* where the primary purpose is to minimize or avoid tax on activities generated by business done in the markets in which they operate. Company subsidiaries based in offshore tax havens are good examples of this.

4. *Global activities* which are more deeply integrated and co-ordinated than any of the above so that *customers* can be offered a global service, regardless of where they are and where production as a result is organized without regard to national frontiers.

It is important to remember that globalization benefits customers, often at the expense of producers. This is the basis of the fundamental conflict of interests within the process that leads to periods of expansion and retreat. For about a hundred years from 1870 global trade grew at 3% per year. Exports rose from 6% of global GDP in the early 19th century to 14% just before World War I. Before 1914, many countries were as open to international flows as today, with Germany, the UK, and Latin America more open than now.[2] As World War II loomed on the political horizon, strategic imperatives reared their heads to reduce the impetus toward globalization. The period between the two World Wars was a period of tariff walls, of disengaging from world trade, partly as a result of inappropriate "beggar my neighbor"[v] policies, but also because policymakers could sense that war was imminent and that interdependence was therefore risky. The UK, for example, found that it had relied too heavily on Germany as a source of dyes and chemicals before World War I,[3] and ensured that this would not happen again.

In attempting to understand why globalization has arisen, it is perhaps worth thinking about what constituent elements create a marketplace, and then to expand to what it is that allows the marketplace to become global. A market involves the exchange of goods and services and the associated property and contractual commitments; communication to inform potential customers that goods or services, with their associated prices, qualities and quantities are available for sale; and informing suppliers that there is a demand for their products.[4] From this we can establish the seven factors needed to allow globalization of markets to occur:

1. ***Buyers must value what it is that suppliers have to offer:*** There needs to be a certain familiarity with what is on offer. This has been made possible by the enormous explosion of information created by the global media and content providers who have provided not just the necessary information about goods and services, but have also given them an aspirational context through the entertainment programs beamed into homes. This information explosion has been turbocharged by IT platforms like Amazon in the West and Alibaba in China.

2. ***Law and order are essential to invest in infrastructure*** needed to take products to market and to manufacture them in local economies. The most important elements in the law are those relating to property rights and contracts if companies are to go abroad. During the 19th century such systems of law and order were established around the world, usually via imperialist mechanisms, which created resistance to the trading entities that had benefited under the imperial/colonial regimes once countries became independent.

3. ***Goods must be available either physically or virtually.*** For this to work, there have to be investments in infrastructure to allow the goods and services to be experienced. The tyrannies of distance and weight must be conquered if the market-space is to extend beyond the local market to the national, then to the regional, and finally to the global. The advent of the

---

v "Beggar thy neighbor is a term used for a set of policies that a country enacts to address its economic woes that, in turn, actually worsens the economic problems of other countries. The term comes from the policy's impact, as it makes a beggar out of neighboring countries." Hayes, A. (2019), "Beggar-Thy-Neighbour," *Investopedia*, October, 24, 2019, https://www.investopedia.com/terms/b/beggarthyneighbor.asp, accessed on March 6, 2020.

steamship, the telegraph, and refrigeration extended the reach of traders, merchants, and agriculturists from the national to the global marketplace in the 19th century.

4. ***Communications make it that much easier to do business*** so investors can become familiar with the environments into which they would be putting their plant and equipment.

> Not only have these developments made the world a smaller place, but they have also enabled globalization as *practice* to develop. The recognition – on the part of say a London businessman – that Manchester in New Hampshire is not much farther away in time and money than Manchester in the UK makes globalization possible as a strategy. Japanese and American companies set up electronic component operations in the countries of Southeast Asia in order to take advantage of large pools of low-cost, semi-skilled labor. *Even local authorities or town councils, hardly exemplars of globalization . . . now find themselves faced with a global marketplace. They compete to attract industry not against an adjacent county or nearby city but rather against locations scattered halfway around the world.*[5]　　　　　　　　　　[Emphasis mine]

5. ***Governments must be prepared to let their economies become interdependent.*** In the middle of the 19th century there was relative peace in Europe and this allowed trade to be based on comparative advantage. With the end of the Cold War in 1989, governments eased up on their strategic imperatives and opened their economies to the benefits of comparative advantage. This may change because of the underlying tensions between the US and China that seem to be a replay of the UK's disengagement from Germany for strategic and military reasons between the two World Wars. Given the complexity of today's supply chains, it is likely to prove difficult for the US and Europe to disengage from China.[6] However, the shock of the 2019–20 coronavirus on travel, highlighting the fragility of global supply chains may accelerate this process of deglobalization; as governments and companies seek to build redundancy into global supply chains to increase their resilience to unexpected shocks.[7]

6. ***Success breeds success.*** The relative failure of autarkic regimes like India in the fifty years after its independence, and the absolute failure of regimes that believe in total self-reliance like North Korea, made the arguments in favor of globalization more compelling. The countries that have opened themselves up to the global marketplace have without exception seen the most astonishing rises in GNP per capita – with China at the forefront.

Looking back through history supports the fact that if wealth creation is the primary objective, then a culture of enlightenment is essential to delivering the goods:

The conscious adoption of the culture of the Enlightenment by a society is the central prerequisite for achieving a sustainable level of wealth. Only thereby is it possible to capitalize upon technology, the single most important factor for economic success. *There is only so far that technology can develop without a broader "scientific" base; and it was this base, essentially the rationalism and modernism of the Enlightenment, that accounted for the triumph of the West.* Technology is central to the globalization of culture. On the one hand, technology "pushes" a global culture through the ubiquity of the English language and Anglo-American media and pop culture. Arguably far more interesting and less obvious, however, is the "pull" argument: that is the conscious choice of modernity in order to reap the benefits of wealth that only technology can give. *The point here is not that technology leads to modernity but rather the very opposite: without adopting modernity a society is in no position to take advantage of technology to prosper. In both ways, technology and the globalization of culture go hand in hand.*[8]   [Emphases mine]

7. *The internet and the emergence of Anglo-Saxon global media and content providers* heighten the importance of English as the language of business. Bismarck,[vi] upon being asked, shortly before his death, what was the most decisive factor in modern history, is reputed to have replied, "The fact that the North Americans speak English." As multinationals made English their language of business, so the world became less unfamiliar and this both created greater homogeneity and allowed for greater diversity at the same time:

> The result is not homogeneity but rather pluralism and cultural diversity, the enrichment of all cultures by their being fertilized by the challenges posed by others. Of course, this is a process of change and can be threatening. . . What is inevitable about the influence of technology is neither cultural imperialism nor any particular brand of global culture but rather cultural competition, resulting in a world culture continuously enriched by multiple and diverse influences. Technology certainly enables the English language and Anglo-American values and lifestyles to set a global cultural baseline, but it equally facilitates this base being constantly influenced from other cultures and societies and being moderated everywhere by local variations.[9]

When considering whether globalization is appropriate for their organizations, boards should remember that the decision to cross borders opens up companies to degrees of complexity they would rather do without. Most firms do not have real multinational exposure; their primary interest is to serve their local market, followed by their regional market and then their national market. It is a special

---

vi Otto Von Bismarck (1815–1898), the first Chancellor of the united Germany he did so much to create by defeating Austria (1866) and France (1870) and perhaps the most powerful statesman in the world at the time of his death.

type of company that chooses to cross borders and take on the added burden of complexity and risk entailed by such a move.

Whether it makes sense or not to go abroad and whether globalization could go into reverse depends on the nature of the industry. Certain industries are more globalized than others as can be seen from Table 4.1.

Table 4.1: Perspectives on globalization (1995).

Industry category	US$ trillions	Status
1. *Physical commodities* – Petroleum, minerals, timber	2.0	Globalized
2. *Scale-driven business goods and services* – Aerospace engines, construction equipment, semiconductors, airframes, shipping, refineries, machine tools	1.0	Globalized
3. *Manufactured commodities* – Refined petroleum products, aluminum, specialty steel, bulk pharmaceuticals, pulp, specialty chemicals	2.8	Globalized
4. *Labor skill/productivity driven consumer goods* – Consumer electronics, PCs, cameras, automobiles, TVs	0.9	Accelerating globalization
5. *"Brandable," largely deregulated consumer goods* – Soft drinks, shoes, luxury goods, pharmaceuticals, film production	0.5	Accelerating globalization
6. *Professional business services* – Investment banking, legal services, consulting services	2.5	Accelerating globalization
7. *"Hard to brand globally," largely regulated consumer goods and services* – Food, personal financial services, TV production, retail distribution	6.3	Early globalization, still local
8. *Local unbranded goods and services* – Construction materials, real estate, funeral homes, education, household services, medical care, utilities	6.4	Early globalization, still local

Source: World Development Report (World Bank); McGraw-Hill/DRI World Economic Outlook 1996; United Nations, 1995, National Income Accounts; McKinsey analysis.

It is clear from this table that certain industries are not just more globalized than others, but also certain industries are more likely to have to be global. Sectors 1, 2, and 3 are already globalized and this status quo is accepted even though it has led to wage stagnation in the US:

> From 1973 to 2013, hourly compensation of a typical (production/nonsupervisory) worker rose just 9 percent while productivity increased 74 percent. This breakdown of pay growth

has been especially evident in the last decade, affecting both college- and non-college-educated workers as well as blue- and white-collar workers. *This means that workers have been producing far more than they receive in their paychecks and benefit packages from their employers.*[10]   [Emphasis mine]

Boards in sectors 1, 2, and 3 do not have to worry excessively about whether they should be concerned with the current problems posed by globalization though they need to recognize their industries have contributed in the past to the rise in inequality:

> In 2007, the last year before the Great Recession, *the average income of the middle 60 percent of American households was $76,443. It would have been $94,310, roughly 23 percent (nearly $18,000) higher had inequality not widened* (i.e., had their incomes grown at the overall average rate – an overall average buoyed by stratospheric growth at the very top). The temporary dip in top incomes during the Great Recession did little to shrink that inequality tax, which stood at 16 percent (nearly $12,000) in 2011.[11]   [Emphasis mine]

These problems occur more acutely in sectors 4, 5, and 6; and boards in companies in these sectors need to pay serious attention as globalization in their industries accelerates. Sectors 7 and 8 are not really suitable for globalization if they are truly local and not tradable across borders or if they are heavily regulated, so their boards do not have to concern themselves with the questions raised by globalization. However, if they are deregulated or likely to be, then boards need to consider the likelihood of cross-border competition brought about by benchmarking and what that means for employment, wages, and inequality.

Already Globalized Sectors

These three sectors are globalized for a variety of reasons and the battles between "winners and losers" have already taken place, with settled outcomes:
1. *Sector 1: Physical commodities:* These by necessity normally must cross borders since locations where they are found are not always the same as markets where they are consumed.
2. *Sector 2: Scale-driven businesses:* This sector needs huge R&D expenditures and exists where there are only a few customers across the world. It requires such large volumes to achieve a competitive edge that it can only be achieved by worldwide scale because domestic markets are not big enough.
3. *Sector 3: Manufactured commodities:* This sector shares many attributes with the second sector. Many companies prominent in this sector are already important in the first and second sectors which gives them a natural

edge in making this sector global. The majority of the companies are in relatively old industries where the need for economies of scale or the need to move commodities from their origin to their market of consumption is well understood. Tensions are not created by the globalization of these sectors, but rather by monopoly power that certain producers try to achieve. There may also be trade tensions, caused by dumping and market share grabbing activities.

In the main, these are capital intensive industries (like steel and ship-building) where the "losers" have already lost out and the employment impacts of further changes are relatively small. There is an accepted equilibrium of sorts regarding who the key players are and which markets they will serve. The battlefields for share and profit were fought over and positions lost and won by the 21st century; outcomes which have contributed to the decline in the share of wages represented in the US and UK economies.[vii] This is not to say that boards in this sector can relax – far from it. They are under great pressure regarding the environment, corporate social responsibility, and sustainable development.

Accelerating Globalized Sectors

These are the sectors where there is genuine debate about the desirability of globalization because it is not yet clear who the "winners" and "losers" will be and therefore what impact there will be on employment, wages, and inequality:

1. *Sector 4: Skill/productivity driven consumer goods:* The arguments here have centered on the "hollowing out" of industries. Countries with traditionally high levels of skill (Germany and Japan) find they are losing out to newer competitors with highly educated workforces and lower social costs – in the case of Germany, to Eastern European countries that joined the EU; and in the case of Japan, first to South Korea and then to China. Even within the EU, the UK used to be accused of "social dumping" in order to capture more than its fair share of EU FDI (foreign direct investment). The tensions here are real because "hollowing out" causes job losses and devalues traditional

---

vii In his speech to the UK's Trade Union Congress on September 10, 2019, Jeremy Corbyn, then leader of the Labour Party, pointed out that wages in the UK in 1976 represented 64% of UK GDP and that by 2019, this had fallen to 54%.

In 1970 in the US, wages were 51.6% of GDP and by 2018 they had fallen to 43.8%. *Economic Research*, Federal Reserve Bank of St. Louis, https://www.tuc.org.uk/speeches/jeremy-corbyns-speech-tuc-congress-2019, accessed on September 10, 2019.

craft-based skills that take a lifetime to acquire. Seen through German eyes in the 1990s, the outlook for labor was not promising:

> Sector by sector, job by job, the world of labor is indeed being revolutionized. Hardly anyone is spared. Politicians and economists look in vain for something to replace the blue-collar jobs that are disappearing at the Vulkan shipyards, the Dasa aircraft hangars or the Volkswagen assembly lines. Fear of redundancy has long haunted white-collar offices, and is spreading to sectors of the economy that used to be most secure. *Jobs for life give way to casual work, and people who yesterday thought they had a career of the future can find that their skills have turned overnight into so much useless knowledge.*[12]
>
> [Emphasis mine]

Although the examples are old and Germany recovered to prosper in the 21st century, the argument is still valid in every threatened or disrupted sector and will continue to be so for the following reasons:

> A brave new world of global supply chains emerged to leverage international differences in costs and skills to produce better and cheaper products
>
> In today's global economy, products are put together in one country from components sourced in other countries and then sold all over the world. *As a result, vastly fewer products are solely "made in America," "made in China," or indeed made in any one country.*[13]
>
> [Emphasis mine]

Appendix 4.1 discusses the breakdown of suppliers in manufacturing an Apple iPhone which shows how complex modern supply chains are and how fragile they can become as a result, if any link in the chain should break, as happened in China in 2020 because of its shutdown caused by the Covid-19 pandemic.

This makes it clear that the belief that balance of payments can be aggregated by country – as in arguing about China benefitting at the expense of the US – no longer makes sense; though it might have been appropriate before the advent of global supply chains. Moreover, given the way value is added and profits are made across global supply chains, it is very hard to disaggregate the benefit by country of origin. For example:

> The value added by assemblers Foxconn and Pegatron is typically estimated at only about 5% of the total cost of making an Apple device. The rest comes from the components, none of which come from China. So much for "made in China."
>
> According to *TechInsights*, the total cost of the iPhone XS Max is $453. Compare that with the retail sticker price of $1099 and it's easy to see why Apple is one of the world's largest companies by market capitalization.[14]

2. ***Sector 5: "Brandable" deregulated consumer goods:*** The jury is still out regarding the feasibility of creating identical brand positionings everywhere

in the world. There have been successes such as Coke, Marlboro, and McDonalds. Yet these successes have been exceptions to prove the rule. These brands have been able to promote identical propositions everywhere because they represented an American way of being. Received wisdom argues for global branding, and yet the problems the major consumer goods firms face in growing their volumes around the world with global brands argues that there is a good deal of resistance to homogeneity. For example, even Coca-Cola has had to drive its soft drinks growth in India through the acquisition of a local brand, Thums Up.[15] Pepsi has also found it difficult to grow its snack business on the basis of a uniform approach.[16] And in China the evidence is that as soon as the local brand is as good as the foreign product, consumers will choose the local product, especially in fast food.[17] New evidence from the snacking sector in China suggests Oreo is having difficulties competing with Three Squirrels, a local upstart.[18] McDonalds have experienced similar problems in the Philippines where the brand leader is Jollibee.[19]

3. ***Sector 6: Professional business services:*** This is a sector where the US has been pushing hard for liberalization. There is probably no great animosity felt toward American accounting firms or consultants. Using them is part of being modern. Legal services are perhaps a little more contentious in that litigation is not the natural way in so much of Asia. On the other hand, there is a great deal of ambivalence regarding investment banking and the financial services industry.

As early as 1986, Peter Drucker was concerned by the volatility created by movements of funds seeking a better marginal rate of return and he felt the sheer size of the movements was perhaps the major threat to the well-being of economies and to the sustainability of the globalization agenda.[20] His concern was that they were not anchored in any economic activity and were therefore able to move at the touch of a computer key. They were subject to panic and systemic risk.

Apologists for bankers argued we had learned the lessons of the "Tequila" crisis in 1994–1995 and the Asian financial crisis in 1998–1999 and that such concern was overplayed. Professor Rick Mishkin[viii] had this to say after the Asian financial crisis in 1998 in an article he wrote for the *Financial Times*:

In the last 20 years, systemic risk has become a growing problem. . .

---

viii Frederic Stanley "Rick" Mishkin is the Alfred Lerner Professor of Banking and Financial Institutions at the Graduate School of Business, Columbia University.

Why has systemic risk become more of a problem? In recent years, *there has been a growing trend towards liberalisation of financial systems in many economies and the globalization of international capital markets. This has provided new opportunities for risk-taking by financial institutions.*

In addition, the expectation by market participants that governments would come to the rescue of their financial sectors and offer a safety net has increased, and these expectations have been validated by huge bail-outs, often conducted with the assistance of international financial organisations such as the IMF. *Financial institutions have more incentive for moral hazard, so substantial increases in systemic risk have occurred. . .*

. . .Further, when systemic risk leads to a financial crisis in which the financial system seizes up, depressions can result, with high unemployment, severe economic hardship and the threat of political instability.

The last 20 years have not been good ones in terms of managing systemic risk. Let us hope that governments, banks and financial institutions have learned the lesson and the future will bring considerable improvement.[21] [Emphases mine]

His concerns were validated by the global financial crisis in 2008–2009.

Jeffrey Garten (former US Undersecretary of Commerce for International Trade) was equally prescient when he wrote:

Finally, while the financial playing field is supposedly more sophisticated now, investors and lenders are no smarter today than in the past. They take the same risks that traders always have, whether in the early 1700s, when European financial wizards went broke investing in the South Sea Company, a speculative real estate venture, in the prolonged spree of the 1920s that led to the crash, or in the current Asian debacle.

Similar features recur in all these crises. To begin with, there is good news, and confidence rises. Then more lenders and investors appear on the scene, attracted by the new opportunities.

Soon, optimism turns to euphoria, and new theories emerge to justify why this particular business cycle will not have a downswing or why these super-high valuations aren't really excessive. (Remember how in the 1970s lending to Latin America exploded on the theory that sovereign nations couldn't go broke? Or how just before the '87 crash, experts declared junk bonds and highly leveraged companies to be the wave of our financial future?) At last, a troublesome event – a default, or a change in investor sentiment – causes the bubble to burst, and everyone rushes for the exit.

The pattern has hardly varied.

Today two new developments reinforce it further.

Computers now insure [sic] that investors, traders and bankers have instant real-time information.

As a result, hundreds of billions of dollars move by keystroke in response to a rumor, thereby worsening the damage caused by lemming-like financial behavior.

Also, lenders have become emboldened to take ever greater risks with increasing sums of money because they believe – with good reason – that in a crisis Uncle Sam and the I.M.F. will bail them out to limit global fallout. . .[22] [Emphases mine]

Since Professor Mishkin and Jeffrey Garten wrote their prophetic words, we have had the GFC which followed their script almost word for word, with two new explicitly articulated concepts: "Too Big to Fail"[ix] and "Too Big to Jail."[x] The resulting Great Recession and the reaction of central banks to prevent another Great Depression increased inequality (more on this later) and fueled resentment against the elites who supported and benefited disproportionately from globalization.

More recently, there is an added source of disenchantment with current globalized finance: the weaponization of global finance by the US administration:

US President Donald Trump's "America First" policy exposed the myth that the US dollar-denominated global money and financial system is a global public good. If the US dollar serves only the national issuers, then the rest of the world needs to think through what this truly means for global monetary and financial stability. . .

. . .Mao Zedong's dictum that "political power stems from the barrel of a gun" can be extended to financial power. In a military conflict between the US and China, where would savings flee to – the US dollar or RMB? The US dollar is defended not by the size of US foreign exchange reserves (small by global standards), but by the biggest military power in the world. Geopolitical rivalry, including the threat of geopolitical conflict, introduces political instability to exchange rates and, hence, to whole financial systems.[23]

McDonaldization

There is another driver of globalization that is less obvious and more subtle – McDonaldization. This is an umbrella term used to cover the rationalization and dehumanization of work.[24] In an extension of Frederick Winslow Taylor's "Scientific Management,"[xi] the McDonald's working environment is one that breaks tasks down into totally predictable repetitive actions that are the same everywhere in the world. In Ritzer's 1993 study of the fast food industry,[25] he identified four drivers: efficiency, quantification, predictability, and the displacement of human labor. These drivers are also evident in universities, hospitals, supermarkets, and increasingly in the cultural industries as well (hence

---

ix During the GFC of 2008–2009, a number of financial institutions were bailed out by the US and the UK governments at taxpayer expense because they were deemed to be systemically so important, they could not be allowed to fail, hence the phrase "Too Big to Fail."
x When Eric Holder, the US Attorney General, sought to indict a number of US financial institutions, he was stopped by Timothy Geithner, then US Treasury Secretary, because of their systemic importance. As a result, the Attorney General called them "Too Big to Jail."
xi Frederick Winslow Taylor (1856–1915) was the originator of so-called "Scientific Management" introducing work study and systematic measurement.

formulaic blockbuster films where special effects are the star; and sitcoms where the tried and tested is what is offered):

> *The McDonald's culture offers efficiency in that it seeks the quickest method possible to sat-isfy the consumer's demands for entertainment, nourishment and transport.* In an increas-ingly fast-paced world consumer needs have to be satisfied quickly, and with the minimum amount of personal disturbance. In terms of media cultures, the development of the Internet offers a fast and streamlined way of receiving up to the minute news, with-out (it seems) the inconvenience of having to search through cumbersome newspapers for the reports that are of interest. The McDonald's culture also offers a service that can be quantified and numerically counted. Culture in this climate is increasingly subject to the procedures of calculation; rather than focusing upon the "experience" a piece of music opens out, we are persuaded to assess our purchase in terms of its value for money, the length of the recording and even the number of easily recognized songs it contains. . . *Human labour that can never be made perfectly predictable is replaced by technology in the workplace, in areas of social control and other avenues of social life. . . The growth of a self-service culture de-skills service workers while imposing drudgery upon the consumer. The ultimate consequence of this process is the elimination of human contact altogether.* Indeed this is precisely what is being promised by home shopping television channels [and online shopping]. . . Such practices offer a smooth seamless culture with few shocks or surprises.[26]   [Emphasis mine]

The key point about this trend toward homogeneity and the removal of human contact in being served is that it becomes less and less important where you are. If all places appear to be the same, if all environments offer the same ser-vice experience, then they become readily interchangeable in people's minds. One Hilton or Hyatt is like another, so it no longer makes a difference whether it is in Shanghai or Chicago. This new feeling that there really is not that much difference between major cities is a key driver in creating the pressure to global-ize on the one hand, and is a mechanism by which the process of globalization changes the way people look at each other and their investment decisions on the other. Relationships based on human interaction and engagement are re-placed by transactions that undermine the sense of community, belonging, and identity.[27] McDonaldization is both a cause and an effect of globalization.

Benchmarking in Deregulating Domestic Sectors

Personal financial services, retail distribution, education, medical care, and utili-ties are all regulated environments where deregulation has arrived in the last twenty-five years. The impact of deregulation has been greater competition. In many markets the service provided was nearly identical and so the advent of com-petition led to prices falling. The fall in prices hurt margins and drove weaker companies into the arms of the stronger. This has led to cross-border mergers and acquisitions in country after country in areas that were traditionally regarded as local markets: buses,[xii] rail,[xiii] gas and electricity,[xiv] water,[xv] waste management,[xvi] health services,[xvii] and telecommunications (fixed and mobile).[xviii] In most cases, the arguments for the deals were superior management, best practice transfer, and benchmarking to compete. Better prices have resulted, so has more rapid innovation, often at the cost of jobs, increasing resentment at globalization.

Globalized trade in goods has led to unparalleled increases in wealth in the period since World War II and, in the case of China, to a unique reduction in the number of people living in poverty. However, it has created "losers" in a number of developed countries who have been unable to compete with former Communist countries and with Mexico and Asian Tigers (the highly developed economies of Hong Kong, Singapore, South Korea, and Taiwan) which led to a squeeze on incomes and a loss of jobs in rustbelt regions in the US and Europe.

---

xii For example, in Europe the biggest international bus companies are Eurolines and Flixbus. Eurolines operates in 29 European countries; Flixbus in 28. The UK's Stagecoach through its Megabus subsidiary operates in four European countries. First Group is the largest UK bus company with operations in the US and Hong Kong.

xiii For example, 70% of the UK's rail routes are owned by the German, French, and Dutch railways. https://www.google.com/search?q=crossborder+train+companies&oq=crossborder +train+companies&aqs=chrome..69i57j33.15238j0j7&sourceid=chrome&ie=UTF-8, accessed on September 5, 2019.

xiv For example, in the UK, EDF (French), E.ON (German), and Iberdrola (Spanish), serve 47.7% of UK customers. British Gas, owned by Shell (an Anglo-Dutch company), serves another 32.5%. https://en.wikipedia.org/wiki/Big_Six_energy_suppliers, accessed on September 5, 2019.

xv For example, in the UK, Corsair, JP Morgan Asset Management, and Lazard (American), Deutsche Bank (German), and YTL (Malaysian) own major water utilities. https://www.google. com/search?ei=TdZwXavIBLSHjLsPoKWZ6As&q=water+suppliers+ownershio&oq=water+sup pliers+owners, accessed on September 5, 2019.

xvi For example, Waste Management (American) operates in Canada and owns 40% of Shanghai Environment Group in China https://en.wikipedia.org/wiki/Waste_Management_ (corporation)#International.

xvii For example, IHH (Malaysian) operates hospitals in Central and Eastern Europe, Central Asia, Middle East, India, Singapore, and Turkey, https://en.wikipedia.org/wiki/IHH_ Healthcare, accessed on September 10, 2019.

xviii For example, Vodafone (British) operates in forty countries. https://www.google.com/ search?ei=Z9xwXcXKEZaV8gLM5J3YBw&q=vodafone+47+countries+list&oq=vodafone+coun tries+list

Telefonica (Spanish) operates in twenty-four countries. https://www.google.com/search? ei=ENxwXbfbMYaVgQahibOIBQ&q=telefonica+countries+list&oq=telefonica+countries+list&

Axiata (Malaysian) operates in eight countries in Asia. https://www.google.com/search?q= axiata+operating+countries&oq=axiata+countries&aqs=chrome.1.69i57j0l2.9539j1j7&sour

Measured in terms of its impact on GDP overall, globalization has been regarded as a force for good. However, increases in GDP do not necessarily translate into better lives,[28] particularly if they do not lead to a reduction in inequality, but instead to an increase and a loss of self-respect for those who have lost their jobs. It is vital that politicians and boards of directors appreciate this if they are to defend the current economic system from populist protectionist siren songs. Therefore, I now turn to the threat posed by inequality.

The Threat Posed by Inequality

Although globalization has reduced the wealth gap between the richest economies and some of the poorest, it has increased inequality within economies. There have been two unintended consequences of globalization with respect to inequality.

The Rise of Global Supply Chains

The first unintended consequence was the arrival of the Chinese and Eastern European workforces into the global marketplace after 1989. It raised the standards of living in those countries as a result of foreign direct investment, technology transfer, and access to previously closed export markets in the West.

I remember discussing this with Dr. Gary Dirks, then head of BP Asia, based in Shanghai in 1996. He compared the impact of this new supply of workers with two columns of water of differing heights. As long as there was zero contact between the two, the differences in height would remain. However, once there was contact between the two columns, no matter how tiny, they would adjust till they both were the same height – it was a simple matter of physics. He said the same would happen to wages in the US and China. Chinese wages would rise and American wages would either stagnate or fall as US companies developed supply chains to capitalize on the lower costs of production first in Mexico, then in China and Eastern Europe. The impact of these supply chains was particularly notable in the case of the US where they led to stagnant wages for workers:

Income inequality has increased more rapidly in North America, China, India, and Russia than anywhere else notes the World Inequality Report 2018 produced by the World Inequality Lab, a research center based at the Paris School of Economics. The difference between Western Europe and the United States in this regard is particularly striking: *"While the top 1% income share was close to 10% in both regions in 1980, it rose only slightly to 12% in 2016 in Western Europe while it shot up to 20% in the United States. Meanwhile, in the United States, the bottom 50% income share decreased from more than 20% in 1980 to 13% in 2016."* Continental Europe, the report emphasized, saw income inequality moderated by educational and wage-setting policies that were relatively more favorable to low and middle-income groups and a lesser decline in the progressivity of its tax code.[29]

In addition to issues of income inequality (for details see, Appendix 4.2) created by globalization are those of wealth inequality:

> According to the WEF index, income inequality has risen or remained stagnant in 20 of the 29 advanced economies while poverty increased in 17. Although most emerging economies have improved in these respects – 84% of them registered a decline in poverty – their absolute levels of inequality remain much higher. In addition, the report states, both in advanced and emerging economies, *wealth* is significantly more unequally distributed than *income*: "This problem has improved little in recent years, with wealth inequality rising in 49 economies."[30]

The rise in wealth inequality is a function of two factors. The first factor was that global supply chains weakened unions and the bargaining power of workers in developed countries. Consequently, the lower costs created by globalization meant the benefits accrued to corporations in the form of higher profits. These higher profits benefited the top 1% of people disproportionately as the equity they owned rose in price. The second factor was the impact of quantitative easing introduced by central banks to prevent the Great Recession becoming another Great Depression after the GFC. Quantitative easing and the attendant low interest rate regimes designed to stimulate economies had the unintended effect of pumping money into existing assets (property and equity) rather than encouraging investment in new assets. As a result, owners of existing assets saw the value of their assets rise, whereas those who did not own shares or property were left behind. Once again, an increase in inequality was the result. This was made worse by the financialization of the economy:

> As yields on long term securities plunge and asset prices surge, very low interest rates encourage companies, private equity, hedge funds and the rich to borrow even more to invest in financial assets, sending prices even higher.
>
> Finance also increases inequality through greater wealth concentration thanks to exclusive wealth management services for rich clients who get favoured access to specialized services and structured, high yield products.
>
> Corporations and wealthy individuals use the best available professional services for tax avoidance and evasion, often facilitated by banking secrecy.
>
> Private banking employs top fund managers to manage the wealth of rich clients, offering double digit returns while ordinary depositors have to accept modest interest rates on their deposits. . .

With finance capturing more profits than manufacturing, unlike before, those working for finance now secure much higher incomes compared to others. "Excessive" financial sector salaries took off in the 1980s, reaching 40% just prior to the 2008 Global Financial Crisis, with "rents" accounting for 30–50% of this "excess."

The protracted decline of real wages in the U.S. and the U.K. has been enabled by new rules and laws favouring wealth owners over labour incomes. In the U.S., capital gains can be taxed a maximum of 20%, while the highest marginal tax rate for wages is 37%.

By contrast, the poor have less, but also costlier access to finance, and contribute more to financial gains for others, e.g., through subprime mortgages, or unsecured personal loans.

Stagnant or declining wages have imposed greater indebtedness on the poor, with finance reaping lucrative profits from such lending to households. Between 1960 and 2007, U.S. household debt rose from 41% to 100% of annual GDP. . .

With real wages for many not rising for decades, increased financial inclusion has meant greater indebtedness for many of them.[31]

This does not just fuel resentment by the disadvantaged against the current economic system, it also reduced the rate of growth because the theoretical "trickle down" benefits of the rich becoming richer failed to materialize; removing the economic justification for channeling more wealth into the hands of the already rich:

Another problem to consider is that when massive proportions of a nation's income and wealth are concentrated in the hands of a few, overall economic growth appears to suffer. A 2015 study by the International Monetary Fund[32] found that "if the income share of the top 20% (the rich) increases, then GDP growth actually declines over the medium term, suggesting that the benefits do not trickle down" while "an increase in the income share of the bottom 20% (the poor) is associated with higher GDP growth."[33]   [Emphasis mine]

Mexico, Chile, the U.S. and Turkey have the highest inequality among the OECD members. And inequality is even higher in emerging economies. On the flip side, Denmark, Slovenia, and Czech Republic have the lowest.

"The evidence shows that high inequality is bad for growth. The case for policy action is as much economic as social. By not addressing inequality, governments are cutting into the social fabric of their countries and hurting their long-term economic growth," Gurría added.[34]   [Emphasis mine]

The internet and the gig economy have made matters worse, as they make it much easier for even small companies to look for the cheapest skills in a global market. Platforms like Fiverr[35] encourage employers of contract labor to race to the bottom:

While freelance websites may have raised wages and broadened the number of potential employers for some people, *they've forced every new worker who signs up into entering a global marketplace with endless competition, low wages, and little stability.* Decades ago, the only companies that outsourced work overseas were multinational corporations with the resources to set up manufacturing shops elsewhere. *Now, independent businesses and*

> individuals are using the power of the internet to find the cheapest services in the world too, and it's not just manufacturing workers who are seeing the downsides to globalization. All over the country, people like graphic designers and voice-over artists and writers and marketers have to keep lowering their rates to compete.[36]   [Emphases mine]

Perhaps this helps explain how globalization has helped increase inequality in the richer countries of the world. It may also help explain why such increases in inequality slow down growth because the people who lose out do not have enough money to spend, eliminating the positive multiplier effect of growth because the marginal propensity to consume of the top 1% is lower than that of the bottom quartile. Support for this view comes from comments in response to Sajid Javid, the UK's Chancellor of the Exchequer's spending review in 2019[37] announcing an end to austerity after ten years:

> While anxiety on the public finances may have been overdone, there has been nowhere near enough focus on family finances. Weekly pay is projected to be almost £25 lower in 2022 than previously expected, still £22.70 below the pre-crisis peak. Addressing this unprecedented living standards squeeze – with action on housing and social security – should be front and centre of the chancellor's response.[38]

The Network Effect

Globalization has increased the impact of the network effect[xix] by increasing the number of members of the network dramatically. The effect of this is that the owners of the networks and the stars featured on the networks have been able to earn disproportionately in a "winner takes all" environment.

On the one hand, it allows leading soccer players to earn astonishing sums each year – for example, Lionel Messi (€40 million), Cristiano Ronaldo (€31 million), and the twenty-year-old Kylian Mbappe (€17.5 million),[39] whereas top nurses and teachers in the UK in 2019 get paid $29,800[40] and $49,700[41] per year because they are not paid for entertaining global audiences. The justification for this difference in earnings is that "this is how the global marketplace works" – enough people around the world are willing to pay a tiny sum individually for watching footballers (or any other entertainer for that matter) that it adds up to these huge earnings. Advertisers know these celebrities have global

---

xix "The network effect is a phenomenon whereby increased numbers of people or participants improve the value of a good or service. The Internet is an example of the network effect. Initially, there were few users on the Internet since it was of little value to anyone outside of the military and some research scientists." Investopedia, https://www.investopedia.com/terms/n/network-effect.asp accessed on March 6, 2020.

reach and so are willing to pay them to act as sponsors. Social media influencers and celebrities who create no long-term value but are rewarded for their reach add to inequity. Global news channels and communications make people aware of this disparity, and TV and social media show the differences in lifestyles, reinforcing the sense of unfairness.

Summary

Globalization is not a new phenomenon. From an economist's perspective "Globalization 1.0" (1870–1914) saw the UK exporting textiles and industrial goods; "Globalization 2.0" (1945–1989) saw the US first and then China exporting, based on factories located in their countries; "Globalization 3.0" (1989–2008) saw the expansion of supply chains designed to feed the US and European markets; and "Globalization 4.0" sees the trade in digital goods and services, led by the US and China – who are each seeking global dominance.

Globalization mainly benefits customers, often at the expense of producers. This is the basis of the fundamental conflict of interests within the process that has led to periods of expansion and of retreat and may well see globalization in retreat once more as a result of populist disaffection with the current economic system caused by the stagnation of wages and rise in inequality.

For globalization to prosper, seven conditions must exist: buyers must value what suppliers in other countries have to offer; law and order enforcing property rights and contracts in exporting countries are essential for companies to invest in infrastructure needed to provide goods and services across borders; good cross-border communications to familiarize both buyers and investors with what is available; governments must be prepared to allow their economies to become interdependent; successful role models to encourage other countries to follow suit; all supported by the internet and global media and content providers.

Certain industries are more globalized than others. They can be grouped into those that are already globalized; those where globalization is accelerating; and those where globalization is difficult. Three industrial sectors were already fully globalized before the 21st century: physical commodities; scale-driven businesses; and some manufactured commodities. Three sectors faced accelerating globalization over the past forty years: skill/productivity driven consumer goods; brandable, deregulated consumer goods; and professional business services. Two sectors were not natural candidates for globalization in the past, though that has been changing in the last twenty years wherever deregulation has taken place: hard to brand globally regulated goods and services; and locally branded or untradeable goods and services.

Boards in the already globalized sectors do not need to concern themselves unduly with the current problems of globalization because the "winners" and "losers" in these three sectors have already been decided. They do, however, have to be sensitive to the resulting fall in the share of wages as a percent of GDP and rise in inequality in developed economies, caused by past changes in their industries as a result of globalization.

Boards in industries where globalization is accelerating must pay great attention to the socio-political implications of the changes forced on them, as opposed to just focusing on the bottom-line impacts. They also need to consider whether their assumptions regarding trends for increasing globalization may be about to go into reverse as a result of populist disaffection and increased protectionism. This is particularly relevant for financial services where the anger against bankers and their contribution to the Great Recession has not been forgotten.

Boards in the two sectors that previously did not have to worry about globalization because they were protected by regulation may find they need to consider the impact of benchmarking and cross-border mergers and takeovers that previously would not have been considered as likely. They need to understand the benefits and drawbacks of McDonaldization and the potential for discontent caused by so-called cultural homogenization where one modern city looks like any other.

Finally, I believe all boards need to be sensitive to the charge that globalization has led to increases in inequality whose impact is made worse by the network effect of global communications and social media. They need to start thinking about how they can help reduce inequality without damaging their businesses rather than supporting fiscal proposals designed to increase inequality further. This requires boards to recognize the complexities involved rather than seeking to oversimplify matters in order to come to grips with the issues in the time available, and I will discuss how this could be done in Part 3 of the book.

Appendix 4.1: Apple's iPhone Supply Chain

Location	Supplier	Components
U.S.	GT Advanced Technologies	Sapphire Crystal Components
U.S.	Samsung	Chips
U.S.	Global Foundries	Chips
U.S.	Texas Instruments	Chips
U.S.	Maxim Integrated	Chips
U.S.	Corning	Gorilla Glass
Japan	Japan Display Inc.	Display
Taiwan	Innolux	Display
South Korea	LG	Display
Japan	Toshiba	Storage
South Korea	SK Hynix	Storage
Taiwan	TSMC	Touch ID
Netherlands	NXP	NFC Chip
France	ST Microelectronics	Gyroscope
U.S.	Invensense	Gyroscope
China	Foxconn	Assembly
China	Pegatron	Assembly
Brazil	Foxconn	Assembly

Source: Based on: Hogan, J. (2016), cited in Garrett, G. (2019), "Why US-China Supply Chains Are Stronger Than the Trade War," *Knowledge@Wharton,* September 5, 2019, https://knowledge.wharton.upenn.edu/article/trade-war-supply-chain-impact/?utm_source=kw_newsletter&utm_medium=email&ut, accessed on September 8, 2019.

Appendix 4.2: Inequality Ranking

(Ratio of the average income of the 10% richest to the 10% poorest)

Ranking	Country	Ratio	Ranking	Country	Ratio
1.	Mexico	30.5	19.	Ireland	7.4
2.	Chile	26.5	20.	Poland	7.4
3.	United States	18.8	21.	Hungary	7.2
4.	Turkey	15.2	22.	Luxembourg	7.1
5.	Israel	14.9	23.	Austria	7.0
6.	Greece	12.3	24.	Switzerland	6.7
7.	Spain	11.7	25.	Netherlands	6.6
8.	Italy	11.4	26.	Germany	6.6
9.	Japan	10.7	27.	Sweden	6.3
10.	United Kingdom	10.5	28.	Norway	6.2
11.	Portugal	10.1	29.	Belgium	5.9
12.	South Korea	10.1	30.	Slovakia	5.7
13.	Estonia	9.7	31.	Iceland	5.6
14.	OECD average	9.6	32.	Finland	5.5
15.	Australia	8.8	33.	Slovenia	5.4
16.	Canada	8.6	34.	Czech Republic	5.4
17.	New Zealand	8.2	35.	Denmark	5.2
18.	France	7.4			

References

1 Zinkin, M. (2001), "Not new and never costless: globalisation," *International Relations,* Vol. 15 (5), pp. 27–36 (London/Thousand Oaks/New Delhi: Sage Publications), original manuscript provided to the author by his father.

2 Maddison, A. (1995), *Explaining the Economic Performance of Nations* (Aldershot: Edward Elgar).

3 Johnson, J. A. (2017), "Military-Industrial Interactions in the Development of Chemical Warfare 1914–1918: Comparing National Cases Within the Technological System of the Great War," in "One Hundred Years of Chemical Warfare: Research, Deployment, Consequences," *Springer Link,* November 28, 2017, https://link.springer.com/chapter/10.1007/978-3-319-51664-6_8, accessed on November 11, 2019.

4 Hodgson, G. (1988), *Economics and Institutions: A Manifesto for Institutional Economics* (Cambridge: Polity Press), p. 174.

5 Talalay, M. (2000), *Technology and Globalization,* in Germain, R., ed. (2000) *Globalization and its Critics, Perspectives from Political Economy* (Palgrave Macmillan), p. 209.

6 Garrett, G. (2019), "Why US-China Supply Chains Are Stronger Than the Trade War," *Knowledge@Wharton,* September 5, 2019, https://knowledge.wharton.upenn.edu/article/

trade-war-supply-chain-impact/?utm_source=kw_newsletter&utm_medium=email&ut, accessed on September 8, 2019.

7 "The new coronavirus could have a lasting impact on global supply chains," *The Economist,* February 15, 2020, https://www.economist.com/international/2020/02/15/the-new-coronavirus-could-have-a-lasting-impact-on-global-supply-chains?cid1=cust/ednew/n/bl/n/2020/02/29n/owned/n/n/nwl/n/n/AP/415278/n, accessed on March 2, 2020.

8 Talalay, M. (2000), op. cit., p. 214.

9 Ibid., p. 211.

10 Mishel, L. et al. (2015), "Wage Stagnation in Nine Charts," *Economic Policy Institute,* January 6, 2015, https://www.epi.org/publication/charting-wage-stagnation/, accessed on September 10, 2019.

11 Ibid.

12 Martin, H-P. and Schumann, H. (1997), *The Global Trap: Globalization and the Assault on Democracy and Prosperity* (London: Zed Books), p. 97.

13 Garrett, G. (2019), op. cit.

14 Ibid.

15 Ghaswalla, A. N. (2013), "No regrets selling Thums Up, says Bisleri chief Ramesh Chauhan" *Financial Times,* June 13, 2013, https://www.thehindubusinessline.com/companies/no-regrets-selling-thums-up-says-bisleri-chief-ramesh-chauhan/article23106362.ece, accessed on March 6, 2020.

16 Collins, G. and Strom, S. (1996), "Can Pepsi Become the Coke of Snacks?" *New York Times,* November 3, 1996, https://www.nytimes.com/1996/11/03/business/can-pepsi-become-the-coke-of-snacks.html, accessed on September 6, 2019.

17 Jourdan, A. (2013), "Local tastes tempt China diners away from Golden Arches," *Reuters,* October 28, 2013, https://uk.news.yahoo.com/local-tastes-tempt-china-diners-away-golden-arches-055247340–finance.html, accessed on September 6, 2019.

18 Wernau, J. (2019), "America is losing the Chinese shopper," *The Wall Street Journal,* https://www.thestar.com.my/business/business-news/2019/10/14/america-is-losing-the-chinese-shopper?utm_source=Smartech&utm, October 14, 2019, accessed on October 15, 2019.

19 Gilchrist, K. (2019), "How two Filipino brothers staved off competition from McDonalds to build global fast food chain Jollibee," *CNBC Make It,* April 30, 2019, https://www.cnbc.com/2019/05/01/how-jollibee-beat-competition-from-mcdonalds-to-build-a-global-brand.html, accessed on March 6, 2020.

20 Drucker, P. (1986), "The Changed World Economy," *Foreign Affairs,* Spring 1986.

21 Mishkin, F. S. (2000), "Securing a safety net against economic free fall," *Financial Times Supplement on Mastering Risk,* June 6, 2000, p. 7.

22 Garten, J. (1998), "Adrift in the Global Economy," *New York Times,* May 11, 1998.

23 Sheng, A. (2020), "Condivergence: Why standard finance theory is incomplete," *Forum, The Edge Malaysia Weekly,* February 24–March 1, 2020, https://www.theedgemarkets.com/article/condivergence-why-standard-finance-theory-incomplete, accessed on March 2, 2020.

24 Stevenson, N. (2000), "Globalization and Cultural Political Economy, Globalization and its Critics," in Germain, R. D., ed., "Globalization and its Critics," *International Political Economy Series* (London: Palgrave McMillan).

25 Ritzer, G. (1993), *The McDonaldization of Society* (Newbury Park, California: Pine Forge Press).

26 Stevenson, N. (2000), op. cit., pp. 94–95.

27 Dirks, G. (2020), in an email reply to the author on January 18, 2020.

28 Sen, A. (1999), *Development As Freedom* (Oxford: Oxford University Press).

29 "Wealth Distribution and Income Inequality by Country 2018," *Global Finance,* September 2, 2019, https://www.gfmag.com/global-data/economic-data/wealth-distribution-income-inequal ity, accessed on September 2, 2019.

30 Ibid.

31 K. S., Jomo. and Lim, M. H. (2020), "Financialization Increases Inequality," http://ipsnews. net/2020/02/financialization-increases-inequality, accessed on February 5, 2020.

32 Dabla-Norris, E. et al. (2015),"Causes and Consequences of Income Inequality: A Global Perspective," June 15, 2015, https://www.imf.org/en/Publications/Staff-Discussion-Notes/ Issues/2016/12/31/Causes-and-Consequences-of-Income-Inequality-A-Global-Perspective- 42986, accessed on September 6, 2019.

33 "Wealth Distribution and Income Inequality by Country 2018," op. cit.

34 Ibid.

35 "Fiverr – Freelance Services for the Lean Entrepreneur," https://www.fiverr.com/.

36 Semuels, A. (2018), "The Online Gig Economy's 'Race to the Bottom': when the whole world is fighting for the same jobs, what happens to the workers?" *The Atlantic,* August 31, 2018, https://www.theatlantic.com/technology/archive/2018/08/fiverr-online-gig-economy/569083/, accessed on September 3, 2018.

37 Javid, S. (2019), "Spending Round 2019: what you need to know," *HM Treasury,* September 4, 2019, https://www.gov.uk/government/news/spending-round-2019-what-you-need-to-know, ac cessed on September 8, 2019.

38 Resolution Foundation quoting UK Office for Budget Responsibility finding, cited in Elliott, L. (2018), "UK pay squeeze to last five more years, warns thinktank," *The Guardian,* November 13, 2017, https://www.theguardian.com/business/2017/nov/13/uk-wages-squeeze-continue- until-2022-resolution-foundation-warns, accessed on September 5, 2019.

39 https://www.google.com/search?q=kylian+mbappe+age&oq=kylian+mbappe&aqs= chrome.2.69i57j0l5.8584j0j7&, accessed on September 8, 2019.

40 "NHS terms and Conditions of Service (AfC) Pay Scales," https://www.nhsemployers.org/ pay-pensions-and-reward/agenda-for-change/pay-scales/annual, accessed on September 10, 2019.

41 "Pay scales 2018–2019," January 25, 2019, https://neu.org.uk/advice/pay-scales-2018-19 accessed on September 10, 2019.

42 Based on Hogan, J. (2016), cited in Garrett, G. (2019), op. cit.

Chapter 5
Employment Sustainability

This chapter is presented in two parts. The first explores the challenges posed by disruptive technology; and the second discusses the unsuitability of education in sustaining employability. It closes with a summary of the discussion.

Chapter 3 discussed environmental sustainability and Chapter 4 explored the impact of globalization on economic sustainability. Implicit in both chapters was the threat to sustainable employment in developed democracies.[i] What both of these threats have in common is that they are systemic, with long-term consequences boards may find difficult to deal with; because so much of their impact on employment is the result of decisions taken outside their organizations by governments, domestically and internationally.

This chapter explores issues affecting sustainable employment that are within the discretion of boards as they decide who to employ, and on achieving the right balance between capital and labor after considering stakeholder concerns. While it is true to say these are decisions boards must take to ensure they are making the right choices for the long-term success of their organizations, they are also decisions that I believe could lead to a "political tragedy of the commons,"[ii] if all organizations take the same decisions at the same time without considering their systemic impact.

Automation and artificial intelligence (AI) disrupt the labor market. Investing in them will affect the demand side for labor in radical ways, affecting the suitability of the supply side. Automation covers investments in technologies designed to replace muscle power, whereas AI covers investments in technologies designed to augment or replace mental power.

This raises issues regarding the role of education in ensuring the supply of labor can satisfy future demand so that there is full employment with good wages. If automation and AI lead to disemployment without creating alternative ways of providing the disemployed with economically and, more important, emotionally satisfying occupations, I fear the current discontent with the existing economic system could lead to its political overthrow.

---

i It is also a threat in countries like India and the Philippines that specialize in call centers.
ii The potential "political tragedy of the commons" could be triggered by any economic and social tragedy of the commons.

https://doi.org/10.1515/9783110670486-005

Impact of Disruptive Technology

The level of development in an economy is a function of its ability to use the three factors of production – land, capital, and labor – to best effect. Over time, the relationship between them changes, as a result of their relative prices. This determines the type of economy and its sustainability. Land is more or less a given, though its agricultural productivity is a function of how capital and labor are applied to increase yields. The relationship between capital and labor varies by country. It is an intensely political issue because it determines the percentage of GDP accruing to profits and wages and therefore affects the level of inequality – discussed in Chapter 4.

Disruptions caused by automation mainly affected workers or animals using muscle power because investments in automation and mechanization were designed to replace it, to raise productivity by improving how people and things were moved. Disruptions caused by AI are new and affect workers who rely on mental processes because investments in AI are designed to improve productivity by improving how intelligence can be better applied.

Automation Disruption

Automation is not new, nor are the arguments about its benefits and drawbacks. Perhaps the most famous example of its benefits for consumers and its drawbacks for producers was the failure by displaced British weavers to stop the introduction of mechanized looms designed to replace workers at the beginning of the Industrial Revolution. Inspired by one Ned Ludd, who allegedly broke two stocking frames in a rage, the Luddites smashed machinery that undercut their ability to earn a living:

> The Luddites were trying to save their livelihoods by smashing industrial machines developed for use in the textile industries of the West Riding of Yorkshire, Nottinghamshire, Leicestershire and Derbyshire. Some Luddites were active in Lancashire also. They smashed stocking-frames and cropping frames among others. There does not seem to have been any political motivation behind the Luddite riots; equally, there was no national organisation.
> *The men merely were attacking what they saw as the reason for the decline in their livelihoods.*[1]   [Emphasis mine]

There was a revival in 1816 of violence and machine breaking following a bad harvest and a recession. On June 28, 1816, the Luddites attacked two mills in Loughborough and smashed 53 frames costing GBP6,000 (worth GBP580,720 in 2020 money[2]). Troops were called in to end the riots; six men were executed and three transported to Australia. Although the British government of the day did nothing to alleviate the conditions of the workers, there were leading thinkers who thought such laissez-faire behavior was inappropriate and unsustainable:

> *Society ought not to exist, if not for the benefit of the whole.* It is and must be against the law of nature, if it exists for the benefit of the few and for the misery of the many. I say, then, distinctly, that *a society, in which the common labourer. . . cannot secure a sufficiency of food and raiment, is a society which ought not to exist; a society contrary to the law of nature; a society whose compact is dissolved.*[3]   [Emphases mine]

This is not unlike the policies of the British Labour party two hundred years later. Equally there was criticism of the government's "do-nothing" approach by the opposition Tory party that was a forerunner of Keynesian thinking of the 1930s:

> In passing from a state of war[iii] to a state of peace, the shock of the revulsion might not improbably have been lessened to all orders of society by somewhat graduating the transition. . . *If stagnant manufactures, and languishing agriculture, and a population suddenly turned loose from the military or naval services of the country, produce a supply of hands for which there is no work, a partial and temporary remedy might perhaps have been found in undertakings of public utility and magnificence – in the improvement of roads, the completion of canals, the erection of our National Monuments for Waterloo[iv] and Trafalgar[v] – undertakings which government might have supplied, if the means had been available.*[4]
>
> [Emphasis mine]

The fears of the Luddites were real and, as it turned out, wrong in the long run if the economy as whole was considered:

> In the long run, not only were there still many (if, on average, less skilled) jobs in the new textile factories but, more important, the productivity gains from mechanisation created huge new wealth. This in turn generated many more jobs across the U.K. economy in the long run than were initially lost in the traditional handloom weaving industry. The standard economic view for most of the last two centuries has therefore been that the Luddites were wrong about the long-term benefits of the new technologies, even if they were right about the short-term impact on their personal livelihoods. Anyone putting such arguments against new technologies has generally been dismissed as believing in the "Luddite fallacy."[5]
>
> While traditional machines, including fixed location industrial robots, replaced our muscles (and those of other animals like horses and oxen), these new smart machines have the potential to replace our minds and to move around freely in the world driven by a combination of advanced sensors, GPS tracking systems and deep learning – if not

---

iii The Napoleonic Wars ended in 1815.

iv The Battle of Waterloo in 1815 in which the Duke of Wellington and General Blucher defeated Napoleon and ended his career.

v The Battle of Trafalgar in 1805 in which Admiral Horatio Nelson defeated the combined French and Spanish fleets, losing his life in the process.

now, then probably within the next decade or two. *Will this just have the same effects as past technological leaps – short term disruption more than offset by long term economic gains? Or is this something more fundamental in terms of taking humans out of the loop not just in manufacturing and routine service sector jobs, but more broadly across the economy?* What exactly will humans have to offer employers if smart machines can perform all or most of their essential tasks better in the future?[6] *In short, has the "Luddite fallacy" finally come true?*[7]   [Emphases mine]

John Maynard Keynes was deeply concerned in 1932 about whether the rate at which technology disrupted jobs was greater than the rate at which it created demand for new jobs to replace them. He predicted widespread technological unemployment:

> due to our discovery of means of economising the use of labour outrunning the pace at which we can find new uses for labour.[8]

Mechanization saw the end of humanity's dependence on the horse, with serious consequences for horses and all those who made a living looking after horses. In 1900, London needed 300,000 horses to keep it moving.[9] Today it needs none. Whatever the impact of mechanization and automation, people can protest and take action to mitigate their effect on them or change jobs to benefit from new industries arising from the wealth creating effects of greater mechanization. Unlike working horses, they can try to ensure they do not become irrelevant.

In 1870 almost 50% of the US population were employed on farms; by 2008, only 1.3% were employed on farms.[10] In the UK it was less than 1% in 2013, versus 20% in 1841.[11] This was the result of mechanization and industrialization of agriculture. The surplus labor was able to move out of agriculture into other occupations and be absorbed elsewhere, although this transition took decades.

As watchers of *Downton Abbey*[vi] will know, a large percentage of the female population in England was employed as domestic servants. In 1901 there were 1,690,686 women or 40.5% working in domestic service,[12] but this changed over the next 50 years. First, women found opportunities elsewhere, notably working in munitions factories – made respectable by the shortage of working

---

vi *Downton Abbey* is the name of a British TV series (2010–2015). This historical drama follows the lives of the Crawley family and their servants in the family's Edwardian country house. The program begins with the 1912 sinking of the Titanic, which leaves Downton Abbey's future in jeopardy, as Lord Grantham's presumptive heir – his cousin James – and his son, Patrick, die aboard the ship, leaving him without male offspring. A new film of the same name was released in 2019.

men who had gone to fight in World War I. Second, after World War II, they were replaced by affordable household appliances in developed economies. As a result, the percentage of working women in domestic service in developed economies fell to 1.4%[13] from the 40.5% in the UK in 1901.

There have been equally significant losses in employment in manufacturing in the US as a result of the closures of factories rendered uneconomic by Asian competition, with 22% fewer factories in the US in 2018 than in 2000,[14] shown in Figure 5.1.

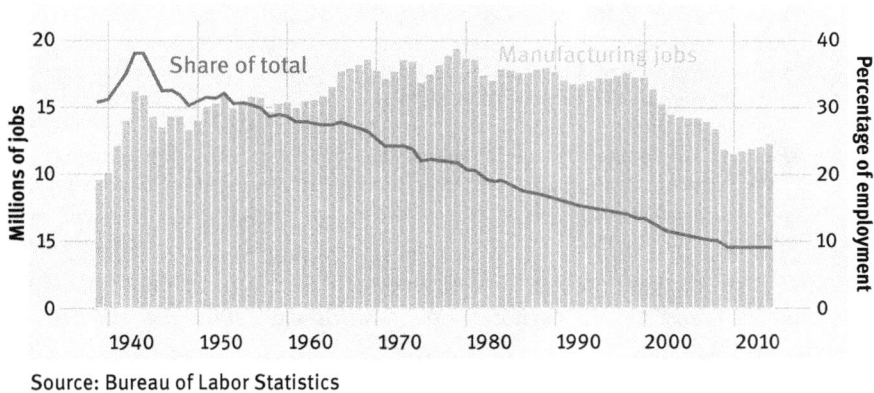

Source: Bureau of Labor Statistics

Figure 5.1: Declining manufacturing jobs in the United States 1940–2010.

US manufacturing jobs peaked in 1979 at just over 19 million and fell by about 7% in the 1990s. Between 2000 and 2018 there was a further drop of nearly five million jobs.[15] Despite these losses, US unemployment figures were at a 49-year low of 3.6% in May 2019,[16] offset by a transition of employment into the service sectors. However, in many cases the income earned and status ascribed to workers who have moved from manufacturing into the service sectors has been less – hence the disaffection in the US rustbelt states as inequality rises, fueling the concerns of experts about the future and that Keynes might be correct:

> Half of these experts (48 percent) envision a future in which robots and digital agents [will] have displaced significant numbers of both blue- and white-collar workers – with many expressing *concern that this will lead to vast increases in income inequality, masses of people who are effectively unemployable, and breakdowns in the social order.*[17]
>
> [Emphasis mine]

The optimists who believe in the benefits of robotization and AI argue that what has happened in the past – a transition from one industry to another to absorb the surplus labor – will happen again:

> Technology adoption can and often does cause significant short-term labor displacement, but history shows that, *in the longer run, it creates a multitude of new jobs and unleashes demand for existing ones, more than offsetting the number of jobs it destroys even as it raises labor productivity.* An examination of the historical record highlights several lessons:
> - All advanced economies have experienced profound sectoral shifts in employment, first out of agriculture and more recently manufacturing, even as overall employment grew. In the United States, the agricultural share of total employment declined from 60 percent in 1850 to less than 5 percent by 1970, while manufacturing fell from 26 percent of total U.S. employment in 1960 to below 10 percent today. Other countries have experienced even faster declines: one third of China's workforce moved out of agriculture between 1990 and 2015.
> - *Such shifts can have painful consequences for some workers. During the Industrial Revolution in England, average real wages stagnated for decades, even as productivity rose. Eventually, wage growth caught up to and then surpassed productivity growth. But the transition period was difficult for individual workers, and eased only after substantial policy reforms.*[18]   [Emphases mine]

The same report suggested that 30% of work activities could be automated by 2030 and as many as 375 million workers worldwide could be affected by emerging technologies:[19]

> In our prior report on automation, we found that about half the activities people are paid to do globally could theoretically be automated using currently demonstrated technologies. Very few occupations – less than 5 percent – consist entirely of activities that can be fully automated. *However, in about 60 percent of occupations, at least one-third of the constituent activities could be automated, implying substantial workplace transformations and changes for all workers.*[20]   [Emphasis mine]

The Automation Dilemma

Boards face a serious dilemma. On the one hand they must automate as fast as possible if they are to remain competitive, as pointed out by a 2019 UK Parliamentary Committee report on productivity:

> Rachel Reeves, the Labour MP who chairs the committee, said: *"The real danger for the U.K. economy and for future jobs growth is not that we have too many robots in the workplace but that we have too few.* The government has failed to provide the leadership needed to help drive investment in automation and robot technologies. If we are to reap the potential benefits in the future of improved living standards, more fulfilling work,

and the four-day working week, the government needs to do more to support British businesses and universities to collaborate and innovate."[21]   [Emphasis mine]

This warning was prompted by the fact that the UK does lag behind its rivals in the adoption of robots. In 2015, for every million hours worked, the UK had only 10 robots, while the US had 131, Germany 133, and Japan 167. By 2017, the UK represented just 0.6% of industrial robotics shipments.[22]

On the other hand, although the UK needs to invest more in automation to maintain its competitiveness, the committee recognized this will lead to serious job losses:

> Automation of industries from retail to manufacturing promises to revolutionise how businesses operate but *also raises the threat of huge job losses as robots replace people* in some functions in factories and warehouses, and driverless vehicles displace humans in many tasks.[23]   [Emphasis mine]

A more conservative view regarding the likelihood and pace of disruption caused by automation (at least in its computerization manifestation) suggests that many fewer jobs will be lost because the pace of change will be less rapid as a result of a number of obstacles. However, the OECD study emphasizes the need to retrain and help those lower status workers who will be most affected by disruption:

> We argue that the estimated share of "jobs at risk" must not be equated with actual or expected employment losses from technological advances for three reasons. *First, the utilisation of new technologies is a slow process*, due to economic, legal and societal hurdles, so that technological substitution often does not take place as expected. *Second, even if new technologies are introduced, workers can adjust to changing technological endowments by switching tasks, thus preventing technological unemployment. Third, technological change also generates additional jobs through demand for new technologies and through higher competitiveness.* The main conclusion from our paper is that automation and digitalisation are unlikely to destroy large numbers of jobs. However, *low qualified workers are likely to bear the brunt of the adjustment costs as the automatibility of their jobs is higher compared to highly qualified workers. Therefore, the likely challenge for the future lies in coping with rising inequality and ensuring sufficient (re-)training especially for low qualified workers.*[24]   [Emphases mine]

The bulk of the jobs at risk, even on this more optimistic interpretation, are those that have repetitive tasks and these are likely to be in manufacturing, clerical, and administrative work:

> We refer to computerisation as job automation by means of computer-controlled equipment. This view finds support in a recent survey by the McKinsey Global Institute,[25] showing *that 44 percent of firms which reduced their headcount since the financial crisis of 2008*

had done so by means of automation. Because the core job tasks of manufacturing occupations follow well-defined repetitive procedures, they can easily be codified in computer software and thus performed by computers.[26] In addition to the computerisation of routine manufacturing tasks, Autor and Dorn document a structural shift in the labour market, with workers reallocating their labour supply from middle-income manufacturing to low-income service occupations.[27] Arguably, this is because the *manual tasks of service occupations are less susceptible to computerisation, as they require a higher degree of flexibility and physical adaptability.*[28] At the same time, with falling prices of computing, problem-solving skills are becoming relatively productive, explaining the substantial employment growth in occupations involving cognitive tasks where skilled labour has a comparative advantage, as well as the persistent increase in returns to education.[29] The title "Lousy and Lovely Jobs"[30] thus *captures the essence of the current trend towards labour market polarization, with growing employment in high-income cognitive jobs and low-income manual occupations, accompanied by a hollowing-out of middle-income routine jobs.*[31]

[Emphases mine]

This new feature of automation – *the hollowing out of middle-income jobs combined with growth in low-income manual jobs* – *is a source for concern.* What matters therefore is how automation and AI are rolled out in the future.

Three Waves of Automation

A PricewaterhouseCoopers (PwC) study foresees three overlapping waves of automation and AI which affect industries and countries differently:

We also identify how this process might unfold over the period to the 2030s in three overlapping waves:

1. *Algorithm wave:* focused on automation of simple computational tasks and analysis of structured data in areas like finance, information and communications – *this is already well underway.*

2. *Augmentation wave:* focused on automation of repeatable tasks such as filling in forms, communicating and exchanging information through dynamic technological support, and statistical analysis of unstructured data in semi-controlled environments such as aerial drones and robots in warehouses – *this is also underway, but is likely to come to full maturity in the 2020s.*

3. *Autonomy wave:* focused on automation of physical labour and manual dexterity, and problem solving in dynamic real-world situations that require responsive actions, such as in manufacturing and transport (e.g. driverless vehicles) – *these technologies are under development already, but may only come to full maturity on an economy-wide scale in the 2030s.*[32]

[Emphases mine]

The effects of these three waves are shown in Table 5.1.

Table 5.1: Effects of three waves of automation.[33]

Wave phases	Description	Industries impacted	Tasks affected
First Wave: Algorithm	Automation of simple computational tasks and analysis of structured data	Data driven sectors: – Financial and insurance – Information and communication – Professional, scientific, and technical services – Legal searches	The more fundamental computational job tasks that will be most impacted first: – Manually conducting mathematical calculations – Using basic software packages – Internet searches

Second Wave: Augmentation	Dynamic interaction with technology for clerical roles and decisions, including robotic roles, e.g., moving objects in controlled environments (warehouses, factories)	Wherever there is a back office with routine tasks:
		– Financial institutions
		– Sectors with a high percentage of repetitive clerical work:
		  – Government
		  – Manufacturing
		  – Transport
		  – Storage
			Routine tasks:
			– Filling in forms and filing
			– Exchanging information
			– Conveyancing
			
			Reduced need for programming languages with automated repetitive program tasks with machine learning and redesigned algorithms

Third Wave: Autonomy	Automation of physical labor and manual dexterity and problem solving in dynamic real world situations that require responsive actions	The advent of fully autonomous vehicles and robots will affect: – Construction – Water, sewage, and waste management – Transportation – Storage	AI and robotics will automate: – Routine tasks further – Tasks involving physical labor or manual dexterity – Simulation of adaptive behaviour by autonomous agents

From this table it is clear certain sectors are more likely to be affected by automation than others and its impact will differ over time depending on which wave is involved and how they overlap. This is also true of countries. The PwC study divides countries into four broad groups:[34]

1. **Industrial:** These countries are typically characterized by jobs that are easier to automate and have a greater percentage of their GDP in sectors (such as automotive) that feature such jobs – for example, Germany, Slovakia, or Italy.
2. **Services-dominated:** These are countries that have both sectors that are easy to automate and a greater concentration on services sectors that are relatively difficult to automate – for example, the US, UK, France, and the Netherlands.
3. **Asian:** These countries overall have relatively few sectors that are easy to automate, but those that are automatable have relatively high concentrations of employment in sectors with high potential for automation – for example, Japan, South Korea, and Singapore in manufacturing; and India and the Philippines for outsourced call centers.
4. **Nordic:** These countries have fewer industries that are automatable in sectors with lower potential for automation – for example, Finland, Norway, and Sweden.

Countries with well-educated populations such as the Nordics, East Asia, and New Zealand are estimated by the PwC study to face 20–25% job losses, while East European countries with their relatively high share of easily automatable manufacturing jobs could face greater than 40% losses. Services-dominated economies, like the US and the UK, with a high proportion of lower skilled workers in services could face a level of job losses of between 30 and 38%.[35]

Varying Impact of Automation

Recognizing these points enables boards to consider how automation will affect their industries and their companies within these industries. Table 5.2 shows how key sectors are likely to be affected:

The impact of automation will differ among demographic groups, shown in Table 5.3.

Table 5.2: Automation impact by sector.[36]

Sector	Comments
Transportation and storage	Particularly high potential for job losses through automation long-term (approx. 52%[37]) when driverless vehicles become common, but this will likely happen in the third *autonomy* wave around 2030. The second *augmentation* wave will make a big difference. There is relatively little impact from the first *algorithmic* wave. *Boards still have some time to prepare for these impacts.*
Manufacturing	High potential for job losses through automation long-term (approx. 45%.[38]) The first *algorithmic* wave will have relatively little impact. Manufacturing will be affected almost equally by the *augmentation* and *autonomy* waves. *Boards still have some time to prepare for these impacts.*
Construction	High potential for job losses through automation long-term (approx. 38%). The first *algorithmic* wave will have relatively little impact. Construction will be affected more by the *autonomy* wave than the *augmentation* wave. *Boards still have some time to prepare for these impacts.*
Administration and support services	Considerable potential for job losses through automation long-term (approx. 35%). The first *algorithmic* wave will have relatively little impact. Administration and support services will be affected equally by the *autonomy* and *augmentation* waves. *Boards may not have much time to prepare for these impacts.*
Wholesale and retail trade	Considerable potential for job losses through automation long-term (approx. 34%[39]) The first *algorithmic* wave will have relatively little impact. Wholesale and retail will be affected most severely by the second *augmentation* wave and somewhat less by the third *autonomy* wave. *Boards still have some time to prepare for these impacts.*
Public administration	Considerable potential for job losses through automation long-term (approx. 32%). The first *algorithmic* wave will have relatively little impact but still more than most other sectors. Public administration and defense will be affected most severely by the second *augmentation* wave and a bit less by the third *autonomy* wave. *Boards need to start preparing for these impacts.*

Table 5.2 (continued)

Sector	Comments
Finance and insurance	Considerable potential for job losses through automation long-term (approx. 30%). The first *algorithmic* wave will have considerable impact. Finance and insurance will be affected most severely by the second *augmentation* wave with very little impact from the third *autonomy* wave. *Boards need to prepare for these impacts now.*
Information and communication	Potential for job losses through automation long-term (approx. 28%). The first *algorithmic* wave will have considerable impact. Information and communication will be affected most severely by the second *augmentation* wave with little impact from the third *autonomy* wave. *Boards need to prepare for these impacts now.*
Professional, scientific, and technical	Potential for job losses through automation long-term (approx. 25%). The first *algorithmic* wave will have considerable impact. Professional, scientific, and technical sectors will be affected most severely by the second *augmentation* wave with little impact from the third *autonomy* wave. *Boards need to prepare for these impacts now.*
Accommodation and food service	Potential for job losses through automation long-term (approx. 22%). The first *algorithmic* wave will have very little impact. Accommodation and food service will be affected equally by the second *augmentation* and third *autonomy* waves. *Boards still have time to prepare for these impacts.*
Human health and social work	Potential for job losses through automation long-term (approx. 21%.[40]) The first *algorithmic* wave will have little impact. Human health and social sectors will be affected most severely by the second *augmentation* wave with some impact from the third *autonomy* wave. *Boards still have time to prepare for these impacts.*
Education	Few job losses through automation long-term (approx. 8%.[41]) The first *algorithmic* wave will have relatively little impact. Education will be affected most severely by the *augmentation* wave with little impact from the third *autonomy* wave. *Boards still have time to prepare for these impacts.*

Table 5.3: Automation impact by demographic.[42]

Demographic	Comments
Gender	Men face a greater likelihood of job losses than women. In the case of men, the *algorithm* wave is not important; the losses are driven by the *augmentation* and *autonomy* waves which means the full impact will take longer to materialize than in the case of women where, although the *algorithm* wave is more important than for men, the really significant impact comes with the *augmentation* wave.
Age	Both the young (people younger than 25) and the old (people older than 55) are more vulnerable to job losses than the core age group (people aged between 25 and 54). In all cases the biggest impact comes from the *augmentation* wave, followed by the *autonomy* wave with the *algorithmic* wave having the least impact.
Education	Education is the most significant factor in determining the exposure of people to automation: – People with low levels of education are most at risk and this occurs in the medium- and long-term because of the impact of the *augmentation* and *autonomy* waves, with the latter being most significant. – People with medium levels of education are still at considerable risk, but in their case, it is the *augmentation* wave that presents the biggest threat, followed by the *autonomy* wave. – The highly educated face the least risk by far with both the *algorithmic* and *autonomy* waves being minor in their impact. The threat comes with the *augmentation* wave. Highly educated workers are presumed to be more adaptable in the face of technological changes. They are more likely to be in senior managerial roles that will still be needed to apply human judgment, as well as to design and supervise AI-based systems.

Low and medium educated male workers are least impacted in the Algorithm wave, as computational tasks typically form a smaller proportion of their daily activity. However, by the end of Augmentation wave, the potential jobs at high risk of automation are comparable between male and female workers with either a low or medium education. *In the final Autonomy wave, low educated males are expected to be at a much greater risk as manual and routine tasks (including driving) become more heavily automated across the economy.*[43]   [Emphasis mine]

At a more detailed level, the PwC study suggests the following levels of potential job loss by occupation, shown in Table 5.4.

Table 5.4: Potential job loss percentage by task by 2030.[44]

Task	Comments
Manual	There is high potential for job losses (approx. 39%) by 2030. The first *algorithmic* wave has little impact. The second *augmentation* wave is serious, but the greatest impact comes with the *autonomy* wave, because of its effect on transportation and storage sectors. *Boards still have time to prepare for the effects of automation.*
Routine	There is high potential for job losses (approx. 37%) by 2030. The first *algorithmic* wave has some impact. The second *augmentation* wave is where the greatest impact comes with the *autonomy* wave still having a serious effect, because of its effect on transportation and storage sectors. *Boards still have time to prepare for the effects of automation.*
Computation	There is considerable potential for job losses (approx. 28%) by 2030. The first *algorithmic* wave has considerable impact, but the main effects are the result of the second *augmentation* wave, with the third *autonomy* wave also having an effect. *Boards need to prepare for the effects of automation now.*
Management	There is considerable potential for job losses (approx. 25%) by 2030. The first *algorithmic* wave has some impact, but the main effects are the result of the second *augmentation* wave, with the third *autonomy* wave also having a considerable effect. *Boards need to start preparing for the effects of automation.*
Social skills	There is some potential for job losses (approx. 17%) by 2030. The first *algorithmic* wave has little impact. The majority of the effect comes with the second *augmentation* wave, with the third *autonomy* wave having considerable impact as well. *Boards still have time to prepare for the effects of automation.*
Literacy skills	There is some potential for job losses (approx. 15%) by 2030. The first *algorithmic* wave has some impact. The majority of the effect comes with the second *augmentation* wave, with the third *autonomy* wave having considerable impact as well. *Boards still have time to prepare for the effects of automation.*

What is clear is that algorithms[vii] will have a huge impact on tasks that have the following four features or combinations of them, shown in Table 5.5.

---

vii Algorithms are step-by-step procedures for solving a problem or accomplishing some end, especially by a computer. "They take a sequence of mathematical operations – using equations, arithmetic, algebra, calculus, logic, and probability – translate them into computer code. They are fed with data from the real world, given an objective, and set to work crunching through the

Table 5.5: Four tasks done better by algorithms.[45]

Prioritization	Classification	Association	Filtering
Making an ordered list: For example, Google Search which ranks one result over another or Netflix which suggests what films subscribers might like to watch next.	**Picking a category:** For example, the algorithms that direct advertisements or political messages on Facebook or YouTube based on user characteristics. There are algorithms that remove inappropriate content, label holiday photos, or scan handwriting by classifying each mark on the page as a letter in the alphabet.	**Finding links:** For example, dating apps which look for connections between members and suggesting matches based on the findings.	**Isolating what's important:** For example, speech recognition algorithms used by Siri, Alexa, and Cortana, which filter out the voice from background noises before deciphering what is being said. Facebook and Twitter filter stories based on people's known interests.

People whose jobs are based primarily on these four characteristics are at risk of being replaced by algorithms because algorithms tend to achieve better results, can be run 24/7, do not get sick and do not need to be managed, hence the challenge to the sustainability of employment and employability. AI will clearly create further pressure for people who already are disaffected with the way the global economy has worked for them. However, that does not mean that people will necessarily become slaves to the machines.

Instead, it is possible that an effective alliance[46] can be created between people and machines where each continues to do what they are best suited to do. Improving algorithms requires choosing between sensitivity and specificity. For example, cancer predicting algorithms are excellent at spotting abnormalities in breast tissue, however tiny and unimportant. They do this much better than even the best pathologists. At the same time, pathologists need the specificity to decide whether perfectly normal tissue with its minor abnormalities is suspicious or not. This is necessary if false negatives (i.e., when there are in fact cancerous cells present, but have not been detected) are to be eliminated. If the algorithm is designed to eliminate all false positives (when the

calculations to achieve their aim." Fry, H. (2018), *Hello World: How to be Human in the Age of the Machine* (London: Doubleday), p. 8.

tissue is perfectly healthy despite the presence of anomalies), it can do so, but only by flagging every breast tissue it recorded as suspicious. The result would mean a great number of women undergoing unnecessary, painful, and emotionally scarring treatment. If, on the other hand, the algorithm is written to eliminate false positives totally, all women would be cleared as healthy, with disastrous results for those who needed treatment.

Given that pathologists do have problems with sensitivity – they do not spot every abnormality however unimportant, but have no problems with specificity; it makes sense to use machines and algorithms to target sensitivity and then have the pathologists decide whether the highly suspicious results provided by the machines justify interventions or not:

> The algorithm doesn't dictate which patients have tumours. It narrows down the vast array of cells to a handful of suspicious areas for the pathologist to check. *The algorithm never gets tired and the pathologist rarely misdiagnoses.* The algorithm and the human work together in partnership, exploiting each other's strengths and embracing each other's flaws.[47] [Emphasis mine]

The latest findings on the ability of algorithms to diagnose breast cancer suggest further improvements so that AI can outperform one radiologist working alone by reducing both false positives by 1.2% and false negatives by 2.7%. However, when compared with the system used by the UK's NHS where two radiologists work together, the new algorithm developed by Google performs only just as well. The result will be that fewer radiologists who take a long time to learn their skills and are expensive to train will be needed; but that a radiologist will still always be in charge.[48]

The additional problem with over-reliance on automated systems is a kind of moral hazard. In the case of driverless cars, the passengers cease to pay attention to the road and what is going on around the car because they no longer have to:

> Imagine sitting in a self-driving car, hearing an alarm and looking up from your book to see a truck ahead shedding its load into your path. In an instant, you'll have to process all the information around you: the motorbike in the left lane, the van braking ahead, the car in the blind spot on your right.[viii] You'd be most unfamiliar with the road at precisely the moment you need to know it best; *add in the lack of practice, and you'll be as poorly equipped as you could be to deal with the situation demanding the highest level of skill.*[49] [Emphasis mine]

---

viii The author is English, so she uses right-hand driving conditions.

The better the technology gets, the worse the problem of over-reliance becomes:

> The worst case is a car that will need driver intervention once every 200,000 miles. . . . An ordinary person who has a [new] car every 100,000 miles would never see it [the automation hand over control]. But every once in a while, maybe once for every two cars that I own, there would be that one time where it suddenly goes "beep beep beep, now it's your turn!" And *the person typically not having seen this for years and years, would not be prepared when that happened.*[50]   [Emphasis mine]

This is not hypothetical. Such an event occurred on May 9, 2009, when an Air France Airbus A330 crashed in the Atlantic returning to Paris from Rio. The co-pilot had accumulated thousands of hours in an Airbus cockpit simulator but his actual experience of flying an A330 manually was minimal. His role in flight had been to monitor the automatic system, so when it disengaged during the flight creating an emergency, he did not know how to fly the plane:[51]

> If a pilot is only expected to take over in exceptional circumstances, they'll no longer maintain the skills they need to operate the system themselves. *So they'll have very little experience to draw on to meet the challenge of an unanticipated emergency.*[52]
>   [Emphasis mine]

As these examples show, there are limits to the extent to which we should aim for machine autonomy and how it is to be achieved, if humans are kept in the loop. Algorithms are good at creating content, but people are still needed to provide the context.

> Until we get to full autonomy, why not flip the equation on its head and aim for a self-driving system that supports the driver rather than the other way around? A safety net, like ABS or traction control, that can patiently monitor the road and stay alert for a danger the driver has missed. *Not so much a chauffeur as a guardian . . . which runs in the background while a human drives, and acts as a safety net, reducing the risk of an accident if anything crops up that the driver hasn't seen.*[53]   [Emphasis mine]

Winners and Losers

Every major disruption creates winners and losers.

The PwC study suggests the gains will outweigh the losses because AI and robotics will create new demand directly or indirectly through the new wealth created by their introduction. The extra wealth will likely be spent on goods and services, increasing the demand for labor. The most likely sectors to benefit from this increased wealth are non-tradable services such as health and education to meet the needs of aging societies in developed economies. The health sector is likely to grow everywhere as life expectancy rises and will absorb some of the workers who have been displaced. As for education, this is most likely to be targeted at older people who need either to be retrained or who are interested in learning new skills and interests for their retirement. At the personal level, jobs that require empathy and social skills will be in demand, so caregivers and nurses should do well, as will coaches and mentors who will be able to guide the displaced through their transitions into new roles.[54]

The occupations facing the biggest disruption, in declining order of serious losses, are machine operators and assemblers, clerical workers, unskilled occupations, craft workers, technicians and associated professionals, service and salespeople, skilled agricultural and fishery workers, professionals, and senior officials and managers.[55]

What is becoming clearer is that occupations that are routine or clerical; that follow a prescribed set of actions; that do not interface with people in environments requiring empathy and nuanced interpretation of what is said; that do not require creativity and out of the box thinking; that do not have to deal with the unusual and unpredictable as a matter of course – these occupations will be at risk from the combination of automation and AI.

The McKinsey Global Institute study in 2017 suggested that given around 50% of current work was automatable by adapting current technologies and that 60% of existing occupations were 30% automatable; one-third of the estimated 2030 global workforce (890 million "full time equivalents"[ix]) could be replaced by the combined effects of automation and AI. However, of the estimated workforce of 2.66 billion in 2030, 8–9% would be in new occupations.[56]

There are two forces to create additional demand for labor that currently does not exist. The first is the forecast rise of a mass affluent consumer class in emerging markets. It could contribute up to 300–365 million new jobs to satisfy the demand for consumer durables, leisure and tourism, financial and telecom services, housing, healthcare, and education. The second is the rising percentage of population above age 65, particularly in developed economies, which could add up to at least 300 million people. This is expected to create additional demand for more spending on healthcare and other personal services, reflected in more opportunities for doctors, nurses, caregivers, and nursing assistants, even as it reduces demand for pediatricians, teachers,[57] and, potentially, radiologists.[x] This is expected to translate into an additional 50–85 million jobs,

---

ix "Full time equivalent" (FTE) is calculated as being the number of hours worked per year by a single individual full time. Thus, two people working half-time for a year would be counted as one FTE.

x Even at this early stage of automation, there is mounting evidence AI does an equal or slightly better job at diagnosing medical conditions from medical images than humans. Davis, N. (2019),

after allowing for fewer jobs needed to look after fewer children as a percentage of the population.

Historically, there is good evidence that *in the end* the winners outnumber the losers, even though there are large movements during the process from the disrupted or declining sectors into new sectors. For example, in the US over the period 1850–2015 four sectors (mining, domestic work, manufacturing, and agriculture) fell from representing around 75% of employment to around 17% in 2015. They were replaced by professional services, utilities, business and service repair, telecoms, health care, entertainment, education, government, and financial services – all of which hardly featured or did not feature at all in 1850.[58] Further support for the transferability of employment is provided by the fact 18% of jobs in the US in 2017 did not exist in 1980.[59]

The example of PCs helps show how this happens. According to the McKinsey Global Institute 2017 report, the introduction of PCs in the US destroyed 3,508,000 jobs, but created 19,263,000 jobs, yielding a net gain of 15,755,000 (roughly 10% of the civilian labor force), divided into 12,176,000 who used PCs; 2,904,000 who were enabled by PCs; 524,000 who benefited indirectly and 151,000 directly.[60]

Despite the optimism expressed in the 2017 McKinsey Global Institute report, there is also the following warning:

> The changes in net occupational growth or decline imply that a very large number of people may need to shift occupational categories and learn new skills in the years ahead. *The shift could be on a scale not seen since the transition of the labor force out of agriculture in the early 1900s in the United States and Europe, and more recently in China.* But unlike those earlier transitions, in which young people left farms and moved to cities for industrial jobs, *the challenge, especially in advanced economies, will be to retrain midcareer workers. There are few precedents in which societies have successfully retrained such large numbers of people.* Frictions in the labor markets – including cultural norms regarding gender stereotypes in work and geographic mismatches between workers and jobs – could also impede the transition.[61]   [Emphases mine]

Unsuitable Education

If developed economies are to navigate the transition successfully, education and re-education have a critical role to play:

"AI equal with human experts in medical diagnosis, study finds," *The Guardian*, September 24, 2019, https://www.theguardian.com/technology/2019/sep/24/ai-equal-with-human-experts-in-medical-diagnosis-study-finds?utm_term=RW, accessed on September 25, 2019.

For advanced economies, the share of the workforce that may need to learn new skills and find work in new occupations is much higher: up to one-third of the 2030 workforce in the United States and Germany, and nearly half in Japan. . .

. . .*But a larger challenge will be ensuring that workers have the skills and support needed to transition to new jobs.* Countries that fail to manage this transition could see rising unemployment and depressed wages.[62]   [Emphasis mine]

Governments and businesses will need to reimagine what education and training are supposed to achieve in preparing the workforce for its future roles, which will differ from the existing ones:

Workers of the future will spend more time on activities that machines are less capable of, such as managing people, applying expertise, and communicating with others. They will spend less time on predictable physical activities, and on collecting and processing data, where machines already exceed human performance. *The skills and capabilities required will also shift, requiring more social and emotional skills, and more advanced cognitive capabilities, such as logical reasoning and creativity.*[63]   [Emphasis mine]

It is not just businesses that will have to rethink what skills they need in their workforces over their working lifetimes and invest in appropriate continuous learning and development programs to keep their existing staff employable, it is universities as well:

. . .we are at a point where we need to find a new pedagogical philosophy that can help students achieve the set of skills required in the twenty-first century for a balanced civic, economic and social life. We have a new world that is based on uncertainty and challenges that change at a rapid pace, and *all this requires creativity, flexibility, the capacity to use and adapt to uncertain contexts. Graduates have to act in a world of value conflicts, information limitations, vast registers of risks, and radical uncertainty.* All this, along with the ongoing possibility of staying within personal and group 'bubbles' and of being exposed to vast operations of manipulation. . .[64]   [Emphasis mine]

Summary

Automation and AI will disrupt labor markets everywhere. Pessimists worry their impact will be to destroy more jobs than they create. Optimists accept there will be a need for considerable migration out of existing jobs and occupations as a result, but that, in the end, more jobs will be created than lost in the economy as a whole. They argue that the best outcome is an alliance between humans and machines rather than machines replacing humans. Should major disemployment occur, they point to historical examples where major migrations of work have been implemented successfully and have led to increased wealth, creating demand for more workers in new fields.

Estimates suggest 30% of jobs could be automated by 2030 affecting up to 375 million workers worldwide. This presents boards with a crucial dilemma. On the one hand they need to automate as fast as possible to remain competitive. On the other hand, they need to be careful they do not contribute to a "political tragedy of the commons" by causing mass unemployment and the political problems that will create. The bulk of the jobs lost through automation will be either low-skill jobs; or routine, repetitive jobs that can be easily codified. This will lead to a new phenomenon – the hollowing out of middle-income jobs combined with growth in low-income manual jobs that are difficult to codify.

Automation and AI are expected to arrive in three waves: first the algorithm wave, second the augmentation wave, and third the autonomy wave. The exact impact and timing of these waves on countries will depend on which of four groupings the countries belong to: industrial; services-dominated; Asian; and Nordics. The three waves will also affect people differently depending on which sector they work in; their demographics; and the tasks they undertake. The tasks most under threat are those that require prioritization, classification, association, and filtering.

There will be winners and losers.

The health sector is likely to grow everywhere as life expectancy rises and will absorb some of the workers who have been displaced. As for education, this is most likely to be targeted at older people who need either to be retrained or who are interested in learning new skills and interests for their retirement. At the personal level, jobs that require empathy and social skills will be in demand, so caregivers and nurses should do well, as will teachers, coaches, and mentors who will be able to guide the displaced through their transitions into new roles. The occupations facing the biggest disruption, in declining order of job losses, are machine operators and assemblers, clerical workers, unskilled occupations, craft workers, technicians and associated professionals, service and salespeople, skilled agricultural and fishery workers, professionals, and senior officials and managers.

What is becoming clearer is that occupations which are routine or clerical; that follow a prescribed set of actions; that do not interface with people in environments requiring empathy and nuanced interpretation of what is said; that do not require creativity and out of the box thinking; that do not have to deal with the unusual and unpredictable as a matter of course – these occupations will be at risk from the combination of automation and AI.

People in the occupations adversely affected by automation will need to be retrained to cope with the new demands placed upon them. People entering the job market for the first time will need to be educated differently if they are to succeed. Failure by governments and boards to rethink the fundamentals of education and how it should be taught and to reverse the decline in investment in training will only increase the level of disruption and discontent caused by automation and AI.

My real concern is that while machines will not take all the jobs in the coming decade, the political process will not be up to the challenge because AI will:

> *Encroach on tasks, and we reorganise our jobs in response, becoming more productive as a result.* But there is good reason to believe that such reorganisations will be wrenching in the decade to come, and also that *some people will be permanently unable to contribute economically in the way they would have hoped and expected. Above all, it is likely that our political institutions will be unable to adapt to the challenge.*[65]　　　[Emphases mine]

If the result of automation and AI in developed economies is that a significant percentage of the population become unemployable because governments and businesses have not helped them make the transition from their pre-automation roles to their post-automation ones, the resulting inequality and poverty may fatally undermine the social contract and lead to a "political tragedy of the commons." There is already enough disenchantment with the existing economic system. A large pool of disemployed and unemployable would be fertile recruiting ground for populists seeking to overthrow the system, claiming, like William Cobbett in 1819, that:

> Society ought not to exist, if not for the benefit of the whole. It is and must be against the law of nature, if it exists for the benefit of the few and for the misery of the many.[66]

References

1 Bloy, M. (2005), "The Luddites 1811–1816," *The Victorian Web,* December 30, 2005, http://www.victorianweb.org/history/riots/luddites.html, accessed on September 15, 2019.
2 UK Inflation Calculator https://www.officialdata.org/uk/inflation/1816?amount=1, accessed on April 2, 2020.
3 Cobbett, W. (1819), *Political Register,* September 11, 1819, quoted in Bloy, M. (2005), op. cit.
4 *Quarterly Review,* Volume 16, 1816, pp. 276–77, quoted in Bloy, M. (2005), op. cit.
5 Hawksworth, J. et al. (2018), "Will robots really steal our jobs? An international analysis of the potential long-term impact of automation," p. 7, https://www.pwc.com/gx/en/news-room/docs/will-robots-really-steal-our-jobs-an-international-analysis-of-the-potential-long-term-impact-of-automation.pdf, accessed on September 12, 2019.
6 Ford, M. (2015), *The Rise of the Robots* (OneWorld Publications), cited in Hawksworth, J. et al. (2018), op. cit., p. 7.
7 Hawksworth, J. et al. (2018), op. cit., p. 7.
8 Keynes, J.M. (1932), "Economic possibilities for our grandchildren" (1930) in "Essays in persuasion" (New York: Harcourt Brace), pp. 358–73.

9 The Horse Trust (1907), "1900s London Needs 300,000 horses to keep it moving," *Horse Trust News,* Case Notes, http://www.horsetrust.org.uk/history/yesterday/yesterday-londonsworkinghorses/, accessed on September 16, 2019.

10 Economic Research Service (2019), "Agriculture and its related industries provide 11 percent of U.S. employment," *United States Department of Agriculture,* August 20, 2019, https://www.ers.usda.gov/data-products/ag-and-food-statistics-charting-the-essentials/ag-and-food-sectors-and-the-economy/, accessed on September 17, 2019.

11 Jones, A. (2013), "Less than 1% of British workers now employed in agriculture for the first time in history," *The Independent,* June 5, 2013, https://www.independent.co.uk/news/uk/home-news/less-than-1-of-british-workers-now-employed-in-agriculture-for-first-time-in-history-8645324.html, accessed on September 17, 2019.

12 The National Archives, "Living in 1901," *Making a Living,* http://www.nationalarchives.gov.uk/pathways/census/living/making/women.htm, accessed on September 17, 2019.

13 Marchant, P. (2013), "Domestic workers across the world: Global and regional statistics and the extent of legal protection," *International Labour Office,* p. 20, https://www.ilo.org/wcmsp5/groups/public/—dgreports/—dcomm/—publ/documents/publication/wcms_173363.pdf, accessed on September 17, 2019.

14 Guilford, G. (2018), "The epic mistake about manufacturing that's cost Americans millions of job," *Quartz,* May 3, 2018, https://qz.com/1269172/the-epic-mistake-about-manufacturing-thats-cost-americans-millions-of-jobs/ accessed on March 6, 2020.

15 Ibid.

16 Moya, S. (2019), "U.S. Jobless Rate Unchanged at 49-Year Low," *Trading Economics,* July 6, 2019, https://tradingeconomics.com/articles/06072019123436.htm, accessed on September 17, 2019.

17 Smith, A. and Anderson, J. (2014), "AI, Robotics, and the Future of Jobs," Pew Research Center, August 6, 2014, quoted in West, D. M. (2018), "Will Robots and AI take your job? The economic and political consequences of automation," *Brookings Institution,* April 18, 2018, https://www.brookings.edu/blog/techtank/2018/04/18/will-robots-and-ai-take-your-job-the-economic-and-political-consequences-of-automation/, accessed on September 17, 2019.

18 Manyika, J. et al. (2017), "Jobs Lost, Jobs Gained: Workforce Transitions in a Time of Automation," *McKinsey Global Institute,* December 2017, p. 4, https://www.mckinsey.com/~/media/mckinsey/featured%20insights/Future%20of%20Organizations/What%20the%20future%20of%20work%20will%20mean%20for%20jobs%20skills%20and%20wages/MGI-Jobs-Lost-Jobs-Gained-Report-December-6-2017.ashx, accessed on September 18, 2019.

19 Manyika, J. et al. (2017), op. cit., p. 2.

20 Ibid., p. 2.

21 Farrell, S. (2019), "U.K. economy has 'too few robots,' warn MPs," *The Guardian,* September 18, 2019, https://www.theguardian.com/business/2019/sep/18/uk-economy-has-too-few-robots-warn-mps, accessed on September 19, 2019.

22 Ibid.

23 Ibid.

24 Arntz, M., Gregory, T., and Zierahn, U. (2016), "The Risk of Automation for Jobs in OECD Countries," *OECD Social, Employment and Migration Working Papers,* No 189 (Paris: OECD Publishing), Arntz, M., T. Gregory and U. Zierahn (2016), "The Risk of Automation for Jobs in OECD Countries: A Comparative Analysis," OECD Social, Employment and Migration Working Papers, No. 189, OECD Publishing, Paris. http://dx.doi.org/10.1787/5jlz9h56dvq7-en, accessed on March 6, 2020.

25 McKinsey Global Institute (2011), "An economy that works: Job creation and America's future," *McKinsey Global Institute*, cited in Frey, C.B. and Osborne, M.A. (2013) op. cit.

26 Acemoglu, D. and Autor, D. (2011), "Skills, tasks and technologies: Implications for employment and earnings," *Handbook of labor economics*, vol. 4, pp. 1043–1171, cited in Frey, C.B. and Osborne, M.A. (2013) op. cit.

27 Autor, D. and Dorn, D. (2013), "The growth of low skill service jobs and the polarization of the U.S. labor market," *American Economic Review*, 103 (5), pp. 1553–1597, cited in Frey, C.B. and Osborne, M.A. (2013) op. cit.

28 Autor, D. et al. (2003), "The skill content of recent technological change: An empirical exploration," *The Quarterly Journal of Economics*, vol. 118, no. 4, pp. 1279–1333; Goos, M. and Manning, A. (2007), "Lousy and Lovely Jobs: The rising polarization of work in Britain," *The Review of Economics and Statistics*, vol. 89, no. 1, pp. 118–133; Autor and Dorn (2013), op. cit., cited in Frey, C.B. and Osborne, M.A. (2013) op. cit.

29 Katz, L F. and Murphy, K.M. (1992), "Changes in relative wages, 1963–1987: supply and demand factors," *The Quarterly Journal of Economics*, vol. 107, no. 1, pp. 35–78, 1992; Acemoglu, D. (2002), "Technical change, inequality, and the labor market," *Journal of Economic Literature*, vol. 40, no. 1, pp. 7–72; Autor, D. and Dorn, D. (2013), op. cit., cited in Frey, C.B. and Osborne, M.A. (2013), op. cit.

30 Goos, M. and Manning, A. (2007), op. cit., cited in Frey, C.B. and Osborne, M.A. (2013) op. cit.

31 Frey, C.B. and Osborne, M.A. (2013), op. cit., pp. 2–3.

32 Hawksworth, J. et al. (2018), op. cit., p. 8.

33 Based on Hawksworth, J. et al. (2018), op. cit., pp. 5–6.

34 Ibid., p. 10.

35 Ibid., p. 16.

36 Based on ibid., p. 3.

37 Ibid., p. 18.

38 Ibid.

39 Ibid.

40 Ibid.

41 Ibid.

42 Based on ibid., p. 4.

43 Ibid., p. 31.

44 Ibid., p. 15.

45 Fry, H. (2018), *Hello World: How to be Human in the Age of the Machine* (London: Doubleday), pp. 8–10.

46 Ibid., pp. 87–88.

47 Ibid., p. 202.

48 Walsh, F. (2020), "AI 'outperforms' doctors diagnosing breast cancer," *BBC News*, January 2, 2020, https://www.bbc.com/news/health-50857759, accessed on January 3, 2019.

49 Ibid., p. 136.

50 Ackerman, E. (2017), "Toyota's Gill Pratt on self-driving cars and the reality of full autonomy," *IEEE Spectrum*, January 23, 2017, https://spectrum.ieee.org/cars-that-think/transportation/sel-driving/toyota-gill-pratt-on-the-reality-of-full-autonomy, accessed on April 2, 2020, quoted in Fry, H. (2018), op. cit., p. 137.

51 Fry, H. (2018), op. cit., p. 132.

52 Ibid., p. 133.

53 Ibid., p. 139.

54 Hawksworth, J. et al. (2018), op. cit., p. 22.

55 Ibid., p. 23.

56 Manyika, J. et al. (2017), op. cit., p. 2.

57 Ibid., p. 7.

58 Ibid., p. 5.

59 Lin, J. (2011), "Technological adaptation, cities and new work," *Review of Economics and Statistics*," volume 93, number 2, May 2011, cited in Manyika, J. et al. (2017), op. cit., p. 4.

60 Manyika, J. et al. (2017), op. cit., p. 5.

61 Ibid., p. 9.

62 Ibid., pp. 11, 12.

63 Ibid., p. 15.

64 Popenici, S. and Kerr, S. (2017), "Exploring the impact of artificial intelligence on teaching and learning in higher education," *Research and Practice in Technology Enhanced Learning* (2017), 12:22, pp. 9–10, https://www.researchgate.net/publication/321258756_Exploring_the_impact_of_ar tificial_intelligence_on_teaching_and_learning_in_higher_education, accessed on September 22, 2019.

65 Harford, T. (2020), "Will the 2020s be the decade that the robots finally come for our jobs," *The Undercover Economist,* January 30, 2020, http://timharford.com/2020/01/will-the-2020s-finally-be-the-decade-that-the-robots-come-for-our-jobs/, accessed on January 30, 2020.

66 Cobbett, W. (1819), op. cit.

Chapter 6
Social Sustainability

This chapter is presented in two parts: the first explores what being a corporate responsible citizen implies; and the second covers the impact of different cultural assumptions. It closes with a summary of the discussions.

Much of the discussion about corporate responsibility has been about defining Corporate Social Responsibility (CSR)[1] and in many cases its primary focus was on what organizations do with their profits – i.e., what to do with the money once it has been made. This can either be genuine philanthropy or PR white-wash to deflect criticism of the way organizations conduct their business – a charge leveled recently against Coke and Volkswagen,[2] and for a long time against tobacco companies[3] and big oil:[4]

> From the perspective of oil companies, the *benefit of social initiatives may be to bring managers closer to political decision-makers, while appearing to be socially responsible.* From the perspective of broader society, a crucial pitfall of using social initiatives as a competitive weapon is that the *development priorities pursued by oil companies may be those of specific government officials and not necessarily those of the people for whose benefit the initiatives are ostensibly undertaken.*[5]   [Emphases mine]

The ISO 26000 definition of CSR has seven elements to consider: corporate governance; human rights; labor practices; environment; fair operating practices; consumer issues; community involvement and development.[6]

My definition builds on the ISO 26000 definition of CSR. It is not about what to do with the money once it has been made (which is philanthropy), but about how the money is made in the first place: what business an organization is in; how it conducts that business; with whom it chooses to do business; how it defends its positions; and only last, what it does with the money it makes as a result. Figure 6.1 illustrates this across an organization's value chain:

When it comes to answering the questions "What business are we in?" and "With whom do we do business?" and "How do we conduct our business?" before answering the last question "Are we providing our shareholders with a satisfactory return on their investment?" boards need to consider carefully the impact of their organizations on:

1. *Natural capital:* the environment.
2. *Social capital:* the communities within which they operate.
3. *Human capital:* the workplace they create.

https://doi.org/10.1515/9783110670486-006

	Raw materials processing	Shipping and Transport	Production	Distribution	Marketing and Sales	Management Policies

1. Natural capital/Environment:	• Depletion
	• Environmental damage
	  ▪ Forestry
	  ▪ Watersheds
	  ▪ Waste
	  ▪ Pollution
	  ▪ GHG emission
		• Pollution/spills
		• GHG emissions
		• Wasted energy
			• Pollution/spills
			• GHG emissions
			• Wasted water
			• Wasted energy
			• Wasted raw materials
			• Excessive packaging
				• Pollution/spills
				• GHG emissions
				• Wasted energy
				• Excessive packaging
					• 'Green' marketing linked to WWF, Marine Stewardship Council, Sustainable Forestry, Roundtable of Sustainable Palm Oil, etc.,	• 3 'R's
						  ▪ Reduce
						  ▪ Reuse
						  ▪ Recycle

2. Social capital/Community:	• Corruption • Social inequality • Abuse of indigenous people	• Corruption • Social inequality	• Corruption • Social inequality • Outsourcing • Offshoring	• Corruption • Social inequality • Destroying local capability by providing better products/processes	• Corruption • Truthful selling • Ethical marketing • Tax avoidance	• No corruption • Obey the laws • Pay taxes due • Avoid politics
3. Human capital/Workplace:	• Discrimination • Human rights • Union rights • Health & safety • Sexual harassment • Working hours • Child labour	• Discrimination • Human rights • Union rights • Health & safety • Sexual harassment • Working hours	• Discrimination • Human rights • Union rights • Health & safety • Sexual harassment • Working hours • Child labour	• Discrimination • Human rights • Union rights • Health & safety • Sexual harassment • Working hours	• Discrimination • Union rights • Health & safety • Sexual harassment • Working hours	• Diversity & Inclusion • Meritocracy • Pay for performance • Respect union rights • Good working conditions and hours • No sexual harassment

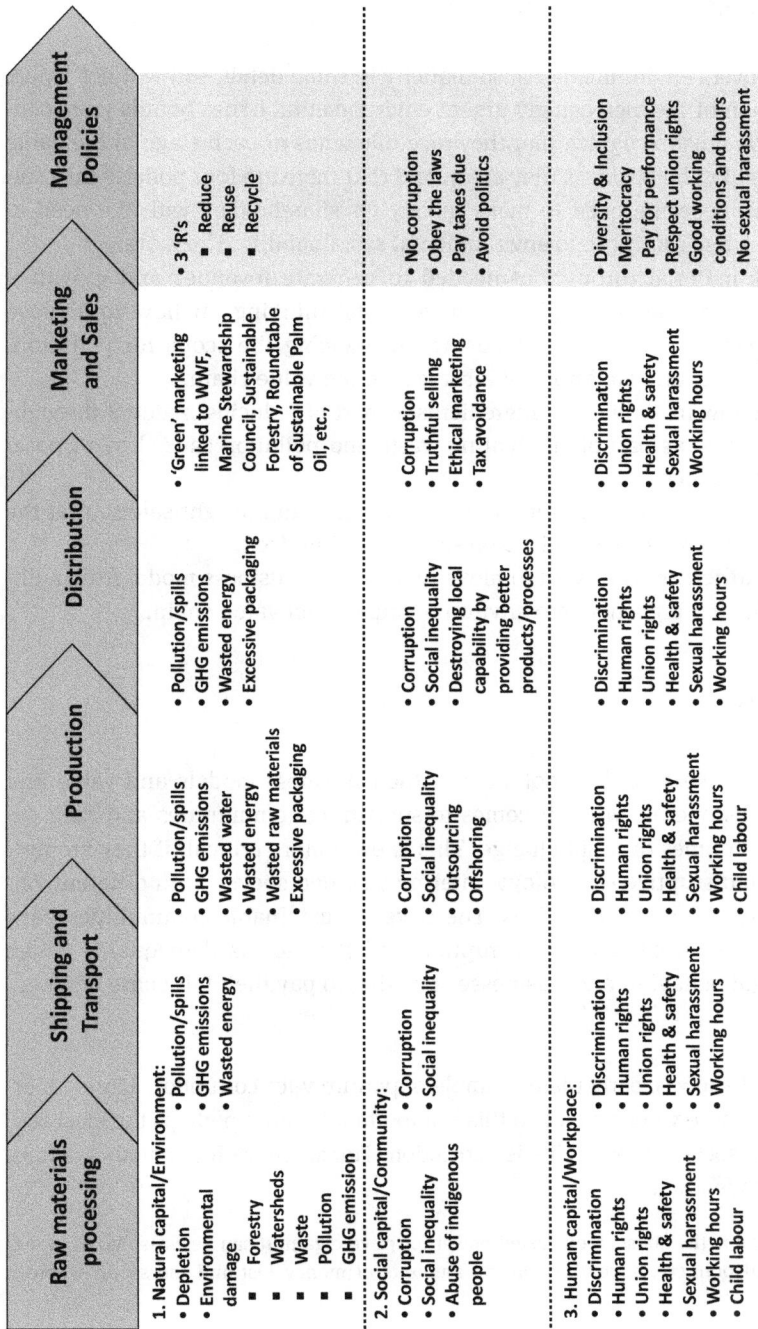

Figure 6.1: Being responsible across the value chain.[7]

Environment

Chapter 3 covers environmental sustainability in some detail, so I will not repeat the discussion of the increasingly urgent environmental issues boards must consider. Boards must recognize that they face dilemmas at each stage of the value chain caused by the business they are in and that there are four policies they can adopt to reconcile the need to make money for shareholders with the need to minimize the risk they pose to environmental sustainability. These are:

1. *Reduce* material throughput needed to generate revenues and growth – boards must therefore focus managements' thinking on how to achieve more with less, as well as focusing on reducing the scope for pollution, spills, waste, and emissions at all stages in the value chain.
2. *Recycle* raw materials and ingredients as part of reducing material throughput, but also as part of eliminating waste and pollution caused by disposal of used products.
3. *Reuse* through the adoption of leasing rather than outright sale so that the pressure to create wasteful obsolescence is minimized.
4. *Remanufacture by design* to move to a circular business model from a linear one, creating a net-zero environmental impact value chain.

Community

Boards must take a careful look at how their business models and value and supply chains operate when it comes to sustaining communities and their social capital in times of rapid change. This is even more critical, if they are new players with disruptive technology entering a settled society with different values and ways of living their lives. The risks to sustainable communities have four main causes: corruption; disruption and the increased inequality it can create; illegal behavior; and businesses refusing to pay their fair share of taxes.

1. Corruption

As Figure 6.1 shows clearly there is ample opportunity for corruption across an organization's entire value chain and this is important because perhaps the most serious threat to social sustainability is corruption. Transparency International defines corruption as follows:

> Corruption is the abuse of entrusted power for private gain. It can be classified as grand, petty and political, depending on the amounts of money lost and the sector where it occurs

Grand corruption consists of acts committed at a high level of government that distort policies or the central functioning of the state, enabling leaders to benefit at the expense of the public good. Petty corruption refers to everyday abuse of entrusted power by low- and mid-level public officials in their interactions with ordinary citizens, who often are trying to access basic goods or services in places like hospitals, schools, police departments and other agencies.

Political corruption is a manipulation of policies, institutions and rules of procedure in the allocation of resources and financing by political decision makers, who abuse their position to sustain their power, status and wealth.[8]

Transparency International goes on to explain the impact of corruption:

Corruption impacts societies in a multitude of ways. In the worst cases, it costs lives. Short of this, it costs people their freedom, health or money. The cost of corruption can be divided into four main categories: political, economic, social and environmental.

On the political front, corruption is a major obstacle to democracy and the rule of law. In a democratic system, offices and institutions lose their legitimacy when they're misused for private advantage. This is harmful in established democracies, but even more so in newly emerging ones. It is extremely challenging to develop accountable political leadership in a corrupt climate.

Economically, corruption depletes national wealth. Corrupt politicians invest scarce public resources in projects that will line their pockets rather than benefit communities, and prioritise high-profile projects such as dams, power plants, pipelines and refineries over less spectacular but more urgent infrastructure projects such as schools, hospitals and roads. Corruption also hinders the development of fair market structures and distorts competition, which in turn deters investment.

Corruption corrodes the social fabric of society. It undermines people's trust in the political system, in its institutions and its leadership. A distrustful or apathetic public can then become yet another hurdle to challenging corruption.

Environmental degradation is another consequence of corrupt systems. The lack of, or non-enforcement of, environmental regulations and legislation means that precious natural resources are carelessly exploited, and entire ecological systems are ravaged. From mining, to logging, to carbon offsets, companies across the globe continue to pay bribes in return for unrestricted destruction.[9]   [Emphases mine]

Corruption harms social sustainability in four ways. It:

1. ***Increases the cost of doing business:*** Estimates by the World Bank are that more than US$1 trillion are paid in bribes every year. The World Economic Forum estimates the cost of all forms of corruption equal 5% of world GDP at US$2.6 trillion.[10] The costs are not just financial. Corruption brings with it risks of prosecution, penalties, blacklisting, and reputation damage. It distorts market mechanisms, rewarding inefficiency, stifling growth, investments, and future growth. IMF research shows that there is almost 5% less investment in countries deemed to be corrupt and the World Economic Forum estimates corruption increases the cost of doing business by up to 10% on average.[11]

2. ***Leads to waste and inefficient use of scarce public resources:*** Corruption leads to bad value for money, to misallocation of scarce resources, to deliberately slowed down approval processes and nepotism; all of which undermine the effectiveness of the state:

> Investments are not allocated to sectors and programmes which present the best value for money or where needs are highest, but to those which offer the best prospects for personal enrichment of corrupt politicians. Thus, *resources go into big infrastructure projects or military procurement where kickbacks are high, to the detriment of sectors like education and health care.* Moreover, public tenders are assigned to the highest bribe payer, neglecting better qualified companies not willing to bribe, *which undermines the quality of the projects carried out.* In some instances, *public funds are simply diverted from their intended use, embezzled and exploited for private enrichment.* Corruption also slows down bureaucratic processes, as *inefficient bureaucracies offer more leverage for corrupt public officials: the longer the queue for a service, the higher the incentive for citizens to bribe to get what they want.* Finally, nepotism – in both private and public organisations – *brings incompetent people into power,* weakening performance and governance.[12]   [Emphases mine]

3. ***Excludes the poor from public services and perpetuates poverty:*** The poor have a problem in corrupt regimes because they lack the resources to get access to decision makers to obtain necessary goods and services. Resources and benefits flow between the rich who have the required resources to gain access. The poor may find themselves cut off from basic services like healthcare and education, which only impoverishes them further, if they cannot afford to pay the bribes required for access.[13] This can affect life expectancy where child mortality is up to one-third higher and infant mortality is twice as high in countries that are corrupt.[14]

4. ***Erodes public trust, undermines the rule of law and delegitimizes the state:*** If rules and regulations are circumvented by bribes, public budget control is undermined by illicit money flows. Political critics and the media are silenced through bribes from protecting democratic systems of checks and balances. Corruption in elections or party financing undermines the rule of the people and thus the very foundation of democracy. If basic public services are not delivered to citizens due to corruption, the state eventually loses its credibility and legitimacy.[15]

Given the harm corruption does, it is not surprising that in recent years there has been an increasing focus on anti-money laundering. Boards now have to consider very carefully whether what they used to do regarding transfer pricing and payment of commissions is not regarded as a form of money laundering where the penalties are severe.

The themes of inequality and economic disruption and their impact on communities were discussed in Chapters 4 and 5. What is special about community sustainability is the need to consider the rights of indigenous peoples, which is often closely associated with environmental sustainability, discussed in detail in Chapter 3. It is a critical issue for companies involved in primary and extractive industries but of not much consequence for most organizations. That leaves two dilemmas boards must still consider: obeying the law and paying taxes:

1. **Obeying the law:** Most people assume that obeying the law is a must.[i] Yet many companies choose to break the law by disregarding environmental, health and safety, and consumer protection regulations and pay the resulting fines instead. There are several reasons for this behavior:

    a. In countries with weak enforcement, directors may calculate it is worth running the risk of prosecution and fines because the likelihood of getting caught is low.

    b. In the event of getting caught, they can buy their way out of trouble before the case gets to court.

    c. If directors focus only on maximizing short-term profits for their shareholders, they may feel they can justify this antisocial behavior on the grounds that this is "just the cost of doing business" and that as long as the bribe or the penalty is less than the bottom line impact of breaking the law, that it is worth doing. It is, after all, the same logic as people who break the law by parking in reserved spots because it is convenient or who are willing to pay for it in order to save time.

    d. They discount the corrosive effect on behavior of their own employees of bribing officers of the law or of believing that it does not really matter as long as they can meet their profit targets. They ignore the risk that small crimes can grow into big ones.

    e. If their organization has little or no brand value to protect unlike Siemens[ii] or Volkswagen,[iii] the reputation damage caused by prosecution

---

i In some countries, laws are introduced as bargaining chips for corrupt discussions on how they can be worked around or ignored for a fee.

ii "The day is past when multinational corporations could regard illicit payments to foreign officials as simply another cost of doing business. The $1.6 billion in combined sanctions that Siemens will pay in the U.S. and Germany should make clear that these corrupt business practices will be rooted out wherever they take place, and the sanctions for them will be severe." Scarboro, C., Associate Director, US SEC Enforcement Division Press Release, December 15, 2008, https://www.sec.gov/news/press/2008/2008-294.htm, accessed on November 1, 2019.

iii Volkswagen incurred US$33 billion in costs in settling its emissions scandal in the US, including fines in Germany of US$1.2 billion for the Volkswagen brand and a further US$926 million for Audi. Raven, B. (2018), "Volkswagen's new $926M fine for Audi brings total dieselgate

may not feature in their thinking. Equally, if their company is not publicly listed, there may be no negative impact on the value of their market capitalization to upset shareholders.

f. They also fail to recognize that companies are unique entities whose very existence is a result of the law, and if the law falls into disrepute, their organizations will be left helpless when politicians decide to limit their freedom to operate.

g. Sometimes multinational companies are caught in a jurisdictional crossfire. Boards face the agonizing dilemma of deciding which set of laws to obey – those of the host country or those of the country where they are headquartered?

Sanctions can also present serious problems if there is a political disagreement about the appropriateness of sanctions between countries. A couple of examples relating to US sanctions against Iran illustrates what boards may have to deal with. The first was BNP Paribas in 2015[16] – a leading French bank – which was fined US$8.9 billion by the US Department of Justice for doing business in Iran. This was perfectly legal in France when the US sanctioned the Iranian government – forbidding any company to trade with the country, using its extraterritorial reach because the trade was done in dollars and therefore came under US jurisdiction. BNP sought the support of the French government in defending its position. This only made matters worse and BNP was fined much more than HSBC – a British bank – which paid US $1.9 billion[iv] without involving the British government.[17]

2. **Paying taxes:** There are three ways in which the issue of companies failing to pay their fair share of taxes arises: tax avoidance; cross-border manipulation of recorded profits; and on-line retailing being exempt from local authority taxes at the expense of brick-and-mortar competitors:

a. *Tax avoidance:* The ultra-rich work hard at avoiding tax, which is legal. They always have. The proliferation of schemes and offshore tax havens does not just deprive governments of much-needed revenues to invest in infrastructure[v] improvements and social safety nets for the less fortunate members of the community; it undermines the principles of democratic control:

---

costs up to $33B," *MLive Michigan,* October 16, 2018, https://www.mlive.com/auto/2018/10/volkswagens_new_926m_fine_for.html, accessed on November 1, 2019.

iv The HSBC fine covered Mexican drug money laundering as well as sanction violations in Iran, which represented less than half of the total fine.

v "In 2016 many authorised the Bank for International Settlements (BIS) to make banking statistics publicly available. Using these data, a new study. . .concludes that tax havens hoard

After interviewing 65 wealth managers in 18 countries, I learned that many *individuals with enormous wealth and power deeply resent any institutions that limit their freedom or hold them accountable to obey the law.* Thus, they form common cause with populist political movements, which attack the authority and legitimacy of policy professionals and politicians. In this effort, *the ultra-rich weaken the actors empowered to impose restrictions on them, liberating themselves to make even more money by flouting regulations, tax obligations, trade embargoes and other inconveniences.* The goal, as a Guardian columnist wrote presciently back in 2012, is to "free the rich from the constraints of democracy" – and that, sooner or later, has the ironic consequence of aligning global elites with authoritarian nationalists. . .

The novelist GK Chesterton had their number over a century ago, when he wrote: "The poor man really has a stake in the country. The rich man hasn't; he can go away to New Guinea on his yacht. The poor have sometimes objected to being governed badly; the rich have always objected to being governed at all. Aristocrats were always anarchists."[18]

If I replace the word "aristocrats" with "multinational corporations," G. K. Chesterton's quotation could apply equally well to some of the world's largest businesses, whose aim is to avoid being governed as much as possible.

b. ***Cross-border manipulation:*** One of the issues created by globalization is the practice of multinationals not paying their fair share of taxes. This behavior is legal but manifestly unfair. Multinationals benefit from operating outside their domestic jurisdictions; they would not do so unless it made commercial sense. Yet through the canny use of transfer pricing in the private markets of their supply chains, they are able to transfer profits from higher tax jurisdictions to the lowest ones at the expense of the countries where they are doing business:

Multinationals can all too easily relocate their headquarters and production to whatever jurisdiction levies the lowest taxes. *And in some cases, they need not even move their business activities, because they can merely alter how they "book" their income on paper.*

Starbucks, for example, can continue to expand in the U.K. while paying hardly any British taxes, because it claims that there are minimal profits there. But if that were true, its ongoing expansion would make no sense. Why increase your presence when there are no profits to be had? Obviously, *there are profits, but they are being funnelled from the U.K. to lower-tax jurisdictions in the form of royalties, franchise fees, and other charges.*

wealth equivalent to about 10% of global GDP," *The Economist*, October 7, 2017, https://www.economist.com/finance-and-economics/2017/10/07/a-new-study-details-the-wealth-hidden-in-tax-havens, accessed on November 3, 2019.

This kind of tax avoidance has become an art form at which the cleverest firms, like Apple, excel. The aggregate costs of such practices are enormous. According to the IMF, governments lose at least $500bn (£406bn) a year as a result of corporate tax shifting. And Gabriel Zucman of the University of California, Berkeley, and his colleagues estimate that *some 40% of overseas profits made by U.S. multinationals are transferred to tax havens. In 2018, 60 of the 500 largest companies – including Amazon, Netflix, and General Motors – paid no U.S. tax, despite reporting joint profits (on a global basis) of some $80bn.* These trends are having a devastating impact on national tax revenues and undermining the public's sense of fairness.[19]   [Emphases mine]

c. ***Asymmetrical competition:*** On-line retailers do not have to pay main street rent and expenses and in some cases do not have to pay sales taxes. This means they can undercut stores with a brick-and-mortar presence, leading to the gradual destruction of city centers, in turn undermining the communities that depend on shops and banks on main street. Making large online retailers pay sales tax may help bring business back to main street and this was argued in the US Supreme Court ruling in 2018, following which, states in the US have begun to tax internet sales.[20]

Workplace

Creating a sustainable workplace requires board policies dealing with discrimination, human rights, union rights, occupational health and safety, sexual harassment, working conditions, and the avoidance of child labor. These policies do not apply only to what happens in their own organizations but across their entire supply chains as well. The majority of policies dealing with union rights, occupational health and safety issues, working conditions, and avoiding the use of child labor are determined by legislation in the domestic jurisdictions of employers and are dealt with accordingly.

As a result, typically, most organizations meet or exceed the minimum standards set by the law and relevant regulations regarding union rights, working conditions, and pay. However, there are industries where sweat shops still exist even in the US[21] and the gig economy and "zero hours contracts" are seen by some as being a violation of workers' rights with respect to pay, working conditions, and other entitlements, such as paid leave, medical, and retirement benefits, that full-time employees enjoy. Companies like Uber[22] or Lyft[23] face litigation in a number of jurisdictions to settle the status of drivers whom they regard as independent contractors. Amazon is regularly criticized for the harshness of its working conditions[24] and there have been alleged cases of its employees' health being put at risk.[25]

Promoting Meritocracy

Most people assume meritocracy and pay for individual performance are the best way to manage organizations. It seems self-evident that people should be hired and promoted on merit and equally obvious that they should be rewarded for their achievements as individuals. Meritocracy originated in China in the sixth century BC when Confucius proposed a series of rigorous exams for prospective officials to qualify for the different levels of the Imperial administration rather than on their inherited status or family connections.[26] The British were the first to adopt the Chinese approach when they created the Indian Civil Service to administer the Indian subcontinent for the British East India Company where company managers hired and promoted employees based on competitive examinations in order to prevent corruption and favouritism.[27]

They then extended it to the British civil service based on the belief that the longevity of the Chinese system of government was based on the advancement of men of talent:

> The long duration of the Chinese empire is solely and altogether owing to the good government which consists in the advancement of men of talent and merit only. . .[28]

So it may come as a surprise, as it did to me, to discover that Michael Young, creator of the term "meritocracy" in his book, "The Rise of the Meritocracy," in 1957, regarded a meritocratic society as dystopian and not something to be desired:

> He meant the term as a pejorative, for underneath the mock academic tract lay bitter social commentary. Though the test-based system of advancement emerging in postwar Britain appeared to provide opportunity for all, it was, Mr. Young argued, simply the centuries-old class system in sheep's clothing.
> Lacking access to the best schools, *underprivileged children routinely did badly on the 11-plus exam, the test given to children after sixth grade that largely determined their professional future. As a result, the disadvantaged remained at the bottom of the social ladder, their poor scores used to justify the status quo.* "The Rise of the Meritocracy" became an international best seller and was credited with leading to the abolition of the 11-plus in Britain.[29]   [Emphasis mine]

With the passage of time, the criticisms of meritocracy have developed further. The whole point of meritocratic assessment is supposed to be its objectivity; dependent on the measurement of performance against standardized tests of competence. However, there appear to be two flaws in the process:
1. *Meritocracy reflects and promotes inequality* because so much of educational performance depends of the socio-economic backgrounds of children. The recent admissions scandals in the US were attempts to reinforce privileged access[30] in what is supposed to be an egalitarian system for

getting onto the educational ladder to better careers. In other words, it is a system that can be gamed; and regularly is by parents with the means to give their children an unfair advantage, whether it is in the US, or China:[31]

> Today's meritocrats still claim to get ahead through talent and effort, using means open to anyone. In practice, however, meritocracy now excludes everyone outside of a narrow elite. Harvard, Princeton, Stanford, and Yale collectively enroll more students from households in the top 1 percent of the income distribution than from households in the bottom 60 percent. Legacy preferences, nepotism, and outright fraud continue to give rich applicants corrupt advantages. But the dominant causes of this skew toward wealth can be traced to meritocracy. On average, children whose parents make more than $200,000 a year score about 250 points higher on the SAT than children whose parents make $40,000 to $60,000. Only about one in 200 children from the poorest third of households achieves SAT scores at Yale's median. Meanwhile, the top banks and law firms, along with other high-paying employers, recruit almost exclusively from a few elite colleges.[32]   [Emphases mine]

2. ***Meritocracy does not measure appropriate competencies*** because it is based on standardized testing:

> Standardized tests can't measure initiative, creativity, imagination, conceptual thinking, curiosity, effort, irony, judgment, commitment, nuance, good will, ethical reflection, or a host of other valuable dispositions and attributes. What they can measure and count are isolated skills, specific facts and function, content knowledge, the least interesting and least significant aspects of learning.[33]

The added problem of the meritocratic approach is that the winners tend look down on the losers, adding insult to the injury of remaining at the bottom of the socio-economic ladder, fueling the resentment of the less fortunate against the elites that have been successful only in part as a result of their own efforts:

> Hardworking outsiders no longer enjoy genuine opportunity. According to one study, only one out of every 100 children born into the poorest fifth of households, and fewer than one out of every 50 children born into the middle fifth, will join the top 5 percent. Absolute economic mobility is also declining – the odds that a middle-class child will outearn his parents have fallen by more than half since mid-century – and the drop is greater among the middle class than among the poor. Meritocracy frames this exclusion as a failure to measure up, adding a moral insult to economic injury.[34]   [Emphases mine]

Promoting Diversity and Inclusion

Much has been written about the benefits of promoting diversity and inclusion. The arguments are compelling, though they tend to ignore the impact of

different cultures on how to do business effectively across cultures and different values (discussed in the next section of this chapter).

A LinkedIn study in 2017 showed US company inclusion efforts focused on
gender (71%); race and ethnicity (49%); age and generational differences
(48%); educational differences (43%); disability (32%); religious affiliation
(19%); other (6%).[35]

The alleged benefits of diversity are shown in Table 6.1.

Table 6.1: Benefits of diversity.

Gender:
1. *Mixed gender balanced teams perform better in terms of sales and profits.*[36]
2. *Having women on teams makes the teams smarter:*
   Collective intelligence increased because members were found to be more
   prone to listen to each other; to be more open-minded; and better able to
   accept constructive criticism rather than trying to dominate the conversation.
   This was in contrast to groups with high IQs only who did not show the
   same sense of teamwork.[37]
3. *The more women there are on boards, the better deals they get in mergers and
   acquisitions, paying less for them:*
   "Our findings show that the prudence exhibited by women directors
   in negotiating mergers and acquisitions has had a substantial positive
   effect on maintaining firm value," says Professor Li. "Female board members
   play a significant role in mitigating the empire building tendency of CEOs
   through the acquisition of other companies. On average, merger and
   acquisition transactions don't create shareholder value, so women are
   having a real impact in protecting shareholder investment and overall firm performance.
   The researchers say their results suggest women are less interested in pursuing risky
   transactions and require the promise of a higher return on investment."[38]
4. *The number of women in senior and board positions also increased the likelihood of
   successful start-ups:*
   "Companies have a greater chance of either going public, operating profitably or being
   sold for more money than they've raised when they have females acting as founders,
   board members, C-level officers, vice presidents and/or directors."[39]
5. *When women were promoted, companies did better financially than companies that did
   not promote women:*
   "Twenty- five subject firms fared better by 34 percent in revenue than companies in the same
   industry that did not promote women. In terms of assets, companies that promoted women
   outperformed companies in the same industry by 18 percent. Individually, 62 percent of the
   subject firms were more profitable in terms of assets than their counterparts. Women friendly
   firms outmatched their counterparts by 26.5 percent in stockholders' equity. Individually,
   they outperformed their counterparts by 68 percent."[40]

Table 6.1 (continued)

6. ***Boards with women directors achieve better annualized returns:*** The most recent evidence for the added value women bring comes from the MSCI Asia Pacific Index companies, where companies with at least one female director on the board achieved a five-year annualized return of 8.9% compared with Bloomberg's 7.3% return for companies with no women on boards[41] As a result, Goldman Sachs announced at the 2020 World Economic Forum that it would not help a company IPO unless it had a gender diverse board.[42]

7. ***Companies with women in senior positions outperform companies without:*** A study by Catalyst of 524 public listed companies with three or more women directors over the period 2004–2008 found they achieved 84% better return on sales; 60% better return on capital; and 46% better return on equity.[43]

Ethnicity, education and age:

1. ***Reducing risk of groupthink:*** Hiring employees with different personalities, ethnic and educational backgrounds, at varied stages in their careers and lifestage helps improve problem-solving and increases creativity.

2. ***Growing the talent pool:*** Individuals from diverse backgrounds can offer a selection of different talents, skills, and experiences, of benefit to the organization and their work performance. Though some crossover of skills can be beneficial when it comes to assisting each other, it is important to hire people with the appropriate skills to fit each of the roles within the company.[44]

3. ***Producing better results:*** Workplace diversity does deliver better results as follows:

    a. *Better financials and 19% higher revenues from innovation:*
    "The biggest takeaway we found is a strong and statistically significant correlation between the diversity of management teams and overall innovation. Companies that reported above-average diversity on their management teams also reported innovation revenue that was 19 percentage points higher than that of companies with below-average leadership diversity – 45% of total revenue versus just 26% . . . EBIT margins that were 9 percentage points higher than those of companies with below-average diversity on their management teams . . . the most significant gains came from changing the makeup of the leadership team in terms of the national origin of executives, range of industry backgrounds, gender balance, and career paths. Age and educational focus showed a lesser effect."[45]

    b. *Better decisions:*
    "When diverse teams (of three or more people) made a business decision, they outperformed individual decision-makers up to 87 per cent of the time. *Diverse teams were also shown to make decisions faster than individual workers, and benefited from a 60 per cent improvement on decision-making . . .* Effective decision-making also increases with greater diversity in a team. All-male teams were shown to make better business decisions than individuals 58 per cent of the time, while gender-diverse teams outperformed individuals 73 per cent of the time. *Teams that were geographically diverse, and included members with different genders and at least one age gap of more than 20 years, were the most successful – making better business decisions than individuals 87 per cent of the time.*"[46] [Emphases mine]

Table 6.1 (continued)

Business Case for Diversity[47]

In their review of diversity and why it matters, McKinsey concluded the following:

1. *Companies in the top quartile for racial and ethnic diversity are 35% more likely to outperform their peers financially.*
2. *Companies in the top quartile for gender diversity are 15% more likely to outperform their peers financially.* The lower outperformance for gender diversity may be the result of greater efforts in underperforming peers to improve gender diversity, which have not occurred to the same extent for ethnic diversity in underperforming companies.
3. *In the US there is a linear relationship between racial and ethnic diversity and better financial performance.* For every 10% increase in the senior management team, there is an 0.8% increase in EBIT.
4. *In the UK there is a stronger linear relationship.* For every 10% increase in senior management diversity, there was a 3.5% increase in EBIT
5. *Diversity is a competitive differentiator in achieving greater market share.*

If the business case for diversity is positive, why is it still an issue? The answer is that it is difficult to promote diversity consistently and coherently. Table 6.2 shows the drawbacks if it is not done well.

Table 6.2: Drawbacks of diversity and inclusion.

---

1. *Lack of respect and acceptance of diverse perspectives:* If senior management show little or no understanding and empathy for different points of view, the introduction of diverse perspectives leads to slower decision making and alienation.
2. *Distrust, prejudice, and discrimination:* While the purpose of promoting diversity and inclusion is to achieve better decision making by minimizing the incidence of groupthink and to better reflect the interests of differing stakeholders and constituencies, lazy stereotyping undermines that objective by encouraging division and distrust leading to prejudice and discrimination.
3. *Miscommunication made worse by language issues:* If the addition of diversity and inclusion increases the number of people who are communicating across linguistic borders, this can create serious misunderstandings because of missed nuances and misunderstood association of ideas across linguistic borders.
4. *Impact of different cultural assumptions and behavioral axioms:* Most serious of all is the fact that people of different cultural backgrounds may have different belief systems and values leading to divergent and mutually incompatible behaviors.

Impact of Different Cultures

Given the increasing importance of embracing diversity and achieving inclusion, boards and management will inevitably have to employ and deal with people whose belief systems and values may diverge from their own. It is even more important in the case of multinationals that have to employ local staff when they venture abroad.

Boards of multinational organizations must therefore consider their impact on the culture and values of employees who come from another jurisdiction and on their interaction with institutions which do not share the same belief systems. Culture matters and finding the best ways to reconcile differences in axioms and beliefs is essential if the relationship between multinational organizations and their foreign host countries is to be beneficial. It also matters if employees from diverse cultures are to give their best when working for an organization whose cultural foundations are different from their own. As part of reconciling their responsibilities to shareholders and to the societies in which they operate, boards need to consider how best to reconcile any cultural differences they discover in the course of doing business.

Boards would do well to remember Peter Drucker's alleged comment:

> Culture eats strategy for breakfast.

This statement has been accepted as critically important for effective execution of strategy by consultants and boards. However, it would seem this acceptance is really more lip service than applied practice:

> Despite culture being in the top three priorities for company boards, only 20% of 450 London-based directors and board members reported spending the time required to manage and improve it.
>
> Some 62% of survey respondents felt that they were primarily responsible for setting culture from the top of an organisation.
>
> However, a similar proportion (63%) either did not consider culture as part of their formal risk assessment or failed to routinely consider the risk associated with their corporate culture.[48]

The risk caused by cultural misunderstanding goes both ways, undermining:

1. *The ability of organizations to work outside jurisdictions with which they are culturally familiar* because they are unable to establish mutual understanding of how business should be done.

2. *Companies' own codes of conduct* as expatriate employees either "go native" or different values are introduced into the organization, conflicting with the values and codes of conduct laid down in headquarters, rather like a virus attacking its host.

Maybe one of the reasons why so few boards report assessing "cultural" risks specifically, is the wide variation of meanings for the word "culture." It helps to define what is meant by "culture":

> Culture is difficult to define, I think it's even more difficult to mandate – but for me *the evidence of culture is how people behave when no-one is watching.*[49]　　　[Emphasis mine]

Every organization has its own code of conduct. It is the result of its history and the myths that bind its people together, answering the questions of "Who are we?" "What do we believe?" and "How should we behave toward each other and our customers?" It must reflect domestic laws and regulations that apply to its industry and, where relevant, international agreements, laws, and regulations of other jurisdictions, if the organization operates in more than one country.

Developing codes of conduct should be relatively straightforward. In theory, all it requires is to look at past business practices, the history of the organization, and all laws and regulations that could apply to its operations. In practice, however, it is much more complicated. Cultural differences come into play, requiring great cross-cultural sensitivity when developing and applying codes of conduct. The key areas of cross-cultural tension are how to reconcile different approaches to:

1. Following the rules or preserving relationships.
2. Measuring performance.
3. Determining status.
4. Reconciling the role of individuals and the community.

Rules versus Relationships

Table 6.3 present a hypothetical car accident in which you might find yourself as a witness. There are three statements that could apply. The questions I would like you to ask yourself are: which do you believe is appropriate, what would you do, and does it make a difference how badly hurt the pedestrian was?

How we respond to the hypothetical example above depends on where we sit on the Universalist-Particularist spectrum. Universalists (typically Northern Europeans and North Americans) tend to believe the rules apply regardless of relationships of friendship or seniority, whereas Particularists (typically Southern Europeans, Latin Americans, Africans, and Asians) tend to find reasons why "in these particular circumstances" the rules should not apply – in this example, the need to be loyal to a close friend. Universalists would counter that being loyal may be important, but greater harm would be created by letting friends get away with breaking the law and allowing them to do it again. It is the differences in the

Table 6.3: Witnessing a car accident.[50]

Situation:
You are in a car with a close friend driving when he hits a pedestrian at more than 70 kph in an area where the speed limit is 50. There are no witnesses and no forensic evidence to prove the speed at which he was driving. His lawyer says if you testify that he was going at less than 50, it will help your friend.

Differing beliefs

Question: Does your friend, as a good friend, have the right to expect you to lie for him?
Answer 1: He has the right to expect me to testify to the lower speed.
Answer 2: He has some right to expect me to testify to the lower speed.
Answer 3: He has no right to expect me to testify to the lower speed.

What would you do?
1. Testify he was going at less than 50 kph?
2. Not testify he was going at less than 50 kph?

How much difference would it make to your answer, if the pedestrian was badly hurt?

underlying beliefs and values that determine what we do. Table 6.4 compares and contrasts the differences in beliefs and behavior of Universalists and Particularists.

If Universalists and Particularists want to work together successfully, they must first of all recognize differences in their basic beliefs by understanding what each side believes in and above all understanding clearly what their own biases and implicit assumptions are. Next they must recognize their validity for each group without becoming judgmental; and then work on reconciling the two approaches.

Differences in Managing Performance

The most important causes of disagreement between organizational cultures on managing performance come from differences in peoples' beliefs regarding time and how to measure performance. Managers need to examine their own assumptions and beliefs regarding the right way to manage performance and recognize the people they supervise may have different beliefs and assumptions if they are to avoid unfortunate misunderstandings and unintentional conflict.

1. *Two Perspectives of Time:* People spend time sequentially or synchronously. Which they choose depends on their assumptions and beliefs about the nature of time. Table 6.5 shows the differences in assumptions between sequential and synchronous approaches to time.

Table 6.4: Differences between universalists and particularists.[51]

Universalist Approach	Particularist Approach
Underlying beliefs:	**Underlying beliefs:**
1. Car accident case	1. Car accident case
a. The truth must be told	a. The need to support my friend comes first
b. The law was broken and the serious condition of the pedestrian underlines the importance of upholding the law.	b. My friend needs my help even more now he is in trouble with the law
c. It is more important to tell the truth the more serious the injuries	c. It is more important to lie for my friend the more serious the injuries
2. What is good and right can be defined and always applies regardless of circumstances	2. Obligations to relationships considering special circumstances come first
3. No exceptions to applying rules; relationships do not matter	3. Waivers are necessary because special circumstances always exist
4. Level playing field is the basis of competition	4. Handicaps are the basis of competition
5. Only one reality – that which has been agreed in a legally binding document	5. Several realities exist based on changing circumstances and relationships
6. Legal contracts are easily drawn up	6. Legal contracts are easily modified
7. Trustworthy person honors their word or contract	7. Trustworthy person honors changing mutual ties
8. Particularists cannot be trusted to adhere to codes of conduct because they will always help their friends out when there is a problem	8. Universalists cannot be trusted because they put the code of conduct first and won't help their friends out when there is a problem
Resulting behavior:	**Resulting behavior:**
1. Focusing on rules rather than relationships – a deal is a deal	1. Focusing on relationships – relationships evolve and so the deal must evolve
2. Using legal proceedings to ensure promises are kept	2. Keeping promises based on personal relationships
a. Contract records agreement in principle and codifies *specific performance*	a. Recognizing good relationships require more than what contracts may demand, *keeping the contract as diffuse as possible*
b. Implies consent and provides recourse	b. Relationships are more lasting
c. Introducing lawyers into the process signals failure to perform is not acceptable and expensive to remedy	c. Seeking process of mutual accommodation; litigation should be avoided
d. Contract takes the place of the relationship	d. Relationship takes the place of the contract

Table 6.4 (continued)

Universalist Approach	Particularist Approach
3. Striving for consistency and uniform procedures 4. Instituting formal ways of changing the way business is done 5. Changing the system so the system will change you 6. Signaling changes publicly 7. Seeking fairness by treating all like cases in the same way	3. Taking offense at detailed penalties and requirements in the contract for specific performance, implying one party will cheat the other 4. Building informal networks and creating private understandings 5. Modifying relations with individuals so that they modify the system 6. Pulling levers privately 7. Seeking fairness by treating all cases on their special merits

Table 6.5: Differences in approaches to time.[52]

Sequential Approach	Synchronous Approach
Underlying beliefs: 1. Time is a scarce resource – "time is money" 2. Time is measurable and tangible 3. Time is linear	**Underlying beliefs:** 1. Time is "space for relating with others" 2. Time is like a "wide ribbon" and intangible 3. Time is circular
Resulting behavior: 1. Corporate ideal is the straight line and most rapid efficient route to achieving objectives 2. Focusing on the quickest way from A to B, efficiency is the driver 3. Leaving the past behind in the attempt to capture the immediate gains in the near future 4. Focusing on the agenda and each step one at a time 5. Seeing product or service as separate from the relationship 6. Insisting each step has its own sequence and its own 'due by' date; project management essential	**Resulting behavior:** 1. Corporate ideal is the interacting circle in which past experience, present opportunities, and future possibilities cross-fertilize 2. Focusing on developing long-term relationships: "What's the hurry?" 3. Refusing to admit the need for change unless it can carry part of the heritage forward 4. Pursuing multiple and often apparently distracting agendas 5. Seeing a product or service as part of an ongoing relationship 6. Seeing separate steps as parallel parts of the whole rather than on their own

Table 6.5 (continued)

Sequential Approach	Synchronous Approach
Performance Appraisal:	**Performance Appraisal:**
1. Employees feel rewarded by achieving planned future goals (MBO)	1. Employees feel rewarded by achieving improved relationships with supervisors/ customers
2. Employees' most recent performance is the major issue, along with whether their commitments for the future can be trusted	2. Employees' entire histories with the firm and future potential are the contexts framing the review of current performance
3. Plan the career of employees jointly with them; stressing landmarks to be reached by certain times, and corrective actions if not achieved	3. Discuss with employees their final aspirations in the context of the company; in what ways can they be realized?

Table 6.6: Specific and diffuse approaches to performance.[53]

Specific Approach	Diffuse Approach
Underlying beliefs:	**Underlying beliefs:**
1. Principles and consistent moral stands, independent of the person being addressed	1. Highly situational morality depending on the person and context
2. Private and business agendas are kept separate	2. Private and business issues are not kept separate
3. The language of performance contracts at work is specific	3. The behavior of the whole person in a relationship including outside work is diffuse
4. *"The Report leads to the Rapport"*	4. *"The Rapport leads to the Report"*
a. Measurement of KPIs [key performance indicators]	a. Trust creates performance
b. Facts/performance create trust	b. Trust provides access to the facts
5. Company is an "Instrumental" system designed to perform functions and tasks in an efficient way. People perform these functions aided by equipment and machines. They are paid for the tasks they perform.	5. Company is a "Social" group of people working together. They have social relations with other people and with the organization. Their effective functioning depends on these relations.

Table 6.6 (continued)

Specific Approach	Diffuse Approach
Resulting behavior:	**Resulting behavior:**
1. Operates on feedback and fact-based analysis	1. Reconciles contradictions in a complex world of networks
2. Seeks truth through analysis: deductive, inductive logic	2. Understands the need for balance; yin and yang coexist
3. Believes in individual responsibility/ accountability	3. Believes in group or team responsibility/ accountability
4. Works with business plans and budgets	4. Works with scenarios
5. Deals in *explicit* knowledge:	5. Deals in *tacit* knowledge:
a. Manuals	a. Relationships
b. Software	b. Culture
c. Libraries	c. Understandings
d. Records	d. Who knows what
e. SLAs [service level agreements], SOPs [standard operating procedures]	e. Institutional memory
6. Communication	6. Communication:
a. Direct, to the point, purposeful in relating	a. Indirect, circuitous, seeming "aimless" forms of relating
b. Precise, blunt, definitive, and transparent	b. Evasive, tactful, ambiguous, even opaque
Performance Appraisal:	**Performance Appraisal:**
1. Only as good as the last performance appraisal	1. Past contributions of employees taken into account
2. Clear, precise, and detailed instructions assure better compliance, allowing employees to disagree in clear terms	2. Ambiguous and vague instructions allow subtle, responsive interpretations through which employees can exercise personal judgment

2. ***Two Ways of Measuring Performance:*** The two different approaches to measuring performance can be serious sources of misunderstanding when appraising people. Some cultures are specific, breaking performance down into its constituent parts, whereas others are more diffuse when defining performance. Table 6.6 compares the two approaches.

Determining Status

There are two ways of looking at status. At one end of the spectrum are those who believe that status, like respect, must be earned. At its most extreme in many professional services firms, people believe it must be earned every day, summarized in the saying, "You are only as good as your last performance review." At the other end of the spectrum are people who believe that some people are entitled to status and respect regardless of what they do. At its most extreme in feudal societies, this can be summarized as, "Every person has his/ her place; and there is a place for everyone."

Sociologists say people's status is either *achieved* or it is *ascribed*. Table 6.7 shows four statements about status. As you read them, choose the one that best fits your and your colleagues' beliefs, which will reflect where you are on the spectrum of Achievement versus Ascription.

Table 6.7: Achievement versus ascription.[54]

a)	Status should lie in the permanent attributes of employees: age, education, background, seniority, position, and the level of ascribed responsibility. Status should not change according to occasion or just because of recent successes. It reflects intrinsic worth, not the latest forays.
b)	Status should lie in the permanent attributes of employees: their education, seniority, age, position and the level of responsibility ascribed. Such status tends to be self-fulfilling, with achievement and leadership resulting from what the corporation values in you and expects of you.
c)	Status is a matter of what the employee has actually achieved, his or her track record. Yet over time this deserved reputation becomes a permanent attribute, allowing success to be renewed and enabling even more achievement to occur.
d)	Achievement or success is the only legitimate source of status in business. The more recent the achievement, the better and more relevant to current challenges. Achievement gets its significance from the humble nature of the individual's birth and background, and from beating the odds.

The statement you choose depends on your cultural background. However, from an organizational perspective, boards and senior managers need to understand the differences in underlying belief systems and the resulting behaviors of employees. Table 6.8 shows the two approaches to status.

Table 6.8: Achieved or ascribed status.[55]

Status is achieved	Status is ascribed
Underlying beliefs	**Underlying beliefs**

1. Status through *Achievement* means you are judged on
   a. Measurement of performance: contracts and KPIs matter
   b. Track record
   c. Recent performance ("only as good as your last . . . ") – technical know-how:
	1. Status through *Ascription* means you are judged on
	   a. What is attributed to you (birth, kinship, gender, age)
	   b. Educational record
	   c. Connections – technical know-who:

"What did you study?" "What do you know?"
2. Individuals can be easily compared based on their ability to "Achieve more" in specific performance terms
3. "I am my functional role"
   a. Hierarchical relationships are functionally specific and *apply only at work*
   b. Success is universally defined according to performance benchmarks
   c. Relationships with others are instrumental – temporary, lasting as long as necessary to complete the task
	"Where did you study?" "Who do you know?"
	2. Individuals are unique and cannot be easily compared with others in specific performance terms as there are other factors to be considered
	3. "I personify the organization, wielding its power"
	   a. Status is independent of task or function and hierarchical relationships which *still apply outside work*
	   b. Role justified through "power to get things done"
	   c. Relationships are social – based on loyalty and affection

4. Subordinates' status is independent of superior's status, rewards may be higher 5. Superiors know what questions to ask, but not the answers 6. Universalist: the rules apply to everybody regardless of relationships	4. Subordinates' status depends on superior's status, rewards must be less 5 Superiors are expected to know the answers and tell their subordinates 6. Particularist: waivers to the rules may be applied to preserve relationships
Career development philosophy	**Career development philosophy**
1. *High fliers* promoted on "Up or Out" basis 2. "Only as good as last performance review" – latest performance best predictor of future performance 3. Measured on achievement of latest KPIs, earlier contributions discounted	1. *Crown Princes* identified based on potential 2. Exposed to different roles and responsibilities to elicit potential; mistakes tolerated 3. Measured on earlier contributions as well as present performance

Table 6.8 (continued)

Status is achieved	Status is ascribed
Resulting behavior	**Resulting behavior**
1. Individualistic, independent, and accountable	1. Communitarian, dependent, and waiting for instruction
2. Most senior managers are of varying age and have proved themselves in specific jobs	2. Most senior managers are qualified by their background rather than past performance
3. Respect for superiors is based on how effectively their jobs are done and how adequate their knowledge	3. Respect for superiors is seen as a measure of commitment to the organization and its mission
4. Use of titles only when relevant to the competence you bring to the task	4. Extensive use of titles, especially to clarify status in the organization
5. Decisions are challenged on technical and functional grounds	5. Decisions only challenged by people with higher authority
6. MBO [management by objectives] and pay-for-performance are effective tools	6. 'Rice bowl' and social rewards from superiors more effective than MBO

Individualism versus the Community

The difference in the importance placed on individual or collective behavior matters. It affects attitudes toward individual accountability, competition versus collaboration, and the role of the individual in the community. Table 6.9 has four statements on competition and collaboration. Which of these statements best reflects your beliefs determines where you belong on the Individualism/Community spectrum. This in turn affects how you feel about competition and collaboration:

The statement that best reflects your thinking – there is no right or wrong answer – depends on what you feel about the merits of competition and collaboration; a function of your belief systems and their impact on behavior, shown in Table 6.10.

Table 6.9: Four statements on competition and collaboration.[56]

a) Competition is the supreme value of any successful economy or company. Attempts by major parties to cooperate usually end in collusion against one or more of them.

b) Competition is the supreme value of any successful economy or company, because this involves serving customers better than our rivals, so assuring the public interest.

c) Cooperation among stakeholders is the supreme value because this shared aim makes companies fiercely competitive toward outsiders, thereby fulfilling personal interests.

d) Cooperation among stakeholders is the supreme value. Personal rivalry and competing for self-advancement are disruptive of effective operations.

Table 6.10: Individual versus community.[57]

Individual	Community
Underlying beliefs:	**Underlying beliefs:**
1. *Person seeking fulfillment is solely responsible for choices made and convictions formed* in the creative, feeling, inquiry, and discovery processes	1. *Society nurtures, educates, and takes responsibility for the spirit engendered among its members* in the social discourse of living
2. Individual is self-made and inner-directed, based on a. Self-reliance b. Self-interest c. Achieving personal growth and fulfillment	2. The social system creates personal outer-directed success, based on a. Social concern b. Altruism c. 'National service' and societal legacy
3. Competing is the basis of success	3. Cooperating is the basis of success
4. Shareholder value and profitability come first	4. Stakeholder value and market share come first
5. Government acts as referee	5. Government acts as coach
Resulting behavior:	**Resulting behavior:**
1. Competing all out as rivals	1. Collaborating as mentor-mentee
2. Achieving alone and assuming personal responsibility	2. Achieving in groups and assuming joint responsibility
3. Making decisions on the spot, acting as representatives of the organization	3. Referring decisions back to the organization, acting as delegates
4. Making decisions based on voting	4. Making decisions by consensus
5. Focusing on completing tasks	5. Focusing on building relationships
6. Talking about "I"	6. Talking about "We"
Managing people:	**Managing people:**
1. Giving people freedom to take personal initiatives	1. Holding up superordinate goals for all to meet
2. Trying to adjust individual needs to organizational needs	2. Seeking to integrate personality with authority within the group
3. Introducing individual incentives (MBO, pay for performance, etc.)	3. Paying attention to esprit de corps, morale, and cohesiveness
4. Expecting high job turnover and mobility	4. Having low job turnover and mobility
5. Seeking out high performers and champions for role models	5. Praising the whole group and avoiding showing favoritism

Summary

Social sustainability depends first on environmental sustainability, followed by economic sustainability. If the environment fails, all is lost. The challenges this poses were covered in Chapter 3. When the economy fails, as it did during the Great Depression, social sustainability deteriorates dramatically, ending in the political disasters of World War II in Europe and Asia. These challenges were covered in Chapters 4 and 5. However, even if the environment is stable and the economy appears to be functioning well, social stability can still be undermined by the actions of businesses damaging communities and creating unsustainable workplaces.

Perhaps the most serious threat to social sustainability is the impact of corruption on communities. Corruption damages them in four ways. First, politically; corruption is a major obstacle to democracy and the rule of law. Second, economically; corruption depletes national wealth. Corrupt politicians invest scarce public resources in projects that will line their pockets rather than benefit communities. Third, socially; corruption corrodes the social fabric. It undermines people's trust in the political system, in its institutions, and its leadership. Finally, environmental degradation is another consequence of corrupt systems. The lack or non-enforcement of environmental regulations and legislation means that precious natural resources are over-exploited, and entire ecological systems are ravaged. Corruption also does real harm by increasing the cost of doing business; leading to waste and inefficient allocation of scarce resources; excluding the poor from public services and perpetuating poverty; eroding and ultimately delegitimizing the state.

Boards need to consider carefully the damage they do to society when they choose to disobey the law, justifying paying fines or bribes on the grounds they are a "just a cost of doing business." They ignore the risk that small crimes can grow into big ones. They also fail to recognize that companies are unique entities – whose very existence is a result of the law – and if the law falls into disrepute, their organizations will be left defenseless when politicians decide to limit their freedom to operate.

Boards also need to consider whether avoiding taxes is still a socially sensible way to behave. The sums involved are now so serious that governments are not just deprived of the revenues they need to maintain their national social contracts; they also fuel popular resentment against the ultra-rich and threaten the political acceptance of neoliberal capitalism.

Social sustainability also depends on what happens in the workplace. Apart from respecting the appropriate regulations and laws covering human and union rights, health and safety, and working conditions, boards need to consider whether their emphasis on meritocracy has the intended results. Evidence suggests that the concept of meritocracy needs to be re-examined. It appears that it reinforces privilege rather than creating a ladder of opportunity for all. The inequality it fosters may explain in part the resentment at elites and the disaffection with the current economic system.

As far as promoting diversity and inclusion are concerned, these are not merely admirable objectives; in the case of diversity, there is a positive business case. Diverse organizations outperform less diverse ones. Increased racial and ethnic diversity yields even better outcomes than gender diversity, itself leading to significantly outperforming organizations. However, managing diversity is not easy and it requires an understanding of the impact of cultural differences on how people behave and how they should be led and managed as a result.

There are four areas boards must consider when they attempt to manage across cultures. First, are the dilemmas created by the differences in approach to the importance of rules versus relationships reflected in whether people are Universalists or Particularists. Second, are the differences in belief systems about managing performance; a function of two different approaches to time – "sequential" versus "synchronic" time; and how performance is measured – "specific" versus "diffuse" performance. Failure to recognize people have very different starting points will only lead to unsatisfactory outcomes. Third, it is critical to recognize there are two completely different approaches to status – "achieved" versus "ascribed" – which can best be summarized in the phrases "technical know-how" versus "technical know-who" and career plans based on "high fliers" versus "crown princes." Finally, boards need to remember different cultures place differing levels of importance on the role of the individual versus the community. Success in reconciling these different viewpoints depends on recognizing their complexity.

References

1 Garriga, E. and Mele, D. (2004), "Corporate Social Responsibility Theories: Mapping the Territory," *Journal of Business Ethics* 53, pp. 51–71.
2 Pontefract, D. (2016), "Faking Corporate Social Responsibility Does Not Fool Employees," *Forbes*, September 24, 2016, https://www.forbes.com/sites/danpontefract/2016/09/24/faking-corporate-social-responsibility-does-not-fool-employees/#77abd64779, accessed on September 30, 2019.
3 WHO (2004), "Tobacco industry and corporate responsibility . . . An inherent contradiction," *Tobacco Free Initiative,* World Health Organization, https://www.who.int/tobacco/communica tions/CSR_report.pdf, accessed on September 30, 2019.
4 Frynas, J.G. (2005), "The false developmental promise of Corporate Social Responsibility: evidence from multinational oil companies," *International Affairs*, 81, 3, pp. 581–598, http://oilandgas.living earth.org.uk/wp-content/uploads/2013/09/FalseDevelopmentPromiseCorporateSocResponsibility-Frynas.pdf, accessed on September 30, 2019.
5 Ibid., p. 584.

6 ISO (2010), "Social Responsibility: 7 Core Subjects," *ISO Publications,* https://www.iso.org/files/live/sites/isoorg/files/store/en/PUB100259.pdf, accessed on September 30, 2019.

7 Zinkin, J. (2019), *Better Governance Across the Board: Creating Value Through Reputation, People and Processes* (Boston/Berlin: Walter de Gruyter Inc.), p. 306.

8 Transparency International (2018), "What is corruption?" https://www.transparency.org/what-is-corruption, accessed on October 3, 2019.

9 Ibid.

10 Yermo, J. and Schroeder, H. (2014), "The Rationale for fighting corruption," *CleanGovBiz,* OECD, p. 2, https://www.oecd.org/cleangovbiz/49693613.pdf, accessed on October 3, 2019.

11 Ibid., p. 2.

12 Ibid., pp. 2, 3.

13 Ibid., p. 3.

14 Ibid., p. 2.

15 Ibid., p. 4.

16 Reuters (2015), "BNP Paribas sentenced in $8.9 billion accord over sanctions violations," Reuters, May 1, 2015, https://www.reuters.com/article/us-bnp-paribas-settlement-sentencing/bnp-paribas-sentenced-in-8-9-billion-accord-over-sanctions-violations-idUSKBN0NM41K20150501, accessed on October 6, 2019.

17 Reuters (2012), "HSBC to pay $1.9 billion U.S. fine in money-laundering case," Reuters, December 11, 2012, https://www.reuters.com/article/us-hsbc-probe/hsbc-to-pay-1-9-billion-u-s-fine-in-money-laundering-case-idUSBRE8BA05M20121211, accessed on October 6, 2019.

18 Harrington, B. (2019), "'Aristocrats are anarchists': Why the wealthy back Trump and Brexit," Big Money. *The Guardian*, February 7, 2019, https://www.theguardian.com/us-news/2019/feb/07/why-the-wealthy-back-trump-and-brexit, accessed on October 22, 2019.

19 Stiglitz, J. (2019), "Corporate tax avoidance: it's no longer enough to take half measures," *Independent Commission for the Reform of International Corporate Taxation,* October 7, 2019, https://www.icrict.com/icrict-in-thenews/2019/10/7/corporate-tax-avoidance-its-no-longer-enough-to-take-half-measures, accessed on October 31, 2019.

20 Murray, J. (2019) "Sales Tax for Internet Transactions – Which States?" *The balancesmall-business*, June 10, 2019, https://www.thebalancesmb.com/internet-sales-tax-what-is-the-law-4164865, accessed on October 31, 2019.

21 Kitroeff, N. (2016), "Factories that made clothes for Forever 21, Ross paid workers $4 and hour, Labor Department says," *Los Angeles Times,* November 16, 2016, https://www.latimes.com/business/la-fi-wage-theft-forever-ross-20161116-story.html, accessed on November 5, 2019.

22 Templeton, B. (2019), "If Uber Drivers Become Employees, Can Uber Escape That? Plus How Employees Compete With Robocars," *Forbes,* September 17, 2019, https://www.forbes.com/sites/bradtempleton/2019/09/17/if-uber-drivers-become-employees-can-uber-escape-that-plus-how-employees-compete-with-robocars, accessed on November 3, 2019.

23 Dickey, M, R. (2019), "Uber and Lyft are putting $60 million toward keeping drivers independent contractors," *TechCrunch,* August 30, 2019, https://techcrunch.com/2019/08/29/uber-and-lyft-are-putting-60-million-toward-keeping-drivers-independent-contractors/, accessed on November 3, 2019.

24 Gurley, L.K. (2019), "60 Amazon Workers Walked Out Over Warehouse Working Conditions," *Vice,* October 4, 2019, https://www.vice.com/en_us/article/pa7qny/60-amazon-workers-walked-out-over-warehouse-working-conditions, accessed on November 3, 2019; Cain, A. and Hamilton, I.A. (2019), "Amazon warehouse employees speak out about the 'brutal' reality of working during the holidays, when 60-hour weeks are mandatory and ambulance calls are common,"

Business Insider, February 19, 2019, https://www.businessinsider.com/amazon-employees-describe-peak-2019-2?IR=T, accessed on November 3, 2019.

25 Sainato, M. (2019), "Revealed: Amazon touts high wages while ignoring issues in its warehouses," *The Guardian,* August, 7, 2019, https://www.theguardian.com/technology/2019/aug/06/amazon-workers-minimum-wage-injuries-working-conditions, accessed on November 3, 2019.

26 Sienkewicz, T. J. (2003), *Encyclopedia of the Ancient World* (Pasadena, Calif: Salem Press), p. 434.

27 Kazin, M., Edwards, R., and Rothman, A. (2010), *The Concise Princeton Encyclopedia of American History* (Princeton, N.J.: Princeton University Press), p. 142.

28 Meadows, T.T. (1847), *Desultory Notes on the People and Government of China,* republished by Forgotten Books (2018).

29 Fox, M. (2002), "Michael Young, 86, Scholar; Mocked 'Meritocracy'," *The New York Times,* January 25, 2002, https://www.nytimes.com/2002/01/25/world/michael-young-86-scholar-coined-mocked-meritocracy.html, accessed on November 5, 2019.

30 Yan, H. (2019), "What we know so far in the college admissions cheating scam," *CNN,* March 13, 2019, https://edition.cnn.com/2019/03/13/us/what-we-know-college-admissions-cheating-scandal/index.html, accessed on November 5, 2019.

31 Thibaud, A. (2016), "Private Tutoring Industry In China: Experiencing Explosive Growth," *Daxue Consulting,* June 1, 2016, https://daxueconsulting.com/private-tutoring-industry-in-china-experiencing-explosive-growth/, accessed on November 5, 2019.

32 Markovits, D. (2019), "How Life Became a Terrible Endless Competition," *The Atlantic,* September 2019 Issue, https://www.theatlantic.com/magazine/archive/2019/09/meritocracys-miserable-winners/594760/, accessed on November 6, 2019.

33 Ayers, W. (1993), "To teach: the journey of a teacher," *Teachers College Press,* p. 116, quoted in "Meritocracy," *Wikipedia,* https://en.wikipedia.org/wiki/Meritocracy#cite_note-49, accessed on November 6, 2019.

34 Markovits, D. (2019), op. cit.

35 LinkedIn (2017), "Where does your company focus its diversity efforts?" *Worldwide Study,* August 24 to September 24, 2017, cited by Regoli, Natalie (2019), "22 Advantages and Disadvantages of Diversity in the Workplace," *Vittana Personal Finance Blog,* https://vittana.org/22-advantages-and-disadvantages-of-diversity-in-the-workplace, accessed on November 6, 2019.

36 Hoogendorn, S. et al. (2014), "The Impact of Gender Diversity on the Performance of Business Teams: Evidence from a Field Experiment," *Management Science,* Articles in advance, published online, March 4, 2013, p. 13, https://papers.tinbergen.nl/11074.pdf, accessed on September 29, 2018.

37 Wooley, A. and Malone, T.W. (2011), "Defend Your Research: What Makes a Team Smarter? More Women," *Harvard Business Review,* June 2011 Issue, https://hbr.org/2011/06/defend-your-research-what-makes-a-team-smarter-more-women, accessed on September 28, 2018.

38 Li, K. (2017), "Women Directors Get Better Deals in Mergers and Acquisitions," *Global Network for Advanced Management,* March 16, 2017, https://globalnetwork.io/perspectives/2017/03/women-directors-get-better-deals-mergers-and-acquisitions accessed on March 6, 2020.

39 Dow Jones (2012), "Women at the Wheel: Do Female Executives Drive Startup Success?" *Dow Jones Venture Source,* 2012, https://www.pedrad.org/Portals/5/Subspecialties/Diversity%20and%20Inclusion/Women%20Executives%20Dow%20Jones%20Report.pdf?ver=2018-02-14-115459-767&ver=2018-02-14-115459-767, accessed on September 28, 2018.

40 Adler, R.D. (2011), "European Research Project on Equal Pay," cited by French, A. (2012), "Research Summary: Women in the Executive Suite Correlate to High Profits," *InPower Coaching,*

January 25, 2012, https://inpowercoaching.com/study-women-in-the-executive-suite-correlate-to-high-profits/, accessed on September 28, 2018.

41 "Fund manager wants to prove gender equality is good for profits," *Star Online*, January 1, 2019, accessed on January 1, 2019.

42 Martinuzzi, E. (2020), "Goldman's Anti-Bro Pledge Isn't Just a Stunt," *Bloomberg*, January 24, 2020, https://www.bloomberg.com/opinion/articles/2020-01-24/goldman-sachs-is-right-to-reject-the-all-white-all-male-board?cmpid=BBD012920_GREENDAILY, accessed on January 30, 2020.

43 Carter, N. M. (2011), "The Bottom Line: Corporate Performance and Women's Representation on Boards, 2004–2008," *Catalyst*, March 11, 2011.

44 Deering, S., "What are the Benefits of Diversity in the Workplace?" *Undercover Recruiter*. https://theundercoverrecruiter.com/benefits-diversity-workplace/, accessed on November 6, 2019.

45 Lorenzo, R. et al. (2018), "How Diverse Leadership Teams Boost Innovation," *BCG*, January 23, 2018, https://www.bcg.com/en-us/publications/2018/how-diverse-leadership-teams-boost-innovation.aspx, accessed on November 6, 2019.

46 "Diversity drives better decisions," *People Management*, October 23, 2017, https://www.peoplemanagement.co.uk/experts/research/diversity-drives-better-decisions, accessed on November 6, 2019.

47 Hunt, V., Layton, D., and Prince, S. (2018), "Delivering through diversity – New in 2018," updated version of "Why diversity matters," *McKinsey & Co,* originally published in January 2015, https://www.mckinsey.com/business-functions/organization/our-insights/why-diversity-matters, accessed on November 6, 2019.

48 Cave, A., "Culture Eats Strategy for Breakfast. So, What's for Lunch?," *Forbes*, November 9, 2017, https://www.forbes.com/sites/andrewcave/2017/11/09/culture-eats-strategy-for-breakfast-so-whats-for-lunch/#738149a47e0f, accessed on July 23, 2018. No longer active.

49 Diamond, R. (2011), "Today Business Lecture 2011," *BBC Radio 4,* http://news.bbc.co.uk/today/hi/today/newsid_9630000/9630673.stm, accessed on July 23, 2018.

50 Based on Trompenaars, F. and Hampden-Turner, C. (1998), *Riding the Waves of Culture* (London: Nicholas Brealey Publishing), p. 33.

51 Based on ibid., pp. 33–49.

52 Based on ibid., pp. 122–140.

53 Based on ibid., pp. 100–101.

54 Ibid., p. 117.

55 Based on ibid., pp. 118–119.

56 Ibid., p. 65.

57 Based on Trompenaars, F. and Hampden-Turner, C. (2000), op. cit., pp. 81–93.

Chapter 7
Dealing with Volatility and Uncertainty

This chapter is presented in two parts. The first deals with volatility; the second with uncertainty. It closes with a summary of the discussion.

Volatility

Four questions combine to create historically unparalleled levels of volatility, uncertainty, complexity, and ambiguity for boards when making decisions.

The first question is whether the environment is sustainable under "business as usual" assumptions. If the challenges to environmental sustainability outlined in Chapter 3 are not resolved, the resulting environmental damage by the end of this century may require drastic changes to how and where business is done.[1]

The second question is whether neoliberal economic orthodoxy is sustainable with its acceptance of globalization and the discontents created by winners and losers and increased inequality, discussed in Chapter 4. If the challenges faced by neoliberal capitalism are not resolved quickly, capitalism as currently practiced may not survive the political stresses caused by the failure to create an economic system that "works for the many rather than the few."

The third question is what will be the likely impact of "Industry 4.0" on the sustainability of employment and employability, explored in Chapter 5. If governments, shareholders and boards fail to resolve the dilemmas posed by doing what is right for individual organizations, but wrong when all organizations take the same actions at the same time, the resulting disemployment may lead to "political tragedies of the commons," similar to those of the Arab Spring – triggered by the despair of the young unemployed in Tunisia with no hope for gainful employment. This is made worse by the increasing number of people over the age of 65 still at work because they wish/need to remain at work[2] or because governments in developed economies cannot afford the increased pension burdens resulting from longer than originally budgeted life expectancy.[3]

The fourth question is whether the recently declared transition from shareholder primacy to stakeholder primacy by leading businesses[4] is more than PR whitewash and whether organizations can reconcile "doing well with doing good" effectively enough to sustain the social capital needed to have flourishing communities that offer more than just GDP growth to their members.

https://doi.org/10.1515/9783110670486-007

Social media and fake news unfortunately amplify the volatility, uncertainty, complexity, and ambiguity boards must deal with as a result of their speed, reach, and focus on creating division and outrage through their algorithms, designed to maximize addictive engagement.[5]

Types of Volatility

Volatility, defined as "the quality or state of being likely to change suddenly, especially by becoming worse,"[6] undermines "business as usual" assumptions politically, economically, socially, technologically, legally, and environmentally.

1. **Political Volatility:** The political environment as we enter the third decade of the 21st century has become unusually volatile as a number of different political pressures are affecting business assumptions for the future. The neoliberal economic assumptions underpinning the belief in globalization and free trade are being increasingly challenged,[7] making it especially difficult for businesses involved in international trade.

   Symptoms of this volatility are many. President Trump's tweets affect businesses he targets in the US.[8] Shifting political blocs within countries are making it much harder for business to decide which way to go: in the UK, there is Brexit[9]; in France, the rise of the "gilets jaunes"[10]; in Italy,[11] Germany,[12] and Spain[13] the traditional parties of left and right are losing the center ground to the Greens on the left and to nativist, xenophobic parties on the right. The Middle East is destabilized by Sunni-Shia struggles[i] for power between Iran supported by its proxies in Yemen, Syria, and Lebanon; and Saudi Arabia supported by the US, Egypt, and the Gulf States[14]; as well as by the Israeli-Palestinian conflict over land.[15] In Asia there are rising tensions between India and Pakistan over Kashmir,[16] North Korea and Japan over missile tests,[17] trade tensions between South Korea and Japan,[18] and the challenge posed by a more assertive China to Vietnam, the Philippines, Indonesia, and Malaysia over the South China Sea.[19] A revanchist Russia[20]

---

i "Two countries that compete for the leadership of Islam, Sunni Saudi Arabia and Shia Iran, have used the sectarian divide to further their ambitions. How their rivalry is settled will likely shape the political balance between Sunnis and Shias and the future of the region, especially in Syria, Iraq, Lebanon, Bahrain, and Yemen . . .

Islam's dominant [Sunni] sect, which has roughly 85 percent of the world's 1.6 billion Muslims follow, viewed Shia Islam with suspicion, and extremist Sunnis have portrayed Shias as heretics and apostates." "The Sunni-Shia Divide," *Council on Foreign Relations*, https://www.cfr.org/interactives/sunni-shia-divide#!/sunni-shia-divide, accessed on March 11, 2020.

seeks to destabilize Western democracies[21] and is pushing the boundaries of asymmetrical warfare in Eastern Europe in the Ukraine,[22] while testing NATO's commitment to defending the Baltic states.[23]

As a result of these different political pressures, the risk of war by mistake remains real in Eastern Europe, Northeast Asia, South Asia and the Middle East. There is also the ever-present threat of further refugees and migrants from North Africa and the Eastern Mediterranean, destabilizing domestic politics in the EU in a repeat performance of 2014–2015 when refugees sought shelter from the murderous civil war in Syria.[24] The same applies to refugees and migrants trying to enter the US from unstable countries in Central America.[25]

Needless to say, changes of government create volatility that boards have to deal with. For example, after the December election in the UK, boards still have to contend with unclear outcomes which will affect their businesses differently – depending on whether the Conservative victory leads to a total disruption to trading relationships with the EU; and a possible breakup of the United Kingdom in the medium term.[26]

The third decade of the 21st century promises to be more politically and economically volatile than the first two.[27]

2. **Economic Volatility:** Economic volatility is mainly the result of political volatility, although political volatility is often a symptom of economic failure to create "an economy that works for the many rather than just the few" – for example in Hong Kong, where the high level of inequality was the fuel for six months of political protests that pushed the territory into a self-inflicted recession.[28] The UK's travails with a Brexit-induced economic slowdown before it even left the EU is another example.[29]

Economic volatility usually manifests itself in currency volatility as a result of diverging growth rates, inflation, and interest rates – for example, the problems faced by Turkey[30] or Argentina.[31] Sometimes, it is the result of straightforward bad governance, as in the case of Venezuela[32] and Zimbabwe.[33] It can also be the result of punitive sanctions, as with Iran.[34]

Every ten years or so, it is the result of a major financial crisis.[35] However, current economic volatility is more likely to be the result of unstable long-term growth assumptions globally, regionally, or nationally, as a result of the end of quantitative easing; and deglobalization, resulting from trade wars and the imposition of tariff barriers or the mere threat of tariffs. Every now and again, it is the result of a "black swan," like the Covid-19 pandemic's impact on demand as a result of fear, and supply at the same time, because of the disruption it creates to supply.

3. **Social Volatility:** Social volatility is both a symptom and a cause of both political and economic volatility created by political choices and their economic consequences. Increased social volatility in much of Europe has been the result of decisions made regarding immigration; the imposition of austerity policies after the GFC by governments trying to get their balance sheets back in order; and the rise in inequality and unemployment in the developed world as a result of globalization (discussed in Chapters 4 and 5). It has been made more acute by the rise of social media[36] with its focus on promoting resentment and outrage to get greater engagement in the siloed echo chambers of Facebook, YouTube, and Twitter.[37] The resulting increased polarization in the US and UK, in particular, has led to an ever more volatile political identity-based discourse where key protagonists treat each other as enemies rather than as people with whom compromise is essential, if democratic norms are to be respected, as explained in the following quote:

> "The spirit of liberty is the spirit which is not too sure that it is right; the spirit of liberty is the spirit which seeks to understand the mind of other men and women; the spirit of liberty is the spirit which weighs their interests alongside its own without bias." That is also the spirit of our representative democracy, and we need politicians who embrace it.[38]

Boards could end up faced with a vicious feedback loop where an increasingly volatile and polarized society leads to populist political decisions that worsen economic conditions, reinforcing social disharmony and unrest.

4. **Technological Volatility:** Even though Schumpeter's "creative destruction"[39] is an integral part of capitalism, technological volatility is less of an issue for boards. New products and processes need to be developed and road tested before they are rolled out. This gives boards time to think about the timing of their introduction and their likely impact. Occasionally, app-based processes may blind-side incumbents, usually in the distribution areas of services, such as online shopping or shared platforms capitalizing on underutilized assets, such as cloud-based computing, Airbnb, or Uber and Lyft. Their impact is severe, but there is considerable warning for boards who scan the horizon for threats to their business models, even in the areas of AI and robotics (discussed in Chapter 5). Technological innovation is more likely to be a cause for concern in the areas of uncertainty and complexity rather than volatility, given the lead-times involved in its adoption.

5. **Legal and Regulatory Volatility:**
   Legal and regulatory volatility are closely connected to political volatility, in particular to changes in governments where manifestos may promote changes

in industry structure and ownership; for example, the nationalization or privatization of utilities (railways, energy and postal services[40]) or the break-up of oligopolies like the tech giants,[41] and the impact of competition watchdogs on mergers and acquisitions.[42] Equally, there may be changes proposed in the role of unions[43] and health and safety legislation that forms part of the political cycle.

6. **Environmental Volatility:** On the one hand, environmental issues have the longest time horizons of all and therefore should not create volatility. On the other hand, extreme weather events, by their very nature, create disasters and emergencies for which boards are very often not prepared at all. For example, the floods in Thailand in 2011 disrupted global automotive supply chains;[44] the impact of the Fukushima earthquake in Japan in 2011 on Japanese fossil fuel imports as a result of the closure of nuclear reactors across Japan;[45] hurricane Dorian in Florida severely damaged the 2019 orange crop;[46] and drought in France cut the 2019 wine harvest by 12%.[47]

Uncertainty

The Cambridge English Dictionary defines uncertainty as "a situation in which something is not known, or something that is not known or certain."[48] This was expanded to include what we know we know (known known), what we know we do not know (known unknown), what we do not know we know (unknown known), and what we do not know we do not know (unknown unknown[ii]) by US Defense Secretary Donald Rumsfeld in a Pentagon briefing in 2002 on the subject of terrorism:

> Reports that say that something hasn't happened are always interesting to me, because as we know, there are known knowns; there are things we know we know. We also know there are known unknowns; that is to say we know there are some things we do not know. But there are also unknown unknowns – the ones we don't know we don't know. . .[49]

---

ii "Black Swans" are the most famous example of unknown unknowns. A "Black Swan" event has three characteristics: "First, it is an *outlier,* as it lies outside the realm of regular expectations, because nothing in the past can convincingly point to its possibility. Second, it carries an extreme impact. Third, in spite of its outlier status, human nature makes us concoct explanations for its occurrence *after* the fact, making it explainable and predictable." Taleb, N.N. (2007), "The Black Swan: The Impact of the Highly Improbable," *New York Times,* April 22, 2007, https://www.nytimes.com/2007/04/22/books/chapters/0422-1st-tale.html, accessed on November 27, 2019.

We should take the idea of knowing one step further by including knowledge we have, but suppress or ignore because it is inconvenient, dangerous to admit, or will cause delay when time is of the essence – in other words, the "known we do not want to know."[50] This is the basis for "turning a blind eye" to existing conditions that break the law or are violations of codes of conduct justified on the grounds that "the ends justify the means" or "are the costs of doing business" or "speaking truth to power will cost me my job," or "we have a deadline to meet." The "known we do not want to know" usually ends badly: either in a scandal like Abu Ghraib[51]; a disaster like NASA's Challenger shuttle, where a defective "O" ring[iii] was ignored[52]; Deepwater Horizon where cost considerations overrode those of safety,[53] or the failures of Merrill Lynch and Lehman Brothers where risks they were taking were misrepresented as being safe.[54]

Uncertainty therefore comes in all shapes and sizes. These include political, economic, social, technological, legal, and environmental uncertainty. Their lack of predictability and the fact that they cannot be relied upon is what makes them so difficult for boards to handle when making decisions that often cannot be reversed.

1. **Political Uncertainty:** The board of any organization that is affected, however indirectly, by changes in the political environment in which it operates, be it globally, nationally, regionally, or locally, will know it must pay attention to who is in power, what their agenda is, and how it could affect their organization. This also means directors must pay attention to the agendas of politicians who are not in power, but could be; making sure that should the opposition achieve power, their organization's business is not disadvantaged as a result.

   Currently, there is serious political uncertainty. The certainties of the neoliberal consensus[iv] following the fall of the Berlin Wall in 1989 seem to be giving way to challenges to global institutions and norms with weakened governments having to deal with hung parliaments and growing discontent

---

iii "The 'O' Ring was not defective; it was not rated for operating under such freezing temperatures and the Shuttle was launched in weather conditions that were beyond the limits of its design." Dirks, G. (2020), in an email to author on January 19, 2020.

iv The neoliberal consensus of the past thirty years is best captured by looking back at the "people from nowhere" – company CEOs, regulators, and politicians who attended the annual gathering of the World Economic Forum in Davos and the topics they discussed; comfortably disconnected from the everyday problems of the "people from somewhere" or of the "just about managing"; to use Prime Minister Theresa May's description in the 2017 general election of the different types of people working in the globalized economy.

with the economic status quo, represented by the rise of the alt-right on the one hand and the Greens on the other.

These uncertainties are the result of the behavior of President Trump both domestically and internationally;[55] of Brexit and its unclear implications going forward for both the UK and the EU post Brexit; of the rise of nativist and extreme right-wing politicians in Europe, challenging the social-democratic assumptions on which the EU was built.[56] This has been made worse by Russian interference in Western democratic processes trying to foment distrust, division, and dissension using targeted social media.[57] The rise of China and the US reaction may force other countries to choose between the US and China; a choice they would much rather avoid.[58] The long-standing problems in the Middle East and with North Korea remain added sources of political uncertainty.

2. **Economic Uncertainty:** Boards have always had to consider macroeconomic variables, such as monetary policy affecting exchange and interest rates; fiscal policy affecting both direct and indirect taxes; and their combined impacts on growth rates and the business cycle, with their effect on supply and demand in their industries, both domestically and globally.

   Forecasting the effect of these macroeconomic variables has always been the subject of uncertainty. However, as we enter the third decade of the 21st century, six sources of increasing uncertainty have yet to reach their conclusion, further raising the levels of economic uncertainty faced by countries and therefore boards. The first is Covid-19 and how it will affect both the short- and medium-term recovery from the impact it is creating for the global economy and what any "new normal" will look like for the next ten years; and it is too early to tell what will happen to the way we live and work or how long the pandemic will last. The second is the US–China trade war; the third is Brexit; the fourth is the 2020 US presidential election; the fifth is whether China can avoid the so-called "middle income trap"[v]; and the sixth is the destabilizing effect of financial globalization, which is still regarded as acceptable.

   a. ***The US–China trade war:*** Will the US and China find an acceptable solution to the threat of endless trade wars, splitting the world into an Anglosphere in conflict with a Sinosphere?[59] Should such a split arise, it

---

v China's "middle income trap" could occur when "growth rates will fall, just as they have in all but a handful countries that have reached the same income level. Growth is harder, they observe, when it can no longer be based on brute-force capital accumulation. Now it must be based on innovation, which is difficult to bring about in an economy that is still centrally directed." Eichengreen, B. (2019) "Will China Confront a Revolution of Rising Expectations?" *Project Syndicate*, November 11, 2019.

will create enormous economic uncertainty as global supply chains will need to be disassembled as assumptions about capital flows will be upended with the Chinese market closed to American investors and Chinese companies listed on US exchanges having to reconsider whether the benefits of the enormous liquidity of US capital markets warrants the risks of possibly being treated like ZTE[60] and Huawei[61] in 2018 and 2019.

b. **Brexit:** How will Brexit play out over the next five to ten years? To what extent will the departure of the UK from the EU divide, damage, and diminish the UK?[62] Will the Brexiteers be right in saying that leaving the single market will be easy or will the Remainers be correct in saying that the UK will be poorer as a result? Will Brexit lead to the disintegration of the United Kingdom, precipitating Scottish independence and the reunification of Ireland? Will that in turn lead to a hard border between Scotland and England and a hard border down the Irish Sea? How badly will the EU and the countries that trade with the UK be affected? What will happen to "frictionless trade" and to the complex integrated supply chains across Europe, most particularly in the automotive sector, where parts and components currently cross borders between the UK and the Continent up to four times without incurring any costs or delays?[63] Even if London survives more or less intact as a financial hub,[64] given its unique location and agglomeration of support services, what will happen to inward investment into the UK once there are significant barriers to frictionless movement of goods, people, and services? How long will it take before boards get clarity regarding the economic assumptions they make regarding GDP growth, exchange rates, supply of skilled labor, and resources?

c. **US Presidential election in 2020**: Will President Trump be re-elected? If not, what are the implications for the resulting economic policies domestically in the US and globally up to 2024 and beyond? What will happen to tariffs on Chinese imports? Will the US Federal Reserve (Fed) be able to continue acting independently as far as monetary policy is concerned? This will matter not just to the US but to all central banks that are affected by policies of the Fed. What are the implications for fiscal policy and for the regulatory environment, in particular for environmental policies that will be critically important in promoting or delaying policies designed to help decarbonize the economy? What will happen to fossil fuel companies and to ones working on a green revolution? What will happen to healthcare and to the industries most affected by any changes in it – pharmaceuticals and health providers? Covid-19 has made it more difficult to evaluate whether or not President Trump's policies are in fact good for the US economy.[65]

d. ***China and the "middle income trap":*** Can China avoid the "middle income trap" or will it face the revolution of rising expectations experienced across many countries – which may reach China with dramatic consequences for the Chinese economy and the global economy as a result?[66] How will China deal with the heavy indebtedness of its corporate sector? Will it be forced to shift the debt burden to the government, thus weakening its finances and investor confidence? How will China deal with its rapidly aging population and the resulting fall in productivity and living standards for those in retirement? Finally, how will it deal with the trade war with the US? Could the wrong combination of events and governmental responses lead to the kind of unrest seen in Hong Kong, France, Chile, Colombia, and Ecuador?

e. ***The destabilizing effect of financial globalization:*** In Chapter 4, I discussed the predictions of Peter Drucker, Rick Mishkin, and Jeffrey Garten on the destabilizing effect of financial globalization. Their predictions proved to be correct, evidenced by the following quote:

> *An important factor in China's rise was the decision not to open the economy to capital flows.*
>
> Consider the following counterfactual history. In the late 1990s, when China's economic miracle was becoming evident, it could easily have succumbed to the prevailing orthodoxy on financial globalization. *Had it done so, the likely outcome would have been a surge in foreign capital chasing high Chinese returns, rapid appreciation of the renminbi, slower export growth, and lost dynamism.* China's export machine would not have become the juggernaut that it is, and its economy may well have suffered through much more volatility as a result of the fickleness of foreign capital. *In fact, Argentina – with its periodic macroeconomic volatility and recurring financial crises – offers a perfect illustration of these downsides.*
>
> *Nearly every major emerging-market financial crisis of the past few decades has been preceded or accompanied by surges in capital inflows. That was true of Latin America in the 1980s, India in 1991, Mexico in 1994, and East Asia and Russia in the late 1990s. It was also true of Brazil, Turkey, and Argentina in the early 2000s; the Baltics, Iceland, Greece, and Spain in the late 2000s and early 2010s; and the "Fragile Five" emerging-market economies (Brazil, India, Indonesia, South Africa, and Turkey) in 2013. And it is true of Argentina today.*
>
> To be sure, capital flows have often reflected deeper policy problems or imbalances within a given emerging market. But they are also usually the necessary transmission mechanism for crises, and thus have magnified the eventual costs to those economies. *Although most tenets of the neoliberal consensus – privatization, deregulation, trade integration, immigration, fiscal discipline, and the primacy of growth over distribution – are now being challenged or outright rejected, financial globalization remains a glaring exception.*[67]   [Emphases mine]

The authors are concerned that China has now chosen to embrace the neoliberal orthodoxy of financial globalization, with the implied criticism that this decision will create further avoidable instability and economic uncertainty in the world's second largest economy.

Currently there are no clear answers to these questions: about trade between the largest (US) and second largest (China) economies in the world;[vi] about the relationship between the sixth largest (UK) economy in the world and the world's largest market (EU);[vii] about the economic direction of the US after 2020; and about the economic health of the world's leading manufacturer;[viii] and whether China is wise to embrace financial globalization.

This lack of clarity increases the level of economic uncertainty dramatically both for the countries themselves and for the global economy, as the wrong policy choices could perpetuate a depression and potentially the next financial crisis;[68] in turn increasing the levels of economic uncertainty in every economy. Every board should therefore consider the need for at least a "Plan B," and maybe for a "Plan C" for the third decade of the 21st century. What is certain is that boards will be unable to assume "business as usual" for the entire decade.

3. **Social Uncertainty:** Three factors are major contributors to social uncertainty: changing values; changing demographics; and social media.

   a. *Changing values:* I believe how people behave toward each other; what they do with their education and disposable income; their attitudes about work and retirement, and about working for a single employer are in large part determined by the values they inherit from role models and that they modify them – based on their experiences of life and the economic opportunities they see before them. After the GFC, governments could have adopted Keynesian solutions to solve the problem – i.e. invested in demand through "shovel-ready" programs to improve dilapidated infrastructure across the US, UK and EU. Instead the neoliberal economists and the GOP forced governments to only apply monetary policy solutions which healed banks, bankers and the owners of existing assets rather than creating new productive ones. As a result, electorates in the US and UK felt there was one set of rules and consequences for bankers and another for the rest, as profits were privatized and losses socialized:[69]

---

vi US and China.
vii UK and EU.
viii China.

Privatizing profits and socializing losses refers to the practice of treating company earnings as the rightful property of shareholders, while losses are treated as a responsibility that society must shoulder. In other words, the profitability of corporations are [sic] strictly for the benefit of their shareholders. But when the companies fail, the fallout – the losses and recovery – are the responsibility of the general public. Popular examples of this include taxpayer-funded subsidies or bailouts.[70]   [Emphasis mine]

This destroyed trust in political institutions, business, the media. and experts in general with just four countries rated as trustful (China, Indonesia, India, and the UAE, in that order), four countries rated as neutral (Singapore, Mexico, Netherlands, and Malaysia, in that order), and twenty out of the twenty-eight surveyed as distrustful.[71] The arrival of post-truth politics and the dissemination of "fake news" has only made matters worse, with electorates unconcerned with the truth, preferring to believe what they read in their social media echo chambers; believing all politicians to be liars and experts as people to be ignored.[72] There is little evidence of increased trust in democratic institutions. If the UK's experience in the last three years is anything to go by, the reverse may sadly be true.[73]

The austerity programs chosen led to the impoverishment of many in the Eurozone with unemployment averaging 12% and more than 50% youth unemployment in the EU periphery.[74] Austerity also caused hysteresis:[ix]

The problem, notes Nouriel Roubini of New York University, is that "*if workers remain unemployed for too long, they lose their skills and human capital.*" And this erosion of the skills base can lead to "hysteresis," such that "a persistent cyclical downturn or weak recovery (like the one we have experienced since 2008) can reduce potential growth."

  Hysteresis . . . can also result from a large-scale switch to inferior employment. Flexible labor markets in the U.S. and the United Kingdom have enabled both economies to return to pre-crisis unemployment levels (in the range of 4–5%). But the official unemployment rate excludes millions of workers who are involuntarily employed part-time, as well as others doing what the anthropologist David Graeber has described as "*bullshit jobs.*"[75]   [Emphases mine]

---

ix "Hysteresis in the field of economics refers to an event in the economy that persists into the future, even after the factors that led to that event have been removed. Hysteresis can occur following a recession when the unemployment rate continues to increase despite growth in the economy." *Investopedia.*

The privatization of profits and socialization of losses and the austerity programs that followed as a result, destroying trust in institutions, and the economic hysteresis combined, have weakened the neoliberal consensus to the point where it is being challenged globally.

b. ***Changing demographics:*** Demographics determine demand for products and services. Boards therefore must understand the threats and opportunities presented by any change in demographics: their share of the market, whether they have more or less disposable income than previously, whether changes in education and lifestyle affect their demand for products and services and their willingness to work for the organization. In terms of changed demographics threatening increased uncertainty through their effect on politics and therefore on the economy, there are two major trends boards must come to terms with:

i. *The arrival of the young-old:* Known in Japan as the "yold,"[x] increases the problems posed for the young and middle-aged by robotics and AI, discussed in Chapter 5. The Baby Boomer yold – over the age of 65 – should be starting to retire, except they are not. They are more numerous, and healthier than in previous generations.[76] They will represent 11% of the population of rich countries in 2020, up from 8% in 2000. Of the 3.7 extra years of life expectancy between 2000 and 2020, 3.2 years were enjoyed in good health according to the World Health Organization.[77] They now have slower cognitive decline as a result and have the cognitive capacity of someone who is a year and a half younger, according to a German study.[78]

The yold will increase business for airlines and tourism and will spend much more on vacations than younger adults, once the world recovers from the impacts of Covid-19. They represent a new market for adult education. They are also transforming insurance companies from passive distributors of fixed annuities to financial advisers to people who want to manage their pensions.[79]

Surprisingly, research in Germany suggests that the yold are more productive than average and that when they work in teams of mixed ages, the teams' productivity increases – perhaps the result of a blend of the wisdom of age with the energy of youth? While this appears to be good news, making societies better off because of less

---

x "The year 2020 will mark the beginning of the decade of the yold, or the 'young old,' as the Japanese call people aged between 65 and 75." Parker, J. (2019), "The decade of the 'young old' begins," *The World in 2020*, https://worldin.economist.com/article/17316/edition2020decade-young-old-begins, accessed on December 2, 2019.

spending needed on pensions and health care,[80] it may well create a problem for the middle-aged who hope to move into jobs previously held by the yold; making it harder for the young to progress up a satisfying career ladder.

ii. *The rise of the Millennials and Gen Z:* This generation appears to have different values and behaviors from Gen X and Baby Boomers. They expect businesses to have a social purpose ahead of being profitable.[81] They go out less to socialize, using their mobile phones instead and drink less as a result.[82] They are less interested in acquiring and in paying the premiums for luxury.[83] They do not prioritize owning a car and drive less than previous generations, yet they like cars, so it is not clear what impact they will have on the future of the car market:

> Experts and studies repeat the same mantra over and again: young people have fallen out of love with cars. . . they'd much rather pay a little for using vehicles than pay a lot for buying them; and for environmental reasons would like to avoid them altogether.
>
> That's the thinking that underpins predictions of an imminent paradigm shift, towards a future dominated by both shared mobility (car-sharing, car-pooling, ride-hailing) and multimodal mobility (combining car usage with public transport, walking, cycling and other modes of transportation).
>
> The big loser in this model: car ownership. *But, as two recent surveys strongly indicate, the millennials that are supposed to be turning away from car ownership actually like the concept.*
>
> Financial constraints are why millennials are more likely to drive sedans than the average consumer, who increasingly goes for crossover SUVs. The top three millennial vehicles are: the Honda Accord, Nissan Altima and Honda Civic.
>
> *While it's true that millennials [prioritize] 'experience over possessions' (i.e. car usage over car ownership), the evidence is that there is no real aversion towards car ownership – downsizing or postponing car ownership is just an easy way to cut cost.* Especially since corporate benefits increasingly include free public transport as a mobility option.[84]   [Emphases mine]

These generations care deeply about the environment,[85] and encouraged by Greta Thunberg they are taking to the streets to protest the lack of action by governments.[86] Increasingly, they change what they buy[xi] with reference to its impact on climate change.[87] After all, they are the generation that will have to literally live with any failure to meet the Paris climate change targets.

---

xi Seventy-five percent of millennials surveyed changed what they eat because of climate change.

c. ***Social media:*** This is a new phenomenon, made possible by the combined inventions of the World Wide Web, released to the public in 1991, and the iPhone which was launched by Apple in 1997.[xii] This has revolutionized how and what we communicate and with whom.

Social media is driven by algorithms designed to maximize the user's engagement and interest. As early as 2011, *The Atlantic* was concerned that the internet might be more suited for the propagation of lies than the truth:

> We continue to believe that the truth will out and the facts will save us. We will have better information and make better decisions, elect better leaders, have better government, be better off. That's a pretty hopeful picture but not one that's in line with how humans – or the world – work. *When you take Mercier and Sperber's theory to heart you understand that narratives, ideas, and ideologies are what fuel the world, not facts.*[88] [Emphasis mine]

By 2016, the concerns about the ability of social media to mislead us were sufficiently serious for the *New Scientist* to quote the following:

> "There's something happening here that's really unprecedented," says Robert Epstein, a psychologist at the American Institute for Behavioral Research and Technology in Vista, California. *"Technologies are rapidly evolving that can impact people's behaviours, opinions, attitudes, beliefs on a massive scale – without their awareness."*[89] [Emphasis mine]

That was before Kellyanne Conway's famous phrase "alternative facts" legitimized post-truth telling of events by politicians to divert attention:

> *The use of the lie in politics is mutating.* Once politicians made questionable claims in the hope that the deceit would pass unchallenged. These days, one of the weapons of political warfare is to make a false claim in the full expectation that it will be rebutted, and the outrage about the lie will crowd out other stories.[90] [Emphasis mine]

Alternative facts compete with the truth to the point where it is often difficult to know what is fact, what is true, and what is fake. Mark Zuckerberg recognizes the problem for Facebook, but unlike Jack Dorsey who had stopped all political ads on Twitter, he defends political advertisements on Facebook that are lies as being an integral part of free

---

[xii] In the US, Google was launched in 1998; Facebook in 2004; YouTube in 2005; Twitter in 2006; Instagram in 2010. In China, TenCent was launched in 1998; Baidu in 2000; Weibo in 2009; WeChat in 2011.

speech and that it is not the role of private companies to censor politicians or the news.[91] This defense ignores the ethnic cleansing caused by fake news on Facebook propagated by Buddhist extremists and the Myanmar military,[92] leading to nearly 700,000 Rohingya fleeing for their lives to Bangladesh since August 2017.[93]

As long as social media is driven by algorithms that play to humanity's basest instincts, and as long as platform owners, like Facebook, refuse to be responsible for the veracity of what is posted on their sites, social media will continue to be source of social uncertainty and harm that boards will have to reckon with.

4. **Technological Uncertainty:**

Technological uncertainty arises in two ways. The first is disruptive technology where boards must consider whether what is being proposed either by the competition or by the organization's own R&D department has the capacity to render the organization and its business model obsolete. The second is more operational in nature, where boards only need to concern themselves with answering three questions "Will what is being proposed work or not?" "How far have we pushed the technology envelope?" and "What is preventing us from doing it?"

a. *Disruptive Technological Uncertainty:* Disruptive technologies do not just improve performance to win the game; they change the game. The threat they pose to organizations and their business models is existential. Failure by boards to understand their impact is a dereliction of duty, not just to shareholders, but also to customers, employees, communities, and to governments who, as stakeholders, have a vested interest in the continued existence of the organization.

Disruptive technologies require boards to scan the environment for potential unrecognized threats to their organizations. Failure to do so will leave them blindsided should a new technology materialize (unknown unknown), perhaps marketed by non-traditional competitors. Once they have identified a potentially threatening innovation, boards need to understand how these identified innovations by potential competitors could affect their customers (known unknown) and on their business models (unknown known), as well as their likely rate of adoption (unknown unknown). Only once the new approaches have been thoroughly tested and successfully marketed by competitors and the resulting disruption is there for all to see (known known), can boards respond, by which time it may be too late.

Established companies therefore have much to fear from upstart disrupters, who threaten their dominance by introducing new products, based in part on having a different business model. They should in theory be prepared to change their business models before the upstarts do it to them, as Jack Welch, one-time CEO of GE put it:

> If the rate of change on the outside exceeds the rate of change on the inside, the end is near.[94]

Yet incumbents find it very difficult to follow this advice. Effective evolution even in companies with a track record of past success in innovation is often blocked by the "Innovator's Dilemma."[95] Internal vested interests will fight such changes when it is not immediately obvious that change is required. And when it becomes obvious that change is required, it may be too late to do anything about it, as examples like Xerox's, Nokia's, or Sony's falls from grace make clear:

> *The problem is they fail to value new innovations properly because incumbents attempt to apply them to their existing customers and product architectures – or value networks.* Often new technologies are too new and weak for the more advanced and mature value networks that incumbents operate.
> *This leads to the ROI needed to advance the innovation to be seen as low.* In other words, management acts sensibly in rejecting the continued investment in these new technologies and act in the company's best fiduciary interests. *Moving into new markets is rejected as they are seen as too small to make a dent for them and their cost structure prohibitive to enter at sensible margins. . .*
> . . .Initially these small upstarts don't pose a threat – the new entrants find new markets to apply these technologies largely by trial and error, at low margins. *Their nimbleness and [low-cost] structures allow them to operate sustainably where incumbents could not.*
> However, the error in valuing these technologies comes from what happens next. By finding the right application use and market, the upstarts advance rapidly and hit the steep part of the classic "S" curve, eventually entering the more mature markets of the incumbents and disrupting them.
> *In essence, the smaller markets are the guinea-pigs and test labs that help the technologies advance enough to play in the big boys' league. In many cases the entry-point markets are left behind as the new technologies move into higher margin up-market territory disrupting due to their superior performance.*[96]   [Emphases mine]

The key difference in the behavior of upstarts is their willingness to tolerate levels of uncertainty that incumbents are not at each stage in the decision-making process.

There are, however, two conditions where delaying adopting disruptive technologies developed by competitors makes sense:

i.   *When the technology is "bleeding edge";* where unknown unknowns affect the safety of the offer. In these circumstances, it is often better to be second to market rather than first. The deHavilland Comet was the first passenger jet plane. In almost every way, it set the technical standards for jet performance for sixty years, right up until the Boeing 787 Dreamliner's launch in 2009.[97] Its test flight was in 1949; its first commercial flight was on May 2, 1952. The Comet 1 flew until 1954. It was twice as fast as piston-engine rivals, loved by passengers and airlines with an 89% load factor. In 1954, however, two Comets crashed; caused by metal fatigue as a result of the way the hull skin was riveted on the roof of the plane under a plate which was painted over. It was impossible to spot the crack's growth in time before it caused the hull to fail and the plane to break up on its 1,290th flight.

Neither the designers of the Comet nor the industry really knew enough about metal fatigue thresholds in an aluminum skin or how it happened before the tests undertaken by the Royal Aircraft Establishment's safety experts determined why the two Comets were brought down. DeHavilland was found to be operating "beyond the limits of knowledge" – operating in the world of unknown unknowns.

As a result of the delays, even though the Comet 4 was the first jet to fly across the Atlantic in early October 1958 for BOAC [British Overseas Airways Corporation], just weeks ahead of Pan Am's inaugural Boeing 707 transatlantic flight, the four lost years allowed Boeing to develop a bigger capacity jet and take the market created by the Comet from deHavilland.[98]

ii. *When rates of adoption take much longer than expected:* Advocates of generic disruptive technologies sometimes expect them to be implemented earlier than is practical. This may be the result of teething problems causing the new technology to underperform in its introductory phase or of it being too expensive initially. It may be the result of path dependency where the initial technological, capital, or skills "infrastructure" is lacking. It may be the result of effective pushback by vested interests. For example, it took eight years before PCs posed an existential threat to minis and mainframe computers – time enough for IBM to join in and make it happen.[xiii]

---

xiii Xerox introduced the Alto in 1973. Only 2,000 were made. IBM introduced the IBM PC using Intel's 8088 chip and Microsoft's MS-DOS in 1981 and created the mass market for personal computers and the so-called Wintel monopoly that lasted until 2012.

It took online retailing 15 years to become the threat it is today to brick-and-mortar retailers.[xiv] The same applies to electric and driverless vehicles. Promoters of electric and driverless vehicles are realizing it will take longer for them to replace the internal combustion engine and drivers than they originally believed; giving traditional car manufacturers time to get their act together.[99]

b. ***Operational Technological Uncertainty:*** When faced with operational technological uncertainty, boards need answers to the questions: "Will what is being proposed work or not?" "How far have we pushed the technology envelope?" and "What is preventing us from doing it?" From a board perspective, I believe it is the last two questions that matter most. Whether what is being proposed will work can be established relatively easily, whereas understanding whether the technology envelope has been pushed beyond its limits can only be answered when there is a design failure. Even if this proves not to be a problem, often innovations fail to meet their objectives because of the lack of the appropriate internal processes to nurture successful outcomes:

  i. *Pushing the technology envelope beyond its known limits:* Take, for example, BP and the Deepwater Horizon disaster. For a long time, BP had been very successful in pushing the exploration envelope, working with its subcontractors even though the risks of disaster were growing. Their success encouraged their crews to ignore the fact they were getting closer to disaster, as were the Transocean crew [the drilling contractor], also involved in the dubious decision making. The federal regulators who supervised drilling in the Gulf of Mexico signed off on their plans at every stage because they believed BP's track record. The essential errors leading to the disaster were BP's focus on speed and cost, combined with the belief they were not pushing the envelope too far and fast because each incremental step had worked, anesthetizing them to the fear of cumulatively small errors leading to catastrophic failure through a process called the 'normalization of deviance,' experienced by NASA in the *Challenger* disaster:[100]

---

xiv Amazon was launched on July 5, 1994. Online sales overtook general merchandise brick-and-mortar retailing in the US on April 2, 2019. Rooney, K. (2019), "Online shopping overtakes a major part of retail for the first time ever," *CNBC,* April 2, 2019, https://www.cnbc.com/2019/04/02/online-shopping-officially-overtakes-brick-and-mortar-retail-for-the-first-time-ever.html, accessed on December 4, 2019.

> Vaughan and other researchers argue that *most high-risk industries are prone to normalizing deviance.* We've all seen this, even in businesses that don't involve life-and-death decisions: *Managers focus on positive data about their operations and tune out small signs of trouble, safety margins get shaved in the name of efficiency, and small deviations from procedural rules are tolerated.* But disaster researchers have also developed strategies to help counteract the tendency: tools to help managers be more aware of "weak signals" hinting at trouble, for example, and policies that empower whistleblowers.[101]
>
> [Emphasis mine]

Just as in banking there are financial crises every ten years or so, caused by a failure of institutional memory of what could go wrong, the same applies in civil engineering, but every thirty years.[102] For example, when engineers develop new approaches to bridge-building they push the frontiers of their understanding to create more aesthetically satisfying bridges, or bridges with longer spans to cross wider rivers. When the first such innovative bridge is built, the designers are careful to document all their assumptions about how the design is supposed to work, erring heavily on the side of caution. Once the new structural approach has proved successful, the next generation of designers push the envelope gradually, lengthening the spans or making new trade-offs to increase the beauty of the structure. However, at some point, they run the risk of taking their success in improving upon the original innovation one step too far – literally building a bridge too far, at which point, the bridge collapses, sometimes with fatalities:

> The accidents happened not because the engineer neglected to provide sufficient strength as prescribed by the accepted design approach, but because of the unwitting introduction of a new type of behaviour. *As time passed during the period of development, the bases of the design methods were forgotten and so were their limits of validity. Following a period of successful construction a designer, perhaps a little complacent, simply extended the design method once too often.*[103]
>
> [Emphasis mine]

Given this tendency to push the design envelope to the point of failure, justified by a track record of previous success, boards must be certain that past success, far from justifying continued moves towards the limits of the technology, are not, in fact, a recipe for imminent failure.

ii. *Lacking internal processes to ensure success:* Once boards are certain that the technology envelope is not going to be torn, they need be sure internal processes are in place that are not going to block progress toward desired outcomes. This requires being sure that the right ideas are being selected for further investment. Surprisingly, most organizations have too many creative ideas to choose from rather than too few when it comes to new product ideas:

> Innovation *is* inherently risky, to be sure, and getting the most from a portfolio of innovation initiatives is more about managing risk than eliminating it. Since no one knows exactly where valuable innovations will emerge, and searching everywhere is impractical, *executives must create some boundary conditions for the opportunity spaces they want to explore.* . . Thoughtfully prioritizing these spaces also allows companies to assess whether they have enough investment behind their most valuable opportunities.[104]
>
> [Emphasis mine]

Typically, organizations fail to select well in one of three ways. They play it safe to minimize uncertainty, filling their product development pipelines with relatively riskless projects, which by their nature will not do more than yield incremental improvements. As a result of technological uncertainty, they spread their resources too thinly, instead of concentrating on those projects with the best returns. They fail to allocate/reallocate sufficient resources each year because of uncertainty, with the resulting stagnation in innovation and its adverse impact on growth compared with companies that actively reallocate resources.

Boards need to be certain their organizations have a disciplined iterative process, involving the interaction of changes in technology and partnerships with customers to define what people are lacking or what customers do not like about either product performance or processes for doing business with the organization. This requires the active use of prototypes to test and validate improvement hypotheses, whether for products or processes in order to reduce operational technological uncertainty. The problem is made worse by the fact that most well-established companies have lost their founder-innovators and are left with time-servers focusing on achieving transactional efficiency rather than transformational effectiveness.

Another way to reduce operational technological uncertainty is to work with outside parties to develop proof of concept ideas, prototype them jointly and develop trials to test whether they work as expected.[105] To reduce technological uncertainty, an increasingly important type of synergy takes place when manufacturers agree with their customers that what they need are the services provided by the products they offer; rather than selling them as much product as possible.[106]

5. **Legal Uncertainty:** Legal uncertainty will only be important for boards in a limited number of circumstances, given that legal certainty is a:

> Foundational rule of law value. It is the idea that the law must be sufficiently clear to provide those subject to legal norms with the means to regulate their own conduct and to protect against the arbitrary exercise of public power – has operated as a foundational rule of law value. As such, legal certainty has played a vital role in determining the space of individual freedom and the scope of state power. In this way, the ideal of legal certainty has been central in stabilizing normative expectations and in providing a framework for social interaction, as well as defining individual freedom and political power in modern societies.[107]

For legal certainty to exist, five conditions must apply: (1) laws and decisions must be made public; (2) laws and decisions must be definite and clear; (3) the decisions of the courts must be regarded as binding; (4) the retroactivity of the laws and decisions must be limited; and (5) legitimate interests and expectations must be protected.[108]

Boards must therefore consider carefully whether they should do business with or have subsidiaries in jurisdictions where these five preconditions for legal certainty do not exist. The short-term benefits of privileged access could well be outweighed by the long-term economic costs and reputation damage[xv] of having been involved in such jurisdictions. Furthermore, such involvement could undermine organizational values, infecting employee behavior with malpractices, weakening good governance and leaving the board open to charges of hypocrisy and double standards.

In addition, boards may need to consider what to do when they are caught in a jurisdictional crossfire or when changes in social expectations of responsible behavior lead to unforeseen litigation:

1. *Caught in jurisdictional crossfire:* What exactly are boards supposed to do if the laws in the country where they are based conflict with laws in countries where their subsidiaries operate? Which laws are they

---

xv Unforeseen economic costs could be caused by arbitrary arrest of key personnel, expropriation of assets, unilateral increases in licensing fees or in the cost of necessary resources supplied by the government or its favored cronies, mandated changes in share ownership or partners with whom work must be done, or politically motivated application of retroactive legislation. Reputation damage could be caused by any of these *and* by scandals involving environmental degradation, human rights abuses, poor safety and working conditions, bribery, corruption, civil war, and ethnic cleansing.

supposed to obey? Take, for example, the problems faced by British and American multinationals operating in Apartheid South Africa. The law in the UK and US forbade them as companies headquartered in the UK and US to discriminate on grounds of race and religion. However, the Apartheid regime in South Africa made it illegal to operate companies unless the extreme racial discrimination was followed. Failure to follow the Apartheid laws would lead to the closure of operations. American investment in South Africa by 1977 was considerable: 312 companies operated there doing US$1.7 billion a year of business with an average profit of 12% – twice the rate they achieved in the US, because of the low cost of black South African labor. Political pressure in the US became so great that by 1986, American multinationals chose to leave South Africa, depriving black South Africans of good jobs, weakening the economy, and hurting the majority black population as a result.[xvi] The leading British multinationals chose to remain and break the South African government's laws, defending their decisions on the grounds that engagement rather than divestment could lead to a better outcome in the long term for black South Africans. Given the departure of the American multinationals, the South African government was less likely to shut down or expel the remaining British companies as this would do too much damage to the economy. Clearly there were benefits for black South Africans who worked for the British multinationals and maybe the engagement by the British companies helped persuade the South African regime to change. However, Steve Biko,[xvii] before his assassination, was quite clear that black South Africans were prepared to suffer the consequences of divestment:

> If Washington is really interested in contributing to the development of a just society in South Africa, it would discourage investment in South Africa. We Blacks are perfectly willing to suffer the consequences! We are quite accustomed to suffering.[109]

---

xvi "In 1986, after years of pressure, Congress responded. They overrode President Reagan's veto to pass the US Comprehensive Anti-Apartheid Act. Banks stopped making loans to South Africa. Other corporations withdrew from the country. Capital – money to be used for investment in new ventures in South Africa – pulled out or dried up." Brown, B. (2013), "The U.S. Responds to Apartheid: Polaroid," *Boston University, African Studies Center,* https://www.bu.edu/africa/files/2013/10/The-US-Responds-to-Apartheid.pdf, accessed on December 6, 2019.
xvii Steve Biko (1946–1977) was a South African anti-apartheid activist. Ideologically an African nationalist and African socialist, he was at the forefront of a grassroots anti-apartheid campaign known as the Black Consciousness Movement during the late 1960s and 1970s. *Wikipedia.*

When interviewed after the end of Apartheid, Archbishop Desmond Tutu also thought divestment was the correct decision:

> In South Africa, we could not have achieved our freedom and just peace without the help of people around the world, who through the use of non-violent means, such as boycotts and divestment, encouraged their governments and other corporate actors to reverse decades-long support for the Apartheid regime.[110]

Sanctions or trade wars with their tariffs also cause legal and regulatory uncertainty. Companies in the UK and EU face serious regulatory uncertainty as a result of Brexit, with nobody knowing whether the UK will leave the EU on WTO terms at the end of 2020 or not. During 2019, British companies had to stockpile products and medicines before the original March 31st deadline and again before the new October 31st deadline for the UK's departure from the EU single market.[111] The legal/regulatory implications of unwinding more than forty years of legislation will take years to sort out, creating more legal uncertainty that boards will have to face when deciding on the viability of their business models.

2. **Unforeseen litigation:** The law reflects what society is thinking – and that changes over time. For example, in the 1950s people thought smoking was cool and good for the nerves, even though the tobacco companies already knew it was harmful. For many years, the companies got away with denying the harmfulness of tobacco, until a class action brought by 46 US states Attorneys General led to a historic settlement of US$206 billion in 1998.[112] Something similar is happening over opioids and affected boards need to decide whether they should settle like Johnson & Johnson[113] and Purdue Pharma[114] or fight. Exxon Mobil faces a class action in Washington D.C. over the impact of fossil fuel usage on climate change on the basis that their climate change advertising misled consumers.[115] That Exxon knew about the impact of fossil fuels on global warming is clear from an internal report from its Imperial Oil subsidiary:

> "There is no doubt that increases in fossil fuel usage and decreases in forest cover are aggravating the potential problem of increased CO_2 in the atmosphere." Excerpt from a 1980 Imperial Oil internal report. The Exxon subsidiary concluded as far back as 1981 that *curbing global warming would require a high carbon tax.*[116]

What makes the harm done by funding climate change denial for so long so serious is that more than half of all the industrial CO_2 ever emitted had already been emitted between 1988 and 2014.[117] The legal uncertainty faced by the oil companies now as a result of this case is serious, given their share of all industrial global greenhouse gas emissions since 1965:[xviii]

> *In November 1965,* the president, Lyndon Johnson, released a report authored by the Environmental Pollution Panel of the President's Science Advisory Committee, which set out the likely impact of continued fossil fuel production on global heating.
>
> *In the same year,* the president of the American Petroleum Institute told its annual gathering: "One of the most important predictions of the [president's report] is that carbon dioxide is being added to the Earth's atmosphere by the burning of coal, oil and natural gas *at such a rate by the year 2000 the heat balance will be so modified as possibly to cause marked changes in climate beyond local or even national efforts.*"[118]   [Emphases mine]

6. **Environmental Uncertainty:** The scientific community seems certain that global warming is taking place and that it is taking place faster than expected:

> The world's average temperature is rising faster than previously thought, headed for a gain that may be triple the goal set by almost 200 countries.
>
> The findings by the World Meteorological Organization suggest an increase of 3 degrees to 5 degrees Celsius (5.4 to 9 degrees Fahrenheit) by the end of the century. It's another indication of how far off track the planet is in meeting its target to contain global warming to 1.5 degrees Celsius since the dawn of the industrial revolution.[119]

This does not, however, remove the uncertainty surrounding whether current extreme events are caused by global warming, such as the out of control wild

---

xviii "The top 20 companies on the list have contributed to 35% of all energy-related carbon dioxide and methane worldwide, totalling 480bn tonnes of carbon dioxide equivalent ($GtCO_2e$) since 1965.

Those identified range from investor-owned firms – household names such as Chevron, Exxon, BP and Shell – to state-owned companies including Saudi Aramco and Gazprom.

Chevron topped the list of the eight investor-owned corporations, followed closely by Exxon, BP and Shell. Together these four global businesses are behind more than 10% of the world's carbon emissions since 1965.

Twelve of the top 20 companies are state-owned and together their extractions are responsible for 20% of total emissions in the same period. The leading state-owned polluter is Saudi Aramco, which has produced 4.38% of the global total on its own."

Taylor, M. and Watts, J. (2019), "Revealed: the 20 firms behind a third of all carbon emissions," *The Guardian,* October 9, 2019, https://www.theguardian.com/environment/2019/oct/09/revealed-20-firms-third-carbon-emissions, accessed on December 7, 2019.

fires in California[120] and Australia[121] or the severe drought in Zimbabwe making the mighty Victoria Falls a disappointing trickle,[122] though it does increasingly seem to be the case. Nor does it provide any certainty about where the next extreme event will occur or how serious it will be. What is certain, however, is that the costs of insuring against such events are rising according to Munich Re [a global provider of reinsurance].[123]

Professor Schellnhuber's equation[xix] to show whether "reaction time is longer than intervention time left" – in which case "we have lost control" over climate change – unfortunately does not reduce uncertainty because there are apparently nine tipping points we must not cross if we are to remain in control; and we have already crossed five of them.[124]

Summary

The challenges to environmental, economic and employment sustainability have increased the levels of volatility, uncertainty and complexity faced by boards as we enter the third decade of the 21st century. These have been made worse by social media and post-truth politics where facts no longer seem to matter.

Volatility in the third decade of the century is likely to be greater than in the first two because of the breakdown of political assumptions about the desirability of globalization and the sustainability of the neoliberal economic order dominant since 1989. Businesses and countries may be forced to choose, however reluctantly, between the US and Chinese spheres of influence. European politics are in disarray as a result of Brexit and the rise of the Greens on the left and the nativist parties on the right, weakening the traditional center-left-right coalitions. The Middle East remains highly unstable. Asia has its own political problems. A revanchist Russia is working hard to destabilize democracies everywhere and is pushing the frontiers of asymmetrical warfare. Increased economic volatility is the result of the uncertainty created by Brexit and the US-China trade war and unanswered questions on where they both will lead.

Social volatility caused by austerity and immigration has added to economic volatility and has been heightened by the divisive nature of social media and populist policies. Technical and legal volatility remain relatively low given the long gestation periods of technical and legal/regulatory change. Although the

---

xix Emergency = R × U = p × D × τ / T, where R = Risk, U = Urgency, p = probability of an event occurring, D = Damage; and τ = reaction time to prevent an event from happening.

environment, including issues such as the coronavirus, remains long-term the world's biggest challenge and therefore should not affect volatility, extreme weather events by their very nature affect businesses in ways they cannot foresee.

Uncertainty poses the biggest headaches for boards. It comes in many shapes and sizes. Political worldwide uncertainty is at its greatest since before World War II, as a result of the increasing geopolitical strategic issues separating the US from its allies and from Russia and China. US, European, and Asian politics all feature uncertain outcomes which will make significant differences to the economic environment in which companies operate. From an economic perspective, the trade war between the US and China, the US election in 2020, Brexit, and the sustainability of China's economic progress all suggest that the next five years will see levels of economic uncertainty not experienced since the 1930s. The resulting lack of clarity, made worse by the Covid-19 pandemic and its impact increases the level of economic uncertainty both for the countries themselves and for the global economy, as the wrong policy choices could perpetuate a depression and potentially the next financial crisis; which could, in turn, increase levels of economic uncertainty in *every* economy.

What *is* certain is that boards will not be able to assume "business as usual" for the entire decade. Social uncertainty is another reason why "business as usual" assumptions are unwise. As a result of austerity and the resulting inequality, values have changed. There is no longer the same confidence in the neoliberal economic model; distrust of politicians and experts is greater than ever, amplified by social media and populist politicians peddling "alternative facts." Changing demographics have also had a role to play.

The impact of three megatrends will have to be considered by boards: the resulting rejection of global values and institutions to help solve global problems; the rise of the "yold" – people over the age of 65 who want to or need to continue working. This will create new market opportunities, but it will also make the impact of "Industry 4.0" harder to manage, especially for the young who need jobs. Moreover, the millennials and Gen Z have different attitudes toward work and working for companies that do not put social purpose at the heart of what they do. Finally, the rise of social media makes dealing with these changes much harder.

Technological uncertainty is not new. Disruption matters greatly, but disruptive technologies take time to mature to the point where they overthrow incumbent market leaders. Boards must therefore be acutely aware of the possibilities that a disrupter may come and destroy their business models. Boards need to make sure they are not requiring excessive returns for adoption of new ideas that are being explored by others before rejecting them. The reason Xerox failed to commercialize so many of its ideas from PARC was because the board wanted the same returns as they were getting from copiers. By ignoring these opportunities they gave the up-starts time to get their acts together and change the game at the incumbents' cost. As far as operational technology uncertainty is concerned, the key question boards must ask is whether the technology has moved from "pushing the envelope," based on previous successes, to "tearing the envelope," because the underlying assumptions have in some way become invalid without anyone realizing it.

Legal uncertainty only matters in a limited number of situations: jurisdictional crossfire where the organization finds itself having to reconcile irreconcilable laws, forcing it to decide whether to divest or not enter that market or to break the law in one of the jurisdictions. It also matters when unexpected class actions based on historic behavior comes to light that causes known harm that could have been avoided – as with tobacco, opioids, and climate change.

References

1 Cribb, J. (2019), "Countries from Siberia to Australia are burning: the age of fire is the bleakest warning yet," *The Guardian,* November 29, 2019, https://www.theguardian.com/commentis free/2019/nov/29/countries-from-siberia-to-australia-are-burning-the-age-of-fire-is-the-bleak est-warning-yet, accessed on November 30, 2019.
2 Brooks, R. (2018), "Never Retire: Why People are Still Working in Their 70s and 80s," *U.S. News & World Report,* August 3, 2018, https://money.usnews.com/money/retirement/baby-boomers/articles/2018-08-03/never-retire-why-people-are-still-working-in-their-70s-and-80s, accessed on December 1, 2019; Hill, A. (2019) "Number of over-70s still in work more than doubles in a decade," *The Guardian,* May 27, 2019, https://www.theguardian.com/money/2019/may/27/number-of-over-70s-still-in-work-more-than-doubles-in-a-decade, accessed on December 1, 2019.
3 Clarke, L. (2019) "Raising the retirement age to 75 won't fix the UK's pension problem," *Wired,* August 23, 2019, https://www.wired.co.uk/article/pension-age-state-raise-uk, accessed on December 1, 2019; Tass (2019), "Law on raising retirement age in Russia comes into effect on January 1, 2019," *Tass,* January 1, 2019, https://tass.com/society/1038728, accessed on December 1, 2019.
4 Business Roundtable (2019), "Business Roundtable Redefines the Purpose of a Corporation to 'Promote an Economy that Serves all Americans'," *Corporate Governance,* August 19, 2019, https://www.businessroundtable.org/business-roundtable-redefines-the-purpose-of-a-corpora tion-to-promote-an-economy-that-serves-all-americans, accessed on November 24, 2019.
5 Cohen, S. B. (2019), "The Greatest Propaganda Machine In History" speech at the Anti-Defamation League's "Never is Now" Summit on November 22, 2019; Obama, B. H. (2019), speech at Salesforce's Dreamforce conference in San Francisco on November 21, 2019 quoted in Chuck, E. (2019), "Greatest Propaganda Machine in History: Sacha Baron Cohen slams Facebook, other social media companies," *NBC News,* November 22, 2019, https://www.nbcnews.com/tech/social-media/greatest-propaganda-machine-history-sacha-baron-cohen-slams-facebook-other-n1089471, accessed on November 25, 2019.

6 Cambridge Dictionary, https://dictionary.cambridge.org/dictionary/english/volatility, accessed on November 26, 2019.

7 Roubini, N. (2019), "The Global Consequences of a Sino-American Cold War," *Project Syndicate*, May 20, 2019, https://www.project-syndicate.org/commentary/united-states-china-cold-war-de globalization-by-nouriel-roubini-2019-05?barrier=accesspaylog, accessed on November 25, 2019.

8 Wolff-Mann, E. (2017), "62 businesses Trump has targeted on Twitter," *Yahoo Finance*, February 9, 2017, https://finance.yahoo.com/news/61-businesses-trump-has-attacked-on-twit ter-181623705.html, accessed on November 26, 2019.

9 Inman, P. (2019), "U.K. companies hit by sharpest activity drop since Brexit vote," *Guardian*, November 22, 2019, https://www.theguardian.com/business/2019/nov/22/uk-service-sec tor-suffers-sharpest-drop-since-brexit-vote?utm_term=RWRpdG9yaWFsX0J1c2luZ, accessed on November 26, 2019.

10 Caldwell, C. (2019), "The People's Emergency," *The New Republic*, April 22, 2019, https://newrepublic.com/article/153507/france-yellow-vests-uprising-emmanuel-macron-techno cratic-insiders, accessed on November 26, 2019.

11 Horowitz, J. (2019), "Italy's Government Collapses, Turning Chaos Into Crisis," *New York Times*, August 20, 2019, https://www.nytimes.com/2019/08/20/world/europe/italy-pm-giu seppe-conte-resign.html, accessed on November 26, 2019.

12 Karnitschnig, M. (2019), "5 Takeaways from Germany's regional elections," *Politico*, September 3, 2019, https://www.politico.eu/article/5-takeaways-regional-elections-branden burg-saxony/, accessed on November 26, 2019.

13 "Spanish election results: Socialists win most seats, PP and Vox make huge gains, C's collapse," *The Local*, November 10, 2019, https://www.thelocal.es/20191110/spanish-election-re sults-exit-poll-shows-socialist-lose-seats-pp-and-vox-make-huge-gains, accessed on November 26, 2019.

14 Rashad, M. and Kalin, S. (2019), "Trump, Saudi Arabia Warn Iran Against Middle East Conflict," *Reuters*, May 19, 2019, https://www.reuters.com/article/us-saudi-oil-emirates-tanker/trump-saudi-arabia-warn-iraq-against-middle-east-conflict-idUSKCN1SP01C, accessed on November 26, 2019.

15 Mladenov, N. (2019), "'Multi-generational tragedy' in Israel and Palestine demands political will for two-state solution," *United Nations*, October 28, 2019, https://news.un.org/en/story/2019/10/1050091, accessed on November 26, 2019.

16 "Kashmir unrest could lead Pakistan, India to 'accidental war'," *Al Jazeera*, September 10, 2019, https://www.aljazeera.com/news/2019/09/kashmir-unrest-lead-pakistan-india-ac cidental-war-190910140000666.html, accessed on November 26, 2019.

17 "North Korea launches two possible 'ballistic' missiles into sea, Japan says," *Reuters*, October 31, 2019, https://www.cnbc.com/2019/10/31/north-korea-launches-two-projectiles-japan-and-south-korea-say.html, accessed on November 26, 2019.

18 "Japan and South Korea promise to work on bilateral ties amid escalating trade tensions," *Reuters*, October 24, 2019, https://www.cnbc.com/2019/10/24/japan-and-korea-promise-to-work-on-bilateral-ties-trade-tensions.html, accessed on November 26, 2019.

19 Heydarian, R. (2019), "Unopposed no more: Beijing's ambitions in the South China Sea increasingly draw U.S. attention," https://www.scmp.com/news/china/diplomacy/article/3037095/unopposed-no-more-beijings-ambitions-south-china-sea, accessed on November 26, 2019.

20 Plokhy, S. and Sarotte, M. E. (2019), "The Shoals of Ukraine: Where American Illusions and Great Power Politics Collide," *Foreign Affairs*, November 22, 2019 https://www.foreignaffairs.com/articles/united-states/2019-11-22/shoals-ukraine, accessed on November 26, 2019.

21 Taylor, M. L. (2019), "Combating disinformation and foreign interference in democracies: Lessons from Europe," *Brookings,* July 31, 2019, https://www.brookings.edu/blog/techtank/2019/07/31/combating-disinformation-and-foreign-interference-in-democracies-lessons-from-europe/, accessed on November 26, 2019.

22 "The U.S. and Russia: A Lesson in Asymmetry," *Stratfor Worldview,* July 28, 2017, https://worldview.stratfor.com/article/us-and-russia-lesson-asymmetry, accessed on November 26, 2019.

23 Judson, J. (2019), "Do the Baltics need more U.S. military support to deter Russia?" *Defense News,* July 16, https://www.defensenews.com/land/2019/07/15/do-the-baltics-need-more-us-military-support-to-deter-russia/, accessed on November 26, 2019.

24 Smale, A. et al. (2015), "Migrants Cross Austria Border from Hungary," *New York Times,* September 4, 2015, https://www.nytimes.com/2015/09/05/world/europe/migrant-crisis-hungary.html?hp&action=click&pgtype=Homepage&module=first-column-region&reg, accessed on November 26, 2019.

25 Doctors Without Borders (2019), "The facts about the humanitarian crisis in Mexico and Central America," February 5, 2019, https://www.doctorswithoutborders.org/what-we-do/news-stories/news/facts-about-humanitarian-crisis-mexico-and-central-america, accessed on November 2019.

26 Williams, C. (2019), "After Brexit, an economic fork in the road," *The World in 2020,* https://worldin.economist.com/article/17320/edition2020after-brexit-economic-fork-road?navigation=true&category=culture, accessed on December 1, 2019.

27 Minton-Beddoes, Z. (2019), "Buckle up for America's ugly elections and faltering economy," *The World in 2020,* https://theworldin.economist.com/edition/2020/article/17309/buckle-americas-ugly-election-and-faltering-economy, accessed on November 30, 2019.

28 "Hong Kong in first recession for a decade amid protests," *BBC News,* November 15, 2019, https://www.bbc.com/news/business-50431614, accessed on November 26, 2019.

29 Partington, R. (2019), "How has Brexit vote affected the UK economy: October verdict," October 25, 2019, https://www.theguardian.com/business/2019/oct/25/how-has-brexit-vote-affected-uk-economy-october-verdict, accessed on November 26, 2019.

30 Goodman, P.S. (2019), "Turkey's Long, Painful Economic Crisis Grinds On," *New York Times,* July 8, 2019, https://www.nytimes.com/2019/07/08/business/turkey-economy-crisis.html, accessed on November 26, 2019.

31 Perez, S. and Dube, R. (2019), "Why Argentina Faces an Economic Crisis. Again." *Wall Street Journal,* September 25, 2019, https://www.wsj.com/articles/why-argentina-faces-an-economic-crisis-again-11569422388, accessed on November 26, 2019.

32 "Venezuela in crisis in 300 words," *BBC News,* January 6, 2020, https://www.bbc.com/news/world-latin-america-48121148, accessed on March 11, 2020.

33 Temin, J. et al. (2019), "Sorry, but the West isn't responsible for Zimbabwe's continuing economic collapse," *The Washington Post,* October 25, 2019, https://www.washingtonpost.com/opinions/2019/10/24/sorry-west-isnt-responsible-zimbabwes-continuing-economic-collapse/, accessed on November 26, 2019.

34 "Six charts that show hard U.S. sanctions have hit Iran," *BBC News,* May 2, 2019, https://www.bbc.com/news/world-middle-east-48119109, accessed on November 26, 2019.

35 "Financial crises occur about once every decade," *The Financial Times,* March 23, 2015, https://www.ft.com/content/5148cd1e-cf01-11e4-893d-00144feab7de, accessed on November 26, 2019.

36 Nye, J. S. (2018), "Is Fake News Here to Stay?" *Project Syndicate,* December 5, 2018, https://www.project-syndicate.org/commentary/fake-news-part-of-the-background-by-joseph-s–nye-2018-12, accessed on December 2, 2019.

37 Cohen, S. B. and Obama, B. (2019), quoted in Chuck, E. (2019), op. cit.

38 Hamilton, L. (2019), "Compromise is the essence of our democracy," *The Montgomery Herald,* September 8, 2019, https://www.montgomery-herald.com/opinion/compromise-is-the-essence-of-our-democracy/article_4a463620-d27e-11e9-a31f-0bf560c14fca.html, accessed on December 2, 2019.

39 Schumpeter, J. A. (1950), *Capitalism, Socialism and Democracy, Third Edition* (New York: HarperCollins).

40 Labour Party (2019), "It's Time for Real Change," https://labour.org.uk/manifesto/, accessed on November 26, 2019.

41 Copeland, R. (2019), "Breakup of Tech Giants 'On the Table', U.S. Antitrust Chief Says," *The Wall Street Journal,* October 22, 2019, https://www.wsj.com/articles/breakup-of-tech-giants-on-the-table-u-s-antitrustchief-says-11571765689, accessed on November 26, 2019.

42 Meredith, S. and Browne, R. (2018), "All you need to know about Fox, Comcast and Disney's battle to own Sky," *CNBC,* September 20, 2018, https://www.cnbc.com/2018/07/18/disney-comcast-and-fox-all-you-need-to-know-about-one-of-the-biggest.html, accessed on November 26, 2019.

43 Rainey, R. (2019), "How Elizabeth Warren would boost labor rights," *Politico,* October 3, 2019, https://www.politico.com/news/2019/10/03/how-elizabeth-warren-would-boost-labor-rights-024199, accessed on November 26, 2019; Labour Party (2019) op. cit.

44 "Thai Floods Threaten Global Automotive Supply Chain, Japanese Firms Worst Hit," *IHS Markit,* October 14, 2011, https://ihsmarkit.com/country-industry-forecasting.html?ID=1065931666, accessed on November 26, 2019.

45 Green, J. (2016), "The economic impacts of the Fukushima disaster," *Nuclear Monitor Issue:* #836 Number:4609, December 16, 2016, https://www.wiseinternational.org/nuclear-monitor/836/economic-impacts-fukushima-disaster, accessed on November 26, 2019.

46 TraderStef (2019),"Florida's Orange Juice Crop at Risk Due to Hurricane Dorian," *Crush the Street,* August 29, 2019, https://www.crushthestreet.com/articles/technical-anal ysis/floridas-orange-juice-crop-at-risk-due-to-hurricane-dorian, accessed on November 26, 2019.

47 "Harsh weather to cut French wine output by 12% this year," *Reuters,* August 27, 2019, https://uk.reuters.com/article/uk-france-wine/harsh-weather-to-cut-french-wine-output-by-12-this-year-idUKKCN1VH140, accessed on November 26, 2019.

48 Cambridge Dictionary, https://dictionary.cambridge.org/dictionary/english/uncertainty, accessed on November 26, 2019.

49 Rumsfeld, D. (2002), DoD News Briefing – Secretary Rumsfeld and General Myers, *U.S. Department of Defense,* February 12, 2002, https://archive.defense.gov/Transcripts/Transcript.aspx?TranscriptID=2636, accessed on November 27, 2019.

50 Daase, C. and Kessler, O. (2007), "Knowns and Unknowns in the 'War on Terror': Uncertainty and the Political Construction of Danger," *Security Dialogue,* December 2007, vol. 38, 4: pp. 411–434.

51 CNN (2019), "Iraq Prison Abuse Scandal Fast Facts," *CNN Library,* March 4, 2019, https://edition.cnn.com/2013/10/30/world/meast/iraq-prison-abuse-scandal-fast-facts/index.html, accessed on November 27, 2019.

52 Baldoni, J. (2019), "The Challenger Disaster: A Dramatic Lesson in the Failure To Communicate," *Forbes,* January 28, 2019, https://www.forbes.com/sites/johnbaldoni/2019/01/28/the-challenger-disaster-a-dramatic-lesson-in-the-failure-to-communicate/#6db9560d184d, accessed on November 27, 2019.

53 Meigs, J. B. (2016), "Blame BP for Deepwater Horizon. But Direct Your Outrage to the Actual Mistake," *Slate,* September 30, 2016, https://slate.com/technology/2016/09/bp-is-to-blame-for-deepwater-horizon-but-its-mistake-was-actually-years-of-small-mistakes.html, accessed November 27, 2019.

54 Zinkin, J. (2014), *Rebuilding Trust in Banks: The Role of Leadership and Governance* (Singapore: John Wiley & Sons), pp. 29–30, 34.

55 Minton-Beddoes, Z. (2019), op. cit.

56 Loxbo, K. et al. (2019), "The decline of Western European social democracy: Exploring the transformed link between welfare state generosity and the electoral strength of social democratic parties, 1945–2014," *Sage Journals,* July 9, 2019, https://journals.sagepub.com/doi/abs/10.1177/1354068819861339?journalCode=ppqa, accessed on December 1, 2019.

57 Mirani, L. (2019), "The real influencers," *The World in 2020* (London: The Economist Newspaper), accessed through the *Economist* app on November 30, 2019.

58 Maestro, O. S. (2019), "South China Sea of Troubles," *The World in 2020,* https://worldin.economist.com/article/17356/edition2020south-china-sea-troubles, accessed on December 2, 2019.

59 Guest, R. (2019), op. cit.

60 Pham, S. (2018), " ZTE took a $2 billion hit but it'll soon be making a profit again," *CNN Business,* August 31, 2018, https://money.cnn.com/2018/08/31/technology/zte-china-earnings/index.html, accessed on November 30, 2019.

61 Merriman, C. (2019), "Microsoft head honcho calls for an end to Huawei trade ban," *The Inquirer,* September 20, 2019, https://www.theinquirer.net/inquirer/news/3081800/microsoft-brad-smith-huawei-ban, accessed on November 30, 2019.

62 Wooldridge, A. (2019), "Divided, damaged and diminished," *The World in 2020,* London: The Economist Newspaper), accessed through the Economist app on November 30, 2019.

63 Ruddick, G. and Oltermann, P. (2017), "A Mini part's incredible journey shows how Brexit will hit the U.K. car industry," *The Guardian,* March 3, 2017, https://www.theguardian.com/business/2017/mar/03/brexit-uk-car-industry-mini-britain-eu, accessed on December 2, 2019.

64 Davies, H. (2019), "Is Post-Brexit London Really Doomed?" *Project Syndicate,* October 3, 2019, https://www.project-syndicate.org/commentary/will-london-financial-center-survive-brexit-by-howard-davies-2019-10, accessed on December 2, 2019.

65 Barro, R. J. (2019), Trump is slowing U.S. Economic Growth," *Project Syndicate,* June 4, 2019; Stiglitz, J. E. (2019), "Trump's Deficit Economy," *Project Syndicate,* August 9, 2019; Tyson, L. and Mendonca, L. (2019), "Expanding America's Expansion," July 25, 2019; O'Neill, J. (2019), "Trump's One-Way Economy," August 13, 2019, https://www.project-syndicate.org/big picture/trump-s-economy, accessed on December 2, 2019.

66 Eichengreen, B. (2019), "Will China Confront a Revolution of Rising Expectations?" *Project Syndicate,* November 11, 2019, https://www.project-syndicate.org/commentary/china-revolution-of-rising-expectations-by-barry-eichengreen-2019-11, accessed on December 2, 2019.

67 Subramanian, A. and Rodrik, D. (2019),"The puzzling lure of financial globalization," *Project Syndicate,* September 25, 2019, https://www.project-syndicate.org/commentary/financial-globalization-neoliberalism-discredited-by-arvind-subramanian-and-dani-rodrik-2019-09?barrier=accesspaylog, accessed on December 2, 2019.

68 Stiglitz, J. E. (2019), op. cit.

69 Stiglitz, J. E. (2010), "U.S. Does Not Have Capitalism Now: Stiglitz," *CNBC,* January 19, 2010, https://www.cnbc.com/id/34921639, accessed on December 2, 2019.

70 Kenton, W. (2019), "What is Privatizing Profits and Socializing Losses?" *Investopedia*, October 1, 2019, https://www.investopedia.com/terms/p/privatizing-profits-and-socializing-losses.asp, accessed on December 2, 2019.

71 Edelman (2018), "2018 Trust Barometer: The State of Trust in Business," p. 5.

72 Jackson H. and Ormerod, P. (2017), "Was Michael Gove right? Have we had enough of experts?" *Prospect*, July 14, 2017, https://www.prospectmagazine.co.uk/magazine/michael-gove-right-about-experts-not-trust-them-academics-peer-review, accessed on December 2, 2019.

73 Moore, S. (2019), "Trust in politics has evaporated, now it offers only fantasy," *The Guardian*, December 2, 2019, https://www.theguardian.com/commentisfree/2019/dec/02/trust-in-politics-has-evaporated-now-it-offers-only-fantasy, accessed on December 3, 2019.

74 Skidelsky, R. (2018), op. cit.

75 Ibid.

76 Parker, J. (2019), "The decade of the 'young old' begins," *The World in 2020*, https://worldin.economist.com/article/17316/edition2020decade-young-old-begins, accessed on December 2, 2019.

77 Ibid.

78 Ibid.

79 Ibid.

80 Ibid.

81 Fromm, J. (2019), "Purpose Series: A Purpose-Driven Brand Is A Successful Brand," *Forbes*, January 16, 2019, https://www.forbes.com/sites/jefffromm/2019/01/16/purpose-series-a-purpose-driven-brand-is-a-successful-brand/#584feb49437d, accessed on December 3, 2019.

82 Reiley, L. (2019), " Millennials have sparked a sober revolution, and alcohol brands have started to notice," *Washington Post*, June 27, 2019, https://www.washingtonpost.com/business/2019/06/27/millennials-have-sparked-sober-revolution-alcohol-brands-are-starting-notice/ accessed on March 11, 2020.

83 Danziger, P. (2017) "Luxury Brands Are in Danger of Losing American Millennials: How to Get Them Back," *Forbes*, September 11, 2017, https://www.forbes.com/sites/pamdanziger/2017/09/11/luxury-brands-are-in-danger-of-losing-it-with-american-millennials-how-to-get-it-back/#7713903457d8, accessed on December 3, 2019.

84 Jacobs, F. (2019), "90% of millennials still want a car," *GlobalFleet*, October 23, 2019 https://www.globalfleet.com/en/smart-mobility/europe/features/90-millennials-still-want-car?a=FJA05&t%5B0%5D=Shared%20Mobility&t%5B1%5D=Multimodality&curl=1, accessed on December 3, 2019.

85 Robison, J. (2019), "Millennials Care About the Environment – Should Your Company?" *Gallup*, May 29, 2019, https://www.gallup.com/workplace/257786/millennials-worry-environment-company.aspx, accessed on December 3, 2019.

86 Taylor, M. and Bartlett, J. (2019), "Fresh wave of climate strikes takes place around the world," *The Guardian*, September 27, 2019, https://www.theguardian.com/environment/2019/sep/27/fresh-wave-of-climate-strikes-take-place-around-the-world, accessed on December 3, 2019.

87 Mullen, C. (2018), "Millennials drive big growth in sustainable products," *Bizwomen*, December 28, 2018, https://www.bizjournals.com/bizwomen/news/latest-news/2018/12/millennials-drive-big-growth-in-sustainable.html?page=all, accessed on December 3, 2019.

88 Rosen, R. J. (2011), "Truth, lies and the Internet," *The Atlantic*, December 29, 2011, https://www.theatlantic.com/technology/archive/2011/12/truth-lies-and-the-internet/250569/, accessed on December 3, 2019.

89 Baraniuk, C. (2016), Web of lies: Is the internet making a world without truth?" *New Scientist,* February 17, 2016, https://www.newscientist.com/article/2077405-web-of-lies-is-the-internet-making-a-world-without-truth/, accessed on December 3, 2019.

90 Harford, T. (2019), "How to survive an election with your sanity intact," *The Financial Times,* November 15, 2019, https://www.ft.com/content/8b9add52-05f4-11ea-a984-fbbaca d9e7dd, accessed on December 6, 2019.

91 Graham, M. (2019), "Facebook CEO Mark Zuckerberg defends himself against Twitter's Jack Dorsey, saying political ad decision is not all about money," *CNBC,* October 30, 2019, https:// www.cnbc.com/2019/10/30/zuckerberg-defends-facebooks-political-ads-approach-after-twit ter-ban.html, accessed on December 3, 2019.

92 Stevenson, A. (2018), "Facebook Admits It Was Used To Incite Violence in Myanmar," *The New York Times,* November 6, 2018, https://www.nytimes.com/2018/11/06/technology/myan mar-facebook.html, accessed on December 3, 2019.

93 BBC (2018), "Myanmar Rohingya: what you need to know about the crisis," *BBC News,* April 24, 2018, https://www.bbc.com/news/world-asia-41566561, accessed on December 3, 2019.

94 Welch, J. https://www.goodreads.com/quotes/185636-if-the-rate-of-change-on-the-outside-exceeds-the, accessed on September 27, 2018.

95 Christensen, C. (1997), *The Innovator's Dilemma* (Boston, Mass: Harvard Business Review Press).

96 Thrasyvoulou, X. (2014), "Understanding the Innovator's Dilemma, *Wired,* https://www. wired.com/insights/2014/12/understanding-the-innovators-dilemma/, accessed on September 27, 2018.

97 Paur, J. (2009), "Boeing's 787 Is as Innovative Inside as Outside," *Wired,* December 24, 2009, https://www.wired.com/2009/12/boeing-787-dreamliner-interior/ accessed on March 12, 2020.

98 Withey, P. (2019), "The deHavilland Comet Disaster," *Aerospace Engineering,* July 1, 2019, https://aerospaceengineeringblog.com/dehavilland-comet-disaster/, accessed on December 5, 2019.

99 Jacobs, F. (2019), op. cit.

100 Meigs, J. B. (2016), "Blame BP for Deepwater Horizon. But Direct Your Outrage to the Actual Mistake," *Slate,* September 30, 2016, http://www.slate.com/articles/health_and_sci ence/science/2016/09/bp_is_to_blame_for_deepwater_horizon_but_its_mistake_was_actu ally_years.html, accessed on July 26, 2018.

101 Ibid.

102 Petroski, H. (2012), *To Forgive Design: Understanding Failure* (Cambridge, Mass: Belknap Press).

103 Sibly, P. G. and Walker, A. C. (1977), "Structural Accidents and Their Causes," *Proceedings of the Institution of Civil Engineers,* 62, Part 1: pp. 191–208, quoted in Petroski, H. (2012), op. cit., p. 339.

104 Ibid.

105 Sutton, M-R. (2019), How to Develop a New Product (From Concept to Market), *Shopify Blog,* February 13, 2019https://www.shopify.com/blog/product-development-process, accessed on March 11, 2020.

106 "Businesses are trying to reduce, reuse and recycle," *The Economist Special Report,* September 29, 2018, https://www.economist.com/special-report/2018/09/29/businesses-are-trying-to-reduce-reuse-and-recycle, accessed on September 29, 2018.

107 Fenwick, M. and Wrbka, S. (2016), "The Shifting Meaning of Legal Certainty," Fenwick, M. and Wrbka, S. (eds.), *Legal Certainty in a Contemporary Context* (Singapore: Springer), https:// link.springer.com/chapter/10.1007/978-981-10-0114-7_1, accessed on December 6, 2019.

108 Maxeiner, J. R. (2008), "Some Realism About Legal Certainty in Globalization of the Rule of Law," Houston Journal of International Law 31, no. 1 (2008), pp. 27–46.

109 Biko, S. (1976), quoted in Brown, B. (2013), "The U.S. Responds to Apartheid: Polaroid," *Boston University, African Studies Center,* https://www.bu.edu/africa/files/2013/10/The-US-Responds-to-Apartheid.pdf, accessed on December 6, 2019.

110 Archbishop Tutu, D., quoted in Brown, B. (2013), op. cit.

111 Zsofia, P. (2019), "Not enough warehouses in the UK. Another round of stockpiling before Brexit," *Trans.info,* August 9, 2019, https://trans.info/en/not-enough-warehouses-in-the-uk-an other-round-of-stockpiling-before-brexit-158095, accessed on December 6, 2019.

112 "Tobacco a done deal," *CNN Money,* November 20, 1998, https://money.cnn.com/1998/11/20/companies/tobacco_deal/, accessed on December 6, 2019.

113 Helmore, E. (2019), "Lawsuits, payouts, opioids crisis what happened to Johnson & Johnson?" *The Guardian,* October 18, 2019, https://www.theguardian.com/business/2019/oct/18/johnson-and-johnson-opioids-lawsuits-product-recalls, accessed on December 6, 2019.

114 Williams Walsh, M. (2019), "Judge Orders Pause in Opioid Litigation Against Purdue Pharma and Sacklers," *The New York Times,* October 11, 2019, https://www.nytimes.com/2019/10/11/health/purdue-bankruptcy-opioids.html, accessed on December 6, 2019.

115 "Exxon Sued Again for 'Misleading' Advertising", *Desmog,* May 20, 2020, https://www.desmogblog.com/2020/05/20/exxon-sued-misleading-advertising-beyond-pesticides, accessed on July 6, 2020.

116 Imperial Oil Document Trove, Climate Investigations Center December 3, 2019, https://climateinvestigations.org/imperial-oil-document-trove/, accessed March 30, 2020.

117 Frumhoff, P. (2014), "Global Warming Fact: More than Half of All Industrial CO_2 Pollution Has Been Emitted Since 1988," *Union of Concerned Scientists,* December 15, 2014, https://blog.ucsusa.org/peter-frumhoff/global-warming-fact-co2-emissions-since-1988-764, accessed on December 7, 2019.

118 Taylor, M. and Watts, J. (2019), "Revealed: the 20 firms behind a third of all carbon emissions," *The Guardian,* October 9, 2019, https://www.theguardian.com/environment/2019/oct/09/revealed-20-firms-third-carbon-emissions, accessed on December 7, 2019.

119 Lombrana, L. M. (2019), "Global Warming Prediction Sounds Alarm for Climate Fight," *Bloomberg Climate Changed,* December 3, 2019, https://www.bloomberg.com/news/articles/2019-12-03/global-temperature-headed-toward-5-degree-increase-wmo-says?utm_medium=email&utm_source=newsletter&utm_term=191205&utm_campaign=climatechanged, accessed on December 6, 2019.

120 Schoen, J. W. and McDonald, J. (2019), "Warming climate, population sprawl threaten California's future with more destructive wildfires," *CNBC,* November 9, 2019, https://www.cnbc.com/2019/11/09/why-californias-wildfires-are-going-to-get-worse.html, accessed on December 7, 2019.

121 Doherty, B. and Davidson, H. (2019), "Australia fires: blazes 'too big to put out' as 140 bushfires rage in NSW and Queensland," *The Guardian,* December 7, 2019, https://www.theguardian.com/australia-news/2019/dec/07/australia-fires-blazes-too-big-to-put-out-as-140-bushfires-rage-in-nsw-and-queensland, accessed on December 7, 2019.

122 Reuters (2019), "Victoria Falls dries to a trickle after worst drought in a century," *The Guardian,* December 7, 2019, https://www.theguardian.com/world/2019/dec/07/victoria-falls-dries-to-a-trickle-after-worst-drought-in-a-century, accessed on December 7, 2019.

123 Nelson, A. (2019), "Climate change could make insurance too expensive for most people – report," *The Guardian,* March 21, 2019, https://www.theguardian.com/environment/2019/mar/

21/climate-change-could-make-insurance-too-expensive-for-ordinary-people-report, accessed on December 7, 2019.
124 Readfearn, G. (2019), "Scientist's theory of climate's Titanic moment the 'tip of a mathematical iceberg'," *The Guardian,* December 1, 2019, https://www.theguardian.com/environ ment/2019/dec/01/scientists-theory-of-climates-titanic-moment-the-tip-of-a-mathematical-ice berg, accessed on December 6, 2019.

Chapter 8
Dealing with Complexity and Ambiguity

This chapter is presented in two parts. The first deals with complexity; the second with ambiguity. It closes with a summary on how boards can handle complexity and ambiguity in their decision making.

Complexity

Complexity is defined as: "the state of having many parts and being difficult to understand or find an answer to,"[1] or as "the study of phenomena which emerge from a collection of interacting objects."[2] However, I define complexity as being "when the whole is made up of interrelated parts so that simple 'cause and effect' chains are replaced by complicated, rapidly changing, interdependent forces and events."[3]

From Chapter 7, it should be apparent that the sources of volatility are so many and so interconnected and linked to the many causes of uncertainty that boards are faced with really complex decisions they must make, without access to all the facts in the time available. In today's world many board decisions satisfy both definitions above of complexity. This is unfortunate because

> Our corporations have built a global production system that is so complex, and geared so tightly and leveraged so finely, that a breakdown anywhere increasingly means a breakdown everywhere. . .[4]

This description does not just apply to the global manufacturing supply chains discussed in Chapter 4, but it also applies to major utilities everywhere; to public transport systems; to power grids, and to the internet, and of course to the environment which affects us all globally in ways we sometimes cannot foresee.

1. **Supply Chain Complexity:** It is perhaps worthwhile to revisit the example of the Apple iPhone discussed in Chapter 4 to illustrate the complexity of global manufacturing supply chains and how simplistic economics about balance of payments between countries cannot resolve imbalances between countries. Manufacturing an iPhone involves eight countries and seventeen companies, shown in Table 8.1.

https://doi.org/10.1515/9783110670486-008

Table 8.1: Complexity of iPhone supply chain.[5]

Location	Supplier	Components
U.S.	GT Advanced Technologies	Sapphire Crystal Components
U.S.	Samsung	Chips
U.S.	Global Foundries	Chips
U.S.	Texas Instruments	Chips
U.S.	Maxim Integrated	Chips
U.S.	Corning	Gorilla glass
Japan	Japan Display Inc	Display
Taiwan	Innolux	Display
South Korea	LG	Display
Japan	Toshiba	Storage
South Korea	SK Hynix	Storage
Taiwan	TSMC	Touch ID
Netherlands	NXP	NFC Chip
France	ST Microelectronics	Gyroscope
U.S.	Invensense	Gyroscope
China	Foxconn	Assembly
China	Pegatron	Assembly
Brazil	Foxconn	Assembly

This does not include Apple's marketing and distribution arrangements around the world that add another level of complex interrelationships and dependencies. A key dependency is that every entity in the supply/value chain must perform as specified, meeting the operating, health and safety standards set by the ultimate buyer at the end of the chain whose brand and market capitalization can be put at risk by a failure to do so at any stage in the value chain.

Two examples of how complexity makes guaranteeing satisfactory outcomes more difficult: drinking a satisfying glass of milk and using public transport.

a. **Enjoying a glass of milk**: Take the experience of drinking a refreshing glass of milk. What must happen in the supply chain from the farm to the glass? There are a number of stages where failure in any one to meet the desired standards will inevitably lead to a bad experience:

Stage 1: Suppliers of feed and veterinarians must ensure that farmers' cows are in good health. Failure to do so could lead to either the milk being of poor quality or worse still to carry bovine tuberculosis.

Stage 2: The farmers must ensure that their cows are kept in good conditions and that they are properly fed and cared for according to the instructions of the feed suppliers and veterinarians. Failure by any single farmer to do this could contaminate the entire supply chain. They must keep the milk fresh, safe and clean, ensuring it is not contaminated in any way. In the disastrous Chinese milk scandal in 2008, farmers adulterated the milk they provided to the dairies with melamine to make more money. As a result:

> Sixteen infants in China's Gansu Province were diagnosed with kidney stones. All of them had been fed milk powder that was later found to have been adulterated with a toxic industrial compound called melamine. Four months later, an estimated 300,000 babies in China were sick from the contaminated milk, and the kidney damage led to six fatalities. The Sanlu Group, one of the largest dairy producers in China, was identified as the chief culprit. But as the scandal unfolded, more Chinese dairy firms became implicated.
>
> The incident not only damaged the reputation of China's food exports, but also dealt a devastating blow to the booming domestic dairy industry, leading to a series of mergers and consolidations. The inelastic baby formula market boosted the demand for foreign products – indeed, after 2009, more than 100 foreign brands flooded into the Chinese market. In hindsight, it is not an overstatement that the 2008 incident is one of the largest food safety scandals in PRC history.[6]

Stage 3: The milk haulers who collect the milk from the farms must test the milk to ensure it passes the required tests and must also ensure that the trucks that will take the milk from the farms to the dairies are properly cleaned and can keep the milk chilled. Any failure here doesn't merely damage the milk, but could lead to further contamination on its journey to the dairies.

Stage 4: The dairies test the milk upon arrival, blending it from different suppliers, pasteurizing and then homogenizing it according to pre-set sanitary and performance standards that must be met at each stage in the process. Using cartons supplied by packaging companies that must satisfy exacting performance standards, they pack the different milks (fresh, UHT [ultra-high temperature pasteurization], whole, 2%, nonfat, etc.) according to grade, fat content, flavor, and pack size; labeling the resulting different milks with the appropriate branding and their sell-by dates. The milks are then ready to be delivered according to orders collated by retail chain and outlet. They are then stored in appropriate conditions, waiting to be collected at the designated time. Failure to meet the required standards in any of these steps will lead to milks that are not fit for human consumption.

Stage 5: The distributors who may belong to the dairies or to the retail chains will collect the milks, check their condition, and deliver them to retail outlets according to orders placed, making sure the orders are handled correctly so there is minimum damage and that the milks are delivered within the agreed time, kept at the right temperatures throughout their journey (in the cold chain if the milks are fresh as opposed to UHT). Failure to meet pre-set standards will lead to either damaged goods or spoiled product, no longer fit for human consumption.

Stage 6: The retailers hold the milks in stock in appropriate conditions, rotating them onto the shelves in line with their sell-by dates; removing those that have gone past their sell-by dates. Failure to meet the pre-set standards will lead to product that is not fit for sale.

Stage 7: The drinkers will take their cartons home and put them in their refrigerators if the milk is fresh or in their pantries if UHT. Paying attention to the sell-by dates, they will open the cartons and enjoy a good glass of milk. They will then close the cartons; making sure they are properly sealed and put them back in the appropriate part of the fridge, away from fish and aromatic foods. Failure to ensure that the cartons, once opened are stored correctly in the fridge will likely lead to the milk being tainted by other food nearby; failure to keep it at the right temperature to drink before it has lost its freshness will spoil the taste. Even failure to make sure the glass has been properly washed and rinsed can spoil the experience.

If such an apparently simple act as enjoying a glass of milk to its fullest is the result of this complex chain of events, where multiple actors must perform as expected to meet what are, in practice, demanding standards; imagine for example how much more complex the chain of events and interactions required to achieve desired outcomes is for chemical plants, power grids, and finance, which are "tightly coupled" systems,[i] and transport systems, whose effectiveness people often take for granted. The complexity is even greater when we remember that all these different supply chains need to operate as an integrated system and it will have to serve 10 billion people by the middle of the century:

> When summed, these supply chains as well as all social services make up the cooperative scheme that we all live in and must live in to survive. The resilience of the scheme is purely an act of faith – a troubling reality when we recognize that in the name of efficiency both business and government have substantially eliminated all redundancy and all of the subsystems (food, water, energy, built environment) need to be transitioned to something robust to [serve] a world of 10 billion people.[7]

The unforeseen and devastating impact of Covid-19 on how business is done, on how life is lived, on the availability of essential products for businesses or citizens, is a perfect example of what happens when incredibly complex and therefore brittle supply chain systems that are *tightly coupled* fail. We saw that countries and companies all over the world were completely unprepared for an event that should have been part of every country and every corporation's risk preparation. Many of those that did not pay enough attention to that risk, failed. Others were just unfortunate victims of the circumstances.

b. ***Transport Systems Complexity:*** If you have ever been a stranger in a large city trying to work out the best ways to get from A to B using an unfamiliar map of the transport infrastructure and have found this to be complex and difficult, you are not alone. The reason is that research suggests that modern transport systems are too complex for the human brain:

> Now, a team of physicists and mathematicians has attempted to quantify this confusion and find out whether there is a point at which navigating a route through a complex urban transport system exceeds our cognitive limits.
>
> After analysing the world's 15 largest metropolitan transport networks, the researchers estimated that the information limit for planning a trip is around 8 bits. (A "bit" is a binary digit – the most basic unit of information.)
>
> Additionally, similar to the "Dunbar number," which estimates a limit to the size of an individual's friendship circle, this cognitive limit for transportation suggests that maps should not consist of more than 250 connection points to be easily readable.

---

i The defining characteristic of a tightly coupled process is that once it starts, it's difficult or impossible to stop.

Using journeys with exactly two connections as their basis (that is, visiting four stations in total), the researchers found that navigating transport networks in major cities – including London – can come perilously close to exceeding humans' cognitive powers.

And when further interchanges or other modes of transport – such as buses or trams – are added to the mix, the complexity of networks can rise well above the 8-bit threshold. The researchers demonstrated this using the multimodal transportation networks from New York City, Tokyo, and Paris.

Mason Porter, Professor of Nonlinear and Complex Systems in the Mathematical Institute at the University of Oxford, said: "*Human cognitive capacity is limited, and cities and their transportation networks have grown to the point where they have reached a level of complexity that is beyond human processing capability to navigate around them. In particular, the search for a simplest path becomes inefficient when multiple modes of transport are involved and when a transportation system has too many interconnections.*"[8]   [Emphases mine]

Given this finding, it is not really surprising that dealing with traffic and congestion prove to be such a challenge. Being good at logistics is difficult. The move to online retailing where customers have come to expect next day home delivery as a result of Amazon Prime does not just undermine the economics of brick-and-mortar retailing, it puts strain on the roads of our cities, creates pollution and congestion, made worse by the policy of returns; none of which are properly accounted for in the economics of online delivery. The reason for the failure to account for the resulting pollution and congestion costs is that it is too complicated to do and there are no accounting methods to properly allocate the costs of these externalities to the P&L [profit and loss statement].

2. **Complexity in Tightly Coupled Systems:** The most serious dangers posed by complexity occur when the system is both complex and "tightly coupled." Three engineering cases and the subprime mortgage crisis are good examples:

    a. ***Piper Alpha Disaster, July 6, 1988:*** *Piper Alpha* was an oil production platform in the North Sea operated by Occidental Petroleum (Caledonia) Limited. It began production in 1976, but on July 6, 1988, it was the site of the world's most lethal offshore disaster – 167 oil rig workers died.

        The defining characteristic of a tightly coupled process is that once it starts, it's difficult or impossible to stop: a domino-toppling display is not especially complex, but it is tightly coupled. So is a loaf of bread rising in the oven. . .

        But what if a system is both complex and tightly coupled. *Complexity means there are many different ways for things to go wrong. Tight coupling means the unintended consequences proliferate so quickly that it is impossible to adapt to the failure or try something different.* On Piper Alpha, the initial explosion need not have destroyed the rig, but it took out the control room, making evacuation difficult, and also making it almost impossible to override the diver-safety catch that was preventing the seawater pumps from starting automatically. Although the rig's crew had, in principle, shut down the flow of oil and gas to the platform, so much pipework had been damaged that gas and oil continued to leak out and feed the inferno. Each interaction was unexpected. Many happened within minutes of the initial mistake. There was no time to react.[9]   [Emphases mine]

b. ***Bhopal disaster, December 3, 1984:*** The disaster at the Union Carbide plant in Bhopal, India, killed perhaps as many as 10,000 people and left another 100,000 injured, many permanently.[10] It was caused by a toxic cloud of methyl isocyanate that drifted over the sleeping citizens in an adjacent shanty town. It was an example of what happens when the whole is made up of complex interrelated parts so that simple "cause and effect" chains are replaced by complex, rapidly changing, interdependent forces and events – i.e., a complex and tightly coupled system:

> The Union Carbide plant in Bhopal, India was equipped with secondary prevention and mitigation systems specifically designed to prevent a release of methyl isocyanate (MIC), a deadly gas. However, inadequate design, component failures, and lagging maintenance activities resulted in every one of these systems being compromised. Specific elements in the causal structure of the eventual release include:
> - the refrigeration unit, designed to maintain an appropriate temperature in the MIC unit and therefore prevent an exotherm, was not in operation,
> - the vent gas line, intended for carrying MIC to an emergency scrubber, leaked directly to the atmosphere,
> - the gas that did get to the scrubber was not neutralized because of a lack of alkali in the scrubber,
> - the vent gas scrubber was designed for a capacity of 5 to 8 tonnes. The MIC tank's capacity was 70 tonnes,
> - the temperature indicator on the MIC tank was not functioning,
> - the flare tower for burning off the released MIC was not functioning, and
> - the water curtain (high pressure water sprayers) for neutralizing MIC could reach a height of only 10 meters whereas MIC leaked from the vent gas line at about 33 meters.[11]

c. ***US and Canada Blackout, August 14, 2003:*** The August 14, 2003 blackout in a large part of the US Midwest and Northeast and in Ontario, Canada is an excellent example of a system that was "tightly coupled, as well as interactively complex,"[12] hence the cascade of failures in eight US states and Ontario, Canada. It affected an estimated 50 million people and 61,800 megawatts of electric load in Connecticut, Massachusetts, Michigan, New York, Ohio, Ontario, Pennsylvania, and Vermont. It took four days before power was restored in some parts of the US and parts of

Ontario suffered rolling blackouts for more than a week. Estimates of the costs in the US were US$4 billion to US$10 billion. Millions of office workers were stranded; Cleveland was left without water; twenty-two nuclear power plants were shut down; sixty-five fires were the result, and in New York City alone first responders had to rescue people from eight hundred elevators:

> The details of the causes of the outage show the familiar string of interacting small errors. It was a hot summer day and demand was high, but that was not unusual. The device for determining the real-time state of the power system in the Midwest Independent Service Operator (MISO) had to be disabled because a mismatch occurred. The device. . .was corrected, but the engineer failed to re-engage it on going to lunch. Normally, this would not be a problem. . .but it just so happened. . .that forty-five minutes later. . .an alarm to indicate an untoward event at FirstEnergy began to malfunction. . .But the failure was of the sort that when the backup server came on, the program was in a restart mode, and under these conditions the software program failed. Moreover, it failed to indicate it had failed, so the operators were unaware that it was not functioning properly.
>
> Meanwhile in the MISO, the state estimator was restarted after lunch, but again indicated a mismatch. . .At this point there was no untoward event that the program would warn about. . .Independently, faulty tree-trimming practices and the hot weather caused one of the FirstEnergy's lines to go down. . .Finally the MISO noticed and took the tripped line out of service, but FirstEnergy's failed program did not allow FirstEnergy to know of either the trip or that the line was taken out of service. Three more lines shorted out on trees because of FirstEnergy's cutbacks in maintenance, but the utility's computers showed no problems. FirstEnergy only became aware when its own power went out. . .and had to switch to emergency power. By then in just seven minutes of cascading failures, eight states and parts of Canada blacked out.[13]

Clearly being interconnected creates enormous additional levels of complexity in the grid. This is made even more complicated when grids begin to depend on renewable sources of electricity supply. They may be available in abundance when the sun is shining or when the wind is blowing or both. But what happens at night if the wind is not blowing? There is no supply, yet there is plenty of demand. In such circumstances, the grid must rely on power generated from fossil or nuclear fuels or from power that has been stored in batteries or in dams. Choosing the optimal configuration for present and future needs depends on relative prices of the different sources of supply in the spot and futures markets for power, affected in turn by the impact of future subsidies and taxation policies; on the best estimates of projected future demand, itself a function of economic growth on the one hand, and improvements in energy efficiency on the other; and on the projected long-run return on investments in the different sources of supply, which are capital intensive with long-term payoffs, subject to assumptions of the likely cost of capital.

d. **Subprime Mortgage Crisis, 2008:** The fragmentation of the financial services value chain into specialists (assumed to be better value creators in their specific niches than generalist organizations that straddled the whole value creation process), may indeed have led to greater innovation and better value, but at the expense of creating a level of complexity and "tight coupling" that people could no longer understand:

> In the wake of what has happened to major companies like Lehman Brothers, AIG and Fortis, we [can] say that *the roots of the credit crisis can be traced back to increasingly opaque supply chains that even bankers admitted they no longer understood.*
>
> Bankrupt financial giants . . . [are] the inevitable results of an economic system that extends around the world and, in the process, ensures that risks are chopped into thin slices and then distributed between the different layers and players in the value chain. *The final – if not always intended – consequence is that few people, if anyone, can understand or control the full extent of those risks.*[14]
>
> [Emphases mine]

Mortgage brokers were incentivized to create mortgages without vouching for their quality. The originating banks did poor risk management because the resulting mortgage backed securities would either be sold to third parties who would bear the consequences or be hidden off balance sheets so the regulators would not ask difficult questions about the asset quality.

Arrangers would shop for rates between the credit rating agencies, putting them under pressure to lower their standards and reconfigure the tranches so that they would be converted into AAA. As the subprime boom built, the rating agencies were under increasing pressure to process volumes as fast as possible. This pressure was made worse by rate shopping creating extra work and conflicts of interest.[15]

Rating agency models were wrong because:

> They were based on past data; and much of the information they received had been structured so that they would achieve the required FICO scores and get past analysts, who were box-ticking under time pressure. *The investment banks were only interested in selling on the high-yielding securities and so did not take the time to do good due diligence, which, given the complexity of some the CDOs, would have required a great deal of time to understand, let alone verify.* The banks trusted the investment bankers and did not verify.[16]   [Emphasis mine]

The complexity of the subprime system that failed is shown in Figure 8.1.

Financial sector failure from seeking higher yields through subprime debt

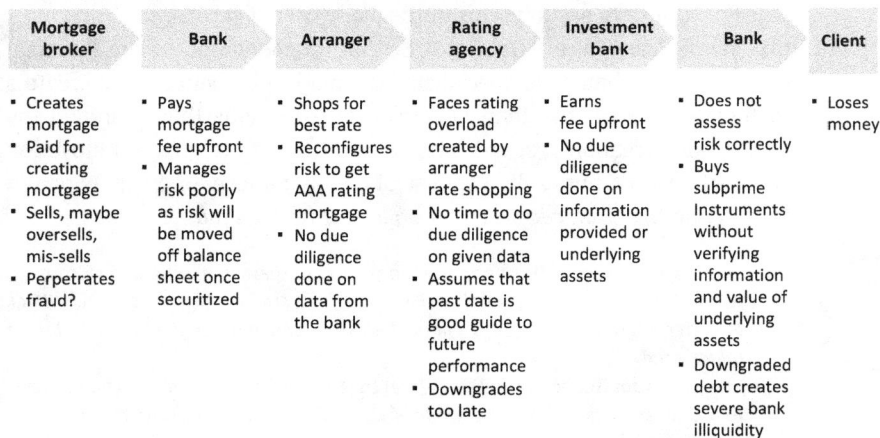

Mortgage broker	Bank	Arranger	Rating agency	Investment bank	Bank	Client
• Creates mortgage • Paid for creating mortgage • Sells, maybe oversells, mis-sells • Perpetrates fraud?	• Pays mortgage fee upfront • Manages risk poorly as risk will be moved off balance sheet once securitized	• Shops for best rate • Reconfigures risk to get AAA rating mortgage • No due diligence done on data from the bank	• Faces rating overload created by arranger rate shopping • No time to do due diligence on given data • Assumes that past date is good guide to future performance • Downgrades too late	• Earns fee upfront • No due diligence done on information provided or underlying assets	• Does not assess risk correctly • Buys subprime Instruments without verifying information and value of underlying assets • Downgraded debt creates severe bank illiquidity	• Loses money

Figure 8.1: Failure of systemic integrity in subprime value chain.[17]

Once the system began to fail, the crisis cascaded from one part of the value chain to the next, just like toppling a stack of dominoes. It was both complex and tightly connected. It nearly destroyed the global financial system, even though it began as just a US falling house prices problem.

The examples above, with the exception of enjoying a glass of milk, show how complex modern systems are. To really understand how they work, their interdependencies, and the unintended consequences of failure at any point in their interconnected and interrelated pieces requires considerable technical expertise and time to explain how things work. The devastating impact of Covid-19 on volatility, uncertainty and its unknown consequences both in the short and medium term regarding public health and the economy is unfortunately an all too powerful example of what happens when complex and tightly coupled systems break down, with nobody knowing where or how the dominoes are going to fall. What is more, the impact of volatility and uncertainty discussed in Chapter 7 makes it even more difficult for directors to appreciate the consequences of decisions taken by their boards. Only experts appreciate the nuances and subtleties of complex systems. In today's world where science keeps pushing the frontiers of knowledge, what we knew yesterday may no longer suffice tomorrow.

The Dangers of Simplification and Bias

The challenge for all directors (and INEDs [independent non-executive directors] in particular, who are not experts in the intricacies and complexities of the organizations on whose boards they sit) is how to come to terms with complex issues presented to them for maybe a couple of hours at the most a few times a year in board meetings.[18] The natural reaction to this problem is for emphasis to be placed on simplifying the complexity so that the main thrusts of the proposals can be understood well enough for boards to make their decisions, based on board papers presented a few working days before the board meeting. To make them easier to absorb, the complexity is further reduced by writing executive summaries – the boards' equivalents of the so-called "elevator pitch" where management has to persuade the CEO during a short ride in the elevator to approve what they are trying to do.

The problem with this approach is that generalists (directors) are being asked to make long-term decisions that may be irreversible, based on the simplification of complex information synthesized by specialists (management and their consultants) who may well fall into the trap of taking what are complex shades of grey, with complicated qualifications whose impact may be difficult to understand in the time available, and presenting them as black and white options.

An excellent example of the power of oversimplification is the 2019 UK general election where the Conservatives had one simple overriding message: "Get Brexit Done!" even though the reality is much more complex. The devastated Labour party lost with the worst result since 1935 had a number of popular policies with no clear message and Jeremy Corbyn's fatal ambiguity regarding his position on Brexit. Nevertheless, the saying "the devil is in the details" expresses an important truth, demonstrating the need for counterbalancing the tendency to oversimplify what is presented to senior management and even more so to boards, where the suppression of complexity and nuance can lead to groupthink.

Napoleon Bonaparte, one of the greatest generals and administrators of all time, totally rejected the use of executive summaries and consensus-based decisions when preparing for battle:[19]

> Napoleon's ability to see the big picture combined with an almost fanatical emphasis on the little picture and hypothesis testing was exceptional.
> *His attention to detail meant he rejected executive summaries, asking for the full report instead, with specifics. He even went so far as to read the muster rolls for an hour every day to know exactly where his forces were deployed.* Napoleon believed in the importance of good information from all sources,[20] but knew it was important to consider the source carefully. . .[21]

Napoleon held no councils of war because they lead to consensus-based second-best solutions.[22] However, his unwillingness to hold councils of war did not mean that he did not seek other opinions. Quite the reverse; he seems to have understood clearly the dynamics of groupthink – he listened to diverse views in private[23]; he wanted ideas that he could then judge for himself and was open to ideas regardless of their origin, as was recognised by his arch-enemy, the Austrian ambassador, Prince von Metternich:

"Seizing the essential point of subjects, stripping them down of useless accessories, developing his thought and never ceasing to elaborate it till he had made it perfectly clear and conclusive, always finding the fitting word for the thing, or inventing one where the image of language had not created it, Napoleon's conversation was ever full of interest. . .Yet he did not fail to listen to the remarks and objections which were addressed to him. . .and I have never felt the least difficulty in saying to him what I believed to be the truth, even when it was not likely to please him."[24]   [Emphases mine]

Napoleon's ability to see both the big picture and the minute details was exceptional. Most CEOs and INEDs do not have this gift. Instead, when faced with volatility and uncertainty that create complexity, they rely on heuristics (rules of thumb) with all the dangers of bias such rules of thumb bring with them. There are six threats to good decisions created by the need to simplify:[25]

1. **Rush to Solve:** This is the tendency to want to find an immediate solution without investing enough in defining the problem, identifying fundamental objectives, and considering alternative approaches. Too often, the solution is to select the first apparently workable alternative without considering carefully enough what the problem to be solved really is and what the objectives should be. As a result, decision makers sometimes solve the wrong problem, or settle for a suboptimal outcome. We tend not to pay sufficient attention to this error because of the way our brains work and our resulting need for norms and causality,[26] even when none exists because events were truly random.[27]

2. **Judgment Triggers:** Every judgment has a trigger initiating the process. This trigger can lead to skipping the early steps of the judgment process. Triggers often appear as an alternative masquerading as a problem definition. As a result, people can take action without a complete understanding of the problem, set themselves inappropriate objectives, or fail to consider all possible alternatives.

   This is often the result of "framing effects" which are the consequence of different ways of presenting the same information. For example,

   The statement that "the odds of survival one month after surgery are 90%' is more reassuring than the equivalent statement that 'mortality within one month of surgery is 10%."[28]

   Both statements mean the same thing; yet their emotional impact is quite different.

3. **Availability Bias:** The "availability tendency" limits the alternatives considered or information gathered to the alternatives or information that come readily to mind. This is also known as "What you see is all there is" (WYSIATI).[29] WYSIATI makes it easier to create coherence and for us to accept a statement as true. It allows us to decide on partial information in a fast-moving world and prevents analysis paralysis. Much of the time it is a good enough heuristic to support reasonable actions, but it also makes us jump to conclusions too quickly. Many disastrous decisions have been taken on the basis of statements like "In the time available and/or with the information we had available . . . " Perhaps the best-known example of this is the primary justification for the US invasion of Iraq was to clear Iraq of weapons of mass destruction that it did not possess.

4. **Overconfidence Bias:** Overconfidence is part of the human condition and leads to suboptimal behavior in every step of the judgment process. It can lead to underinvestment in defining the problem in the first place, in identifying fundamental objectives correctly, in considering sufficient alternatives, and in searching thoroughly for enough information:

   > Overconfidence: As the WYSIATI rule implies, neither the quantity nor the quality of the evidence counts for much in subjective confidence. The confidence that individuals have in their beliefs depends mostly on the quality of the story they can tell about what they see, even if they see little. *We often fail to allow for the possibility that evidence that should be critical to our judgment is missing – what we see is all there is.* Furthermore, our associative system tends to settle on a coherent pattern of activation and suppresses doubt and ambiguity.[30]   [Emphasis mine]

5. **Confirmation Bias:** The "confirmation tendency" affects how we gather and evaluate information and reach conclusions. Human beings seek and give excessive credence to confirming information in the information gathering and evaluation steps and to then favor conclusions that are consistent with initial prejudices:

   > Contrary to the rules of philosophers of science, who advise testing hypotheses by trying to refute them, people (and scientists quite often) seek data that are likely to be compatible with the beliefs they currently hold. *The confirmatory bias of [the unconscious mind] favors uncritical acceptance of suggestions and exaggerates the likelihood of extreme and improbable events.*[31]   [Emphasis mine]

6. **Anchoring Bias:** The "anchoring tendency" and related potential judgment bias affect how we gather information. In gathering and evaluating information the tendency is to anchor on an initial value and stay too close to it when attempting to adjust away from it while making the final assessments. Unless

boards demand that management practice zero-based budgeting, they are unwitting victims of anchoring bias – the anchor being the previous year's budget and actual numbers.

Table 8.2 summarizes the effect of the unconscious mind on our ability or inability to make sound decisions.

Table 8.2: Role of the unconscious mind in decision making.[32]

The Unconscious Mind:
1. Generates impressions, feeling and inclinations, which become beliefs, attitudes, and intention when endorsed by the conscious mind;
2. Is programmed by the conscious mind to mobilize attention when a pattern is observed;
3. Executes skilled responses and generates skilled intuitions after adequate training;
4. Creates a pattern of activated ideas in the associative memory;
5. Links a sense of easy mental processing (cognitive ease) to illusions of truth, pleasant feelings, and lowers vigilance;
6. Distinguishes the surprising from the normal;
7. Infers and invents causes and intentions;
8. Neglects ambiguity and suppresses doubt;
9. Is biased to believe and confirm;
10. Exaggerates emotional consistency through the "horns and halos" effect;
11. Focuses on existing evidence and ignores absent evidence (WYSIATI);
12. Generates a limited set of basic assessments and options;
13. Represents sets by norms and prototypes and does not integrate;
14. Computes more than intended (mental shotgun);
15. Substitutes on occasion an easier question to answer than the correct, but harder one;
16. Is more sensitive to changes in states than to states themselves (prospect theory);
17. Overweights low probability events;
18. Responds more strongly to loss than gain (between 1.5 and 2.5 times more);[33]
19. Frames decision problems narrowly, in isolation from one another.

Ambiguity

Ambiguity is defined as: "Two words that within context are opposites that expose a fundamental division in the author's mind."[34] I define ambiguity as "words or ideas that are capable of being interpreted in more than one way."

A significant example of ambiguity leading to a positive outcome was UN Resolution 242, adopted unanimously by the UN Security Council on November 22, 1967, which ended the Six Day War between Israel and Egypt, Jordan, and Syria. The ambiguity comes from the difference in the English and French versions of the resolution[ii] which allowed both the Israelis and the Arabs to agree to a ceasefire, based on their different interpretations about territorial withdrawal by the Israeli army. Based on the English version, the Israelis understood it to mean "from not all" the occupied territories, whereas the Arabs using the French version understood it to mean withdrawal "from all" occupied territories. Although this ambiguity allowed the parties to stop fighting, it did nothing to resolve the different long-term objectives of the Israelis and Palestinians.

As part of the continuing process of attempting to find a long-term peaceful solution to the Israeli-Palestinian conflict, Henry Kissinger adopted "constructive ambiguity" as the negotiating approach for the Oslo Accords. Constructive ambiguity may work in some circumstances, but not when the endpoints are fundamentally incompatible because it undermines trust:

> Whatever its virtues in other settings, in the context of Israeli-Palestinian negotiations, "constructive ambiguity" has succeeded only in producing confusion and eroding trust between the parties. Throughout the Oslo process of 1990s, disagreements over how to interpret various provisions led to endless delays as well as the renegotiation and outright lack of implementation of signed agreements.[35]

Boards could be presented with potential ambiguity of corporate purpose, with ambiguity over values and codes of conduct (discussed in Chapter 6), with ambiguity over different stakeholder priorities, with ambiguity over forecasts and interpretations of facts, and ambiguity of roles when communicating to different audiences.

1. ***Ambiguity of Corporate Purpose:*** For many years, the only ambiguity of corporate purpose could be summed up in the contrasting philosophies of Peter Drucker and Milton Friedman. Drucker argued that the purpose of business was "to create and maintain satisfied customers," whereas Friedman argued that it was "to maximize shareholder value." This disagreement was made

---

ii The English version of the clause: "Withdrawal of Israeli armed forces from territories occupied in the recent conflict" is given in French as: "Retrait des forces armées israéliennes des territoires occupés lors du récent conflit."

The difference between the two versions lies in the absence of a definite article ("the") in the English version, while the word "des" present in the French version in the expression "des territoires occupés" can only mean "from the occupied territories". . .If the meaning of "from some occupied territories" were intended, the only way to say so in French would have been "**de** territoires occupés."

Although some have dismissed the controversy by suggesting that the use of the word "des" in the French version is a translation error and should therefore be ignored in interpreting the document, the debate has retained its force since both versions are of equal legal force, as recognized languages of the United Nations and in international law. *Wikipedia.*

more complicated by further arguments over the time horizons involved. Was the purpose of business to achieve either or both of these apparently irreconcilable objectives in the short or long term? The view of investors, when shareholder capitalism was all the rage, seems to have crystallized around the need to focus on short-term profits, regardless of unintended consequences, exemplified by the following:

> *The U.S. economic system favors short-run indicators and mobile capital flows. Managers are both creating this culture and driven by it.* Thus, the short-run savings that accumulate with cutting corners on maintenance and safety can be expected to dominate management thinking at the top, middle and, bottom. *Since any untoward consequences of short-run savings are unlikely to appear, if they ever do, until the distant future, management can escape accountability.* This has to be expected as a risk that most large organizations will take, and those with the most market power will be able to more easily absorb the consequences or deflect criticism.[36]   [Emphases mine]

> Safety cultures can only be developed where top management wants them, or at least will tolerate them. (Those of us who worked with NASA after the *Columbia* disaster will testify that *changing a culture is extremely difficult when "efficiency," "privatization," and "cost reduction" remain the top management's primary concern; their culture can trump all others. . .).*[37]   [Emphasis mine]

Even when boards had longer time horizons, CEOs had shorter ones because of their contracts:

> What's more, *there's often a mismatch between the time horizons of board members (longer) and of top executives (shorter), and that lack of alignment can diminish a board's ability to engage in well-informed give-and-take about strategic trade-offs.* "The chairman of my company has effectively been given a decade," says the CEO of a steelmaker in Asia, "and I have three years – tops – to make my mark. If I come up with a strategy that looks beyond the current cycle, I can never deliver the results expected from me. Yet I am supposed to work with him to create long-term shareholder value. How am I supposed to make this work?" It's a fair question, particularly since recent McKinsey research shows that major strategic moves involving active capital reallocation deliver higher shareholder returns than more passive approaches over the long haul, but lower returns over time frames of less than three years.[38]   [Emphasis mine]

The consensus appears to have shifted back toward Drucker's view that maximizing profit is not the purpose of business with the US Business Roundtable's Declaration on August 19, 2019, that the purpose of the corporation is to promote an economy that serves all Americans. Whether this change of heart is real or PR whitewash, only time will tell. Some skepticism is probably warranted as long as the reward and remuneration systems for senior management and CEOs continues to reflect a focus on short-term bottom-line results, reinforcing ambiguity regarding the real purpose of business.

2. ***Ambiguity between Stakeholder Priorities:*** I find the parallels between the 2019 Business Roundtable Declaration and Johnson & Johnson's 1943 *Credo* quite striking, shown in Table 8.3.

Table 8.3: J&J's *Credo* and Business Roundtable Declaration compared.

Johnson & Johnson Credo (1943) [39]	Roundtable Declaration (2019) [40]
"We believe our first responsibility is to the patients, doctors and nurses, to mothers and fathers and all others who use our products and services. In meeting their needs everything we do must be of high quality. We must constantly strive to provide value, reduce our costs and maintain reasonable prices. Customers' orders must be serviced promptly and accurately. Our business partners must have an opportunity to make a fair profit. *We are responsible to our employees who work with us throughout the world.* We must provide an inclusive work environment where each person must be considered as an individual. *We must respect their diversity and dignity and recognize their merit.* They must have a sense of security, fulfillment and purpose in their jobs. Compensation must be fair and adequate and working conditions clean, orderly and safe. We must support the health and well-being of our employees and help them fulfill their family and other personal responsibilities. Employees must feel free to make suggestions and complaints. There must be equal opportunity for employment, development and advancement for those qualified. We must provide highly capable leaders and their actions must be just and ethical.	"Businesses play a vital role in the economy by creating jobs, fostering innovation and providing essential goods and services. Businesses make and sell consumer products; manufacture equipment and vehicles; support the national defense; grow and produce food; provide health care; generate and deliver energy; and offer financial, communications and other services that underpin economic growth. While each of our individual companies serves its own corporate purpose, we share a fundamental commitment to all of our stakeholders. We commit to: – *Delivering value to our customers.* We will further the tradition of American companies leading the way in meeting or exceeding customer expectations. – *Investing in our employees.* This starts with compensating them fairly and providing important benefits. It also includes supporting them through training and education that help develop new skills for a rapidly changing world. *We foster diversity and inclusion, dignity and respect.* – *Dealing fairly and ethically with our suppliers.* We are dedicated to serving as good partners to the other companies, large and small, that help us meet our missions.

Table 8.3 (continued)

Johnson & Johnson Credo (1943) [39]	Roundtable Declaration (2019) [40]
We are responsible to the communities in which we live and work and to the world community as well. We must help people be healthier by supporting better, access and care in more places around the world. We must be good citizens – support good works and charities, better health and education, and bear our fair share of taxes. We must maintain in good order the property we are privileged to use, protecting the environment and natural resources. *Our final responsibility is to our stockholders. Business must make a sound profit.* We must experiment with new ideas. Research must be carried on, innovative programs developed, investments made for the future and mistakes paid for. New equipment must be purchased, new facilities provided and new products launched. Reserves must be created to provide for adverse times. *When we operate according to these principles, the stockholders should realize a fair return."* [Emphases mine]	– *Supporting the communities in which we work.* We respect the people in our communities and protect the environment by embracing sustainable practices across our businesses. – *Generating long-term value for shareholders,* who provide the capital that allows companies to invest, grow and innovate. We are committed to transparency and effective engagement with shareholders. Each of our stakeholders is essential. We commit to deliver value to all of them, for the future success of our companies, our communities and our country." [Emphases mine]

The themes in both statements are similar as are the defined stakeholders, with one exception, the Business Roundtable emphasizes suppliers more. However, the *Credo* is very clear and avoids ambiguities of priority between stakeholders, unlike the Declaration. In the *Credo*, customers come first, then employees, then communities, and finally shareholders (stockholders). It also makes it clear that shareholders are only entitled to a fair return and not the maximum return. In short, the Roundtable Declaration still has ambiguities boards may have difficulty reconciling, given the non-prioritization of stakeholders and its sidestepping of the problem of time horizon and profit maximization by focusing on long-term value creation. As long as CEO rewards and remuneration stay the same, ambiguity about the measurable purpose of the corporation will remain.

3. ***Ambiguity of Facts:*** It is difficult enough for generalists to know what to make of disagreements between specialists about how to interpret the

facts. Bona fide experts disagree about the economy and the stock market; about the impact of AI on employment; about nutrition, wellness, and health. In part this is because as new facts emerge, different conclusions are the result; and in part it is because it is not clear whether what has been observed is merely correlation rather than causation. If the results are only correlation, then cause-and-effect conclusions cannot be drawn:

> In his book ["Reasonable Disagreement"] the philosopher [Chris McMahon], argues that circumstances will arise when two rational and competent reasoners can, after exploring and sharing, reasonably disagree. I am concerned that often there is not enough discussion about how conclusions are reached by protagonists. Too much effort is expended on disagreeing and not enough on exploring where exactly divergence occurred and why.[41]

This is because our brains are programmed to reject randomness; we need stories that make sense, that provide plausible cause and effect, even when none exists, or that reinforce our confirmation biases. It is the foundation on which vested interests deny the facts defending tobacco,[42] deny climate change,[43] or divert attention away from the harmful effects of sugar to the effects of fats and cholesterol,[44] or even deny that the Holocaust happened.[45] This is the basis of conspiracy theories and how conmen operate.[46] Its adverse impact on decision making is made more severe by the propagation of fake news and alternative facts by social media that flourish in today's post-truth world.

4. ***Ambiguity of Roles:*** Boards must recognize that although their top management and, in particular, the CEO and Chair have different audiences to deal with, they must be able to communicate effectively and consistently with all stakeholder constituencies. This can be challenging, given that each constituency has different interests and needs which may conflict with those of the others. Each constituency would like to hear what it wants to hear; regardless of what the others would like to hear. Consequently, the Chair and CEO must reconcile the different needs and expectations of their publics when communicating with them. The Chair and CEO, the investor relations, public relations, marketing and sales, and HR departments, must between them create an internally consistent, coherent message reflecting the organization's purpose and values:

> *Today, the people who lead large companies must play many roles: diplomat, policy maker, motivational captain of their employees and an assuring public face to customers.* Leaders – particularly those like Zuckerberg whose products are so widely used and influential – are expected to be capable of thinking deeply about problems in the world, not only to devise clever product and business strategies.
>
> *It's a nearly impossible ask, but that doesn't mean we should lower the bar for these executives.*[47]   [Emphases mine]

Summary

The increased volatility and uncertainty in political, economic, social, and environmental matters (discussed in Chapter 7), combined with the fact that many industries have developed global supply and value chains, has created such complexity that it is often hard for boards to understand the unintended consequences of decisions they make.

Dealing with the resulting complexity is difficult for directors who are not intimately familiar with the details of the organizations on whose boards they sit. The solution is often to simplify the issues so directors can get their heads around what is being proposed in the time available. This poses two problems. The first is that they miss the nuances – the "devil in the details" of the choices before them – too often they see only strawmen and black-and-white alternatives, when reality is in shades of grey. The second is that it makes robust constructive challenge more difficult when directors themselves recognize the limits of their understanding. They are then forced to apply rules of thumb in digesting what they read and hear, leaving them vulnerable to judgment traps and biases, and making wrong decisions as a result.

The greater uncertainty and complexity in business today compounds the effect of ambiguity on decision making. There is a new source of tension in decision making. Directors now have to deal with ambiguity of corporate purpose with no clear guide on how to prioritize between different stakeholders, while CEOs and investors tend to focus more on short-term shareholder value maximization, when what may be needed is a long-term view.

There have always been sources of ambiguity in facts and their interpretation where generalist directors have to evaluate competing arguments presented by experts (management and their consultants) and where they have to differentiate between correlation and causality when listening to explanations. Finally, directors, in particular Chairs and CEOs, face ambiguity in their roles when dealing with the different audiences they have to face; reconciling the different messages each audience wants to hear with the need for a consistent and coherent overall theme.

Considering all these factors, boards may need a different approach to dealing with volatility, uncertainty, complexity, and ambiguity with at least a "Plan B," and maybe a "Plan C," for the third decade of the 21st century. They may also need to approach doing business differently, if they are to continue creating long-term sustainable value. This will be discussed in Part 3.

References

1 Cambridge dictionary, https://dictionary.cambridge.org/dictionary/english/complexity, accessed on December 4, 2019.

2 Johnson, N. F. (2009), *Simply complexity: a clear guide to complexity theory* (London: One World Publications), p3.

3 Zinkin, J. (2019), "Emerging Risk and Future Board: Boardroom Governance in a VUCA world," *SIDC, presentation* to B.A.T. Malaysia Berhad Board, November 27, 2019.

4 Lynn, B. (2005), *End of the Line: The rise and coming fall of the global corporation* (New York: Doubleday), p. 3, quoted in Perrow, C. (2011), *The Next Catastrophe: Reducing Our Vulnerabilities to Natural, Industrial and Terrorist Disasters* (Princeton: Princeton University Press), p. 302.

5 Based on Hogan (2016), cited in Garrett, G. (2019), "Why US-China Supply Chains Are Stronger Than the Trade War," *Knowledge@Wharton,* September 5, 2019, https://knowledge.wharton.upenn.edu/article/trade-war-supply-chain-impact/?utm_source=kw_newsletter&utm_medium=email&ut, accessed on September 8, 2019.

6 Huang, Y. (2014), "The 2008 Milk Scandal Revisited," *Forbes,* July 16, 2014, https://www.forbes.com/sites/yanzhonghuang/2014/07/16/the-2008-milk-scandal-revisited/#289afe324105, accessed on December 12, 2019.

7 Dirks, G. (2020), in an email to the author on January 20, 2020.

8 University of Oxford (2016),"Are big-city transportation systems too complex for human minds?" *ScienceDaily,* February 19, 2016, https://www.sciencedaily.com/releases/2016/02/160219185214.htm, accessed on December 14, 2019.

9 Harford, T. (2011), *Adapt: Why Success Always Starts With Failure* (London: Little Brown), pp. 185–186.

10 Perrow, C. (2007), *The Next Catastrophe* (Princeton, New Jersey: Princeton University Press), p. 177.

11 Ashford, N. et al. (1993), "The Encouragement of Technological Change for Preventing Chemical Accidents: Moving Firms from Secondary Prevention and Mitigation to Primary Prevention," *Center for Technology, Policy and Industrial Development* (Cambridge, Massachusetts: Massachusetts Institute of Technology), pp. II–9,https://pdfs.semanticscholar.org/7b25/d67aa922651dbca38cede6fd23993eaffec9.pdf, accessed on December 14, 2019.

12 Perrow, C. (2007), op. cit., p. 213.

13 Ibid., p. 212.

14 Elkington, J. (2008), "Time to Tackle Subprime Supply Chains," October 18, 2008, http://www.sustainability.com/blog/time-to-tackle-subprime-supply-chains#.UNz1_OTqn48, accessed on December 14, 2019.

15 Zinkin, J. (2014), *Rebuilding Trust in Banks: The Role of Leadership and Governance* (Singapore: John Wiley & Sons), pp. 71–75.

16 Zinkin, J. (2014), op. cit., p. 74.

17 Based on ibid., p. 74.

18 Bhagat, C. et al. (2013), "Tapping the strategic potential of boards," *McKinsey Quarterly,* February 2013, https://www.mckinsey.com/business-functions/strategy-and-corporate-finance/our-insights/tapping-the-strategic-potential-of-boards?, accessed on December 16, 2019.

19 Axelrod, A. (2011), *Napoleon, CEO* (New York: Sterling), cited in Zinkin, J. (2014), op. cit., p. 9.

20 *Military Maxim LXXVI,* http://www.military-info.com/freebies/maximsn.htm, accessed on February 15, 2013.

21 *Military Maxim LXIII,* ibid.

22 *Military Maxim LXV,* ibid.

23 "Never hold a council of war, but listen to the views of each in private." *Letter to Joseph Bonaparte,* January 12, 1806, cited in Axelrod, A. (2011), op. cit., p. 110, cited in Zinkin, J. (2014), op. cit., p. 10.

24 Prince von Metternich quoted by Felix Markham (1963), *Napoleon* (New York: Penguin Books), quoted in Axelrod, A. (2011), op. cit., p. 200, quoted in Zinkin, J. (2014), op. cit., p. 10.

25 COSO (2012), "Enhancing Board Oversight: Avoiding judgment Traps and Biases," *Committee of Sponsoring Organizations of the Treadway Commission,* March 2012, cited in Zinkin, J. (2014), op. cit., pp. 209–212.

26 Kahneman, D. (2011), *Thinking, Fast and Slow* (London: Allen Lane), pp. 71–88.

27 Taleb, N. N. (2005), *Fooled by Randomness: The Hidden Role of Chance in Life and in the Markets* (New York: Random House).

28 Kahneman, D. (2011), op. cit., p. 88.

29 Ibid., p. 87.

30 Ibid., pp. 87–88.

31 Ibid., p. 81.

32 Ibid., p. 105.

33 Ibid., p. 284.

34 Empsom, W. (1947), *Seven Types of Ambiguity* (London: Chatto & Windus), Chapter VII.

35 Elgindy, K. (2014), "When ambiguity is destructive," *Brookings,* January 22, 2014, https://www.brookings.edu/opinions/when-ambiguity-is-destructive/, accessed on December 12, 2019.

36 Perrow, C. (2011), *The Next Catastrophe: Reducing Our Vulnerabilities to Natural, Industrial and Terrorist Disasters* (Princeton: Princeton University Press), p. 144.

37 Ibid., p. 164.

38 Bhagat, C. et al. (2013), op. cit.

39 Johnson, R. W. (1943), "Our Credo," *Johnson & Johnson website,* https://www.jnj.com/credo/, accessed on December 8, 2019.

40 Business Roundtable (2019), "Business Roundtable Redefines the Purpose of a Corporation to Promote 'An Economy That Serves All Americans'," *Business Roundtable,* August 19, 2019, https://www.businessroundtable.org/business-roundtable-redefines-the-purpose-of-a-corporation-to-promote-an-economy-that-serves-all-americans, accessed on December 16, 2019.

41 Dirks, G. (2020), in an email reply to the author on January 21, 2020.

42 Drew, E. (1965), "The Quiet Victory of the Cigarette Lobby: How it found the Best Filter Yet – Congress," *The Atlantic,* September 1965 Issue, https://www.theatlantic.com/magazine/archive/1965/09/the-quiet-victory-of-the-cigarette-lobby-how-it-found-the-best-filter-yet-congress/304762/, accessed on December 16, 2019.

43 Ketchell, M. (2019), "The Five Corrupt Pillars of Climate Change Denial," *The Conversation,* November 29, 2019, https://theconversation.com/the-five-corrupt-pillars-of-climate-change-denial-122893, accessed on December 16, 2019.

44 Kirts, L. (2016), "The Sugar Conspiracy is Real," *GOOD,* December 9, 2016, https://www.good.is/food/sugar-industry-influenced-research, accessed on December 16, 2019.

45 "Denial of the Holocaust and the genocide in Auschwitz," http://auschwitz.org/en/history/holocaust-denial/, accessed on December 16, 2019.

46 Harford, T. (2019), "Why we fall for cons," *FT Magazine,* November 16/17, http://timhar ford.com/2019/12/why-we-fall-for-cons/, accessed on December 16, 2019.

47 Ovide, S. (2019), "Zuck isn't always boring," *Bloomberg Technology,* December 5, 2019, https://www.bloomberg.com/news/newsletters/2019-12-05/zuck-isn-t-always-boring, accessed on December 6, 2019.

Part 3: **Achieving Sustainability in a Complicated World**

Part 3 consists of four chapters with suggestions for boards on how best to meet the challenges of environmental, economic, employment, and social sustainability in a complicated world.

Chapter 9, "Adopting a Proactive Approach to VUCA," combines volatility with vision, using the "Five P" framework (Purpose, Principles, Power, People, and Processes); uncertainty with understanding; complexity with courage and commitment; and ambiguity with adaptability to create a new and better way of making decisions.

Chapter 10, "Adopting New Processes," introduces suggestions for additional processes boards could consider to improve their ability to meet the challenges of environmental, economic, employment, and social sustainability.

Chapter 11, "Valuing People Properly," challenges the underlying assumptions boards have about how to treat people and suggests sustainable ways of investing in people.

Chapter 12, "Making Capitalism Sustainable," makes the urgent case for reform of capitalism, arguing for an end to "predatory value extraction," and emphasizes the importance of companies embracing a sustainable purpose. It closes with conclusions on how to avert a social and "political tragedy of the commons."

Chapter 9
Adopting a Proactive Approach to VUCA

This chapter is a discussion of how to move from a reactive to a proactive ap-proach to VUCA (volatility, uncertainty, complexity, ambiguity), presented in four parts. The first part combines dealing with volatility by developing vision; the sec-ond reconciles dealing with uncertainty by increasing understanding; the third deals with complexity and the need for courage and commitment in decision mak-ing; and the fourth reconciles ambiguity with adaptability. It closes with a sum-mary on how boards can limit risk to achieve a sustainable future.

Chapter 7 explored the issues boards face when making decisions created by volatility and uncertainty, while Chapter 8 looked at the problems posed by complexity and ambiguity. If Chapters 3–8 are even half right, the uncertainty and complexity faced by boards is much greater than it was 30 years ago when there were no worries about the impact of climate change and belief in the neo-liberal consensus was at its strongest,[1] whereas now it is being challenged. The geopolitical concerns we face now in Europe, Asia, and the Middle East were nonexistent with the exceptions of oil and the Arab-Israeli conflict; and there was no threat to future employment and employability of "Industry 4.0" on the horizon.

It is true, however, that economic volatility (Covid-19 aside) is lower than in the past because of the actions of the leading central banks in keeping inter-est costs low and ensuring there is adequate liquidity.[2] However, this has been at the cost of rising inequality,[3] which has increased political volatility to the point where it might yet become a threat to economic stability.

Previously, discussions on the problems boards face when dealing with VUCA, were reactive. I believe, in the future, boards have to do more than what Bill George called VUCA 1.0.[4] Instead, they will need to adopt a two-pronged approach – one that still deals with VUCA reactively to limit the impact of VUCA-based risk (VUCA 1.0), and then builds on VUCA 1.0 strategies proac-tively to create a sustainable future – an approach he called VUCA 2.0. Stage 1 for each of the elements is reactive, designed to limit the impact of VUCA-based risk, while stage 2 is proactive, designed to create a sustainable future, despite the difficulties posed by VUCA in the third decade of the 21st century.

https://doi.org/10.1515/9783110670486-009

Volatility + Vision

Stage 1 is the traditional, reactive approach to dealing with volatility. It seeks to minimize the risk posed by volatility to "business as usual" business models. This is achieved by building slack and redundancy into processes and systems; stockpiling inventory and talent on a "just in case" basis which needs to be reconciled with "just in time" and "lean management" thinking. The level of investment that is regarded as desirable is determined by the level of risk.[5] If businesses had understood the risks created by adopting excessively complex and tightly coupled global supply chains, the impact of Covid-19 could have been greatly reduced. The domino effects might have been avoided. Making China the "manufacturer for the world" also concentrated risks in one country, so that when it had to shut down, the knock-on effects were global. Although building slack and redundancy is expensive because of the duplication of resources, which may never need to be used; it is relatively easy to manage; and as Covid-19 teaches us, *essential* for good risk management in the event of a "black swan" that is beyond our control:

> While *volatility* is a reality of business, it's far more predictable than most leaders believe. The causes of seasonal fluctuations, supply chain disruptions, natural disasters or shifts in demand are often out of your control and can lead to major month-to-month revenue or cost disruptions. But it's possible to see and heed early warning signs. Leaders who seek clarity about internal and external conditions and track those with high potential to create disruption are better able to recognize volatile conditions and respond accordingly.[6]

Stage 2 is the proactive approach to dealing with volatility – by focusing on developing an "evergreen" vision that is sufficiently well crafted that it can withstand the vagaries of volatility; minimized, but not eliminated by an effectively implemented stage 1:

> Today's business leaders need the ability to see through the chaos to have a clear vision for their organizations. They must define the True North of their organization: its mission, values, and strategy. *They should create clarity around this True North and refuse to let external events pull them off course or cause them to neglect or abandon their mission, which must be their guiding light.*[7]   [Emphasis mine]

Defining the mission is essential if the organization is to develop an "evergreen" vision and set of values which are the basis of its code of conduct. The mission answers the questions, "Who does the organization serve?" "What products or services does it offer to serve its beneficiaries?" and "How does it provide such products and services?" It does this more specifically by answering the following seven questions:[8]

1. *Does the organization have a clear business focus* and is it understood by everybody?
2. *Has the organization developed a compelling, differentiated mission* setting it apart from the competition?
3. *Does the organization understand who are its competitors for market margin?*[i]
4. *What are the organization's ambitions: to be technology leader or follower;* and which segment of the customer universe is it targeting in the product/category life cycle: early adopter, growth, maturity, or decline?
5. *Which market segment does the organization want to operate in:* prestige, premium, value for money, low cost mass market; and what psychographics is it seeking to satisfy?
6. *How adaptable is the organization's mission to changes in the external environment* or does it run the risk of "stuckness"?[ii]
7. *Does the mission ensure the organization's long-term "license to operate"?* This is determined by answering four subordinate questions in the following order. The first two are ethical and the second two are commercial:
   a. What does the organization's top management team want to do? (ethically determined);
   b. What will society allow it to do? (ethically determined);
   c. Is the opportunity worthwhile in terms of absolute size and longevity? (commercially determined);
   d. Does the organization possess the core competencies needed to execute successfully? (commercially determined).

The point to note is that boards ignore the ethical dimensions of the company mission at their peril because behavior that is unethical but legal may become

---

i Michael Porter's "Five Forces" framework explains why competitors are not just the head-to-head competitors who offer similar products and services, but include suppliers and customers of an organization. They compete for market margin between the original suppliers of resources and raw materials to the organization and between the organization and its customers in their respective terms of trade in the value chain. Market margin is also constrained by the ability of new players to enter the market, bringing with them additional capacity or disruptive technologies to depress market margin; and by substitutes and alternatives that limit the extent to which market margin can be raised by anti-competitive behavior.

ii "Stuckness" occurs when the board allocates strategic resources that cannot be reallocated once they have been committed. It preserves excess capacity, creating expensive barriers to exit, and explains why some industries yield low ROI, regardless of how well the companies in those industries are managed.

illegal as society turns its back on such activities.[iii] They also need to reflect on the employee implications of having an unethical but legal mission. They are likely to have to pay more to recruit and retain people because of the ethical stigma around the company's activities and they may not be able attract top talent who are likely to go elsewhere to avoid that stigma.

Once the mission has been established by the board, including whether it will deliver a sustainable long-term "license to operate," it must be translated into a vision that is compelling both emotionally and rationally. The custodian of the vision is the board; with the CEO responsible for guarding it. The CEO's role is to:

> *Ensure that everybody understands "what's in it for them" in achieving the Vision,* and equally what are the consequences for them and the organization as whole for failing. It is the responsibility of the CEO to operationalize the Vision, by ensuring it is broken down into milestones and targets with due dates. *Perhaps the most important and often neglected part in this is to ensure that every employee has a clear "line of sight" between achieving the Vision and their own job.*
>
> *CEOs who are not wholehearted in their support of the Vision have no business being in the company, as they can do tremendous damage to what makes it unique.*[9]
>
> [Emphases mine]

When the board has agreed to the organization's mission and vision, it must ensure its "purpose" reflects them – in other words, the board must decide with whom the organization will do business and with whom it will not. Next, it must articulate its values or "principles," defining how it will do business and what it stands for. The board must then decide on the organizational design or

---

iii An example of this potential conflict between what is commercially acceptable in the short-term, but poor business in the long run were Goldman Sachs' 2007 Abacus and Timberwolf deals during the subprime crisis (Goldstein, M. [2010], "Abacus might have had other benefits for Goldman," *Reuters,* April 14, 2010, https://www.reuters.com/article/us-goldman-circular-exclusive/abacus-might-have-had-other-benefits-for-goldman-idUSTRE63M4U820100424, accessed on December 19, 2019). They were legally defensible, but ethically indefensible because there was a serious conflict of interest. They were scrutinized in detail by Congress (Congressional Financial Inquiry Commission, January 2011).

The damage to Goldman's reputation was considerable. More important, when Senator Carl Levin, chairing the Congressional hearings, was given the answer that what Goldman had done was legal, his reaction was that in that case the law needed changing. This proved to be an important turning point in the development of the 2010 Dodd-Frank legislation, regulating banks more toughly. Goldman's lawyers helped Goldman win the battle regarding Abacus and Timberwolf, but contributed to losing the war over tougher regulation.

Macdonald, E. (2013),"Goldman Sachs Accused of Misleading Congress, Clients," *Fox Business,* April 14, 2011, http://www.foxbusiness.com/markets/2011/04/14/goldman-sachs-accused-lying-congress, accessed on January 7, 2013.

structure needed to allocate resources effectively and to determine appropriate reporting relationships and job descriptions – i.e., the "power" structure of the organization. The "power" structure then needs to be staffed with suitable "people" and the whole entity needs "processes" to hold it together. The resulting "Five P"s[10] capture the board's need to define "purpose," "principles," "power," "people," and "processes"; providing five lenses through which the board can review the company's performance, establishing where things are going according to plan and where more investment or corrective actions are needed.

Figure 9.1 shows how the board-agreed mission and vision can only be achieved if the organization's "Five Ps" are aligned properly.

Aligning the organization to achieve the mission and vision

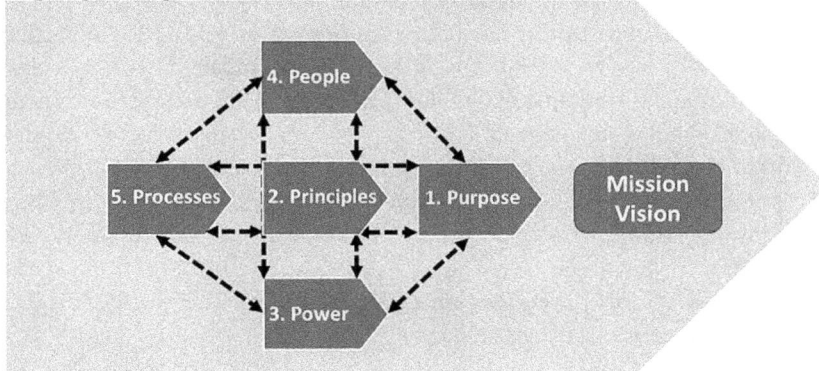

Figure 9.1: The "Five Ps": five lenses to track performance.

If any one of the "Five Ps" is misaligned and does not point toward the mission and vision, the mission and vision will not be achieved. Working together, the "Five Ps" determine and reinforce acceptable behavior and values. Working separately, they will create inconsistent behavior and undermine the values of the organization.

The "Five Ps" cover:

1. **"Purpose":** The best way for directors to ensure their enterprise's "purpose" will be aligned with its mission and vision when starting on its journey is to ask a series of questions of management. It is also important each time directors review proposals brought to them by management that they ask these questions again to reassure themselves the organization is not straying from its originally intended destination, even if the justification is

that such a diversion will be very profitable. If these six questions sound like "Blue Ocean" strategy questions, it is because the thought process is similar. The questions are as follows:

a. ***Who are the intended beneficiaries of our organization?*** You may be asking yourself why "beneficiaries" rather than "customers"? There are two reasons for choosing "beneficiaries":

    i. *CG applies to more than just companies with customers in the tradi-tional sense of the word;*

    ii. *Modern stakeholder capitalism requires directors to consider the in-terests of all stakeholders.* Consequently, the board must include customers, employees, suppliers, and the communities where they operate in deciding who are the intended beneficiaries and how to reconcile their different considerations.

b. ***What difference in their lives are we hoping to make?*** This question requires the board to think carefully about the impact and change they want to make on their stakeholders and to think about how to reconcile the different needs of each. It also forces directors to consider how sus-tainable such differences will be and to consider issues like congestion, pollution, and public health consequences of the products and services they offer and the effect on people of the way they make and sell such products.

c. ***What value will they place on that difference?*** This question forces boards to consider Peter Drucker's quote:

> *It is the customer who determines what a business is. It is the customer alone whose willingness to pay for a good or service converts economic resources into wealth, things into goods.* What the business thinks it produces is not of first im-portance – especially not to the future of the business and to its success. . . *What the customer thinks he/she is buying, what he/she considers value, is deci-sive – it determines what a business is, what it produces and whether it will prosper.*[11]   [Emphases mine]

It is essential boards understand what it is that stakeholders value; it is even more important they understand that this can change dramati-cally over time.

d. ***How will we make that difference?*** Companies have choices. Directors need to decide on the following options before considering the issues covered under "power" later in this section:

    i. *How to avoid being "stuck in the middle":* This is one of the most difficult decisions boards face. Ever since Michael Porter argued firms can achieve competitive advantage either by being low cost leaders or by differentiating their offer,[12] management has been concerned with the problem of being "stuck in the middle." Although there is merit in his argument, it is not the whole story, as the following quote makes clear:

> *Being stuck in an unattractive business without a viable exit is one of the worst situations for a firm.* Think of nuclear power and petrochemical plants, and many manufacturing operations whose owners face exit costs that can ruin the economics of a business as it approaches its end. . . A technology company can become stuck because of a commitment to obsolete technology. *Many of these examples of "stuckness" arise because managers made an inflexible commitment to what they thought would always be an attractive business.*
>
> Irreversible market positions entail commitments that expose the firm to risks. In contrast, *flexible positions can be altered as conditions change. You can think of flexibility as a call option on an alternative strategy* – it is enabled, for instance, by holding excess manufacturing capacity, excess inventory, or excess cash.
>
> *The challenge for business leadership is not to avoid the middle, but rather, to develop flexibility – such as a sensible "Plan B" – if the dice turn against you. The middle is bad if you are* stuck in *some important way. The inability to respond flexibly and appropriately to new competitive conditions is the grave threat.*[13]   [Emphases mine]

So when boards consider how they will make the difference to create happy stakeholders, they do not just need to decide what the basis of their offer is: low cost leadership, differentiation, or focus.[iv] They also need to remember to have flexibility – in case they have no easy way out because they are held hostage by their earlier decisions.

ii. *To be first-to-market or a follower:* Many believe that it is important to have first-mover advantage. Historically, some companies have demonstrated they were good at being first movers: Sony, in its heyday, and Apple. Others chose to be rapid followers, learning from the mistakes of first movers, notably Exxon and Matsushita. This was understandable because there have been many times when being first creates unexpected headaches: there may be technological glitches that need fixing, allowing the company that

---

iv For a fuller discussion of the merits of the three strategic options, see, Zinkin, J. (2019), *Better Governance Across the Board: Creating Value Through Reputation, People and Processes* (Boston/Berlin: Walter De Gruyter Inc.), pp. 160–161.

is second into the market to benefit from the mistakes of the first.[v] Sometimes the market is not yet ready and it needs the competitive noise and investment when the second player overwhelms the first. Who remembers that P&G's *Pampers* was in fact late into the disposable diaper market (the first successful disposable diaper was *Paddi* launched in the UK in 1950 and in the US in 1951[14]). MS-DOS was not the first PC operating system, nor was it the best, but by making it available to all IBM compatible PCs, Bill Gates was able to capture undreamed of network effects, defeating the incumbent, Digital Research Inc.'s original and IBM's later, better products.[15]

e. ***How much will it cost to achieve that difference?*** The answer to this question depends on the choices of the board regarding how it will make the difference in the lives of its chosen beneficiaries: its organizational design; its staffing levels; its remuneration and pension policies; where it chooses to locate its production; its cost of capital; and whether and when it is able to capture economies of scale, scope, and learning, taking into account the lifetime of its investments and the rate of obsolescence. It also depends on how it finances its investments, itself a reflection of the riskiness of the projects and the choices it makes between debt and equity; how much of the debt is long-term and how much short-term; the credit terms it gets from its suppliers and the credit terms it offers its customers.

f. ***What return can we expect as a result?*** Directors need to think not just about the operational ratios involved, but also about matching the risk appetite of the investors/shareholders they answer to. This means thinking carefully about whether the shareholders have realistic expectations of the business risk-reward ratio and what level of leverage makes sense to satisfy them. It also means thinking about transfer pricing policies and where to pay taxes to optimize shareholder returns.

Johnson and Johnson's *Credo*, discussed in Chapter 8, is a good example of the founder answering these questions.

2. **"Principles":** These are the values at the heart of the way the organization functions. They determine what kind of business the board chooses to do and with whom it will do business. The "principles" determine:

---

v For example, the case of the Boeing 707 benefiting from the crashes of the Comet (discussed in Chapter 7).

a. ***What the company stands for and its culture:*** Some companies have good reputations for honest dealing, creating quality products, treating their employees well, and being good corporate citizens. Others do not. The difference comes from their "principles" – the values they profess and live by.

> *Firms whose managers act on the principle that employees are self-interested opportunists who must be forced to do their job will tend to create just that.* Conversely a company that functions on the basis of trust and co-operation creates a system in which honest, co-operative people flourish. Self-fulfilling prophecy makes every company a force for either good or ill.
>
> Since the 1980s, the assumptions baked into the management model are the pessimistic ones. In the crash of 2008, we can see where the template based on them (incentives, compliance with letter rather than spirit, rejection of ethical considerations) leads. If the 21st century that management makes possible is to end happily, managers will have to absorb its most important lesson from the 20th: *what matters most in management is not what you make but what you believe.*[16] [Emphases mine]

The key point is companies get what they expect: if they do not believe employees will work based on trust, collaboration, and values, but only based on greed and self-seeking, they will develop reward and recognition systems that reinforce such behavior; they will promote the selfish and greedy who believe the way to the top was the way shown in *The Apprentice*. The reverse is also true:

> How we do business – and what business does to us – has everything to do with how we think about business, talk about business, conceive of business, practice business. *If we think, talk, conceive, and practice business as a ruthless, cutthroat, dog-eat-dog activity, then that, of course, is what it will become. And so, too, it is what we will become, no matter how often (in our off hours and personal lives) we insist otherwise.* If, on the other hand, business is conceived – as it often has been conceived – as an enterprise based on trust and mutual benefits, an enterprise for civilized, virtuous people, then that in turn, will be equally self-fulfilling. It will also be much more amiable, secure, enjoyable, and last, but not least, profitable.[17] [Emphasis mine]

b. ***The "tone at the top" and the "tone in the middle":*** It is not enough for the board to exhort employees to behave with integrity. The board, the Chair, the CEO, and all directors must abide by the values they declare they believe in. Directors must be covered by the code of conduct in exactly the same way as the rest of the organization. They must review it on a regular basis and give the compliance function and internal audit the authority, resources, and tools to do their jobs properly, lest the "tone in the middle" becomes a source of malpractice.

c.   ***Careers of employees and how they are treated:*** Talent management must reflect the needs of the business strategy. However, the board must also ensure that the people who are recruited and promoted share the same values as those of the company. This is essential if the "tone at the top" is to be preserved.

d.   ***Being a responsible citizen:*** This recognizes that if the company is to maintain its social "license to operate," the board must consider the needs of the community in which it operates and of the impact the company has on the environment in terms of degradation, pollution, and congestion. This also requires the board to think carefully about the conditions prevailing in its supply chain, including the working conditions at its suppliers and the ways its suppliers do business.

3.   **"Power":** This deals with questions regarding organizational design, job descriptions, roles and responsibilities, and reporting relationships, as well as how people are treated by their superiors, hence the term "power." Boards must ensure whatever organizational design they approve, it will be sufficiently flexible to avoid the problem of so-called "stuckness" if the business strategy requires a change of direction. Perhaps the most obvious questions in this regard for directors to answer are the following:

a.   ***To make or buy?*** Directors must consider whether by choosing to outsource they are losing control of key intellectual property or losing a core competency leaving them exposed later when the unexpected happens, because although the lost competency was not core, it was, however, mission-critical.

b.   ***To do research and development or license?*** Companies doing their own R&D have to invest a great deal of time, effort, and money (all scarce resources) with no certainty the investment will bear fruit. If they have deep pockets and can survive the likelihood that for every success, they may have to finance up to twenty failed projects,[vi] then choosing to do their own R&D makes sense. However, if time is of the

---

vi "According to Harvard Business School professor Clayton Christensen, there are over 30,000 new products introduced every year, and 95% fail. According to University of Toronto Professor Inez Blackburn, the failure rate of new grocery store products is 70 to 80%." Emmer, M. (2018), "95 Percent of New Products Fail. Here Are 6 Steps to Make Sure Yours Don't," *Inc*, July 6, 2018, https://www.inc.com/marc-emmer/95-percent-of-new-products-fail-here-are-6-steps-to-make-sure-yours-dont.html, accessed 3/30/2020.

essence, or if the company does not have the financial or human resources to do the R&D, then licensing may be a sensible solution.

   c. ***To own fixed assets or rent/lease them?*** The choice will determine the breakeven point and profitability of the P&L and it will also affect the asset intensity of the business, maybe yielding a return on assets that is higher than if the assets were fully owned – depending on the tax treatment of leases. It might also affect the "stuckness" of the business by removing a barrier to exit – depending on the length of the rental or lease agreement.

   d. ***To go direct, through distributors, franchisees, or via the internet?*** The answer to this question has a huge impact on the size of the sales force and on the physical assets (bricks and mortar) the board needs to worry about.

4. **"People":** There are three questions directors must answer, with the help of the Nomination Committee and HR:

   a. ***Do we have the right number of people?*** In answering this question, directors must consider the current business strategy and how they expect it to evolve over time and how that will affect the organizational design of the company. This will determine the number of jobs/roles needed to fulfill the agreed mission and vision, and if not, what can be done about it.

   b. ***Do our people have the right skills and competencies to do the job properly?*** Too often when people are recruited or promoted, the most important criterion is their ability to perform the job based on their past performance,[vii] without paying sufficient attention to whether the nature of the job is changing. This means the board must insist there is an up-to-date competency dictionary used in assessing the current skills base of its key employees. Even if such a dictionary exists, directors must recognize that in some industries change is so rapid, some of yesterday's competencies may no longer be suited for today's responsibilities and certainly will not be suited for tomorrow.

   c. ***Do our people have the right character to work in line with our "principles"?*** It is my belief that we often hire and promote people based on their ability to meet targets they are set; their past track record; or their apparent list of competencies, *without considering enough whether they*

---

vii This explains the famous "Peter Principle" which states people are promoted to their level of incompetence.

have the right character to fit with the "principles" espoused by the organization. Too often, we excuse people whose behavior does not fit with our values either on the grounds of their seniority or on their ability to make a positive impact on the short-term bottom line.

5. **"Processes":** These are the glue that binds the organization together. To be effective, "processes" must include strategic planning, budgeting, and financial reporting; board-approved policies and procedures, regularly inspected by internal audits reported to the audit committee on lapses and loopholes and the corrective action being taken. They also include all forms of internal formal and informal feedback mechanisms, covering reward, remuneration, and appraisal systems; the setting and review of KPIs and scorecards; as well as training and personal development schemes; career development and talent management; and appropriate documentation of standard operating procedures and service level agreements.

It is essential the measurement and remuneration processes align with the mission and vision, if the board is to avoid falling into the trap of "rewarding A while hoping for B," shown in Table 9.1.

Table 9.1: "Rewarding A while hoping for B."[18]

What we hope for	What we often reward
1. Sustainable growth	1. Quarterly earnings
2. Teamwork	2. Individual effort; bell curve
3. Meeting challenging "stretch" objectives	3. Achieving goals; "making the numbers"
4. Maximizing productivity	4. Maximizing Hay points (a job evaluation method)
5. Achieving total quality	5. Shipping on time
6. Candor; welcoming the messenger of bad news	6. Agreeing with the boss; "shooting the messenger"

Uncertainty + Understanding

The traditional, reactive approach to uncertainty in VUCA 1.0 is to invest in information; to collect, interpret, and share it, supported by a knowledge management infrastructure in more sophisticated organizations. The resulting structural changes help reduce the levels of uncertainty:[19]

Many "uncertainties" can be clarified and planned for. Instead of being a passive bystander, leaders can invest resources to collect and analyze competitive intelligence. . .

Looking ahead is a vital survival skill that can greatly clarify the necessary path forward and avert sudden surprise.[20]

Dealing with uncertainty proactively requires boards to use contrarian thinking regarding business model assumptions, to listen to customers and non-customers as well, to engage with employees and suppliers and academics and innovation centers:

> With their vision in hand, leaders need in-depth understanding of their organization's capabilities and strategies to take advantage of rapidly changing circumstances by playing to their strengths while minimizing their weaknesses. *Listening only to information sources and opinions that reinforce their own views carries great risk of missing alternate points of view.* Instead, leaders need to tap into myriad sources covering the full spectrum of viewpoints by engaging directly with their customers and employees to ensure they are attuned to changes in their markets. *Spending time in the marketplace, retail stores, factories, innovation centers, and research labs, or just wandering around offices talking to people is essential.*[21] [Emphases mine]

While it clearly makes sense for directors to be involved in these processes, there are real difficulties for them in acquiring up to date and accurate information. So we have to build on the reactive approach of VUCA 1.0 to achieve the proactive approach of VUCA 2.0 by testing contrarian hypotheses forcefully in the board and by being better at interpreting what probabilities mean:

1. **Testing contrarian hypotheses:** The best ways to deal with uncertainty are to test contrarian hypotheses, as well as by developing a range of plans or scenarios combined with appropriate pre-mortems and suitable contingency plans as a result. The problem for directors in these situations is information asymmetry and confirmation bias, if the information has been prepared by management, since management will tend to present information in ways that make them look good or lead to their having a quiet session at the board meeting. The problem is more acute for INEDs who have neither the time nor the exposure to be able to challenge the information effectively.

   As an example, I remember a conversation with a conscientious INED who wanted to know what was really going on in the business below the board. She asked her Chair if she could visit the branches, receive the papers and minutes presented at the management executive meetings, and even attend as an observer. Initially, the Chair agreed, provided she said nothing during those meetings, did not lobby other directors based on her superior access to what was happening, and only discussed her findings with him. The process was so effective that she ended up attending so many meetings that the Chair had to stop it because it threatened her status as an INED. As a result, she resigned from the board because she felt uncomfortable with her lack of detailed understanding when she was no longer able to look into what was really happening. However, there are three process ways of getting around this problem that generate constructive contrarian challenge within the board:

a. **The "Alfred Sloan Solution":** Alfred Sloan, the founder of General Motors understood the importance of robust, constructive challenge in improving the quality of decisions. His solution to the problem, which he introduced after his first board meeting where all the directors had agreed with what was being proposed, was to ask them to return with "reasons why not" at the next board meeting:

> If we are all in agreement on the decision – then I propose we postpone further discussion of this matter until our next meeting *to give us time to develop disagreement and perhaps gain some understanding of what the decision is all about.*[22]
>
> [Emphasis mine]

Sadly, not all Chairs have the self-confidence or ability to synthesize complex arguments as quickly as Alfred Sloan; and so there are very few, if any boards that operate in this way. However, there is a process solution to this problem.

b. **Rotating "Devil's Advocacy":** The purpose of this approach is to achieve the same result as Alfred Sloan's approach:

> The advantage of such a process is clear: the ensuing discussion *focuses on all the reasons why the decision might be undesirable, highlighting what could go wrong; and as a result, forcing the board to improve the proposal to overcome identified defects, develop contingency plans in case those defects cannot be eliminated and materialize later, or to reconsider adopting the idea.*
>
> To do this effectively, directors must spend extra time deliberating diligently. If they are to be a high impact board, they will be forced to understand fully the strategies of their company, how it creates value and the impact of the issues faced by its industry.[viii] The benefit of making it an ad hoc rotating process, is no single director gets tarred with the negative halo of always being the

---

viii "At boards with very high impact, directors spend even more time on their work than their peers at lower-impact boards (40 days per year, compared with only 19 days). Other results suggest that these extra days are not spent on basic compliance but on strategic issues instead. Compared with their peers, the directors at higher-impact boards say they evaluate resource decisions, debate strategic alternatives, and assess management's understanding of value creation much more often. These respondents are also likelier than others to say their boards ensure that organizational resources are in place to deliver on strategy and that they manage strategic performance." Barton, D. and Wiseman, M. (2015), "Where Boards Fall Short," *Harvard Business Review*, January–February Issue, 2015.

naysayer "Devil's Advocate." Making who will be called upon to argue the case against the proposal ad hoc ensures all directors are well-prepared for the discussion. *However, to be able to do their "due diligence" on proposals put before them, they will need to understand the real costs of doing business; the financial assumptions of the budget and how the objectives, KPIs and resulting targets and outcomes have been derived.*[23]   [Emphases mine]

For such an approach to work really well, the directors do need to do proper due diligence and the problem then becomes one of how they get the appropriate information in the detail needed to satisfy the modern legal requirements of fulfilling their fiduciary duty. The standard to which they are held in Australia and other Commonwealth countries where Australian rulings are regarded as either precedent or "persuasive" is best illustrated by the words of Justice Middleton in the Centro case:[24]

Nothing that I decide in this case should indicate that directors are required to have infinite knowledge or ability. Directors are entitled to delegate to others the preparation of books and accounts and the carrying on of the day-to-day affairs of the company. *What each director is expected to do is to take a diligent and intelligent interest in the information available to him or her, to understand that information, and apply an enquiring mind to the responsibilities placed upon him or her.*   [Emphasis mine]

If they have to rely on management, the problem of information asymmetry arises; if they have to depend on external experts, there is a question of costs and they are still not off the hook, as is clear from the following words of Lord Goldsmith, the UK Attorney General, during the debate on the 2006 Companies Act:

The duty does not prevent a director from relying on the advice of work of others, but the final judgment must be his responsibility. . . *As with all advice, slavish reliance is not acceptable, and obtaining of outside advice does not absolve directors from exercising their judgment on the basis of such advice.*[25]
                                                                                 [Emphasis mine]

In this case, there is a structural solution to the problem.

c. ***Board "Cabinet Secretariat":*** When Unilever's chief executive function was run as a triumvirate consisting of the Chairmen of Unilever NV (the Dutch part listed in Rotterdam), and Unilever Limited (the English part listed in London), and the Deputy Chairman from either part called the Special Committee, it had the so-called Special Committee Secretariat to serve it. The Special Committee Secretariat answered to the Special

Committee only. It was led by a director-level ex-line manager who understood the issues of line management, but who in addition had been a senior civil servant in the Indian Civil Service before India's independence. He understood the importance of being seen to be neutral in any argument between executive directors over strategic direction and allocation of resources, just like the Cabinet Secretary to the British Government. The role was to create informed discussion by providing well-researched facts neutrally rather than to exercise power.[26] Burmah Castrol used to have what was called the "Chairman's Private Office" before it was sold to BP.[27] It had the same purpose: to help board members make informed decisions by providing the Chairman and the directors with counterfactual arguments and commentary on the proposals brought to the board by management.

This structural solution provided board members with all the arguments and facts, based on a detailed understanding of the working of the businesses and the board dynamics they needed to challenge management (unlike external consultants). It also allowed management to "clear" their draft proposals with the secretariat who could advise them on the board dynamics and point out where their cases were weak or factually inadequate and send them back to management for improvement before they were finally presented to the board. It also achieved the same purpose as Alfred Sloan's method, but without having to wait until the next board meeting. The end result was better board papers from management and robust constructive challenge from board members who felt confident enough to challenge management because they had been properly briefed by the commentaries the secretariat provided for them.

2. **Interpreting probabilities better:** There is plenty of evidence to suggest that human beings are bad at understanding probabilities,[28] even without them being manipulated by the ways in which the probabilities have been stated:

> [He] divided the audience in half, and asked both halves separately to estimate the number of countries in Africa. This is a standard "wisdom of the crowds" sort of question, where the mean should be somewhere close to the actual number. Instead, the two groups had wildly divergent means, with one half of the audience answering well above the actual answer, the second significantly below.
>
> . . .Prior to asking the actual number, [he] had. . .subtly primed each group. For one half of the audience, he asked if they thought there were more than 180 countries in Africa; this group ended up with a much higher mean. The second half was asked if there were more than five. Their answers were, on average, too low.

Although this was a case of conscious manipulation, it's easy to see how a similar effect could be generated accidentally[ix]. . .

. . .[He] consistently noted that language was important when it comes to dealing with probabilities. . .

He described the probabilities associated with a breast cancer test: one percent of women tested have the disease, and the test is 90 percent accurate, with a nine percent false positive rate. With all that information, what do you tell a woman who tests positive about the likelihood they have the disease?. . .

[He] then rephrased the statistics: if we ignore the negative tests, nine times out of ten, a positive test for cancer is a false positive. Put that way, it's easy to see that you can tell the person who got a positive result in the test that there's still only a ten percent chance that she has cancer. *The use of language makes all the difference.*[29]

[Emphasis mine]

So how do normal people, or even exceptional people like President Obama deal with probability, especially if there are a range of expert views on the subject, as there were when he was being advised that Osama Bin Laden was probably in Abbottabad in Pakistan?[30] He was advised that the range of probability was between 30% and 95%. His reaction was, "This is 50:50. Look guys, this is a flip of the coin." This reaction to treating probabilities as evenly split when they are uncertain is normal, even if, as a result, they lead to making the wrong decisions:

Researchers have in the past suggested that odds of 50:50 are really code for "I don't know." That may well have been what was going through Mr. Obama's mind when faced with such a wide range of estimates. Forecasters put odds on events because words like "probable" and "likely" are interpreted very differently by different people. But numbers mean nothing without confidence.[31]

Given that so few people are comfortable with probabilities and that dynamic probabilistic decision trees are often essential in determining which of a number of scenarios is likely to yield the best risk-adjusted expected values of the courses of action under consideration, it may be necessary for the "board cabinet secretariat" to work with management in interpreting them to directors. Then the directors may feel sufficiently confident to challenge probabilistic assumptions robustly.

---

ix The difference in the two results is the result of "anchoring bias." The first group was anchored around 180; the second around 5.

Complexity + Courage + Commitment

The traditional reactive approach to dealing with complexity in VUCA 1.0 is to invest in specialists and resources to try to understand its causes and consequences better, to simplify[x] the business by eliminating sources of complexity; and to build in redundancy so that if things go wrong there is backup to keep things going.

When things go wrong and lessons are learned, the other solution is to add in safety measures to make sure that the same mistakes cannot happen again. The problem with this approach is that safety systems can bite back by introducing unexpected ways for things to go wrong in the future, even with simple systems:

> Galileo described an early example of this principle in 1638. Masons at that time would store stone columns horizontally, raised above the soil by two piles of stone. The columns often cracked in the middle under their own weight. The "solution" was to reinforce the support with a third pile of stone in the centre. But that didn't help. The two end supports would often settle a little, and the column, balanced like a see-saw on the central pile, would then snap as the ends sagged.[32]

Imagine how much worse things can be made by making complex systems "tightly coupled," creating what engineers call a new "failure mode." This happened in the GFC with credit default swaps (CDS). They are a type of insurance against loans not being repaid. The first CDS was agreed to between the European Bank for Reconstruction and Development (EBRD) and JP Morgan in 1994. JP Morgan paid fees to the EBRD and in return the EBRD agreed to make good any losses in the event Exxon defaulted on a possible $4.8 billion loan. The CDS offloaded the risk to the EBRD, freeing up JP Morgan's cash.[33] The regulators approved, believing this to be a safe way of managing risk. They were proved wrong. First, banks increased their levels of risk because they felt protected by the insurance – a classic case of moral hazard.[xi] Second, they introduced new ways of failing:

> The CDS contracts increased both the complexity and the tight coupling of the financial system. Institutions that hadn't previously been connected turned out to be bound together, and new chains of cause and effect emerged that nobody had anticipated. . .

---

x The "elevator pitch" and instructions to have PowerPoints with only three bullets per slide that are only a dozen slides long are examples of oversimplification that ignore the "devil is in the details" which may lead to difficulties later on.
xi Moral hazard occurs when someone increases their exposure to risk when insured, especially when a person takes more risks because someone else bears the cost of those risks. *Wikipedia.*

. . .As the banks cranked out complex new mortgage-related bonds, they turned to insurance companies. . .to provide insurance using credit default swaps. . .

. . .If an insurance company has mistakenly insured too many risky bonds, it will find itself flirting with bankruptcy, and so it will lose its high credit rating. . .as its rating is downgraded, so is the rating of all the bonds it has insured. As large numbers of bonds were downgraded in unison, banks were legally forced to sell them in unison by sensible-seeming regulations forbidding banks to hold too many risky bonds. . .the combination of safety system and safety regulation provided a recipe for a price collapse. . .

. . .The same thing was true. . .for the infamous collateralized debt obligations, or CDOs, which repackaged financial flows from "risky" subprime mortgages. . .

In both cases, the safety systems made investors and banks careless – and more fundamentally, they transformed small problems into catastrophes.[34]   [Emphasis mine]

Dealing effectively with complexity needs more than the reactive simplification of VUCA 1.0 and it also needs more than investing in safety mechanisms. Bill George makes the point that courage is also needed to challenge received wisdom:

Now more than ever, leaders need the courage to step up to these challenges and make audacious decisions that embody risks and often go against the grain. They cannot afford to keep their heads down, using traditional management techniques while avoiding criticism and risk-taking. In fact, their greatest risk lies in not having the courage to make bold moves. This era belongs to the bold, not the meek and timid.[35]

While it may be true that leaders need to show courage and challenge conventional wisdom, such advice should not be translated into a justification for foolhardiness. The responsibility of directors is to prevent charismatic, over-confident CEOs who have been successful in the past from "betting the shop" by being contrarian. The collapses of Bear Stearns, Merrill Lynch, and Lehman Brothers in the US and Royal Bank of Scotland in the UK were the result of CEOs taking bold positions without being properly challenged by their boards; precisely because they had a track record of past success and dominant personalities.[36]

The reason why they were able to get away with reckless behavior for so long was that the members of their boards lacked the commitment to put in the time necessary to understand the details of their banks' business models, to challenge diligently the assumptions underlying the risks their organizations were taking and how those risks were changing over time.

In the case of the collapse of Lehman Brothers, the role of the board is described in the following damning words by the New Jersey Department of Investment:

The supine Board that defendant Fuld handpicked provided no backstop to Lehman's executives' zealous approach to the Company's risk profile, real estate portfolio, and their own compensation. The Director Defendants were considered inattentive, elderly, and woefully short on relevant structured finance background. The composition of the Board according to a recent filing in the Lehman bankruptcy allowed "Fuld to marginalize the Directors, who tolerated an absence of checks and balances at Lehman." Due to his long tenure and ubiquity at Lehman, defendant Fuld has been able to consolidate his power to a remarkable degree. Defendant Fuld was both the Chairman of the Board and the CEO . . . The Director Defendants acted as a rubber stamp for the actions of Lehman's senior management. There was little turnover on the Board. By the date of Lehman's collapse, more than half of the Director Defendants had served for twelve or more years.[37]

In the case of the Royal Bank of Scotland acquisition of ABN Amro, the findings were that the board did not even do a thorough due diligence in determining the valuation they placed on ABN Amro:

The FSA cites three reasons for the poor quality of the Board's decision-making:
1. Excessive confidence in their ability to acquire another bank in a hostile take-over because of "the firm's track record of successful acquisition and integration, particularly of NatWest, and the CEO's personal contribution to it";
2. Insufficient discussion of the risks involved to identify "show-stoppers," given its complexity, scale and how it was financed. Instead the focus was on identifying scope for synergies and cost-cutting. The Board appears to have taken too much comfort from the fact that ABN AMRO was regulated by the DNB (the Dutch banking regulator) and the FSA; filed its records with the U.S. SEC; conformed with Sarbanes-Oxley requirements; from rating agency reports and from the fact that their great rival Barclays was persisting in their bid. This despite the fact that the minutes of the March 28th 2007 Board minutes record that the CEO:
    "provided background to the project. . .A bid for [ABN AMRO] was not seen as a 'must do' deal." The CEO advised the Board that *"execution risk would be high"* and that *"any bid for [ABN AMRO] and subsequent integration would be more difficult than previous transactions."*
    "However, the Review Team has not found evidence that the Board undertook any penetrating analysis of the risks on an enterprise-wide basis in respect of capital and liquidity."
3. The third key factor highlighted by the report *was lack of sensitivity to the importance of understanding counterparty risk and the importance of customer and counterparty confidence in the bank.*[38]
    [Emphases mine]

What these two examples show is a lack of commitment by the directors of both boards to master the context in which their banks were operating, the intricacies of their banks' business models and to understand the assumptions of management, and therefore to appreciate the risks being run.

In a VUCA 2.0 world, boards must take appropriate steps to simplify where possible, have the courage to challenge received wisdom, and most important of all, have the commitment, in the words of Justice Middleton (of the Federal Court of Australia), to *"take a diligent and intelligent interest in the information available to him or her, to understand that information, and apply an enquiring mind to the responsibilities placed upon him or her."*

Ambiguity + Adaptability

Ambiguity will always exist and it makes for inefficiency:

> It's easier to assume you know or to operate with a bias than it is to ask questions that may force a peer or team member to rethink what they're doing or why they're doing it. *But the costs of operating with ambiguity are enormous. Ambiguity in the form of a vague job posting leads to an underperforming hire. Ambiguity about the purpose of a project results in wasted time and money. Ambiguity about a customer "requirement" leads to unnecessary features that bring no benefit because the so-called "requirement" wasn't one.*
>
> And unlike volatility, uncertainty, and complexity – all genuine realities that are mainly outside of your control – ambiguity is man-made. *People create ambiguity.*
>
> *Fortunately, they can also abolish it with clarity.*[39]   [Emphases mine]

The task for boards is to minimize the impact of ambiguity and to determine where ambiguity is permissible and where it is not. The "Five Ps" are useful in helping decide what needs to be unambiguous. When boards decide on the organization's long-term mission and vision, they need to make them unambiguous so that all resources are allocated in the short, medium, and long term to deliver the mission and vision. This is where clarity of "purpose" is essential so that everybody in the organization knows what business the organization is in; and, just as important, what business it is not in. Everybody knows who the organization wishes to do business with and how; what it stands for; and how it treats its beneficiaries and employees – in other words its "principles" or values.

Whatever is "evergreen" must be unambiguous. Consequently, the organization's "purpose" must be unambiguous and so must its "principles." Otherwise its code of conduct will be meaningless.

That does not mean, however, that there can be no adaptation to meet changing circumstances. So, in moving from VUCA 1.0 to VUCA 2.0, boards must find a judicious blend of that which is "evergreen," clear, and unambiguous, namely, its "purpose" and "principles"; and that which can be adapted to suit new conditions, namely, its organization design or "power"; the number of employees and their desired competences or "people"; and policies, procedures and processes – "processes."

The need to adapt is the result of unforeseen combinations of volatility, uncertainty, and complexity. The best way to create adaptive capacity is to develop multiple business plans with strong balance sheets that do not "bet the business," where failure is survivable rather than an experience that bankrupts the business, where organizations can learn from trial and error. Indeed, adaptability allows failure to be the parent of success, provided failures are small and can be learned from quickly. In essence, this approach mimics that of biological survival of the species: maximizing variation through endless random experimentation combined with selection of experiments that lead to improved chances of survival and abandonment of those that do not.[40]

> If ever there were a need for leaders to be flexible in adapting to this rapidly changing environment, this is it. Long-range plans are often obsolete by the time they are approved. Instead, flexible tactics are required for rapid adaptation to changing external circumstances, without altering strategic course. This is not a time for continuing the financial engineering so prevalent in the past decade. Rather, leaders need multiple contingency plans while preserving strong balance sheets to cope with unforeseen events.[41]

Above all, what is most important is that whatever changes are created by adapting the organization's "power," "people," and "processes," strategic and operational flexibility are preserved so that the "stuckness" trap is avoided.

Summary

In the current conditions, I believe boards need to move from a VUCA 1.0 reactive approach designed to limit the impact of VUCA-based risk to a two-stage VUCA 2.0 proactive approach, by building on their VUCA 1.0 strategies to create a sustainable future. Taking each of the four elements of VUCA in turn:

Volatility + Vision: To reconcile both means moving from dealing with volatility alone to providing a clearly defined unambiguous vision and mission to guide the organization and everybody who works in it to navigate through periods of volatility and uncertainty, making sense of inevitable complexity by clarifying ambiguity of "purpose" and "principles." To do this effectively boards must answer seven questions:

1. *Is there a clear business focus?*
2. *Is the mission compelling and unique?*
3. *Does the organization understand who its competitors are for market margin?*
4. *Has the organization chosen to be a technology leader or follower?*
5. *Which market segments has it chosen to serve?*
6. *How adaptable are its organizational design and processes to changes in the environment?*
7. *Do the mission and vision protect the organization's long-term "license to operate"?*

Using the "Five Ps" provides helpful ways to ensure "purpose," "principles," "power," "people," and "processes" are properly aligned to deliver the mission and vision in volatile conditions.

Uncertainty + Understanding: To reconcile both uncertainty and understanding means moving from the reactive approach of investing in the collection, evaluation, and sharing of information reinforced by knowledge management processes and structures, to using contrarian thinking regarding business model assumptions; to listening to customers and non-customers; to engaging with employees and suppliers and academics and innovation centers. Developing and testing contrarian approaches so that directors have access to all the relevant information to overcome the usual information asymmetry when challenging management assumptions can be achieved in three ways:

1. *Alfred Sloan's solution* asking the board to present why what has been agreed on should be challenged at the next board meeting;
2. *Rotating "Devil's Advocacy"* where one director on a rotating basis is required to challenge the underlying assumptions presented by management in detail;
3. *Establishing a "board cabinet secretariat"* whose purpose is to provide the board with an independent evaluation of proposals presented by management.

Complexity + Courage + Commitment: In this case, it is not sufficient to move to courage alone from the reactive approach of investing in specialists and resources to try to understand its causes and consequences better, of simplifying the business by eliminating sources of complexity, and of building in redundancy so that if things go wrong there is backup to keep things going. While it is true that leaders need to show courage and challenge conventional wisdom, such advice should not be translated into a justification for foolhardiness. The responsibility of directors is to prevent charismatic, over-confident CEOs who have been successful in the past from "betting the shop" by being contrarian. This requires personal courage in the boardroom, especially if colleagues shy away from robust and constructive challenge, either as a result of temperamental constraints or lack of knowledge. Courageous constructive challenge of dominant charismatic CEOs can only add value if directors have proper exposure to the details and workings in practice of the organization's business model, to the assumptions of management, and to proper analysis of external trends that could invalidate such assumptions. That is why a third element is essential if complexity is to be managed effectively, namely, commitment – the commitment to taking the time and making the emotional and intellectual effort needed to master the intricacies of the organization's strategy, risk management, succession planning, and financials. Only then is each director able to *"take a diligent and intelligent interest in the information available to him or her, to understand that information, and apply an enquiring mind to the responsibilities placed upon him or her."*

Ambiguity + Adaptability: The task for boards is to minimize the impact of ambiguity and to determine where ambiguity is permissible and where it is not. The "Five Ps" are useful in helping decide what needs to be unambiguous. When boards decide on the organization's long-term mission and vision, they need to make them unambiguous so that all resources are allocated in the short, medium, and long term to deliver the mission and vision. This is where clarity of "purpose" is essential so that everybody in the organization knows what business the organization is in, and, just as important, what business it is not in; everybody knows who the organization wishes to do business with and how; what it stands for; and how it treats its beneficiaries and employees – in other words its "principles" or values. Whatever is "evergreen" must be unambiguous. Consequently, the organization's "purpose" must be unambiguous and so must its "principles."

That does not mean, however, that there can be no adaptation to meet changing circumstances. The ability to adapt is essential in its organization design or "power"; the number of employees and their desired competences or "people"; and policies, procedures and processes – "processes." The best way to create adaptive capacity is to develop multiple business plans with strong balance sheets that do not "bet the business"; where failure is survivable rather than an experience that bankrupts the business; where organizations can learn from trial and error. Indeed, adaptability allows failure to be the parent of success, provided failures are small and can be learned from quickly.

References

1 Fukuyama, F. (1992), *The End of History and the Last Man* (New York: Free Press).

2 Lorgan, L. (2019), "Large central bank balance sheets and market functioning," *Bank for International Settlements*, October 2019, https://www.bis.org/publ/mktc11.pdf, accessed on December 17, 2019.

3 Stockhammer, E. (2013), "Rising inequality as a cause of the present crisis," *Cambridge Journal of Economics* 2013, 1 of 24, doi:10.1093/cje/bet052, http://www.countdownnet.net/Allegati/45%20stockuneq.pdf, accessed on December 17, 2019.

4 George, B. (2017), "VUCA 2.0: A Strategy for Steady Leadership In An Unsteady World," *Forbes*, February 17, 2017, https://www.forbes.com/sites/hbsworkingknowledge/2017/02/17/vuca-2-0-a-strategy-for-steady-leadership-in-an-unsteady-world/#85e137713d84, accessed on December 16, 2019.

5 Bennett, N. and Lemoine, G.J. (2014), "What VUCA Really Means For You," *HBR*, January–February 2014 Issue, https://hbr.org/resources/images/article_assets/hbr/1401/F1401C_A_LG.gif, accessed on December 18, 2019.

6 Martin, K. (2019), op. cit.

7 George, B. (2017), op. cit.

8 Zinkin, J. (2014), *Rebuilding Trust in Banks: The Role of Leadership and Governance* (Singapore: John Wiley & Sons), pp. 136–138.

9 Zinkin, J. (2014), op. cit., p. 140.

10 For a more detailed discussion of the "Five P" performance framework, see, Zinkin, J. (2019), *Better Governance Across the Board: Creating Value Through Reputation, People and Processes* (Boston/Berlin: Walter De Gruyter Inc.), pp. 125–138.

11 Drucker, P. (1955), *The Practice of Management* (Oxford: Butterworth Heinemann), p. 35, quoted in Zinkin, J. (2019), op. cit., p. 127.

12 Porter, M. (1985), *Competitive Advantage: Creating and Sustaining Superior Performance* (New York: The Free Press), pp. 41–42.

13 Bruner, B. (2012), "Stuck in the Middle? Take the Flexible Approach," January 16, 2012, https://blogs.darden.virginia.edu/brunerblog/2012/01/stuck-in-the-middle/, a guest post quoted by Symonds, M. *Forbes*, February 24, 2012, https://www.forbes.com/sites/mattsymonds/2012/02/24/stuck-in-the-middle-take-the-flexible-approach/#4d1184142ebd, accessed on July 5, 2018.

14 "Valerie Hunter Gordon, inventor of the disposable nappy – obituary," *The Telegraph*, October 20, 2016, https://www.telegraph.co.uk/obituaries/2016/10/20/valerie-hunter-gordon-inventor-of-the-disposable-nappy–obituary/, accessed on July 7, 2018.

15 Miller, M. (2011), "The Rise of DOS: How Microsoft Got the IBM PC OS Contract," *PCMAG*, August 11, 2011, https://uk.pcmag.com/opinion/111712/the-rise-of-dos-how-microsoft-got-the-ibm-pc-os-contract, accessed on December 20, 2019.

16 Caulkin, S. (2012) "The wrong direction: Management has lost its way – and its power has sent business down a dangerous road," *FT Business Education*, December 3, 2012, p. 12.

17 Solomon, R.C. (1999) *A Better Way to Think About Business: How Personal Integrity Leads to Corporate Success* (New York: Oxford University Press, 1999), p. xxii.

18 Ibid.

19 Bennett, N. and Lemoine, G.J. (2014), op. cit.

20 Ibid.

21 George, B. (2017), op. cit.

22 Sloan, A., quoted in Zinkin, J. (2019), op. cit., p. 341.

23 Zinkin, J. (2019), op. cit., p. 341.

24 Downie, A. (2011), Justice Middleton judgment in paragraph 20 quoted in "The Centro Matter: ASIC v Healey [2011] FCA 717 and breach of directors' duties," *The Civil Lawyer*, June 28, 2011, http://www.the-civil-lawyer.net/2011/06/centro-matter-asic-v-healey-2011-fca.html, accessed on December 21, 2019.

25 Lord Goldsmith, UK Attorney General quoted in Zinkin, J. (2019), op. cit., p. 58.

26 Based on conversations between the author's late father who headed up the Special Committee Secretariat and the author.

27 Based on a conversation between Chris Bennett who had been a member of the Chairman's Private Office and the author on December 18, 2019.

28 Sorrel, C. (2016), "People Are Really Bad at Probability, And This Study Shows How Easy it to Trick Us," *Fast Company*, June 27, 2016, https://www.fastcompany.com/3061263/people-are-really-bad-at-probability-and-this-study-shows-how-easy-it-is-to-trick-us, accessed on December 22, 2019.

29 Timmer, J. (2011), "Risk, Probability and How Brains Are Easily Misled," *Wired*, June 8, 2011, https://www.wired.com/2011/06/brain-risk-probability/, accessed on December 22, 2019.

30 Gans, J. A. (2012), "This is 50–50: Behind Obama's Decision to Kill Bin Laden," *The Atlantic,* October 10, 2012, https://www.theatlantic.com/international/archive/2012/10/this-is-50-50-behind-obamas-decision-to-kill-bin-laden/263449/, accessed on December 21, 2019.

31 "Why are people attracted to 50:50 probabilities?" *The Economist,* December 12, 2019, https://www.economist.com/finance-and-economics/2019/12/12/why-are-people-attracted-to-50-50-probabilities, accessed on December 22, 2019.

32 Harford, T. (2011), *Adapt: Why Success Always Starts With Failure* (London: Little Brown), p. 187.

33 Romm, J. (2010), "JP Morgan invented credit-default swaps to give Exxon credit line for Valdez liability," *ThinkProgress,* May 26, 2010, https://thinkprogress.org/jp-morgan-invented-credit-default-swaps-to-give-exxon-credit-line-for-valdez-liability-dfe0333d25c7/, accessed on December 22, 2019.

34 Ibid., pp. 187–190.

35 George, B. (2017), op. cit.

36 Zinkin, J. (2014), op. cit., pp. 25–43.

37 Wayne, L., "New Jersey Sues Over Its Lehman Losses," *New York Times,* March 17, 2009, https://www.nytimes.com/2009/03/18/business/18lehman.html?dlbk, and *The Supine Board,* New Jersey complaint (2009), 111 cited in Gillespie, J. and Zweig, D., *Money for Nothing: How the failure of corporate boards is ruining American business and costing us trillions* (New York: Free Press, 2010), p. 16, quoted in Zinkin, J. (2014), op. cit., pp. 35–36.

38 Zinkin, J. (2014), p. 41.

39 George, B. (2017), op. cit.

40 Harford, T. (2011), op. cit., pp. 18–20.

41 George, B. (2017), op. cit.

Chapter 10
Adopting New Processes

This chapter is presented in five parts. The first explores how boards may need new processes to deliver environmental sustainability; the second economic sustainability; the third employment sustainability; the fourth social sustainability; the fifth closes with conclusions discussing processes boards need to consider in addition to traditional, internally focused processes.

This chapter concerns itself only with those areas where boards have control over ways of improving processes directly or indirectly to create sustainable value. It only mentions areas where governments and society have to make choices if sustainability is to be achieved, without making recommendations, as that is beyond the scope of this book.

How should boards deal with externalities that matter when the sustainability of the environment, economy, employability, and community is concerned? Some, like Warren Buffett,[1] argue it is the responsibility of boards of individual organizations to improve internal processes solely and that externalities are no concern of boards. However, this ignores free-riders who compete unfairly with responsible organizations by adopting lower standards of governance. It also disregards externalities imposed on the community by boards doing what makes sense for their individual organizations and not for the environment, economy, employability, or community, if all other companies followed suit at the same time.

Although it is the role of governments to deal with externalities and free-riders, I believe it is also the role of boards to be sensitive to such issues; to be responsible by dealing with them constructively, rather than doing their best through lobbying and regulatory capture to protect their short-term vested interests at the expense of solving the challenges posed for sustainability of the environment, economy, employability, and community. However, if boards are to deal effectively with externalities, they need to work with government, civil society, and academia to develop appropriate new processes.

As a result, I believe boards need to consider additional processes to the traditional, internally focused processes they already adopt to create sustainable value.[2] Both government intervention and changes in board attitudes are necessary if a "political tragedy of the commons" is to be avoided.

If boards are to meet the four sustainability challenges discussed in Chapters 3–6, they will have to consider adding new processes to the processes

https://doi.org/10.1515/9783110670486-010

already discussed in Chapter 9 dealing with VUCA.[i] These are needed to deal with "business unusual" conditions created by environmental issues; the impact of deglobalization and rising inequality; the need to deal with unemployment and unemployability and managing cultural diversity.

There is increasing external pressure on boards to consider ESG issues not just in terms of reporting, but in terms of what changes to their business models they are proposing so that investors and insurers understand the risks they face and the actions they are taking to mitigate them to reassure their bankers and insurers that they will not end up with worthless "stranded assets."[ii]

Environmental Sustainability

When considering new processes to deal with environmental sustainability it helps to distinguish between climate change, moving to a circular economy, and conservation.

Climate Change

Boards must recognize that the regulatory context regarding climate change is changing. Countries are beginning to mandate what has to happen by 2050 to mitigate climate change. For example, the UK was the first major country to

---

i For a detailed discussion of traditional processes high performance boards adopt to deliver sustainable long-term value based on "business as usual" assumptions, refer to Zinkin, J. (2019), *Better Governance Across the Board: Creating Value Through Reputation, People and Processes* (Boston/Berlin: Walter De Gruyter Inc.), pp. 339–359.

ii "Stranded assets are now generally accepted to be fossil fuel supply and generation resources which, at some time prior to the end of their economic life . . . are no longer able to earn an economic return . . . as a result of changes associated with the transition to a low-carbon economy . . .

Investors have recognised the value of companies considering a range of scenarios, including a 2°C scenario, by supporting initiatives and resolutions which ask companies to report on the implications of this future for their business. Financial regulators have also endorsed the importance of scenario analysis for assessing climate risk through the Financial Stability Board Task Force on Climate-Related Financial Disclosures. *Mark Carney, the FSB chair stated that a carbon budget consistent with a 2°C target "would render the vast majority of reserves 'stranded' – oil, gas and coal that will be literally unburnable without expensive carbon capture technology, which itself alters fossil fuel economics."* [Emphasis mine] https://www.carbontracker.org/terms/stranded-assets/, accessed on December 30, 2019.

legislate that it will be a net zero economy by 2050.[3] The EU will follow[4] and even parts of the US are likely to make similar commitments in due course.[5]

Companies are going to have to have convincing plans to deal with the fact that by 2050, the UK and other countries must achieve net zero carbon status:

> "If we were to burn all those oil and gas [reserves], there's no way we would meet carbon budget," he said. *"Up to 80% of coal assets will be stranded, [and] up to half of developed oil reserves."*
>
> "A question for every company, every financial institution, every asset manager, pension fund or insurer: what's your plan?"
>
> "Four to five years ago, only leading institutions had begun to think about these issues and could report on them."
>
> *"Now $120tn worth of balance sheets of banks and asset managers are wanting this disclosure [of investments in fossil fuels]. But it's not moving fast enough."*[6]
>
> [Emphases mine]

The Bank of England and the European Central Bank are starting to insist that commercial banks, insurers and pension funds disclose the extent to which their investments and policies are at risk because of climate change. They are making it clear that these companies are not disclosing fast enough how they are rebalancing their investments to mitigate the risk posed by climate change. As a result, the boards of these financial institutions must have convincing processes in place to explain what they are proposing to do with proper progress tracking mechanisms to satisfy their regulators (see Appendix A: "Setting KPIs and Targets Using a Ten-Step Process"). This, in turn, means the clients of banks and insurance companies and the businesses in which pension funds invest will also have to have convincing processes in place to disclose what they are doing to reduce the risks they face to deal with climate change and the likely regulatory interventions caused by climate change concerns.

The companies most at risk are in fossil fuels exploration and distribution, chemicals, transportation, automotive, and builders (concrete and housing). They are at risk from both a regulatory perspective and a financial perspective. Banks will be less willing to lend, insurers will raise the cost of insurance or refuse to insure them, and pension funds will withdraw their funds. This is already happening. Goldman Sachs has said it will no longer lend to coal companies anywhere in the world and will not finance drilling in the Arctic.[7] Credit Suisse will no longer finance coal-fired power stations[8] despite successful stonewalling at the 2019 Madrid climate change conference by climate change deniers.[9] Pension funds are indicating they will pull almost US$1 trillion in the next decade from fossil fuels.[10] BlackRock is doing the same.[11] The impact of such decisions on the viability of the affected companies and their market capitalization is likely to be severe. Boards will have to review the regulatory and stakeholder environment on a regular basis in order to develop appropriate, timely contingency plans to minimize the impact of having "stranded assets."

No longer can boards argue that the time horizon for action is so lengthy that they can ignore the impact of climate change because neither they nor their investors will be around when the damage is done. Instead, they will have to begin developing plans now to mitigate the short-medium term risks of being unable to get financing from banks, of being uninsured/uninsurable, or of falling share prices. The changing external regulatory context is bringing the future to the present in ways boards have to consider carefully – they will need processes capable of developing multiple scenarios with strong balance sheets, including possibly exiting the business, which in turn would likely slash supply similarly to, or worse than the 1979 oil crisis,

Boards in many countries will also have to devote much more time to the issue on a regular basis. They will need to incorporate still-to-be-developed accounting processes designed to internalize the costs of externalities created by climate change, such as carbon taxes or cap-and-trade systems, into their financial planning assumptions. They will have to develop and implement carbon capture processes to eliminate greenhouse gas (GHG) emissions in their supply and value chains, and move to synthetic fuels using solar-generated electricity. They will also need to develop ways to capture and remove carbon from the atmosphere – even if we arrive at zero GHG emissions for humanity to limit global warming to the 2°C target increase agreed in the Paris Accords signed in 2016.[12] This is because there are two problems: the first is eliminating GHG emissions, and the second is reducing the accumulated carbon dioxide since the Industrial Revolution from the atmosphere.[iii]

Companies leading the field in developing and adopting these processes will increase in value, whereas those that lag will be punished; and may very well become worthless according to Bank of England Governor.[13] However, if the UK is typical, only 6% of UK CEOs have a financial incentive to focus on environmental initiatives.[14] There is a long way still to go and it would be much better if boards decided on which measures of sustainability applied to their businesses rather than waiting for governments to do it for them:

> *"It would be much more effective if firms thought about exactly how the climate crisis will affect them and then look to first develop a sustainability strategy. Then, after identifying these, firms can select the relevant KPIs to include in CEOs' remuneration."*

---

iii Current estimates are that capturing emissions at the source can be done profitably now; the problem is that removing past emissions is still too expensive.

Edward Houghton, head of research at the CIPD, agreed that such activity should be business-led. But the government also has an important role to play, he said.

"There is space for progressive policy to promote the type of measures we want. . . We need to see organisations looking at values around sustainability, and incorporating these values into how [they] measure leadership performance," he said.[15]   [Emphases mine]

For this to work well, businesses must have the vision to make needed investments and governments need to encourage such investments through the use of either subsidies to make them more attractive or taxes to make continuing with "business as usual" less attractive.

Moving to a Circular Business Model

The importance of considering moving to a circular business model and how to do it has already been covered in Chapter 3. What boards need to recognize is that if their competitors have already adopted circular business practices successfully, this will put pressure on their organizations to move away from their linear business practices that create depletion, pollution and waste toward the "Reduce, Recycle, Reuse, and Remanufacture" circular business model. This pressure is most likely to be translated into measurements of the organizational "footprint," covering all environmental and social impacts throughout the organization's value chain. At its simplest, the buildings, land, and equipment owned by organizations; the resources they consume; the emissions they produce; and any resulting waste created by the energy, water, and materials used to source, manufacture, market, sell, transport, and dispose of their products and services are the basis of the "footprint." The more advanced lifecycle view of "footprint" extends this analysis to include the organization's entire supply and value chain:[16]

"Closed loop" thinking to do this was already being practiced successfully in the 1990s.[17] Reducing the use of materials of all types can be achieved by moving away from the outright sale of products where manufacturers have no interest in making their products and services last long. As discussed in Chapter 3, this move away can be achieved as follows:

1. Leasing instead of selling.
2. Extending product liability.
3. Joint ownership or use, though the disastrous impact of Covid-19 exposes the limitations of such an approach.
4. Remanufacturing.

Conservation

Conservation issues affect the long-term viability of organizations only indirectly. From a CG perspective, boards can only consider the issues of industrial agriculture, pollution and waste, and dealing with intensive farming on land and sea. The industrial agriculture issues are covered in detail in Chapter 3.

As far as pollution and waste are concerned, once boards appreciate the possible sources of waste and pollution in their organizations' value chains, they need to agree on policies to reduce their impact, with setting measurable targets for reduction in each area, supported by tracking and reward/compliance systems designed to highlight to the board progress against the targets set; including proposed corrective actions where targets are missed; making it clear who is responsible for undertaking them and by when. This approach and methodology must cover all participants in their organizations' supply chains as well.

In the case of water management, substantial progress is already being made in the reduction of water usage in industrial and household environments. Papermaking in Germany went from using 500–1000 liters per kilo of paper in 1900 to 1.5 liters per kilo in 1995. Gillette used 96% less water to make a razor blade in 1993 than in 1972 and 90% less water to make Paper Mate pens in 1993 than in 1974. Residential water use can be reduced by 50–67%. Mobile homes have been developed, using space technology to eliminate all external supplies, so that they recycle their water and wastes. A German textile manufacturer, Brinkhaus, was able to make 80% savings in water consumption and reduce wastewater by 92%.[18]

As a result of these types of improvements in the way water is used, total water use in the US in 2010 was lower than it was in 1970, despite economic and population growth, leading to continued reductions in per capita water use, so that it was lower in 2010 than in 1945. The economic productivity of water (dollars of gross domestic product per unit of water used) nearly tripled over thirty years, from only $4.00 in 1980 (in 2009 dollars) to more than $11.00 (in 2009 dollars) of GDP per hundred gallons used 2010.[19]

> More can be achieved by working on the life cycle of water consumption. By switching from cotton produced in high-precipitation countries to cotton from semiarid areas where subsurface drip irrigation is in use, topsoil losses can be reduced by more than a factor of 15. . .[20]

The biggest gains to be achieved in the areas of agricultural water use are through switching our dietary habits. It takes ten times more water to grow one ton of rice than a ton of wheat, so switching from rice to wheat would

help. It would help even more if we switched from meat to cereals and le-
gumes and nuts for protein:

> It takes up to a hundred times more water to produce a pound of meat as it does to pro-
> duce a pound of wheat. Rice takes more water than any other grain, but even rice requires
> only a tenth as much water per pound of production as meat.[21]

A number of improvements are being successfully applied. Drip irrigation can
save 80% of the water used in conventional irrigation.[22] Timing matters, both
in terms of season and weather but also by irrigating at night so there is less
evaporation. Selecting drought tolerant plant varieties and developing GMO
strains that can flourish in arid regions makes a difference. Rotational grazing,
composting, and mulching all improve the soil's ability to hold moisture, making it easier to use dry farming methods that rely on soil moisture alone. Cover
crops protect the soil from erosion and compaction, as well as reducing weeds
and increasing fertility. As a result, fields in California planted with cover crops
were found to be 11–14% more productive than conventionally planted fields in
times of drought. Going organic helps long-term.[23]

Boards are beginning to take water conservation seriously, though most
have yet to adopt a "water stewardship" approach, which may well become necessary as a result of climate change.[24]

It is important that the environmental processes and tracking systems
boards institute in their organizations are transparent and reported regularly as
part of the organization's external ESG reporting.

Economic Sustainability

The challenge must be serious when the Nikkei Asian Review has the problems
faced by capitalism in its first review of 2020 with the following comments:

> More than 400 years since the British and Dutch East India companies became the first
> publicly traded companies, and two decades since the fall of the Berlin Wall appeared to
> end the great ideological struggle between capitalism and communism, pressure is build-
> ing toward another economic watershed. *A combination of tech behemoths, growing
> wealth disparities, climate change and rampant protectionism is calling into question the
> very nature of capitalism itself.*
> *It was not supposed to be this way.*[25]   [Emphasis mine]

That capitalism is in crisis is a view shared by the historian, Niall Ferguson,
when interviewed by McKinsey in July 2019:[26]

Capitalism is in crisis, as usual. . .

To understand where we are now, you need to go back to the late 19th century, which saw a period of extraordinary globalization: enormous increases in trade, in capital flows, in migration. . .in 1873, there was a financial crisis, one of the first really global financial crises, and in the aftermath. . .populism on both sides of the Atlantic came to the fore. *It was the usual cocktail: nativism on immigration. . .; backlash against free trade. . .; attacks on corrupt elites. . . And outsiders came to the fore politically. This is the standard formula for populism.*

What tends to happen in the wake of a crisis as the dust settles, once people recover from their financial difficulties and turn to politics, is that they castigate big business. . .

From the vantage point of a chief executive, reputation is extraordinarily important. When it comes to the shifting sands of legislation and regulation, unpopular companies are vulnerable in a way that popular companies are not. The obvious lesson from the Gilded Age is don't be the villain of the piece. John D. Rockefeller became the villain of the original anti-trust movement in a way that Andrew Carnegie avoided. . . Why? I think it's partly about bad luck. . . *But it's also because Carnegie understood the power of philanthropy to offset the unpopularity that you inevitably accumulate as a successful businessman. . . In a wonderful essay on wealth,[iv] Carnegie argued that you should spend the first third of your life educating yourself, the second third making money, and the third third giving it all away. . .*

I think there's a lesson here, and we see some people, such as Bill Gates, learning it well.[27]   [Emphases mine]

Four key points emerged from that interview: capitalism is regularly in crisis as a result of Schumpeterian "creative destruction"; the resulting populism consists of a backlash against globalization with attacks on corrupt elites and the rise of outsider politicians; in these conditions there is a real danger of companies becoming the "villains of the piece" (currently they are likely to be big oil, big banks, and big tech); and finally, the importance of philanthropy, practiced effectively and distinctively to neutralize any hostility. The missing element in this analysis is the need to establish an effective process for handling workforce transitions through effective programs of life-long learning.

The only thing that has changed in terms of targets of anger are the addition of big tech and excessively paid CEOs to the previous list of "villains." The populist ingredients have remained the same. However, the threats posed by bad behavior are perceived to be existential because of the much greater adverse consequences of environmental and employment externalities on environmental sustainability and employability. Perhaps the other important change is that effective ESG has replaced philanthropy as the mitigating factor because its benefits are preventative – before the fact; whereas philanthropy can only compensate for damage done – after the fact.

---

iv Carnegie, A. (1889), "The Gospel of Wealth," *North American Review,* June 1889, https://www.carnegie.org/about/our-history/gospelofwealth/, accessed on January 2, 2020.

Given the poor reputation of business in general, it is no longer enough for companies to justify the damage they do to sustainability of the environment, economy and society through philanthropic CSR (corporate social responsibility). As a result, companies must proactively justify the benefits of their existence and purpose by doing more than just maximizing shareholder value, which is now somewhat discredited. This is made more critical, given the August 2019 US Business Roundtable Declaration that all stakeholders have equal importance and that the purpose of business is no longer to maximize shareholder value.

I believe that, as a result, boards that wish to avoid their companies being cast as "villains" will need to revisit their "purpose," prioritize stakeholder interests, redefine key measurements, and internalize externalities.

Revisiting "Purpose"

As explained in Chapter 2, organizational "purpose" depends on ownership structures and types of capitalism:

1. *Family and owner capitalism's "purpose":* "The first priority is the family stays together, with appropriate, satisfying and rewarding work for every adult member who chooses to work in the company. The second priority is that the worth of the company, and the worth of each family member's shares, grows at a rate comparable to indexed funds."[28]
2. *Managerial capitalism's "purpose":* "The corporation came to be run to profit its managers, in complicity if not conspiracy with accountants and the managers of other corporations."[29]
3. *Shareholder capitalism's "purpose":* "The ultimate aim of the company is return on shareholder equity better than the return for firms of similar risk characteristics. Risk characteristics for comparison will include similar size, industry, and maturity of market. Better return will mean above the median for such firms, rather than above the average."[30]
4. *State capitalism's "purpose":* "The ultimate purpose of state ownership of enterprises should be to maximize value for society, through an efficient allocation of resources."[31] The first priority is to promote and create business and job opportunities for the nation's industries and provide quality products and services at a fair price. The second priority is to enlarge the nation's industrial base and ensure a clean and safe environment.[32]
5. *Stakeholder capitalism's "purpose":* "Promoting business prosperity and corporate accountability with the ultimate objective of realizing long-term shareholder value while [considering] the interest of other stakeholders."[33]

The model of capitalism will determine the priorities given to stakeholders. For example, family capitalism and shareholder capitalism will give most weight to the interests of shareholders/owners. Managerial capitalism will give most weight to managers, while state capitalism and stakeholder capitalism will have to reconcile the competing interests of different stakeholders and, as a result, they will have to agree how to prioritize stakeholder interests.

Prioritizing Stakeholder Interests

If you accept Peter Drucker's argument that the "purpose of business is to create and maintain satisfied customers," customers must come first. This is reinforced further if you accept his additional point that it is the customer who determines what a business does and how it creates value:[34]

> *It is the customer who determines what a business is. For it is the customer, and he alone, who through being willing to pay for a good or service, converts economic resources into wealth, things into goods.* What the business thinks it produces is not of the first importance – especially not to the future of the business and to its success. What the customer thinks he is buying what he considers "value" is decisive – it determines what a business is, what it produces, and whether it will prosper.
>
> *The customer is the foundation of a business and keeps it in existence. He alone gives employment. And it is to supply the* consumer that society entrusts wealth-producing resources to the business enterprise.   [Emphases mine]

Johnson & Johnson's *Credo* (see Chapter 8) makes the same case. It puts customers first, employees second, communities and the environment third, and shareholders last.[35] Even the August 2019 US Business Roundtable puts stakeholders in the same order with customers first, employees second, suppliers third, communities fourth, and shareholders fifth.[36] However, putting employees second requires new processes boards must consider:

1. ***Recording employees as assets on the balance sheet*** to be invested in rather than only as payroll costs to be minimized.[37]

2. ***Revisiting the percentage of revenue committed to payroll***. One of the major contributors to the dissatisfaction with the current economic system in the US and UK is that the percentage of GDP that goes to wages is lower than in the past and that average workers are worse off today in real terms than they were twenty or thirty years ago.[38] The gains in productivity have led to increased profits and these have been distributed to shareholders and CEOs, increasing the inequality that threatens the social contract.

3. ***Revisiting how much CEOs should be paid***. Peter Drucker believed CEOs should be paid twenty times the average worker's pay than it was in 1965.

It peaked at 383:1 in 2000 in the US[39] and dropped to 265 in 2018. In Germany it is 136.[40] Something seems to have gone badly wrong with CEO remuneration as a result of stock options and needs redressing if trust in business is to be re-established. It is a sad reflection on the failures of boards' succession planning that they feel they must pay these exorbitant sums to compensate outsiders for the thinness of their talent pipeline.[41]

4. *Ensuring that organizations invest properly in skills and life-time opportunities for employees* given the pace of change in the way business is done and the disruptions that will materialize as a result of "Industry 4.0." In other words, boards should stop treating employees as disposable costs and treat them as assets requiring maintenance and upgrading to remain valuable.[42] Universities and technical colleges need to revisit their teaching and training models to help business create effective platforms for life-time opportunities for employees facing disruptive change.[43]

5. *Developing proper succession plans and managing talent to reflect the organization's current and future business strategies.* Boards must consider the appropriate current and future organizational design needed to deliver their mission and vision. This requires processes designed to determine the right number of people with the right competencies and character in the right roles now and in the future. To do this, boards need to spend much more time on establishing what skills are needed at both the organizational level and at the individual employee level for employees deemed to be of pivotal importance.[44]

6. *Developing support programs for the disemployed as a result of the impact of "Industry 4.0" on existing employment.* This requires careful coordination with trade associations, local authorities, and government to minimize the impact on communities of job losses and on individuals' sense of self-worth.

These subjects are discussed in greater detail in Chapter 11.

Redefining Key Measurements

If we are concerned with achieving long-term economic sustainability, then the measurements boards use to assess performance must reflect that objective. Currently, many do not; they encourage behavior designed to have the opposite effect.

1. *Move away from ROE:* If what really matters is maximizing the efficiency with which scarce resources are utilized by organizations, the best ratios

are either Return on Investment (ROI), Return on Capital Employed (ROCE), or Return on Net Assets (RONA), rather than the most popular ratio of Return on Equity (ROE). However, if maximizing shareholder returns is all that matters, then ROE becomes more important. Nevertheless, there are two problems with the use of ROE since Milton Friedman argued in 1970[45] that the purpose of business is to maximize shareholder value:

a. *ROE is a form of financial engineering:* It does not measure the efficiency with which scarce resources are utilized. Instead, it reflects the proportion of debt to equity, itself distorted as a measure of efficiency by the tax treatment of debt, which encourages using debt over equity.

b. *ROE encourages CEOs to take unsustainable long-term risks:* Remunerating CEOs with stock options based on their relative ROE performance is to reward them three times over for unsustainable behavior. First, by focusing on ROE without considering whether their financial engineering does improve asset utilization, *ROE rewards them with higher share prices for doing nothing to improve the economic value of the business.* Second, they can and do reward themselves by increasing dividends and doing share buybacks which transfer the employees' contribution to improved profits to shareholders (including themselves); and *ROE encourages them to sacrifice investment for the future in R&D and upgrading of fixed assets to focus on short-term investor time horizons.* This weakens the long-term competitive position of companies. Third, by reducing the amount of equity through increased dividends and buybacks, *ROE encourages CEOs to risk bankrupting the business when there is a liquidity crunch,* which is exactly what happened in 2009 with banks.[46]

2. ***Measure reductions in inputs:*** As part of ESG reporting, boards will need to set targets for reducing material inputs of fuel, energy, water, and raw materials to achieve the same levels of revenue and profit. They will then need to measure progress against these targets and record how they have done, where they fall short, and their corrective action plans and timetables for achieving such targets.

What investors look for in such reporting are three things:[47]

a. *Financial materiality:* Investors and regulators are looking to understand how companies' sustainability reporting relates to creating financial performance.

> The European Union's 2014 directive on nonfinancial reporting and the Financial Stability Board's creation of the Task Force on Climate-related Financial Disclosures in 2015 are two signals that financial regulators realize

sustainability-related activities can materially affect the financial standing of companies and should be reported accordingly.[48]

b. *Consistency:* Given the number of reporting frameworks, investors are looking for consistency to make comparability easier.

> As the head of sustainable investing at a major asset manager explained, "We have positions in over 4,500 companies. Unless [sustainability information] is comparable, hard data, it is of little use to us."[49]

c. *Reliability:* Ninety-seven percent of investors surveyed by McKinsey wanted sustainability audits and 67% expected them to be as rigorous as financial audits and that they should be undertaken using one uniform, comparable standard. This would not just save investors time and effort when comparing organizations; it would also reduce the amount of work companies have to do to meet different sets of standards; making it less expensive for them to employ independent auditors to verify their claims.[50]

3. ***Measure costs of externalities:*** What still needs to be done with the help of academics and economists is for boards to develop reasonably accurate costing systems to put a price on the externalities their organizations create through depletion, waste, pollution, congestion, and unemployment. Until that is done, society will not be able to evaluate properly whether activities being undertaken contribute to long-term sustainability.

Internalizing Externalities

Perhaps the most serious problem with internalizing external costs that hurt environmental and economic sustainability is the lack of easy to use mechanisms to do so and disagreement about the suitability of those that do exist. Moreover, boards cannot solve this on their own. They must work with governments, economists, and accountants to achieve consensus on pricing congestion, pollution, and global warming. Once pricing consensus has been achieved, regulators must enforce the adoption of such prices; and investors must understand why they are necessary and adjust their expectations of ROI accordingly.

This lack of suitable mechanisms and enforcement are major threats to sustainability of the environment, economy, employment, and the social contract. Unfortunately, there does not seem to be much progress in developing solutions.

Employment Sustainability

> The digitalization of economies, however, has increased the value of knowledge and data while decreasing that of physical labor. The IT sector needs only a relative handful of workers with advanced skills to control artificial intelligence and other cutting-edge technology.
>
> *Society, overall, is starting to lose its ability to create employment.*[51] [Emphasis mine]

This stark warning is perhaps an oversimplification. The RSA (Royal Society for the encouragement of Arts, Manufactures and Commerce) envisages four scenarios for the future of work in the UK by 2035.[52] Their scenarios may have general validity beyond the UK

The four scenarios are the "Big Tech," "Precision," "Exodus," and "Empathy" economies. Each has different implications for employment and employability and what companies and governments need to do to minimize the disruptions to employment and employability. Table 10.1 shows how they compare in their impact on employment and employability.

The challenge for policymakers is to find a way of ensuring that whichever of the four scenarios materializes, there will still be meaningful and rewarding work that both creates a successful economy and protects human dignity. Based on the RSA's scenarios, clearly the "Precision" and "Empathy" economies are preferred outcomes. The "Big Tech" economy with its undertones of George Orwell's *1984* may not be allowed to occur, with governments taking regulatory action to break up tech giants. The "Exodus" economy brings with it a threat of collapse to social sustainability and should be avoided at all costs. This may well require:

1. Employer commitment to supporting lifelong personal learning for employees.
2. Introducing a licensing system for gig economy occupations.
3. Creating a settlement covering the self-employed.
4. Revitalizing the role of unions.
5. Perhaps increasing worker representation on boards.

These suggestions would help redress the increased inequality that could otherwise occur in all four scenarios. In any event, boards will have to work with governments, trade associations, and civil society to bring these about. They cannot do this on their own.

Table 10.1: RSA's four futures of work.[53]

"Big Tech"	"Precision"	"Exodus"	"Empathy"
"Unemployment and economic insecurity creep upwards, and the spoils of growth are offshored and concentrated in a handful of U.S. and Chinese tech behemoths. The dizzying pace of change takes workers and unions by surprise, leaving them largely incapable of responding."	"Gig platforms take on more prominence and rating systems become pervasive in the workplace. While some lament these trends as invasive, removing agency from workers and creating overly competitive workplace cultures, others believe they have ushered in a more meritocratic society where effort is more generously rewarded."	Following another crash on the scale of 2008, "with another bout of austerity, workers lose faith in the ability of capitalism to improve their lives, and alternative economic models gather interest. Cooperatives and mutuals emerge in large numbers to serve people's core economic needs in food, energy, and banking. While some workers struggle on poverty wages, others discover ways to live more self-sufficiently, including by moving away from urban areas."	"Tech companies self-regulate to stem concerns and work hand-in-hand with external stakeholders to create new products that work on everyone's terms. Automation takes places at a modest scale but is carefully managed in partnership with workers and unions. Disposable income, kept aloft by high employment, flows into 'empathy sectors' like education, care, and entertainment."
Impact on employment	**Impact on employment**	**Impact on employment**	**Impact on employment**
Automation eliminates cognitive and non-cognitive jobs as well as routine and non-routine jobs; 20-hour working week the norm.[54]	Modest automation; Most jobs requiring creativity or dexterity are secure; Workers subject to algorithmic oversight, with pervasive ratings systems; Piece-work labor conditions as firms know who they need, at what times, and at what skill level.[55]	Increases in strikes, unemployment, and zero hours contracts; Workers leave big cities because they cannot afford to live there; Fall in material living standards.[56]	Moderate automation as companies work with unions and employees to achieve mutually beneficial results; Percentage of GDP and jobs in care and education sectors grows; Work is more emotionally demanding as workers manage own emotions while boosting the feelings of those whom they serve.[57]

Employer Commitment to Lifelong Learning

It is clear that the nature of work will change and that people will need to recognize they will have to embrace lifelong learning. Gone are the days where employees could work for one employer all their lives, doing the same things each year. If employers are to invest in their employees (discussed further in Chapter 11), they need to demonstrate that they no longer treat them as disposable costs, but as assets instead. To do this, it may make sense for employers to contribute to portable personal lifelong learning accounts, funded in part by governments when employees move from one employer to another:

> Singapore has introduced "personal learning accounts" – budgets for training for every worker to help adapt to tomorrow's jobs – while in Sweden, the state encourages employers to contribute to funds to help workers transition during periods of redundancy.[58]

The question companies will have to answer is, "What kind of learning should be provided on a lifelong basis?" It would appear that companies and educators will have to move away from vocational styles to "first principles" learning where people are encouraged to use blank sheets of paper to work out answers to the "Why/Why Not?" and "What?" questions rather than the "How?" questions, since it is precisely the answers to the "How?" questions that are threatened as a result of "Industry 4.0" in the RSA's four different scenarios.

Perhaps the problem comes from the fact the way our brains operate is not recognized enough in what we teach both at school and in universities. The brain works as follows:

> The Φ neurons (sensations) activate the Ψ neurons (memory), which in turn activates the Ω neurons (awareness). In other words, *consciousness originates in the unconscious circuits, not the conscious ones.* This flow set[s] a precedent for three interwoven ideas that proved decisive in the study of awareness:
> 1) Almost all mental activity is unconscious.
> 2) The unconscious is the true motor of our actions.
> 3) The conscious mind inherits and, to a certain extent, *takes charge* of those sparks from the unconscious. *Consciousness thus, is not the genuine author of our (conscious) actions. But it, at least, has the ability to edit, modify and censure them.*[59]
>
> [Emphasis mine]

The irony is that education systems focus on the operations of the conscious mind rather than the unconscious mind. As a result, people are locked into "frozen thinking" which prevents them from challenging received wisdom and thinking outside the box, when it is precisely these skills people will need in dealing with "Industry 4.0." Companies will need to encourage so-called "elastic" thinking[60] in their employees and ensure that the training programs they invest in do so. Universities will have to move from past current ways of teaching to ones that recognize the need to focus on the unconscious mind if people are to embrace change. To do this effectively, they will have to work closely with industry to design programs emphasizing key soft skills of being able to "connect the dots," curiosity, creativity, empathy, problem-solving, and communication.[61] They will also have to encourage adaptability to cope with volatility and uncertainty and promote an increase in tolerance of ambiguity arising from the need to learn new skills on a lifelong basis.

Occupational Licensing

Companies like Amazon, Uber, and Lyft have not merely denied their contractors the benefits that employees have, but have also created a level of competition between contractors that undermines their ability to negotiate better terms and conditions. Occupational licensing may help redress the balance between companies that offer "zero hours" contracts and those who work for them, as well as enhancing the self-respect of those who work in the gig economy that has so many of the features of hated 19th century piece work – including the lack of job security:[62]

> More people are in a job than ever, but below the surface of record employment figures, *increasingly we are seeing the link between hard work and fair pay collapse; work alone is no longer a route out of poverty.*
>
> This could not come at a worse time for millions of families amid Brexit uncertainty, the potential for another recession and the increasing prospect of automation of many routine roles.
>
> Economic insecurity is creeping-up the income scale and is no longer just confined to those on low-incomes. Many of those "just managing" are a financial shock away from failing to pay rent or pay a childcare bill, while even people on higher incomes fear the grinding effect of inflation, flatlining pay and falling living standards.
>
> *Neither the labour market nor the welfare state alone can turn automation from a problem to an opportunity for workers. We need to see government creating the framework for employers, civil society, unions, social enterprises and digital start-ups to provide more help, including retraining and income support, while legislating for stronger rights for workers and a genuine living wage.*[63]   [Emphases mine]

Boards will need to think through how they should respond, should governments introduce occupational licenses with defined terms and conditions of work, if their companies rely on zero hours contracts or their equivalent.

Revitalized Role of Unions

The decline of unions in developed economies in the last thirty years has been one of the features of the neoliberal economy, leading to wage stagnation.[64] Workers have lost their voice as a result and it may be desirable to encourage unionization once again – provided unions are committed to developing a new social contract with a stronger and more collaborative worker voice on boards. Outside the US, there is a gradual recognition that it might be desirable to redistribute some power back to workers by either appointing workers to boards or by allocating a given percentage of equity to employees. Stronger unions may also help achieve a move to shorter working weeks – potentially a work-sharing solution to the threat of disemployment caused by "Industry 4.0."

Chapter 11 explores in more detail how to value people properly in order to achieve sustainable employment and employability.

Increased Worker Representation on Boards

This may be needed to ensure whatever solutions are implemented are seen to be "win-win" by all stakeholders rather than just shareholders and the senior management of increasingly concentrated industries, dominated by a few companies who often dictate employment terms and conditions by using harsh non-compete clauses, preventing employees from exercising their rights to seek better conditions.[65]

Social Sustainability

If the "Big Tech" economy is the future, my concern is that it may lead to a breakdown in the social contract and to a totalitarian government of either the extreme left or right, reinforced by the surveillance capabilities of "big tech." However, there are more immediate concerns that boards face in terms of ensuring that they do not undermine societies. The first is dealing with corruption and the "frozen thinking" of institutional vested interests that resist change. The second is managing diversity effectively.

Corruption and Institutional Vested Interests

In principle, most boards have explicit policies specifying a "zero tolerance" for corruption, reinforced by laws prohibiting bribery and corruption. In practice, many companies find ways to work around the laws, and sometimes governments turn a blind eye to extreme cases of corruption, defending their decisions on the importance of the continued relationship to national security, jobs, and the economy:

> December 2006 – SFO [Serious Fraud Office] drops the Saudi probe after "representations" from the British government about the need to safeguard national security. The decision followed a Daily Telegraph article, citing unnamed authoritative sources, saying Saudi Arabia had given Britain 10 days to halt the SFO inquiry or lose a contract for 72 Eurofighter Typhoon combat jets being jointly developed by BAE Systems.[66]

The key distinction that companies must always bear in mind in developing processes to deal with corruption is maintaining transparency with a clear statement of the expected performance and results to be delivered in return for a given consideration, and any consideration must benefit the organization and not the individual. In such conditions, any facilitation payment where the price is clearly stated in return for specific different levels of treatment or speed of response is no different from paying more for flying first class rather than economy or traveling on a high speed train in Europe rather than on a regional train that stops at every station.

Lobbying can turn into regulatory capture when companies get too close to their regulators. The Boeing 737 MAX crashes are a tragic example of what happens when a company captures its regulator:

> The aftermath of the aircraft maker's twin 737 MAX crashes, which killed 346 people, laid bare a culture in which safety concerns were discounted – and federal regulators were treated as little more than malleable rubber stamps.[67]

The extent to which Boeing behaved badly because of its presumed power over its regulators is revealed in the following email exchanges. Boeing persuaded Lion Air and the regulators that simulator training was not needed:

> In one exchange, an unnamed employee wrote: "Now friggin [Lion Air] might need a sim to fly the MAX, and maybe because of their own stupidity. I'm scrambling trying to figure out how to unscrew this now! Idiots. . ."
>
> . . .In a March 2017 internal email released in the documents, Boeing's 737 chief technical pilot wrote: "I want to stress the importance of holding firm that there will not be any type of simulator training required to transition from NG to MAX. *Boeing will not allow that to happen. We'll go face to face with any regulator who tries to make that a requirement.*"[68]   [Emphasis mine]

That training might have saved the 346 lives lost in the Lion Air and Ethiopian Airlines crashes had Boeing put safety before profits and share price.[69] Boeing has now reluctantly conceded that the simulator training is needed – at a cost to Boeing of US$5 billion.[70]

Managing Diversity Effectively

Chapter 6 discussed issues raised by encouraging diversity within organizations. If boards are to incorporate people of diverse backgrounds, cultures, and belief systems successfully, they must recognize the fact that any differences come from fundamental characteristics in belief systems based on history and identity that should be taken seriously. Only if this is done, can boards begin to reconcile the differences in approach and create added value as a result.

From a corporate perspective, four fundamental differences created by diversity of background and belief systems matter. They are differences in attitudes to the importance of rules versus relationships; differences in measuring and managing personal performance; differences in approaches to status; and differences in the role of individuals and the community:

1. Reconciling Universalists with Particularists

As discussed in Chapter 6, universalists and particularists have very different approaches to the importance of rules and relationships (for details, see Table 6.4), that can create serious problems when they are not recognized. Table 10.2 suggests three ways each approach can modify its default behaviors to maximize chances of implementing successful long-term adherence to centrally designed codes of conduct that are essential for multinational organizations if they are to operate with the same values across the world.

Table 10.2: Three suggested modifications.[71]

Universalists dealing with Particularists:	Particularists dealing with Universalists:
1. Being prepared for personal "meandering" or "irrelevancies" that seem to be going nowhere	1. Being prepared for "rational," "professional" arguments that push for your acquiescence
2. Not taking personal "get to know you" attitudes as small talk	2. Not taking impersonal "get down to business" attitudes as insulting
3. Carefully considering the personal implications of legal safeguards.	3. Carefully preparing the ground with a lawyer if in doubt.

Figure 10.1 goes one step further and shows how to reconcile the two approaches.

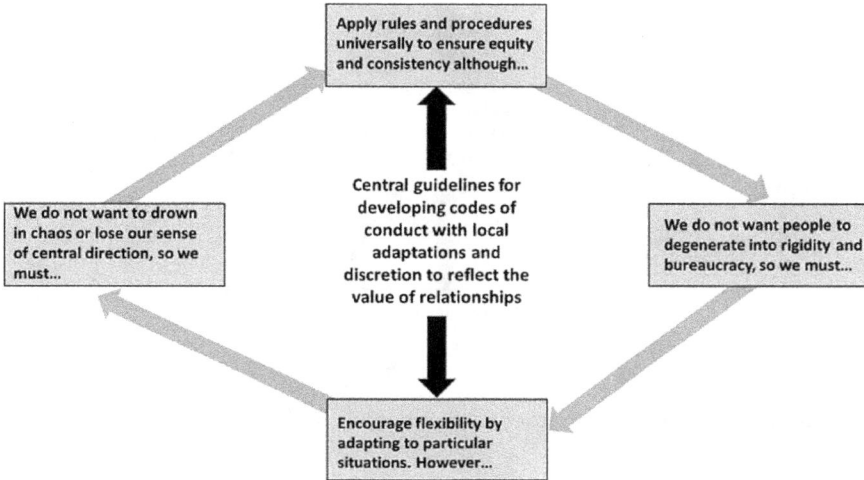

Figure 10.1: Reconciling universalist and particularist approaches.[72]

2. Reconciling Specific and Diffuse Measurement of Performance

As discussed in Chapter 6, the two different approaches to measuring performance can be serious sources of misunderstanding when appraising people. Some cultures are specific, breaking performance down into its constituent parts, whereas others are more diffuse when defining performance (for details, see Table 6.6).

Figure 10.2 shows how the two approaches to measuring performance can be reconciled.

3. Reconciling Achieved and Ascribed Status

As discussed in Chapter 6, there are two ways of looking at status (for details, see Table 6.8). Senior managers, who believe status and respect at work must be earned and want to avoid misunderstandings and rejection of ideas when dealing with colleagues who believe status is ascribed, should do the following:[74]

1. Never underestimate the need of their counterparts to live up to their ascribed status. Giving face is critical, even if it is undeserved.

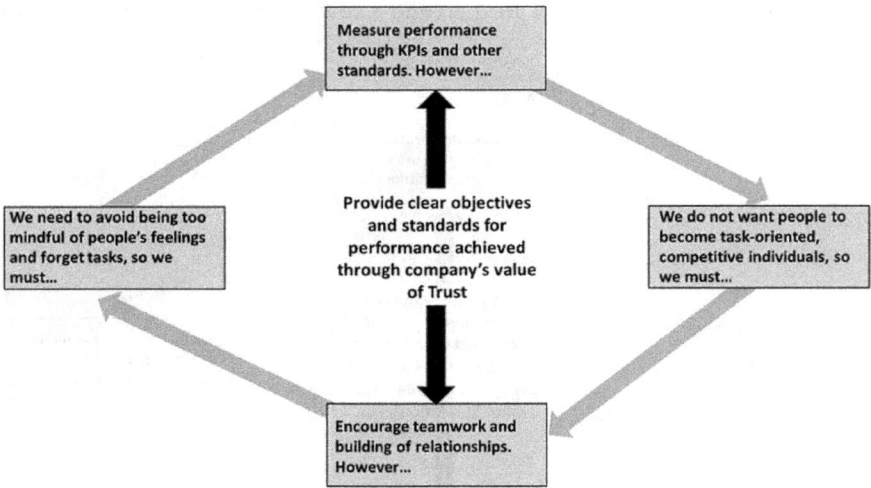

Figure 10.2: Reconciling two approaches to measuring performance.[73]

2. Even if they suspect they are short of knowledge, *respect the status and influence* of their counterparts. *Never* show them up in meetings. Take time out to help them understand what more they need to know *in private*.
3. Choose the title that reflects their own degree of *influence* in their organization.

Senior managers who believe status is ascribed, when dealing with colleagues who believe status should be earned, should do the following:

1. Never underestimate achievers' needs, as individuals, to do better than expected.
2. Even if they think they lack influence, *respect the knowledge and information* of their counterparts.
3. Choose the title that reflects their own *competence* as individuals when dealing with achievers.
4. Successful organizations are able to reconcile the *high flier* (identified high performer whose performance is reviewed regularly) and *crown prince* (selected individual whose career advance has been pre-ordained because of who s/he is) approaches to developing senior careers. Figure 10.3 summarizes how to reconcile these two approaches to status and their impact on career development and behavior.

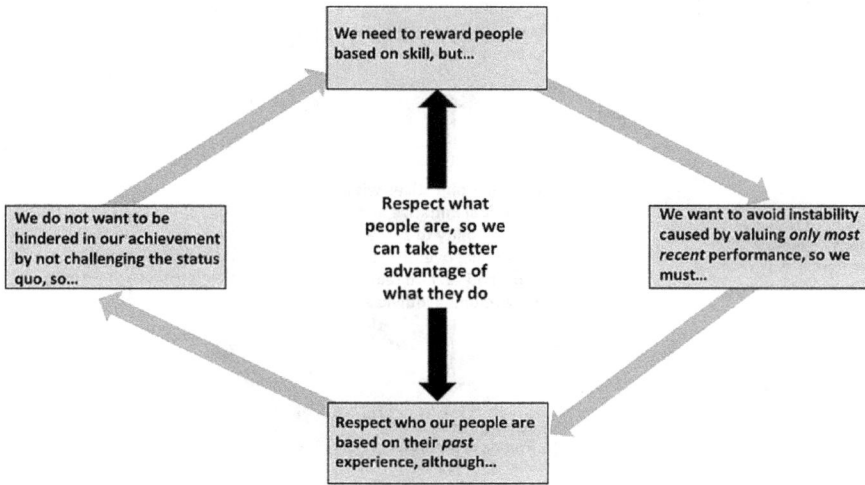

Figure 10.3: Reconciling achievement and ascription.[75]

4. *Reconciling the Role of Individuals with the Community*

The difference in the importance placed on individual or collective behavior matters. It affects attitudes towards individual accountability, competition versus collaboration, and the role of the individual in the community.

As discussed in Chapter 6, there are two approaches to assessing the relative importance of individuals versus the community (for details, see Table 6.10). Reconciling individual effort with team performance can be achieved by rewarding individuals for helping the team, while making sure the team then celebrates the success of those individuals. As a result, there is no longer a basis for jealousy of individual success, since it creates success for all; and individuals are properly recognized for what they have achieved.

Figure 10.4 shows how to reconcile individual objectives with those of the team.

Summary

Boards need to consider additional and perhaps alternative processes to the traditional, internally focused processes they already adopt to create sustainable value. Both government intervention and changes in board attitudes are necessary if a "political tragedy of the commons" is to be avoided.

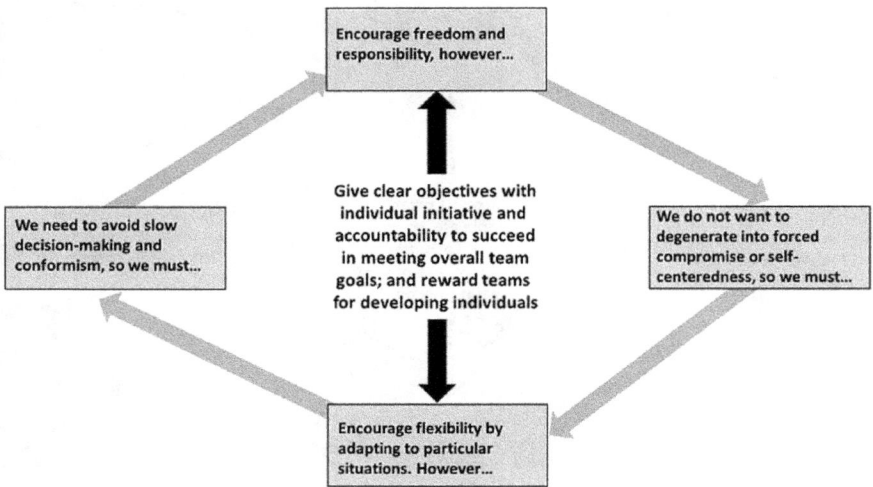

Figure 10.4: Reconciling individual and team objectives.[76]

Environmental Sustainability

Whether boards like it or not, there is increasing external pressure on them to consider ESG issues not just in terms of reporting, but in terms of what changes to their business models they are proposing so that investors and insurers understand the risks they face and the actions they are taking to mitigate them; and to reassure their bankers and insurers that they will not end up with worthless "stranded" assets.

Central banks are starting to insist that commercial banks, insurers, and pension funds disclose the extent to which their investments and policies are at risk because of climate change. *No longer will boards be able to argue that the time horizon for action is so lengthy that they can ignore the impact of climate change because neither they nor their investors will be around when the damage is done.* Instead, they will have to begin developing plans now to mitigate the short-medium term risks of being unable to get financing from banks, of being uninsured/uninsurable, or of falling share prices. The changing external regulatory context is bringing the future to the present in ways boards will have to consider carefully – *they will need processes capable of developing multiple scenarios with strong balance sheets, including possibly exiting the business.*

Boards will need to pay greater attention to the pressures to move from linear to circular business models and this will require more transparent reporting and tracking of progress in ESG reports. It will require tracking progress in each part of the "reduce, recycle, reuse and remanufacture" cycle. This pressure is likely to be translated into measurements of the organizational "footprint," using "closed loop" thinking covering all environmental and social impacts throughout the organization's value chain. Boards are also beginning to take water conservation seriously, though most have yet to adopt a "water stewardship" approach, which may well become necessary as a result of climate change.

Economic Sustainability

Perhaps effective ESG has replaced philanthropy when it comes to dealing with economic externalities because its benefits are preventative – before the fact; whereas philanthropy can only compensate for damage done – after the fact. Boards that wish to avoid their companies being cast as "villains" will need to revisit their "purpose," prioritize stakeholder interests, redefine key measurements, and internalize externalities. The model of capitalism will determine the priorities given to stakeholders. The recent move toward stakeholder capitalism means boards will have to reconcile the competing interests of different stakeholders, perhaps modeling their approach on Johnson & Johnson's *Credo*. In addition, boards will have to revisit financial and other KPIs, moving away from ROE and adding measurements designed to track reductions in inputs. Measuring the costs of externalities will remain a challenge, as will internalizing them.

Employment Sustainability

There are four possible scenarios for the future of work: the "big tech," "precision," "exodus," and "empathy" economies. Each has different implications for employment and employability and what companies and governments need to do to minimize the disruptions to employment and employability. The challenge for policymakers is to find a way of ensuring that whichever of the four scenarios materializes, there will still be meaningful and rewarding work that both creates a successful economy and protects human dignity. Based on the RSA's scenarios, the "precision" and "empathy" economies are to be preferred.

Sustaining employment and employability may well require employer commitment to lifelong learning for employees with changes in training and education, focusing on soft skills and "first principles thinking," a licensing system for gig economy occupations, creating a new settlement for the self-employed, revitalizing the role of unions, and perhaps increasing worker representation on boards. In designing training, there will be a need to emphasize adaptability to cope with volatility and uncertainty and to raise tolerance of ambiguity in order to learn new skills on a lifelong basis.

Social Sustainability

The key distinction that companies must always bear in mind in developing processes to deal with corruption is maintaining transparency with a clear statement of the expected performance and results to be delivered in return for a given consideration. Any consideration must benefit the organization and not the individual.

Managing diversity raises different issues. If boards are to capture the benefits and advantages of a diverse workforce, they must develop processes designed to reconcile different belief systems. The four areas of potential misunderstanding come from the differences in approaches to: rules versus relationships; to measuring performance; the basis of status; and the roles of individuals versus the community.

Reconciling rules versus relationships can be achieved by adopting central guidelines for developing codes of conduct with local adaptations and discretion to reflect the value of relationships. Reconciling specific and diffuse measurements of performance can be achieved by providing clear objectives and standards for performance achieved through company's value of trust. Reconciling achieved and ascribed status can be achieved by respecting what people are so that boards can take better advantage of what they do. Reconciling the roles of individuals and the group can be achieved by giving clear objectives with individual initiative and accountability to succeed in meeting overall team goals while rewarding teams for developing individuals.

References

1 Armstrong, R. (2019), "Warren Buffett on why companies cannot be moral arbiters," *The Financial Times*, December 19, 2019, https://www.ft.com/content/ebbc9b46-1754-11ea-9ee4-11f260415385, accessed on January 7, 2020.

2 For a full discussion of these already adopted processes, see Zinkin, J. (2018), *Better Governance Across The Board: Creating Value Through Reputation, People and Processes* (Boston/Berlin: Walter De Gruyter Inc).

3 "UK becomes first major economy to pass net zero emission law," *Department for Business, Energy and Industrial Strategy*, June 27, 2019, https://www.gov.uk/government/news/uk-becomes-first-major-economy-to-pass-net-zero-emissions-law, accessed on December 30, 2019.

4 Hutchinson, L. (2019), "'Europe's man on the moon moment': Von der Leyen reveals unveils EU Green Deal," *The Parliament Magazine,* December 11, 2019, https://www.theparliamentma gazine.eu/articles/news/%E2%80%98europe%E2%80%99s-man-moon-moment%E2%80%99- von-der-leyen-unveils-eu-green-deal, accessed on December 30, 2019.

5 Rosen, J. (2019), "Cities, states and companies vow to meet U.S. climate goals without Trump. Can they?" *The Los Angeles Times,* November 4, 2019, https://www.latimes.com/environment/ story/2019-11-04/cities-states-companies-us-climate-goals-trump, accessed on December 30, 2019.

6 Carney, M. quoted in Harrabin, R. (2019), "Bank of England chief Mark Carney issues climate change warning," *BBC News,* December 30, 2019, https://www.bbc.com/news/business- 50868717, accessed on December 30, 2019.

7 Ward, R. (2019), "Goldman Sachs Curbs New Lending on Coal and Arctic Oil," *Bloomberg,* December 16, 2019, https://www.bloomberg.com/news/articles/2019-12-16/goldman-sachs- strengthens-climate-policy-as-global-talks-falter, accessed on December 30, 2019.

8 Holger, D. (2019), "Credit Suisse Ends Funding for New Coal Plants," *Morningstar,* December 11, 2019, https://www.morningstar.com/news/dow-jones/201912112524/credit-suisse- ends-funding-for-new-coal-plants, accessed on January 13, 2020.

9 Chandrasekhar, A. (2019), "The UN climate talks ended in deadlock. Is this really the best the world can manage?" *The Guardian,* December 21, 2019, https://www.theguardian.com/commen tisfree/2019/dec/21/un-climate-talks-deadlock-cop25, accessed on January 6, 2020.

10 Cobley. M. (2019), "Investors will pull almost $1trn from fossil fuels in the next decade," *Financial News,* October 14, 2019, https://www.fnlondon.com/articles/investors-say-they-will- pull-almost-1tn-from-fossil-fuels-in-the-next-decade-20191014, accessed on December 30, 2019.

11 Fink, L. (2018), "A Fundamental Reshaping of Finance," *Black Rock,* https://www.black rock.com/corporate/investor-relations/larry-fink-ceo-letter, accessed on January 15, 2020.

12 Dirks, G. (2019), based on a phone conversation between Dr. Gary Dirks, Senior Director, Global Futures Laboratory, Wrigley Chair, Arizona State University, and the author on December 30, 2019.

13 Gregory, A. (2019), "Climate change could render assets 'worthless', Bank of England Governor warns," *The Independent,* December 30, 2019, https://www.independent.co.uk/en vironment/climate-change-finance-assets-worthless-mark-carney-bio-divestment-a9263861. html, accessed on December 31, 2019.

14 Brown, J. (2019), "Most CEOs have no financial incentives around sustainability, research shows," *People Management,* December 13, 2019, https://www.peoplemanagement.co.uk/ news/articles/most-ceos-no-financial-incentives-sustainability-research-shows, accessed on January 7, 2020.

15 Ibid.

16 Hedstrom, G. S. (2019), *Sustainability: What It Is and How to Measure It* (Boston/Berlin: Walter De Gruyter Inc.), p. 21.

17 Hawken, P., Lovins A. B. and Lovins L. H. (1999), *Natural Capitalism: The Next Industrial Revolution* (London: Earthscan Publications).

18 Von Weizsacker, E. (1998), op. cit., pp. 83–89.

19 Donnelly, K. and Coley, H. (2015), "Water Use Trends in the United States," *Pacific Institute,* p. 1, https://pacinst.org/wp-content/uploads/2015/04/Water-Use-Trends-Full- Report.pdf, accessed on December 31, 2019.

20 Von Weizsacker, E. (1998), p. 89.

21 Robbins. J. (1987), *Diet for a New America* (Tiburon, Calif: H.J., Kramer Inc.), p. 367.

22 Shiozaki, J. (2014), "10 Ways Farmers Are Saving Water," *CUESA*, August 15, 2014, https://cuesa.org/article/10-ways-farmers-are-saving-water, accessed on August 22, 2019.

23 Ibid.

24 Ibid.

25 Nikkei staff writers (2020), "System glitches: Capitalism shows its age in the digital era," *Nikkei Asian Review*, January 1, 2020, https://asia.nikkei.com/Spotlight/Neo-Capitalism/System-glitches-Capitalism-shows-its-age-in-the-digital-era?utm_campaign=RN%20Free%20newsle, accessed on January 1, 2020.

26 Ferguson, N. (2019), "'Don't be the villain': Niall Ferguson looks forward and back at capitalism in crisis," *McKinsey Quarterly*, November 2019, https://www.mckinsey.com/featured-insights/long-term-capitalism/dont-be-the-villain-niall-ferguson-looks-forward-and-back-at-capitalism-in-crisis, accessed on January 2, 2020.

27 Ibid.

28 Zinkin, J. (2019), *Better Governance Across the Board: Creating Value Through Reputation, People and Processes* (Boston/Berlin: Walter De Gruyter Inc.), p. 49.

29 Bogle, J. (2003), Speech given to 2003 National Investor Relations Conference, Orlando, Florida, June 11, 2003, *Bogle Financial Center*, http://johncbogle.com/wordpress/wp-content/uploads/2019/08/niri-6-03.pdf, accessed on April 1, 2020.

30 Zinkin, J. (2019), op. cit., p. 49.

31 OECD (2015), *OECD Guidelines on Corporate Governance of State owned Enterprises, 2015 Edition* (Paris: OECD Publishing), p. 17, https://www.oecd-ilibrary.org/docserver/9789264244160-en.pdf?expires=1542261379&id=id&accname=guest&checksum=29D7D3455C42A7989C3D141939B2AAC9, accessed on November 15, 2018.

32 Zinkin, J. (2019) op. cit., p. 49.

33 Securities Commission Malaysia (2017), *Malaysian Code on Corporate Governance*, p. 1.

34 Drucker, P. (1955), *The Practice of Management* (Oxford: Butterworth Heinemann), p. 35 quoted in Zinkin, J. (2010), *Challenges in Implementing Corporate Governance: Whose Business Is It Anyway?* (Singapore: John Wiley & Sons), p. 24.

35 Johnson, R. W. (1943), "Our Credo," *Johnson & Johnson website*, https://www.jnj.com/credo/, accessed on December 8, 2019.

36 Business Roundtable (2019), "Business Roundtable Redefines the Purpose of a Corporation to Promote 'An Economy That Serves All Americans'," *Business Roundtable*, August 19, 2019, https://www.businessroundtable.org/business-roundtable-redefines-the-purpose-of-a-corporation-to-promote-an-economy-that-serves-all-americans, accessed on December 16, 2019.

37 Zinkin, J. (2019), op. cit., pp. 317–323.

38 Ibid., pp. 303–305.

39 Kets De Vries, M. F. R. (2018), "Do CEOs Deserve Their Pay?" *INSEAD Knowledge*, February 7, 2018, https://knowledge.insead.edu/blog/insead-blog/do-ceos-deserve-their-pay-8351, accessed on January 6, 2020.

40 "Ratio between CEO and average worker pay, by country 2018," *Statista*, January 2019, https://www.statista.com/statistics/424159/pay-gap-between-ceos-and-average-workers-in-world-by-country/, accessed on January 6, 2020.

41 Dirks, G. (2020), in an email to the author on February 7, 2020.

42 Zinkin, J. (2019)., op. cit., pp. 320–321.

43 Dirks, G. (2020), op. cit.

44 Zinkin, J. (2019), op. cit., pp. 236–38.

45 Friedman, M. (1970), "The Social Responsibility of Business Is to Increase its Profits," *New York Times Magazine,* September 13, 1970, http://umich.edu/~thecore/doc/Friedman.pdf, accessed on January 3, 2020.

46 Zinkin, J. (2014), *Rebuilding Trust in Banks: The Role of Leadership and Governance* (Singapore: John Wiley & Sons), pp. 28–42.

47 Bernow, S. et al. (2019), "The value-based sustainability reporting that investors want," *McKinsey & Co.,* August 2019, https://www.mckinsey.com/business-functions/sustainability/ our-insights/more-than-values-the-value-based-sustainability-reporting-that-investors-want, accessed on January 3, 2020.

48 Ibid.

49 Ibid.

50 Ibid.

51 Nikkei staff writers (2020), op. cit.

52 Dellot, B. et al. (2019), "The Four Futures of Work: Coping with uncertainty in an age of radical technologies," *RSA Action and Research Centre,* March 2019, https://www.thersa.org/ globalassets/pdfs/reports/rsa_four-futures-of-work.pdf, accessed on January 3, 2020.

53 Ibid., p. 7.

54 Ibid., p. 42.

55 Ibid., p. 46.

56 Ibid., p. 49.

57 Ibid., p. 52.

58 RSA (2019), "Economic insecurity is rising with gig economy workers least prepared for automation or Brexit challenges, think-tank warns," *RSA,* August 16, 2019, https://www.thersa. org/about-us/media/coverage-press-releases/2019/economic-insecurity-is-rising-with-gig-economy-workers-least-prepared-for-automation-or-brexit-challenges-think-tank-warns, accessed on January 6, 2020.

59 Sigman, M. (2017), *The Secret Life of the Mind: How Your Brain Thinks, Feels and Decides* (New York/Boston/London: Little, Brown and Company), p. 104.

60 Mlodinow, L. (2018), *Elastic: Unlocking Your Brain's Ability to Embrace Change* (New York: Vintage Books).

61 Foutty, J. (2019), "Aspire to Lead in 'Industry 4.0'? Hone Your Soft Skills," *The Wall Street Journal,* January 23, 2019, https://deloitte.wsj.com/riskandcompliance/2019/01/23/aspire-to-lead-in-industry-4-0-hone-your-soft-skills/, accessed on January 6, 2020.

62 RSA (2019), op. cit.

63 Ibid.

64 Da Costa, P.N. (2019), "U.S. Inequality, Wage Stagnation Tied To Falling Union Membership in the Private Sector," *Forbes,* August 29, 2019, https://www.forbes.com/sites/ pedrodacosta/2019/08/29/u-s-inequality-wage-stagnation-tied-to-falling-union-membership-in-the-private-sector/#4040397, accessed on January 7, 2020.

65 Maggard, J. and Vering, J. (2018), "Overreaching Covenants Not To Compete Under Attack From All Sides," *American Bar Association,* December 26, 2018, https://www.americanbar.org/ groups/litigation/committees/business-torts-unfair-competition/practice/2018/overreaching-covenants-not-to-compete/, accessed on January 5, 2020.

66 Reuters (2009), "Timeline: Allegations of Corruption at BAE Systems," https://www.reu ters.com/article/us-baesystems-timeline-sb/timeline-allegations-of-corruption-at-bae-systems-idUSTRE5904OW20091001, accessed on January 5, 2020.

67 Primack, D. (2019), quoted in "Boeing CEO Dennis Muilenburg Is Out," *Axios*, December 23, 2019, https://www.axios.com/boeing-dennis-muilenburg-resigns-737-max-crashes-d1208e87-7b7e-4aa6-9baa-2e257fbe594f.html, accessed on January 15, 2020.

68 Baker, S. (2020), "A Boeing employee called Lion Air, the airline in the first 737 MAX crash 'idiots' for asking to have its pilots trained in flying the plane," *Business Insider US*, January 14, 2020, https://www.businessinsider.my/boeing-737-max-employee-called-lion-air-idiots-training-request-2020-1/?r=US&IR=T, accessed on January 15, 2020.

69 Rushe, D. (2019), "Man whose family died in 737 MAX crash accuses Boeing of 'utter disrespect'," *The Guardian*, July 17, 2019, https://www.theguardian.com/business/2019/jul/17/boeing-737-max-congressional-hearing-testimony, accessed on January 15, 2020.

70 Schlangenstein, M. (2020), "Boeing Seen Facing $5 Billion Tab on 737 MAX Simulator Training," *Bloomberg*, January 9, 2020.

71 Based on ibid., p. 49.

72 Ibid., p. 44.

73 Trompenaars, F. and Hampden-Turner, C. (2006), *Riding the Waves of Culture* (London: Nicholas Brealey Publishing), p. 91.

74 Based on ibid., pp. 118–119.

75 Ibid., p. 116.

76 Trompenaars, F. and Hampden-Turner, C. (2006), op cit., p. 58.

Chapter 11
Valuing People Properly

This chapter is presented in two parts: The first discusses changing the underlying assumptions made by boards about "people" and their value to the business; the second considers how best to invest in "people." It closes with a summary on how boards can regard people as assets to be invested in rather than costs to be minimized.

Every time I ask the question of directors, "What is your most important asset?" they answer "people." Incorrectly in my view, because the most important asset of an organization is its reputation. However, "people" are the second most important asset. Henry Ford was of the same opinion:

> The two most important things in any company do not appear in its balance sheet: its reputation and its people.[1]

Yet, from my experience, boards spend less than 10% of their time on people issues; at a time where advances in blockchain applications, robotics, and AI make people with up-to-date skills perhaps the most important strategic issue boards have to face to stay competitive. Equally, what society does with the unemployed who lose their jobs as a result of automation and AI is, I believe, one the greatest challenges to economic and social sustainability in the next thirty years. This is the result of underlying assumptions boards have about "people."

Changing Underlying Assumptions About People

Clearly something has gone wrong in the way "people" are discussed at the board level. If directors truly believe what they say about the importance of "people" as assets, and I am sure at some level they do, they would put their "people," summarized in the payroll cost, on the balance sheet as well as in the P&L – as an asset to be invested in, upgraded, and protected from obsolescence. That does not happen. This is in part the fault of universities who have not adjusted their curricula to meet the needs of lifelong learning and it is also the fault of companies that have cut down on the levels of lifelong training and development of employees as a result of the ending of lifetime employment with one employer. For example, in the days when IBM promised lifetime employment, it invested up to four years of training in its employees:

https://doi.org/10.1515/9783110670486-011

> In the middle of the last century, management saturated American corporations. Every worker, from the CEO down to production personnel, served partly as a manager, participating in planning and coordination along an unbroken continuum in which each job closely resembled its nearest neighbor. Elaborately layered middle managers – or *"organization men"* – coordinated production among long-term employees. In turn, companies taught workers the skills they needed to rise up the ranks. At IBM, for example, a 40-year worker might spend more than four years, or 10 percent, of his work life in fully paid, IBM-provided training.[2]

This is going to become even more critical if the sustainability challenge to employment and employability discussed in Chapter 5 is even half right, as more than a third of people gainfully employed are likely to be rendered obsolete. Given the tremendous pressures boards will be under to reduce costs to remain competitive by adopting robots and AI, it may be unrealistic to expect boards to treat payroll in the same way as they treat plant, machinery, and goodwill; i.e., as an aggregated financial sum that is not treated solely as a cost. They are also unlikely to regard people as a long-term obligation rather than as a variable cost to be disposed of when no longer needed, and this has been the result of companies relying more than ever on management consultants:

> In effect, management consulting is a tool that allows corporations to replace lifetime employees with short-term, part-time, and even subcontracted workers, hired under ever more tightly controlled arrangements, who sell particular skills and even specified outputs, and who manage nothing at all.[3]

Yet, if all boards dispose of the numbers of employees forecast in Chapter 5 in the short time frame expected, there are likely to be two extremely serious consequences. The first consequence is that aggregate demand in the economy will collapse, as the unemployed lose their ability to pay for goods and services, while the robots and algorithms replacing them will consume nothing, except for electricity and maintenance. The second is that this could precipitate a revolution against capitalism as we know it, ushering in totalitarian regimes of either the extreme right or left, justifying their revolutions with the words of William Cobbett in 1819:

> Society ought not to exist, if not for the benefit of the whole. It is and must be against the law of nature, if it exists for the benefit of the few and for the misery of the many.[4]

If this is to be avoided, boards must change how they look at people. Currently, despite claiming people are their most important assets, they actually treat them as costs and as being disposable.

People as a Cost

I suspect this accounting treatment – as a cost – has unconscious psychological implications on how boards look at people. They are only recorded as *expenses and not as assets* in the financials. Thus, there is subconscious and conscious pressure all the time to minimize these expenses in order to maximize shareholder returns. This pressure can be taken to extremes, as exemplified by Amazon's past treatment of some of its workers in the US, where despite benefitting from generous tax breaks[i] to set up warehouses in communities, it also relied in part on food stamps provided by the supplemental nutrition assistance program (SNAP) to subsidize its part-time workers who did not get paid enough to buy their groceries:

> The new data showing Amazon employees' extensive reliance on SNAP demonstrates an additional public cost of the corporation's rapid expansion. Even as generous subsidies help its warehouses turn a profit, its workers still must turn to the federal safety net to put food on the table. In Pennsylvania, for instance, an estimated $24.8 million in subsidies support 13 warehouses employing around 10,000 workers.[5] *At the same time, more than 1,000 of those workers don't make enough money to buy groceries, according to public data provided by the state.*[6]   [Emphasis mine]

As a result of being targeted by Senator Bernie Sanders who proposed the BEZOS Act to stop him from underpaying workers,[7] Jeff Bezos announced on October 2, 2018, that Amazon would raise minimum wages to US$15.00 - per hour in the US starting November 1, 2018, and to £10.50 in the UK for the London area and £9.50 in the rest of the UK,[8] rather than taking several years to do this. This was at a time when the US minimum wage was still $7.25, turning Amazon from villain into almost a hero on pay. Maybe Jeff Bezos had a change of heart. Even if he had not,[ii] the reputation gains and improvement in Amazon's image as an employer make the affordable extra cost worthwhile.[9]

---

i "Amazon, for example, earned over $10 billion in income in 2018. But by taking advantage of tax credits, the company zeroed out its income taxes and earned a rebate of $129 million, according to tax filings published by the Securities and Exchange Commission." Holmes, A. (2019), November 24, 2019, "From Amazon to GM, here are all the major tech and transportation companies who paid $0 in federal income taxes last year," https://www.businessin sider.my/tech-companies-dont-pay-federal-income-taxes-amazon-gm-2019-11/?r=US&IR=T, accessed on December 26, 2019.

ii The initial favorable reaction to Amazon's announcement was tempered by the realization existing hourly workers would forfeit their monthly bonuses and stock options which would go some way to funding the wage increase. Kim, E. (2018), "Amazon hourly workers lose monthly bonuses and stock awards as minimum wage increases," *CNBC*, October 4, 2018,

Another category of employers justifies paying their employees less than market rates on the grounds they provide "psychic income" to compensate for the fact they pay less. This applies to all vocational careers, for example – nurses and caregivers, teachers and academics, soldiers, first responders, and people who work for charities. It also applies to the fashion industry, where except for the owners of the luxury brands and the big-name designers like the late Karl Lagerfeld, there are many people lower down in the high fashion value chain who find it difficult to make ends meet because they do not get paid a salary, but in clothes vouchers instead. The justification for this treatment is that fashion is "exceptional," as this quote makes clear:

> The message is, you don't have to be paid because you are lucky to be there at all. Working in fashion is hyper socially validating, even if you're unpaid. . . Fashion presents itself as something exceptional, a world outside the ordinary. . . There is a kind of confused denial of the norms of labour conditions. *The dream that French fashion, especially, projects is that of a life of effortless luxury – mundane everyday facts of life such as working for a living, or indeed even money, are considered vulgar, taboo, even dirty subjects.*[10]   [Emphasis mine]

The internet and the gig economy have made matters worse, by making it much easier for even small companies to look for the cheapest skills in a global market. Platforms like Fiverr[11] encourage employers of casual labor to race to the bottom:

> While freelance websites may have raised wages and broadened the number of potential employers for some people, *they've forced every new worker who signs up into entering a global marketplace with endless competition, low wages, and little stability.* Decades ago, the only companies that outsourced work overseas were multinational corporations with the resources to set up manufacturing shops elsewhere. *Now, independent businesses and individuals are using the power of the internet to find the cheapest services in the world too, and it's not just manufacturing workers who are seeing the downsides to globalization.* All over the country, people like graphic designers and voice-over artists and writers and marketers have to keep lowering their rates to compete.
>   . . .most buyers are located in high-income countries like the United States, and most sellers are in countries such as India, Nigeria, and the Philippines. *While digital-labor markets are intended to allow sellers to auction off their work to whoever will pay the highest price for it, . . . they also help buyers find the cheapest sellers.*[12]   [Emphases mine]

https://www.cnbc.com/2018/10/03/amazon-hourly-workers-lose-monthly-bonuses-stock-awards.html, accessed on October 5, 2018.

People as Economic Animals

The way economists talk about people tends to be in the aggregate as either labor and its share of national income or as a disembodied "factor of production." This approach informs government debates about the economy and is indoctrinated into us when we study economics. The nearest economists get to talking about individuals, about people and their lives, is shown in the following quote by Professors Paul Samuelson and William Nordhaus in their classic college textbook *Economics International Edition 2002:*

> Is there an invisible hand in the marketplace that ensures that the most deserving people will obtain their just rewards? Or that those who toil long hours or nights and weekends or in tedious or dangerous work will receive a decent standard of living? No. In fact, competitive markets do not guarantee that income and consumption will necessarily go to the neediest or most deserving. Laissez-faire competition might lead to massive inequality, to malnourished children who grow up to produce more malnourished children, and to the perpetuation of inequality of incomes and wealth for generation after generation. The rich man may get richer as the poor get poorer. In a market economy, the distribution of income and consumption reflects hard work, ingenuity, and cunning, along with initial endowments of inherited wealth and a variety of factors such as race, gender, location, effort, health, and luck.
>
> Those who tout the wonders of the market point to the major gains in efficiency that have come with deregulation, privatization, reduced trade barriers, and decline in unions over the last two decades. *But the movement toward greater market competition has been accompanied by greater inequality of incomes in countries as different as the United States, Sweden, and Russia.* In many "winner-take-all" markets, the rewards have gone predominantly to a tiny group of superstars who won patents, lawsuits, elections, software contests, or athletic races by a hair's breadth.
>
> While the market can work wonders in producing a growing array of goods and services in the most efficient manner, there is no invisible hand which ensures that a laissez-faire economy will produce a fair and equitable distribution of income and property.[13]

Since they wrote this in 2002, the inequality of distribution of both income and, more important, wealth has become much worse as a result of the "winner-take-all" dynamics of globalization on the one hand and the effects of austerity and quantitative easing after the GFC on the other (discussed in Chapter 6). It is also the result of the way management consultants have changed the way companies approach the practice of management:

> Running a company on a concentrated model requires a cadre of managers who possess the capacity and taste to work with the intensity demanded of top executives today. At the same time, corporate reorganizations have deprived companies of an internal supply of managerial workers. When restructurings eradicated workplace training and purged the middle rungs of the corporate ladder, they also forced companies to look beyond their walls for managerial talent – to elite colleges, business schools, and (of course) to

management-consulting firms. That is to say: The administrative techniques that management consultants invented created a huge demand for precisely the services that the consultants supply.[14]

In my view, what is even more serious is that as a result, the discourse has tended to be in the language of economics and rational argument, based on the idea that human beings are rational and that they are primarily motivated by economic and material self-interest; i.e., that we are "economic animals" when we are so much more than that:[15]

> Man differs fundamentally from the animals, however, because in addition he desires the desire of other men, that is, he wants to be "recognized." In particular, he wants to be recognized as a *human being*, that is, as a being with a certain worth or dignity. This worth in the first instance is related to his willingness to risk his life in a struggle over pure prestige. For only man is able to overcome his most basic animal instincts – chief among them his instinct for self-preservation – for the sake of higher, abstract principles and goals. . .
>
> . . .The desire for recognition. . .was first described by Plato. . .when he noted that there were three parts to the soul, a desiring part, a reasoning part, and a part that he called *thymos,* or "spiritedness." Much of human behavior can be explained as a combination of the first two parts, desire and reason: desire induces men to seek things outside themselves, while reason or calculation shows them the best way to get them. But in addition, human beings seek recognition of their own worth. . . what we would call "self-esteem" . . .People believe that they have a certain worth, and when other people treat them as though they are worth less than that, they experience the emotion of *anger.* Conversely, when people fail to live up to their own sense of worth, they feel *shame,* and when they are evaluated correctly in proportion to their worth, they feel *pride.* The desire for recognition, and the accompanying emotions of anger, shame and pride, are parts of the human personality critical to political life.[16]

Treating employees as costs to be minimized does little to improve their sense of self-esteem, however rational it may seem from an economic perspective. It should not be a surprise therefore that the "losers" in globalized laissez-faire markets are angry and willing to believe populist slogans that appeal to their anger. Boards and governments must do more to recognize the importance of respecting people at all levels if they are to avoid a "political tragedy of the commons." In particular, they should stop using meritocracy as a way of justifying "winners" and "losers," as all this does is exacerbate the anger and resentment of the so-called "losers" against elites and the current economic system (discussed in Chapter 6).

People Are Disposable

There are many arguments in favor of the "hire and fire" culture typical of Anglosphere free market thinking. Flexible labor laws allow companies to employ people when times are good, making the economy better off as a whole because they are not worried about what happens when times are bad. They allow firms to be more innovative because if the risk taken does not pay off, the firm is not burdened with unproductive employees. They allow the young to get a job, even if it is on "zero-hours"[iii] contracts, despite "zero-hours" contracts being bad for physical and mental health.[17] However, by allowing such flexibility, firms lose continuity – the continuity of engagement with employees that creates loyalty and makes it good economic sense for the company to invest in the skills of its employees over the long term. The lack of continuity also allows boards to continue regarding their employees as disposable costs to rise and fall with the market, so continuity of engagement does not make sense to them.

There is another way, however, "Rhenish capitalism" – practiced in Austria, Germany, the Netherlands, Scandinavia, and Switzerland:

> The German labour market . . . still places more emphasis on employers' freedom to build long-term loyalty between employers and workers. These relationships are embedded in a strikingly different cultural approach to industrial training, closely tied to the German tradition of family-owned Mittelstand businesses *buttressed by long-term savings that take a generational approach to assembling skills and technology.* . .
>
> . . .*Employers who do not have a sense of social responsibility for training are unlikely to be durably persuaded to hire apprentices through one-off state payments.* Instead, governments should consider building comprehensive vocational training schemes that could be funded through a reduction in the social costs ensuing from unemployment. Tinkering with apprenticeship programmes on a piecemeal basis, as has been done in the UK, is unlikely to yield long-term results, as such half-hearted reforms result in expensive and wasteful systems that lack both scale and content. . .
>
> . . .*One of the main reasons why Germany's economy was able to recover so quickly after the downturn was the system of short-time working support (Kurzarbeit), introduced in the 1920s and extended in recent years.* . .
>
> . . .Imagine a small engineering firm that ran into financial trouble in 2008: rather than letting go of the 17-year-old apprentice who had recently joined the firm, it would have been able to keep employees on board and then benefit from their experience when

---

iii Q&A: What are zero-hours contracts? "Zero-hours contracts, or casual contracts, allow employers to hire staff with no guarantee of work. They mean employees work only when they are needed by employers, often at short notice. *Their pay depends on how many* hours *they work.*" [Emphasis mine] *BBC News,* April 1, 2015, https://www.bbc.com/news/business-23573442, accessed on November 3, 2018.

the economy was back on its feet. *Even if the company had gone bust, the apprentice would by law have been sent to another company.*

Sir Anthony Bamford, chairman of U.K. excavator maker JCB, points out that his company was forced to shed more than 20% of staff in Britain when production halved in 2009. *By contrast, the Kurzarbeit system enabled him to keep all his labour force in Germany.*[18] [Emphases mine]

The key question at the macroeconomic level is which of these two different systems is likely to deliver more sustainable value creation for its people as a whole? The answer is that, on balance, the Rhenish capitalist countries deliver better lives for their people than those in the Anglosphere.[iv]

Shareholders Come First; Employees Last

The unfairness of laissez-faire markets in distributing wealth and income pointed out by Professors Samuelson and Nordhaus earlier has been aggravated greatly by the behavior of firms interpreting Milton Friedman's 1970 theory to mean that the purpose of business was to maximize shareholder value regardless. Companies were open to accusations that share buybacks are socially irresponsible behavior, thus robbing workers of well-deserved pay increases and society of investment in future jobs and new improved products, just to satisfy short-term shareholders and to inflate the remuneration of overpaid CEOs:[19]

Between 2015 and 2017, U.S. publicly traded companies across all industries spent three-fifths of their profits on buybacks. The low-wage restaurant, retail, and food manufacturing industries spent 137%, 79%, and 58%, respectively. The restaurant industry borrowed money or used cash on its balance sheet to exceed the amount of its bottom line.

These actions disproportionately favor senior management and direct funds away from more productive purposes, such as corporate investment, job creation, or increased worker pay.

"*Lowe's, CVS and Home Depot could have provided each of their workers a raise of $18,000 a year,'* Annie Lowrey writes, covering the report for *The Atlantic.* '*Starbucks could have given each of its employees $7,000 a year, and McDonald's could have given $4,000 to each of its nearly 2 million employees.*"[20] [Emphases mine]

This accusation undermines the moral case for capitalism and raises questions about the legal basis of companies:

---

iv For a detailed justification of this claim, see Zinkin, J. (2019) *Better Governance Across the Board: Creating Value Through Reputation, People and Processes* (Boston/Berlin: Walter De Gruyter Inc.), pp. 321–324.

For much of U.S. history, . . .corporations sought to succeed in the marketplace, but they also recognized their obligations to employees, customers and the community. As recently as 1981, the Business Roundtable – which represents large U.S. companies – stated that corporations "have a responsibility, first of all, to make available to the public quality goods and services at fair prices, thereby earning a profit that attracts investment to continue and enhance the enterprise, provide jobs, and build the economy." This approach worked. American companies and workers thrived.

Late in the 20th century, the dynamic changed. Building on work by conservative economist Milton Friedman, a new theory emerged that corporate directors had only one obligation: to maximize shareholder returns. By 1997 the Business Roundtable declared that the "principal objective of a business enterprise is to generate economic returns to its owners."That shift has had a tremendous effect on the economy. *In the early 1980s, large American companies sent less than half their earnings to shareholders, spending the rest on their employees and other priorities. But between 2007 and 2016, large American companies dedicated 93% of their earnings to shareholders. Because the wealthiest 10% of U.S. households own 84% of American-held shares, the obsession with maximizing shareholder returns effectively means America's biggest companies have dedicated themselves to making the rich even richer. . .*

*. . .Before "shareholder value maximization" ideology took hold, wages and productivity grew at roughly the same rate. But since the early 1980s, real wages have stagnated even as productivity has continued to rise. Workers aren't getting what they've earned.*Companies also are setting themselves up to fail. Retained earnings were once the foundation for long-term investments. *But from 1990 to 2015, nonfinancial U.S. companies invested trillions less than projected, funneling earnings to shareholders instead. This underinvestment handcuffs U.S. enterprise and bestows an advantage on foreign competitors.*[21]   [Emphases mine]

Boards need to be sensitive to charges they have been increasing social inequality and injustice through either paying off rent-seeking elites in emerging markets or by making the richest 1% richer[v] through share buybacks at the expense of their employees. Senator Elizabeth Warren made the point in her interview with Franklin Foer of *The Atlantic*:

The reason is because the rules are not working now. We were talking about how when GDP goes up, productivity goes up and workers' wages go up. In the '80s, that just flattens out. GDP continues to go up, productivity continues to go up, but workers fall behind and the gap has now become enormous. *Eighty-four percent of the wealth in the stock market goes to 10 percent of the population.*

Half of all America owns not one share of stock. Not one. Not even in a 401(k) or an employer retirement plan, and yet a huge portion of the worth of the corporation is being directly diverted to the shareholders. That was not always true. *There was a time in*

---

v "The percentage of total income received by the top 1 percent of earners in the U.S. has risen from under 8 percent in the 1970s to over 18 percent today. The percentage of total wealth held by the richest 0.01 percent (the elite 1 percent of the 1 percent) has soared from under 3 percent to over 11 percent over this interval." Hopp, W. (2016), "How corporate America can curb income inequality and make more money too," *The Conversation*, September 21, 2016.

America when that wealth was shared among those who helped produce it. The workers and the investors. That's just not true today.[22]   [Emphases mine]

That is, because *the rich and corporate CEOs use their influence to promote their self-interest, inequality is built into the very DNA of capitalism.* And to return to our metaphor, the rich scorpions sting the rest of us[vi]– by exacerbating income inequality through pay policies, stock buybacks and other actions – because it's simply their nature.
    But there's plenty of evidence income inequality undermines the economy and, as a result, harms companies and the wealthy too. Eventually, we all sink together.[23]

[Emphases mine]

"Trickle Up" Economics Make Inequality Worse

What makes this tendency to reinforce income inequality worse is that it is often justified on the basis of Arthur Laffer's "trickle down" economics first popularized by President Ronald Reagan; based on fallacious assumptions underlying "trickle down" economics and arguments about the poor deserving to be poor. In fact, the reverse appears to be the case. Far from "trickle down" economics being true, it appears that "trickle up" economics are the natural order of things because of the way mathematical probabilities work:[24]

> We find it noteworthy that the best-fitting model for empirical wealth distribution discovered so far is one that would be completely unstable without redistribution rather than one based on a supposed equilibrium of market forces. In fact, *these mathematical models demonstrate that far from wealth trickling down to the poor, the natural inclination of wealth is to flow upward, so that the "natural" wealth distribution in a free-market economy is one of complete oligarchy. It is only redistribution that sets limits on inequality.*
>
> The mathematical models also call attention to the enormous extent to which wealth distribution is caused by symmetry breaking, chance and early advantage (from, for example, inheritance). *And the presence of symmetry breaking puts paid to arguments for the justness of wealth inequality that appeal to "voluntariness" – the notion that individuals bear all responsibility for their economic outcomes simply because they enter into transactions voluntarily – or to the idea that wealth accumulation must be the result of cleverness and industriousness.* It is true that an individual's location on the wealth spectrum correlates to some extent with such attributes, but the overall shape of that spectrum can be explained to better than 0.33 percent by a statistical model that completely ignores them.

---

vi Refers to Aesop's fable of the scorpion and the frog: Scorpion met Frog on a river bank and asked him for a ride to the other side. "How do I know you won't sting me?" asked Frog. "Because," replied Scorpion, "if I do, I will drown." Satisfied, Frog set out across the water with Scorpion on his back. Halfway across, Scorpion stung Frog. "Why did you do that?" gasped Frog as he started to sink. "Now we'll both die." "I can't help it," replied Scorpion. "It's my nature."

Luck plays a much more important role than it is usually accorded, so that the virtue commonly attributed to wealth in modern society – and, likewise, the stigma attributed to poverty – is completely unjustified.

Moreover, only a carefully designed mechanism for redistribution can compensate for the natural tendency of wealth to flow from the poor to the rich in a market economy. Redistribution is often confused with taxes, but the two concepts ought to be kept quite separate. Taxes flow from people to their governments to finance those governments' activities. *Redistribution, in contrast, may be implemented by governments, but it is best thought of as a flow of wealth from people to people to compensate for the unfairness inherent in market economics. In a flat redistribution scheme, all those possessing wealth below the mean would receive net funds, whereas those above the mean would pay.* And precisely because current levels of inequality are so extreme, far more people would receive than would pay.[25]   [Emphases mine]

The inequality of CEO pay in the US and the UK has been justified in the past in part for their cleverness and industry. Based on these findings, it becomes even harder to justify the levels of remuneration for CEOs and it also becomes morally more difficult to justify continuing policies designed to weaken the social safety nets for the poor – policies adopted since the GFC at a time when the overpaid CEOs of financial institutions got away scot free with having brought the world economy to its knees in 2009.

Perhaps, in part, as a result, the August 2019 US Business Roundtable Declaration that the purpose of business is no longer just to maximize shareholder value, but to consider the interests of all stakeholders may signal the beginning of a change in behavior that has hurt employees over the past thirty years. Perhaps, given the recent findings that macroeconomics are best described by their "trickle up" rather than "trickle down" effects, it might be time to increase the distribution of profits as a share of national income to employees rather than to shareholders and to prioritize employees among stakeholders.

Investing in People

I believe boards need to invest in people if they are to build successful businesses operating in successful economies rather than treating them as disposable costs. The question is how best to do this? I believe boards must recognize there are four types of leadership, not just one. I also believe management and HR should not waste time, effort, and money on trying to "fit square pegs into round holes"; and finally, the top management team must demonstrate that training and development really matter. Investing in people is not just something boards must do differently; it is also something governments must do differently; and universities must be encouraged to change what they teach.

Recognize Four Types of Leadership

I am surprised how often people think of only captains or generals when they describe leadership and how often the behavior they recommend is that of an extrovert, forgetting that there are four types of leaders needed for an organization to succeed: "captains," "navigators," "engineers," and "builders" – and introverts can be effective too. Table 11.1 compares these four types of leaders.

Table 11.1: Four types of leader compared.[26]

"Captain"	"Navigator"	"Engineer"	"Builder"
Just as a ship must have a captain who exercises the ultimate authority over the crew and whose role it is to call them to action, so must a business. The defining role of the captain is to wield power, to articulate the mission and timetable for action, to allocate responsibilities accordingly, to inspire the crew, to lay down the code of conduct, and enforce it. It is also to be the focus of energy in a crisis around whom the crew can rally to get things done quickly.	Once the captain has set the destination and the timetable, it is the responsibility of the navigator to chart the best route, accounting for the wind, weather forecasts, tides, currents and safe channels, reconciling the need for speed with economy and safety. "Navigators" are likely to be in staff functions rather than management. Their responsibility is to develop key assumptions of the plan, to ask the "what if?" questions, examine scenarios, and develop appropriate contingencies. In essence, they do what navigators do on ships when they identify a threatening storm	Both "captains" and "navigators," however, have to rely on "engineers" in the engine room to keep the ship moving – what Peter Senge called "line leaders": "However, engaging local line leaders may be difficult. As pragmatists, they often find ideas like systems thinking, mental models, and dialogue intangible and "hard to get their hands around . . . . . . Simon's view is typical of many line leaders at the outset: he was skeptical, but he recognized that he had problems that he could not solve. He also had a trusted colleague who was willing to engage with him. Again, and again, we have found that healthy, open-minded skeptics can become the most effective leaders and, eventually, champions of this work. They keep the horse in front of the cart by focusing first and foremost on business results.	Never forget the ship-builder. The reason the *Titanic* was such a disaster was primarily flawed design.[27] In business, "builders" are the planners, enterprise risk managers, and auditors whose job it is to ensure there are appropriate processes, procedures, and service level agreements between departments, supported and reinforced by agreed codes of conduct and compliance mechanisms, creating the organizational 'infrastructure' for the business model to achieve its agreed mission and vision: "With little or no infrastructure to support ongoing learning, one might ask, "Why should successful new practices spread in organizations?" Who

Table 11.1 (continued)

"Captain"	"Navigator"	"Engineer"	"Builder"
It is the captain's responsibility to save the crew in a tempest, that is why the captain is the last to leave a sinking ship.	and implement course corrections to avoid the storm, yet stay on track to reach the designated port.	*Such people invariably have more staying power than the "fans" who get excited about new ideas but whose excitement wanes once the newness wears off."*[28] [Emphasis mine]	studies these innovations to document why they worked? Where are the learning processes that will enable others to follow in the footsteps of successful innovators? Who is responsible for creating these learning processes? There can be little doubt of the long-term business impact of executive leadership in developing learning infrastructure."[29]

Stop "Fitting Square Pegs Into Round Holes"

This tendency manifests itself in two ways: believing the only way to progress in an organization is to become a manager of other people; and force-fitting people into unsuitable roles, ignoring the impact of default personalities on productivity.

The number of people who really do not want to manage other people is surprisingly high.[30] There may be two factors to explain this. The first is the lack of training of managers in managing others:

> A recent study by CareerBuilder.com shows that a whopping 58 percent of managers said they didn't receive any management training. Digest that for a second. *Most managers in the workforce were promoted because they were good at what they did, and not necessarily good at making the people around them better.* This statistic obviously unveils a harsh reality. We have a bunch of leaders who aren't trained on how to lead.[31]

The second is that many people actually do not like managing others because it takes them away from what they love, which is "doing" rather than getting others to do:

> *Being a manager caused me to feel disconnected from what career analyst Daniel Pink has identified as the three primary motivators of behavior: autonomy, mastery and purpose. . .*
>
> . . .Why do we reward success on the job with a promotion *out* of the job and into management?. . .Companies continue to cling to the notion that one of the *only* mechanisms they have to acknowledge employees' talent is to make them managers and then to continue to promote them into ever-higher levels of management – *reflecting the misguided assumption that being good at something also means being able to (and wanting to) manage others doing the same thing.* Once in management, its trappings. . .don't really satisfy many of us who, like me, miss the *doing*. . . Management titles allow us to mark our growth, and our maturity. . .
>
> . . .I know now . . . that as corporate executive I felt like I had to pretend to be something I wasn't – *I didn't like being a manager, but I was a manager, so I had to appear to be interested in all the stuff that went along with being a manager. This is something social scientists call "emotion labor"* – what you experience when you feel obliged to act differently from your natural inclinations.[32]   [Emphases mine]

The best way to avoid making such a mistake is to invest in two career ladders: the traditional managerial ladder which has an ever-increasing number of people to be managed as individuals climb the ladder; and to have a parallel technical ladder where individuals grow and are promoted based on their technical expertise, allowing them to focus on what they do best and like doing.

Professional service firms (for example, law and accountancy partnerships, management consultants, advertising and PR agencies, and IT companies) have long practiced this approach, where careers are based on becoming the "go-to" technical experts (practice leaders), effective "rainmakers" (client leaders), as well as managerial leaders (office managers).

Too often, management advised by HR departments spend time trying to close performance gaps in staff caused by their default personalities. Instead they should spend more time focusing on harnessing the power of those personalities by putting employees in roles they are temperamentally suited to doing and will enjoy being in. As Aristotle pointed out more than two thousand years ago:

> Pleasure in the job puts perfection in the work.

We know this to be true: a job we do not like is a chore, whereas a job we enjoy doing does not feel like work; it is something we look forward to doing, for which we do not have to be compensated.[vii] Peter Drucker has made the same point:

> Altogether, an increasing number of people who are full-time employees have to be managed as if they were *volunteers*. They are paid, to be sure. But. . .[w]e have known for fifty years that money alone does not motivate to perform. . . What motivates – and especially what motivates knowledge workers – is what motivates volunteers. Volunteers, we know, have to get *more* satisfaction from their work than paid employees, precisely because they do not get a paycheck. They need, above all, challenge. They need to know the organization's mission and to believe in it.[33]

The critical challenge is to make sure that people are equipped with competencies suited to the new world of AI and automation. For this to happen, boards need to demonstrate that development and training matter; to ensure employees invest in lifelong learning where governments also have a role to play.

Demonstrate Training and Development Matter

Staff development and training is often neglected under the pressure of day-to-day operations and the belief that trained staff leave for better jobs elsewhere once they have undergone expensive formal training. This is a mirror image of the search for the perfect candidate who has been trained by some other company.

> The search for the mythical "perfect candidate" has been fueled, in part, by cutbacks in staff training programs, borne out of companies' desire to hire people who essentially don't need any training.
>
> However, what hiring managers are increasingly discovering is that the perfect candidate rarely exists. What is available is good talent that – with some training and coaching – can be shaped into a productive member of a company's workforce.[34]

Given the perfect candidate does not exist, companies should save themselves the frustration of looking for perfection; recognizing instead they should hire good candidates who will need to be trained from day one, just as new plant

---

vii "Compensate" in English means "give (someone) something, typically money, in recognition of loss, suffering, or injury incurred; recompense." HR should stop using "compensation and benefits" as a mental model as it implies coming to work harms the people who come to work. If people are forced to do work they do not like or that is not suited for their temperament, then maybe it is correct. Personally, I prefer the concept of "reward and recognition" rather than "compensation."

and machinery need to be run in from day one. They should also recognize what could be happening with so-called "on-the-job training":

> While on-the-job training is unquestionably valuable, a problem arises when this be-comes an organization's exclusive approach to refining and expanding the skills of its workforce. The dirty little secret about on-the-job training is that *many managers rely on it* because *they don't really have an employee training program.*
>
> That revelation is not lost on employees, who can surely distinguish between such haphazard attempts at skill development, compared to more organized and thoughtful approaches.
>
> There's no substitute for hands-on training. However, it's bound to be more effective when paired with traditional instruction methods, such as those delivered through class-room venues, e-learning tools and formal procedural documentation.[35] [Emphasis mine]

Companies often conflate new product rollout training with employee develop-ment. New product training is important, as people must know how to use or sell new products. However, focusing on product training alone is to ignore the soft skills training and investment in improving competencies needed for em-ployees to become more effective and more loyal:

> A robust employee development program helps staff expand their horizons beyond just the latest product launch. It might help them cultivate much-needed soft skills, such as customer service, communication or negotiation. It might augment knowledge that, while not directly related to their current role, helps position the employee for future opportuni-ties that are aligned with their aspirations (thus improving retention).[36]

Finally, they must give employees enough time to engage with their trainers, free of interruptions, when they are being trained and also "quiet time" to prac-tice what they have learned, without the pressures of learning it when they are likely to be distracted by the job. "Maintenance on the go" practices come in the form of:

> Directives that employees complete self-training (often delivered online) "as time allows" during their regular workday. It can also be seen in classroom training programs where participants are encouraged to stay in constant touch with the office. . .
>
> . . .It is a disservice to employees when an organization neglects to give them "quiet time" to participate in skill development programs. Indeed, the value of those programs (and the investment a company makes in them) is greatly diminished without the benefit of employees' undivided attention.[37]

In my experience, the best way to indicate to employees that their training and development is taken seriously is for superiors to attend the entire training of their subordinates. This has two benefits: first, it signals to the subordinates that the time they are spending in formal training is not time wasted – it is im-portant enough for their superiors to attend; second, their superiors will know what they have been taught and what they are expected to do differently as a result. Both of these are effective spurs to paying attention and concentrating on what needs to be learned, improving training ROI.

Invest in Lifelong Learning and Education

From a training perspective, workforces need to learn how to be flexible, adaptable, and agile so they can move from occupation to occupation as automation and AI affect sectors and occupations. How training is done will also need to change:

> In the future world of work, it is likely that *an individual will need to move from skill to skill with ease, with flexibility that will allow them to adapt to new or changing careers as opportunities come and go.* But for this to become a reality, there needs to be a change in the way that we approach education and skills training.
>
> While educators have already begun to establish closer links with industry, in the future learning methods will need to become even more flexible. *Practical, project-based learning, which emphasises applied knowledge rather than rote learning, will become the norm,* and success will be measured not in grades, but in how well training has addressed business needs.[38]   [Emphases mine]

The unstated implication here is that people will need to spend their entire working lives learning. Gone are the days of working for one employer, doing one type of job. No longer can people assume that their life's learning is divided into kindergarten, primary, secondary, and tertiary education and after that they work, retire, and die without any further learning being needed. Continuous professional and vocational development will become essential if people are to keep pace with the impact of automation and AI on their jobs. They will also need to learn to deal with uncertainty and ambiguity in ways they never had to in the past:

> The pace of change is so great that even *those joining the workforce today will need to continuously update and evolve their skill sets over the course of their working lives, so that they too are not left behind.*
>
> With little time, and pressured work environments, we believe that distance and online flexible learning are likely to be key. Affordable for companies and more accessible for employees, *the concept of anytime-anywhere learning is likely to further proliferate the employment landscape.*
>
> Apprenticeships will also form a vital part of the puzzle in this new learning landscape. *The training now spans different levels* – from GCSE level right through to master's degree level – *so employees can undertake multiple apprenticeships throughout their working lives,* growing their skills and keeping their knowledge up-to-date.[39]
>
>   [Emphases mine]

When dealing with the fear employees may have of automation and AI, boards and management can dismiss the fears, tell reassuring lies, or help employees prepare for the future. If they choose to help, they have five options:[40]

1. **Step up:** Explain to employees that automation frees them up to deal with "higher order" matters, to think about the big picture and how to create added value by taking on added responsibilities or by spending more time and energy thinking about how to improve their working conditions and processes.

2. **Step aside:** However, not all employees who are freed up are in jobs where they can take on additional responsibilities. In these cases, boards should get management to encourage them to think about other unique personal skills (interpersonal, intuitive, creative, etc.) they can bring to bear on creating added value for the organization. Counseling, coaching, and training can then bring out these unique talents and focus them on organizational priorities. The key point is that these unique personal skills are not codifiable, and therefore will not be replaced by AI:

> *One thing machines cannot do: replace human connection and direction.* As industries further adopt AI, it's more important than ever for workers to develop their emotional intelligence. In a rapidly changing workforce, the "soft skills" of listening to employees, motivating team members, interpreting results that relate to your company culture and values, and facilitating collaboration will make an individual irreplaceable.[41]
>
> [Emphasis mine]

3. **Step in:** Boards can choose to train their workforces to become the brains or support behind the operations undertaken by robots. Workers can figure out better ways of using computers, and machines need to be repaired and maintained properly. Using the example of automated vehicles, mechanics are still needed to fix and maintain them. Skilled drivers could be used to to install sensors and monitor the roadways, clearing the debris, wreckage, towage, and maintaining safe passage.

4. **Step narrowly:** Boards should take a long hard look at which functions should not be automated. Once they have identified the areas where no AI is likely to be applied because it will not be economically justified, management should be encouraged to train and develop employees who will be able to undertake those specialist roles where the on-the-job learning they experience will provide unparalleled value and longevity:

> "Although most [workers] have the benefit of a formal education," the authors write, "the expertise that fuels their earning power is [actually] gained through on-the-job training –

and the discipline of focus. If this is your strategy, *start making a name for yourself as the person who goes a mile deep on a subject an inch wide.*"[42]   [Emphasis mine]

5. ***Step forward:*** This option only applies to those organizations and employees who are in the business of developing robots and software that goes with them, namely to encourage employees to embrace AI and work on developing the next generation of robots and AI.

Which option boards choose depends on the impact of automation on their organization and on how committed they are to treating their employees as assets to be invested in rather than costs to be minimized.

Government Has a Role to Play

The size of the challenge in retraining the unemployed fast enough to avoid social unrest means boards cannot meet it on their own. Government also has a role to play. The US has faced a similar challenge twice before in its history. First, in the early 1900s when there was a major migration out of agriculture. The so-called "High School Movement" raised the rate of enrollment of 14- to 17-year-olds from 18% in 1910 to 73% in 1940.[43] Second, the GI Bill helped eight million veterans returning from World War II to go to college or be retrained. The combination gave the US the best-educated workforce after World War II, allowing it to achieve levels of productivity unmatched in other countries until the 1980s.[44]

A similar mobilization of resources will be essential to ensure a smooth transition of people from sectors affected adversely by automation to ones that are growing. This challenge is made that much more critical because across all OECD countries, with the exception of Denmark, the percentage of GDP devoted to training and retraining has been in decline as both public and corporate spending have fallen in the last twenty or so years. It is all the more serious since the basic assumptions about what education is supposed to do in preparing people for work have not changed in the past 100 years.[45]

Encourage Universities to Change What They Teach

What does this mean for tertiary education in particular? Universities (at least in the UK) can be divided into Oxford and Cambridge and some others, established in the days when only 5% of the population went to university. As a result, they did not focus on teaching skills that could be translated immediately into qualifications for a job upon graduation. Instead, they aimed to teach students what I would call "first principles thinking," working from a blank sheet of paper to establish answers to the questions "Why?" and/or "Why not?" "What?" and only then going on to answer the question "How?"

When I was at Oxford, it was made clear that what my professors were looking for was not how much I knew, but how I used what I knew to make an effective case – in other words, what mattered was whether I had written a "good" answer as opposed to a "bad" one; rather than a "right" answer as opposed to a "wrong" one. Only later, when politicians declared that 50% of the annual cohort should go to university was there a huge expansion in universities; teaching what were in effect vocational subjects, focusing on "How?" rather than on "Why/Why Not?" and "What?" As a second consequence, students started being taught there were "right" and "wrong" answers, which makes sense if what was being experienced was a high-level form of apprenticeship, but it limits creative, "elastic" thinking, encouraging "frozen" thinking instead.[46]

In tomorrow's world, I believe this is exactly the wrong approach. Tertiary education will need to focus much more on the "First Principles" approach, encouraging students to work out for themselves what matters and why rather than how something should be done. This is because the former is something AI cannot do, whereas the latter is what AI can do better than humans.

Summary

The underlying assumptions about people need to change. However, the underlying assumption that people are costs on the P&L to be minimized or externalized will continue as long as financial accounts do not find a way of recording them on the balance sheet as assets. As a result, boards often fail to regard people as assets to be invested in from day one to the day they retire. In addition, there is an entire category of employment where the "psychic income" afforded by following a vocation, doing "national service," or working for an NGO or charity has justified underpaying people.

The internet and gig economy have made matters worse, reinforcing the assumption workers are a cost to be minimized in a global "race to the bottom." This encourages boards to think people are disposable – an attitude most prevalent in the Anglosphere economies. However, "Rhenish" capitalist countries have adopted a different approach, building long-term loyalty through effective apprenticeship programs.

The inexorable rise in inequality resulting from "trickle up" economics is made worse by the view shareholders come first and employees last, demonstrated by companies buying back shares while real wages stagnate or decline for blue-collar and lower white-collar workers may lead to a "political tragedy of the commons" where what makes *economic* sense for an individual board does not make *political* sense when all boards follow suit. Redistribution is essential if a "political tragedy of the commons" is to be avoided.

Once we accept that we need to invest in people, the question is how best to do it. It helps if boards recognize there are four types of leader. It would also help improve morale and productivity if companies stopped trying to "fit square pegs into round holes," by recognizing most people do not want to be managers. Organizations that recognize this problem have invested in more than one career ladder – people can get to the top of a technical career ladder without having to climb the managerial career ladder they dislike.

When investing in training, companies must remember new product training is not the same as training employees in the soft skills and new competencies they need to face in the future and companies must stop treating them as the same thing, just as they must also stop searching for the "perfect" employees who need no training – they do not exist. Finally, senior management must demonstrate their commitment to training and development, recognizing the importance of lifelong learning. They also need to encourage universities to change what they teach to "first principles thinking" from "frozen thinking" typical of vocational styles of teaching.

Perhaps there will be no real change in the underlying attitudes of boards to investing in people until accountants find a way of showing people as assets on the balance sheet and capturing the externalities created by treating people as disposable, and boards remember that human beings are more than just "economic animals." They need recognition and respect as well.

References

1 Ford, H., https://www.azquotes.com/quote/1430055, accessed April 2, 2020.
2 Markovits, D. (2020), "How McKinsey Destroyed The Middle Class," *The Atlantic*, https://www.theatlantic.com/ideas/archive/2020/02/how-mckinsey-destroyed-middle-class/605878/, accessed on February 4, 2020.
3 Ibid.
4 Cobbett, W. (1819), *Political Register*, September 11, 1819, quoted in Bloy, M. (2005), "The Luddites 1811–1816," *The Victorian Web*, December 30, 2005, http://www.victorianweb.org/history/riots/luddites.html, accessed on September 15, 2019.

5 Douglas, C. (2017), "Tracking Amazon's rapidly expanding footprint," *The Business Journals,* October 11, 2017, https://www.bizjournals.com/bizjournals/maps/the-amazon-effect, accessed on September 3, 2018, cited in Zinkin, J. (2019), *Better Governance Across the Board: Creating Value Through Reputation, People and Processes* (Boston/Berlin: Walter De Gruyter Inc.), p. 318.

6 Brown, C. (2018), "Amazon gets tax breaks while its employees rely on food stamps, new data shows," *The Intercept,* April 19, 2018, https://theintercept.com/2018/04/19/amazon-snap-subsidies-warehousing-wages/, accessed on October 3, 2018, quoted in Zinkin, J. (2019), op. cit., p. 318.

7 Squawk Box Team (2018), "Sen. Bernie Sanders targets low wages in BEZOS Act," *CNBC Markets,* September 6, 2018, https://www.cnbc.com/video/2018/09/06/sen-bernie-sanders-targets-low-wages-in-bezos-act.html, accessed on October 3, 2018, cited in Zinkin, J. (2019), op. cit., p. 318.

8 Lauerman, J. and Kahn, J. (2018), "Bezos Blinks and Raises Amazon's Minimum Wage in U.S., U.K.," *Bloomberg,* October 2, 2018, https://www.bloomberg.com/news/articles/2018-10-02/ama zon-raises-minimum-wage-to-15-for-all-u-s-employees-jmrk3z14, accessed on October 3, 2018, cited in Zinkin, J. (2019), op. cit., p. 318.

9 Ovide, S. (2018), "Amazon's Pay Raise Is a Small Price to Pay for its Reputation," *Bloomberg Opinion,* October 2, 2018, https://www.bloomberg.com/view/articles/2018-10-02/amazon-pay-raise-is-a-small-price-to-pay-for-its-reputation?utm_medium=email&utm_source=newsletter&utm_term=181002&utm_campaign=sharetheview, accessed on October 3, 2018, cited in Zinkin, J. (2019), p. 319.

10 Marsh, S. (2018), "Chanel shoes, but no salary: how one woman exposed the scandal of the French fashion industry," *The Guardian,* September 2, 2018, https://www.theguardian.com/fashion/2018/sep/02/academic-exposing-ugly-reality-high-fashion-giulia-mensitieri, accessed on September 3, 2018, quoted in Zinkin, J. (2019), op. cit., p. 319.

11 "Fiverr – Freelance Services for the Lean Entrepreneur," https//www.fiverr.com/, accessed on September 3, 2018, cited in Zinkin, J. (2019), op. cit., p. 319.

12 Semuels, A. (2018), "The Online Gig Economy's 'Race to the Bottom': when the whole world is fighting for the same jobs, what happens to the workers?" *The Atlantic,* August 31, 2018, https://www.theatlantic.com/technology/archive/2018/08/fiverr-online-gig-economy/569083/, accessed on September 3, 2018, quoted in Zinkin, J. (2019), op. cit., p. 319.

13 Samuelson, P. A. and Nordhaus, W. D. (2002), *Economics International Edition 2002* (New York: McGraw Hill), p. 239.

14 Markovits, D. (2020), op. cit.

15 Fukuyama, F. (1992), *The End of History and The Last Man* (London: Penguin Books), p. xvi.

16 Ibid., pp. xvi–xvii.

17 ITV report (2017), "Young adults on zero-hour contracts suffer worse physical and mental health, study finds," *ITV News,* July 5, 2017, http://www.itv.com/news/2017-07-05/young-adults-on-zero-hour-contracts-suffer-worse-physical-and-mental-health-study-finds/, accessed on September 4, 2018, quoted in Zinkin, J. (2019), op. cit., p. 319.

18 Marsh, D. and Bischof, R. (2012), "'Hire and fire' has destroyed Britain's job economy," *The Guardian,* January 26, 2012, https://www.theguardian.com/commentisfree/2012/jan/26/hire-and-fire-destroyed-uk-jobs, accessed on September 4, 2018, quoted in Zinkin, J. (2019), op. cit., p. 321.

19 Lazonick, W. and Shin, J-S. (2019), *Predatory Value Extraction: How the Looting of the Business Corporation Became the U.S. Norm and How Sustainable Prosperity Can be Restored* (Oxford: Oxford University Press), p. 4, pp. 190–196.

20 Hansen, D. (2018), op. cit.

21 Warren, E. (2018), "Companies Shouldn't Be Accountable to Shareholders Only," *Wall Street Journal,* August 14, 2018, https://www.wsj.com/articles/companies-shouldnt-be-accountable-only-to-shareholders-1534287687, accessed on August 29, 2018.

22 Foer, F. (2018), "Elizabeth Warren's Theory of Capitalism," *The Atlantic,* August 28, 2018, https://www.theatlantic.com/politics/archive/2018/08/elizabeth-warrens-theory-of-capitalism /568573/, accessed on August 30, 2018.

23 Hopp, W. (2016), "How corporate America can curb income inequality and make more money too," *The Conversation,* September 21, 2016, http://theconversation.com/how-corporate -america-can-curb-income-inequality-and-make-more-money-too-62339, accessed on August 30, 2018.

24 Boghossian, B.M. (2019), "Is Inequality Inevitable?" *Scientific American,* November 1, 2019, https://www.scientificamerican.com/article/is-inequality-inevitable/, accessed on December 29, 2019.

25 Ibid.

26 Zinkin, J. (2019), based on op. cit., pp. 324–326.

27 Senge, P. (1995), op. cit., in Zinkin, J. (2019), op. cit., p. 325.

28 Woytowich, R. (2018), "Titanic Sinking Tied To Engineering, Structural Failures (DIAGRAMS)," *Science,* December 6, 2017, https://www.huffingtonpost.com/2012/04/09/ti tanic-sunk-new-theory_n_1412622.html, accessed on September 5, 2018, cited in Zinkin, J. (2019), op. cit., p. 325.

29 Senge, P. (1995), op. cit., in Zinkin, J. (2019), op. cit., p. 325.

30 Torres, N. (2014), "Most People Don't Want to Be Managers," *Harvard Business Review,* September 18, 2014, https://hbr.org/2014/09/most-people-dont-want-to-be-managers, accessed on September 10, 2019, cited in Zinkin, J. (2019), op. cit., p. 329.

31 Sturt, D. and Nordstrom, T. (2018), "10 Shocking Workplace Stats You Need To Know," *Forbes,* March 8, 2018, https://www.forbes.com/sites/davidsturt/2018/03/08/10-shocking-workplace-stats-you-need-to-know/#67941965f3af, accessed on September 10, 2018, quoted in Zinkin, J. (2019), op. cit., p. 329.

32 Kreamer, A. (2012), "What If You Don't Want to Be a Manager?" *Harvard Business Review,* December 13, 2012, https://hbr.org/2012/12/what-if-you-dont-want-to-be-a, accessed on September 10, 2018, quoted in Zinkin, J. (2019), op. cit., p. 329.

33 Drucker, P. (1992), *Management Challenges of the 21st Century* (Oxford: Butterworth Heinemann), p. 21.

34 Picoult, J. "Your Workforce: The Most Important Asset You're Not Maintaining," *Monster,* https://hiring.monster.com/hr/hr-best-practices/workforce-management/hr-management-skills/ employee-engagement-strategy.aspx, accessed on September 11, 2018.

35 Ibid.

36 Ibid.

37 Ibid.

38 Willett, D. (2019), "Automation, education and the future of work," *Training Journal,* June 7, 2019, https://www.trainingjournal.com/articles/opinion/automation-education-and-future-work, accessed on September 22, 2019.

39 Ibid.

40 Meneghello, R. (2018), "5 Options for Helping Your Workforce Cope With Automation," *TLNT Talent Management and HR*, September 13, 2018, https://www.tlnt.com/5-options-for-helping-your-workforce-cope-with-automation/, accessed on September 22, 2019.
41 Stokes, C. (2018), "Don't Fight the Robots, Embrace Them," *TLNT Talent Management and HR*, May 10, 2018, https://www.tlnt.com/dont-fight-the-robots-embrace-them/, accessed on September 22, 2019.
42 Meneghello, R. (2018), op. cit.
43 Ibid., p. 17.
44 Piketty, T. (2017), "Of productivity in France and in Germany," *Le Monde*, January 9, 2017, https://www.lemonde.fr/blog/piketty/2017/01/09/of-productivity-in-france-and-in-germany/, accessed on September 23, 2019.
45 Ibid., p. 18.
46 Mlodinow, L. (2018), *Elastic: Unlocking Your Brain's Ability to Embrace Change* (London: Vintage Books).

Chapter 12
Making Capitalism Sustainable

This chapter is presented in three parts. The first explores the need for reform in corporate governance if it is to be compatible with sustainability. The second argues for ending predatory value extraction to satisfy short-term shareholders. The third makes the case for companies having a sustainable purpose. It concludes that meaningful reform can only be achieved if boards embrace a sustainable purpose.

Chapters 1 and 2 discussed the evolution of corporate governance as an idea, and the fact that there is no one single best way of implementing it. Chapters 3–8 explored the challenges boards have when considering how to reconcile their fiduciary duty to shareholders when faced with the immense challenges to sustainability of the environment, economy, employment, and society. Chapters 9–11 suggested some new ways of meeting those challenges in an increasingly complicated world: dealing with VUCA proactively, developing new processes, and treating employees as assets and not as costs.

Recognizing the Need for Urgent Reform

In Chapter 1, I discussed the challenge posed by populism to the way the current economic system works. I return to it now, because I believe we must recognize the need for urgent reform, lest the system is taken over by populist, authoritarian governments of either the left or the right, capitalizing on widespread discontent across the world:

> Popular anger is boiling over against elites seen as irredeemably greedy, corrupt, and indifferent to the plight of most people struggling to get by. The anger has fueled uprisings in Chile, Spain, Ecuador, Lebanon, Egypt, and Bolivia; environmental protests in the U.K., Germany, Austria, France, and New Zealand; and xenophobic politics in the U.S., the U.K., Brazil, and Hungary.[1]

This discontent helps explain in part the election of President Trump in the US; Brexit in the UK; the "gilets jaunes" in France; the decline of Democratic Socialism in the EU, including the collapse of the Labour party in the UK and the SPD in Germany; the rise of populist parties in Europe; the attraction of illiberal democratic ideas in Russia, Hungary, and Poland in Eastern Europe, as well as in Turkey and India; and the protests in Hong Kong and Chile.

https://doi.org/10.1515/9783110670486-012

More than just reform of the economic system is needed, however, given the current discontent, as a result of its *failure to satisfy the economic and emotional needs of large parts of electorates in developed economies.* The concern for the sustainability of the present economic system is perhaps best expressed in the following quotation from the Nikkei Asian Review:

> A combination of tech behemoths, growing wealth disparities, climate change and rampant protectionism is calling into question the very nature of capitalism itself. It was not supposed to be this way.[2]

I believe there are three things that must happen to reconcile capitalism with sustainability:
1. *Businesses and governments must recognize the need for reform* in the relationships between business, nature, and the community.
2. *Investors must stop rewarding companies for "predatory value extraction"* that benefits only short-term shareholders and rewards CEOs for unsustainable behavior.
3. *Boards must define a sustainable purpose* for their organizations and prioritize stakeholders' interests accordingly.

Failure to do this may lead to a social and "political tragedy of the commons," given the evidence of increased discontent with the status quo. The parlous state in which neoliberal capitalism appears to find itself is reinforced by the 2020 Edelman Trust Barometer findings[3]:
1. In developed markets, trust has become uncoupled from GDP growth because people feel they are not getting their fair share of growing prosperity.
2. National income inequality is now the more important factor in institutional trust.
3. Fears are stifling hope, as long-held assumptions about the benefits of hard work and citizenship have been upended.
4. Eighty-three percent of employees globally are worried about job loss due to concerns such as the lack of training, cheaper foreign competition, immigration, automation, and the gig economy.
5. More than 50% of respondents said that they are losing the respect and dignity they once felt for their country.
6. Seventy-five percent are worried that "fake news" will be used as a weapon.
7. Sixty percent fear the pace of technological change, they are no longer in control of their destiny.
8. Fifty-six percent say that capitalism does more harm than good.

9. Seventy-eight percent agree that "elites are getting richer while regular people struggle to pay their bills."
10. In 15 of 28 markets, the majority are pessimistic about their financial future, with most believing they will not be better off in five years' time than they are today. In the US, this represents a seven-point drop in optimism since the previous survey.

Based on these symptoms, capitalism faces another one of its many moments of crisis.[4] It will overcome this crisis, as long as it recognizes the need for urgent reform. When Jack Bogle,[i] Ray Dalio,[ii] and Larry Fink,[iii] three of the greatest investors since World War II, are also seriously concerned about the problems faced by the current economic system, we must pay attention to what they have to say:

Jack Bogle:

A new system developed – *managers* capitalism – in which "the corporation came to be run to profit its managers, in complicity if not conspiracy with accountants and the managers of other corporations.". . .

That transmogrification – that *grotesque transformation* – of a system of owners capitalism into a system of managers capitalism required only two ingredients: (1) the diffusion of corporate ownership among a large number of investors, none holding a controlling share of the voting power; and (2) the unwillingness of the agents of the owners – the boards of directors – to honor their responsibility to serve, above all else, the interests of their *principals* – the shareowners themselves.

When most owners either don't or won't or can't stand up for their rights, and when directors lose sight of whom they represent, the resulting power vacuum quickly gets filled by corporate managers. . . *"When we have strong managers, weak directors, co-opted accountants, and passive owners, don't be surprised when the looting begins."*

. . .*When we consider. . .the average CEO's compensation has risen from 42 times that of the average worker in 1980 to 121 times in 1988, and to an astonishing 531 times in 2000 (now it's "only" about 411 times) – it's certainly fair to say that there has been an extraordinary increase in the portion of corporate earnings that corporate managers have arrogated to themselves. . .*

---

i John C. "Jack" Bogle (1929–2019) was an American investor, business magnate, and philanthropist. He was the founder and chief executive of The Vanguard Group, and is *credited with creating the first index fund, revolutionizing the mutual fund world by creating index investing*, which allows investors to buy mutual funds that track the broader market. *Investopedia.*
ii Ray Dalio is the founder, co-Chief Investment Officer and co-Chairman of Bridgewater Associates, which is a global macro investment firm and is the *world's largest hedge fund. LinkedIn.*
iii Laurence Douglas Fink is the Chairman and CEO of BlackRock, an American multinational investment management corporation. BlackRock is the *largest money-management firm in the world* with more than \$6.5 trillion in assets under management. *Wikipedia.*

> . . .*Much of the compensation increase has been fueled by executive stock options.* . . Options are almost universally described as "linking the interests of management to the interests of shareholders." *But the fact is that there is no such linkage.* Rather than holding onto their shares, executives typically sell them at the earliest moment the options can be exercised, too often leaving their shareholders holding the bag.[5]   [Emphases mine]

Jack Bogle makes the following critical points:

1. *Managerial capitalism was run for the benefit of management and an invitation to loot the company,* leading to the meteoric, unjustifiable rise in CEO pay.

2. *Executive stock options allowed this looting to continue when managerial capitalism became shareholder capitalism.* The theory that executive stock options linked interests of management to the interests of the shareholder proved to be wrong. In practice, there was no such link because managers sell their stock the moment the options can be exercised, leaving the shareholders "holding the bag."

The use of executive stock options was even more harmful than this. It led to "predatory value extraction" (discussed in the next section). This encouraged management to raise dividends and/or execute share buybacks with either the company's spare cash flow or, worse still, borrow to distribute money raised to shareholders rather than retaining and reinvesting it in the future of the company.

Ray Dalio:

> Contrary to what populists of the left and populists of the right are saying, these unacceptable outcomes aren't due to either a) evil rich people doing bad things to poor people or b) lazy poor people and bureaucratic inefficiencies, as much as they are due to how the capitalist system is now working. . . As a result of this dynamic, *the system is producing self-reinforcing spirals up for the haves and down for the have-nots, which are leading to harmful excesses at the top and harmful deprivations at the bottom.* More specifically, I believe that:
>
> 1. *The pursuit of profit and greater efficiencies has led to the invention of new technologies that replace people,* which has made companies run more efficiently, rewarded those who invented these technologies, and hurt those who were replaced by them. *This force will accelerate over the next several years, and there is no plan to deal with it well.*
>
> 2. *The pursuit of greater profits and greater company efficiencies has also led companies to produce in other countries and to replace American workers with cost-effective foreign workers, which was good for these companies' profits and efficiencies but bad for the American workers' incomes.* Of course, this globalization also allowed less expensive and perhaps better quality foreign goods to come into the US, which has been *good for both the foreign sellers and the American buyers of them and bad for the American companies and workers who compete with them.*[6]   [Emphases mine]

Ray Dalio makes the following critical points about the implications for the future, if there is no change:
1. The current system will increase inequality.
2. There will be increasing unemployment and no plan exists to deal with it well.
3. The system has been bad for American workers' wages.
4. The system has hurt American producers and those who work for them.

He makes it clear that this can not continue and fundamental reforms are needed if the system is to survive.[7]

Larry Fink:

Larry Fink in his 2019 Letter to CEOs, "A Fundamental Reshaping of Finance," explained why "business as usual" assumptions regarding climate change were no longer possible:

> The money we manage is not our own. It belongs to people in dozens of countries trying to finance long-term goals like retirement. And *we have a deep responsibility to these institutions and individuals – who are shareholders in your company and thousands of others – to promote long-term value. . .*
>
> *Investors are. . .recognizing that climate risk is investment risk. Indeed, climate change is almost invariably the top issue that clients around the world raise with BlackRock. . .* They are seeking to understand both the physical risks associated with climate change as well as the ways that climate policy will impact prices, costs, and demand across the entire economy.
>
> *These questions are driving a profound reassessment of risk and asset values. And because capital markets pull future risk forward, we will see changes in capital allocation more quickly than we see changes to the climate itself. In the near future – and sooner than most anticipate – there will be a significant reallocation of capital.*

Climate Risk Is Investment Risk

> As a fiduciary, our responsibility is to help clients navigate this transition. Our investment conviction is that sustainability- and climate-integrated portfolios can provide better risk-adjusted returns to investors. And with the impact of sustainability on investment returns increasing, we believe that sustainable investing is the strongest foundation for client portfolios going forward.
>
> In a *letter to our clients* today, BlackRock announced a number of initiatives to place sustainability at the center of our investment approach, including: *making sustainability integral to portfolio construction and risk management; exiting investments that present a high sustainability-related risk, such as thermal coal producers; launching new investment products that screen fossil fuels; and strengthening our commitment to sustainability and transparency in our investment stewardship activities. . .*

Under any scenario, the energy transition will still take decades. Despite recent rapid advances, the technology does not yet exist to cost-effectively replace many of today's essential uses of hydrocarbons. We need to be mindful of the economic, scientific, social and political realities of the energy transition. *Governments and the private sector must work together to pursue a transition that is both fair and just – we cannot leave behind parts of society, or entire countries in developing markets, as we pursue the path to a low-carbon world.*

. . .*we signed the Vatican's 2019 statement advocating carbon pricing regimes, which we believe are essential to combating climate change.*

BlackRock has joined with France, Germany, and global foundations to establish the Climate Finance Partnership, which is one of several public-private efforts to improve financing mechanisms for infrastructure investment. The need is particularly urgent for cities, because the *many components of municipal infrastructure – from roads to sewers to transit – have been built for tolerances and weather conditions that do not align with the new climate reality.* In the short term, some of the work to mitigate climate risk could create more economic activity. Yet we are facing the ultimate long-term problem. We don't yet know which predictions about the climate will be most accurate, nor what effects we have failed to consider. But there is no denying the direction we are heading. *Every government, company, and shareholder must confront climate change. . .*

. . . Over the 40 years of my career in finance, I have witnessed a number of financial crises and challenges. . . Even when these episodes lasted for many years, they were all, in the broad scheme of things, short-term in nature. *Climate change is different.* Even if only a fraction of the projected impacts is realized, this is a much more structural, long-term crisis. *Companies, investors, and governments must prepare for a significant reallocation of capital.*

In the discussions BlackRock has with clients around the world, more and more of them are looking to reallocate their capital into sustainable strategies. *If ten percent of global investors do so – or even five percent – we will witness massive capital shifts.* And this dynamic will accelerate as the next generation takes the helm of government and business. . .*as trillions of dollars shift to millennials over the next few decades, as they become CEOs and CIOs, as they become the policymakers and heads of state, they will further reshape the world's approach to sustainability.*

As we approach a period of significant capital reallocation, companies have a responsibility – and an economic imperative – to give shareholders a clear picture of their preparedness.[8]

Larry Fink makes the following critical points:

1. BlackRock has a deep responsibility to promote long-term value as activist investors.[iv]
2. Climate risk is investment risk.
3. Sustainability is at the center of BlackRock's investment approach.
4. The energy transition will take decades.

---

iv BlackRock's passive index funds must follow the market; it is BlackRock's activist investment philosophy that is changing.

5. The transition must be fair and just (Lord Browne made the same point in his 1997 Stanford speech quoted in Chapter 3).
6. Every government, company, and shareholder must confront climate change.
7. Significant reallocations of capital will take place sooner than many expect.
8. Millennials will reshape investment decisions.

Given BlackRock manages $7 trillion of the nearly $80 trillion on the planet,[9] what BlackRock thinks matters.

What seems to have changed, and it is something boards will have to recognize quickly, is that the focus of attention is moving decisively away from shareholders; and stakeholders want action to reform the system now.

Ending "Predatory Value Extraction"[10]

Milton Friedman's 1970 definition of the social responsibility of business has been the basis of the move to maximizing shareholder value (MSV) that occurred in the last forty years. It is worth restating what he wrote, since it seems to argue that businesses are irresponsible if they spend shareholders' money to prevent inflation by not increasing prices, or to reduce pollution beyond the minimum required by law, or to mitigate the effects of unemployment by hiring "hard core unemployed":

> The social responsibility of business is to increase its profits. . .*What does it mean to say that the corporate executive has a "social responsibility" in his capacity as businessman? If this statement is not pure rhetoric, it must mean that he is to act in some way that is not in the interest of his employers.* For example, that he is to refrain from increasing the price of the product in order to contribute to the social objective of preventing inflation, even though a price increase would be in the best interests of the corporation. Or that he is to make expenditures on reducing pollution beyond the amount that is in the best interests of the corporation or that is required by law in order to contribute to the social objective of improving the environment. Or that, at the expense of corporate profits, he is to hire "hardcore" unemployed instead of better qualified available workmen to contribute to the social objective of reducing poverty. *In each of these cases, the corporate executive would be spending someone else's money for a general social interest. Insofar as his actions in accord with his "social responsibility" reduce returns to stockholders, he is spending their money. Insofar as his actions raise the price to customers, he is spending the customers' money. Insofar as his actions lower the wages of some employees, he is spending their money.*[11]   [Emphases mine]

To be fair, Milton Friedman did *not* argue that only the shareholders' money mattered; he made it clear that the customers' and employees' money matter as well. That seems to have been forgotten by those who have used his article to justify that the purpose of business is MSV. He also stipulated that the laws must be obeyed when doing business, but that management had no business going beyond what the law required and become moral arbiters – a view shared by Warren Buffett.[12]

I believe the four sustainability challenges to neoliberal capitalism's survival in the current political environment in Chapters 3–6 are sufficiently serious to invalidate Milton Friedman's central contention that managers who pay attention to stakeholder issues are spending someone else's money. While that may be true of philanthropic CSR, responsible strategizing on behalf of the owners, customers, and employees requires boards and management to engage stakeholders to establish the best routes to long-term sustainability; maintaining the social and political "license to operate," without which, none of their interests are well-served.

I also believe that only obeying the law is not sufficient. Laws lag science and legislators only respond to crises once they have happened. Yet, we know the four sustainability challenges discussed in Chapters 3–6 are either upon us or imminent. Laws have not caught up because of the complicated and time-consuming processes of dealing with vested interests, and the need to overcome ignorance and inertia. I believe that boards (who, in principle, should know better than the general public) therefore have a duty to be at least one step ahead of legislation needed to achieve sustainability. However, this can only be achieved if investors and shareholders stop demanding "predatory value extraction"[13] by boards and management.

Boards have four functions when they set and review strategy:

1. *Avoiding destroying value:* Booz Allen Hamilton found that boards destroy value in three ways: by choosing the wrong strategy (67% of value destruction); by implementing strategy poorly (20% of value destruction); and by failing to comply with regulations (13% of value destruction).[14]

2. *Creating value:* The creation of value, and, in particular, the creation of long-term value is the responsibility of boards. Its significance goes beyond satisfying short-term shareholder expectations. When organizations create sustainable long-term value, they satisfy customers and improve their lives; they give employees good jobs, security and self-respect; they enrich communities in which they operate; they help the economy through the jobs they create in their value and supply chains; and they pay taxes.

3. *Extracting value:* Boards are responsible for ensuring the efficiency and effectiveness of management, lest 20% of potential value is destroyed through incompetence, waste, or inefficiency. The need to ensure that value is created efficiently and effectively is to enable the surplus arising from value-creating strategies to be retained and reinvested in further R&D, market development,

acquisitions, and training and development of employees. These investments are needed to keep the organization competitive and able to adapt to changing conditions. As the Johnson & Johnson *Credo* made clear, the resulting profits need to be retained to pay for the inevitable failures that all successful organizations have:

> Business must make a sound profit. *We must experiment with new ideas. Research must be carried on, innovative programs developed, investments made for the future and mistakes paid for. New equipment must be purchased, new facilities provided and new products launched. Reserves must be created to provide for adverse times.*[15] [Emphasis mine]

The *Credo* then goes on to state:

> When we operate according to these principles, the *stockholders should realize a fair return.*[16]

It specifically states *a fair return*, not a *maximum* return. It also puts shareholders last in terms of priorities and not first.

Instead, as a result of MSV, "extracting value" seems to have been interpreted as a license to maximize the short-term distribution of cash to shareholders and CEOs via dividends, buybacks, and stock options at the expense of sustainability and ignores the need to retain cash to perform R&D, develop innovative programs, invest for the future, pay for mistakes, buy new equipment, launch new products, and have reserves to carry the company through hard times. If shareholders behaved as owners, instead of as speculators who rent stocks to short, they would understand and support the *Credo*. The late Jack Bogle, founder of Vanguard and an icon of investing on behalf of ordinary people, had this to say about shareholders:

> We are a *rent*-a-stock industry, a world away from Warren Buffett's favorite holding period. Forever.
>
> But while a fund that *owns* stocks has little choice but to regard proper corporate governance. One that *rents* stocks could hardly care less.[17]

As renters, shareholders have little interest in the long-term viability of the business. That is only to be expected if the average time shareholders in the US hold a stock is only four months.[18] The fact that banks and fund managers lend their clients' securities to activist investors who are looking to short shares[19] makes these players behave even less like owners. This is a huge market[v] and

---

v Lenders earned $9.16 billion in securities lending revenues in 2016: $4.67 billion in North America; $2.64 billion in Europe; $1.67 billion in Asia Pacific; and $182 million in the rest of

its existence undermines the concept of ownership – essential to good governance and a focus on sustainable value creation.[vi] As a result, activist shareholders mean something quite different when they talk about extracting value:

> Since the late 1970s, *the richest American households have increased their power to extract value that the American working class has helped to create.* This change. . .has manifested itself in an *ever-increasing gap between the growth of labor productivity and the rate of growth of real wages, with wage growth falling further and further behind productivity growth.* . . The prime cause. . .was the abandonment of the 'retain-and-reinvest' regime, in which CWOC ['career-with-one-company'] was rooted, and the transition to the 'downsize-and-distribute' resource allocation regime, characterized by contingent employment relations.
>
> *Under the retain-and-reinvest regime senior executives made corporate resource allocation decisions that, by retaining people and profits within the company, permitted reinvestment in productive capabilities that could generate competitive. . .products.* . . . The retain-and-reinvest regime, combined with the CWOC norm, enabled both white-collar and blue-collar workers to join a growing middle class.[vii] In sharp contrast, *under downsize-and-distribute, a company is prone to downsize its labor force and to distribute to shareholders, in the form of cash dividends and stock buybacks,*[viii] *corporate cash that it might previously have retained.*[20]   [Emphases mine]

4. *Distributing value:* Boards are required to distribute value once it has been created. They can choose between retaining and reinvesting or authorizing the payment of dividends or buying back shares to reward shareholders. Even if they do neither, but retain and reinvest the value, they can still reward patient capital through increased market capitalization, translated into higher share prices. This is the route adopted by some of the tech unicorns. Alternatively, they can choose to change the proportion of the value created that is distributed outside the business, as most boards in the US

---

the world. The value of securities made available for borrowing was $16 trillion, up $2.75 trillion year on year. More than 45,000 unique securities are available for loan worldwide. Walsh, P. (2017), "Global securities lending hits $2 trillion mark," *Global Custodian,* March 13, 2017, https://www.globalcustodian.com/global-securities-lending-hits-2-trillion-mark/.

vi In Chapter 2, family firms were shown to be better at creating sustainable value than companies with dispersed shareholdings.

vii It also provided workers with job security, in-house promotion possibilities, health insurance, and defined benefit pensions.

viii The buybacks in the US have been huge. In the period 2008–2017, S&P 500 corporations have repurchased $4.0 trillion, equal to 53% of net income – on top of the 41% of net income paid in dividends. The benefits went to senior management through their exercising of stock options at times of their choosing and to hedge funds and investment bankers, in the business of influencing stock prices and timing the sale and purchase of stock. Lazonick, W. and Shin, J-S. (2019), op. cit., p. 3.

have done since 1988 when there has been an unprecedented "reallocation of rents" to shareholders at the expense of real value creation:

> From the beginning of 1989 to the end of 2017, 23 trillion dollars of real equity wealth was created by the nonfinancial corporate sector. *We estimate that 54% of this increase was attributable to a reallocation of rents to shareholders in a decelerating economy.* Economic growth accounts for just 24%, followed by lower interest rates (11%) and a lower risk premium (11%). *From 1952 to 1988 less than half as much wealth was created, but economic growth accounted for 92% of it.*[21] [Emphases mine]

So, in the period 1989–2017, "reallocation of rents" represented 54% of equity gains. Only 24% came from economic growth – i.e., new value creation; whereas in the period 1952–1988, 92% of equity gains came from real growth – i.e., new value creation. Only 8% came from a "reallocation of rents."

What this means is that for the stock market to continue to do as well in the coming years, economic growth and real value creation will have to accelerate. Alternatively, CEOs and boards will have to "reallocate rents" even more from workers and other stakeholders to satisfy their shareholders. What does this imply?

> This is likely to require even more downward pressure on wages, more payoffs to politicians for tax cuts and subsidies and further rollbacks of environmental regulations. All of which will worsen the prevailing discontent.,[22]

Let us hope the business leaders at the World Economic Forum in Davos really mean what they say about the need to serve all stakeholders and not just shareholders, and that Milton Friedman's worldview is now outdated.[23] However, Robert Reich, former US Secretary of Labor, might be correct when he wrote:

> Expect endless speeches touting the "long-term" benefits of stakeholder capitalism to corporate bottom lines: happy workers are more productive. A growing middle class can buy more goods and services. Climate change is beginning to cost a bundle in terms of environmental calamities and insurance, so it must be stopped.
>
> *All true, but the assembled CEOs know they'll get richer far quicker if they boost equity values in the short term by buying back their shares of stock, suppressing wages, fighting unions, resisting environmental regulations and buying off politicians for tax cuts and subsidies.*[24] [Emphasis mine]

Embracing a Sustainable Purpose

Creating a sustainable purpose requires business to become part of the solution, rather than continuing to be part of the problem by lobbying against sustainability. Delaying solving the four sustainability challenges does not only increase the cost of doing so, it could also precipitate a "political tragedy of the commons." A key part in changing attitudes at the board level and among investors is to actively re-verse policies of "predatory value extraction." Finally, improving disclosure will make it easier for investors to see which companies are making progress and should be helped in their journey; and which are not, and should not be supported.

Businesses Becoming Part of the Solution

Given the past emphasis in company law on the primacy of shareholders, it should not surprise us that boards have focused on shareholder value only. Judgments in the Delaware Chancery made it almost impossible for directors to do otherwise:

> Having chosen a for-profit corporate form . . . directors are bound by the fiduciary duties and standards that accompany that form. *Those standards include acting to promote the value of the corporation for the benefit of the stockholders.* The "Inc." after the company name has to mean at least that. *Thus, I cannot accept as valid . . . a corporate policy that specifically, clearly and admittedly seeks not to maximize the economic value of a for-profit Delaware corporation for the benefit of its stockholders. . .*[25]   [Emphasis mine]

As a result, companies have adopted policies that ignored the needs of other stakeholders. They have lobbied extensively to roll back environmental protection regulations in the name of economic growth and increased shareholder value, ignoring the potential harm to communities that could result from increased pollution[26] and reduced water availability.[ix,27] They have worked successfully to challenge the science behind climate change. As a result, mitigating actions which could have been taken as early as 1965, when President Lyndon Johnson was warned of the consequences of climate change by the American Association for the Advancement of Science, have still to be implemented in 2020:

> *Pollutants have altered on a global scale the carbon dioxide content of the air* and the lead concentrations in ocean waters and human populations. . .
> Through his worldwide industrial civilization, Man is unwittingly conducting a vast geophysical experiment. Within a few generations he is burning the fossil fuels that slowly accumulated in the earth over the past 500 million years . . . *The climatic changes that may be produced by the increased CO_2 content could be deleterious from the point of view of human beings.* The possibilities of deliberately bringing about countervailing climatic changes therefore need to be thoroughly explored.[28]   [Emphases mine]

---

ix In Nestlé's case the extraction of water from California's Strawberry Creek left it bone dry, adding to pollution because the water was sold in single use plastic bottles.

Exxon knew what would happen if industry continued to rely on fossil fuels for energy.[29] The Koch brothers began their successful program of denial and delay to cripple government action on climate change as early as 1991.[30] The remedial costs, which taxpayers and communities will have to bear, if remediation is possible, are now much higher as a result of delays that only benefited shareholders.

Such behavior is understandable, given the legal primacy of shareholders and the belief that the purpose of business is to maximize shareholder value. It is reinforced by board inertia and uncertainty in making complicated decisions. However, sustainability time horizons are now shortening, so decisions can no longer be delayed in the same way as before.

As far as the environment is concerned, this is in part a result of changes in regulatory and public concerns regarding climate change and conservation. As Larry Fink made clear in his 2019 Letter to CEOs, "capital markets pull future risk forward" and they are being pressured to do so even faster by central banks. It is also the result of heightened public awareness[31] of environmental issues. This awareness has been translated into activist behavior in Austria, Germany, New Zealand, and the UK[32] that may force boards to pay attention now and stop delaying.

As far as the sustainability of the economy is concerned, the discontent is a clear and present danger with uprisings in countries as diverse as Bolivia, Brazil, Chile, Ecuador, Egypt, France, Lebanon, and Spain, and the rise of xenophobic politics in Hungary, the UK, and the US. The forecasts (discussed in Chapter 5) regarding the impact of automation and AI suggest that the window in which to take effective action is only ten years.

Boards have to start acting now to help their organizations become part of the solution as opposed to continuing to be part of the problem. They can do this by adopting a proactive approach to VUCA (discussed in Chapter 9); by developing new processes designed to meet the four sustainability challenges (covered in Chapter 10); and in valuing people properly (explored in Chapter 11). But, above all, they must reverse the practice of "predatory value extraction." For that to happen, company law must change first.

Reversing "Predatory Value Extraction"

"Predatory value extraction,"[33] since the mid-1980s, has led to a practice of "downsize-and-distribute" with unfortunate effects on employability, income distribution, and productivity. Some have argued that the Boeing 737 MAX disasters were the result of the change from Boeing being a great engineering firm, focused on building great aircraft; to being run as a business focused on maximizing shareholder value:

> Indeed, some go so far as to blame the mistakes that led to the 737 Max disasters on GE-style focus on managerial efficiency ("bean-counting" to its critics) that infused Boeing as a result of the McDonnell Douglas tie-up, ending a long period of dominance by Boeing's engineers. . .
>
> Taking a cue from Mr Welch, in 2001 Boeing moved its headquarters from Seattle to Chicago, putting distance between the suits in the C-suite and the engineers. As Mr Stonecipher put it in 2004: "When people say I changed the culture of Boeing, that was the intent, so it's run like a business rather than a great engineering firm." Shareholders loved it. Over the 15 years since, Richard Abaloufia of the Teal Group, an aviation consultancy, says $78bn was returned to shareholders, doing wonders for Boeing's share price. But in the process, engineers' input into decision-making was relegated, which may have contributed to the 737 Max's tragic design flaws. "The seeds of the Max disaster were planted years ago," he wrote recently.[34]   [Emphases mine]

As part of reforming neoliberal capitalism, boards need to bring value creation and value extraction back into balance to lay the foundations for sustainable growth.[35] Key to redressing the balance is the need to redesign CEO remuneration. The problem with the current approach is that stock-based pay rewards value extraction, not value creation:[36]

> U.S.-style stock options, therefore, provide incentives to executives to take advantage of what they think may be short-term surges in the company's stock price. And stock buybacks, the timing of the exercise of which these executives control, are an ideal mode of making these surges happen. By design, U.S.-style executive stock options incentivize value extraction, not value creation.
>
> So too with stock awards.[37]   [Emphases mine]

The justification for rewarding CEOs with stock is that this will reward them for performance aligned with the interests of shareholders. However, the evidence is that there is no clear link between CEO remuneration and performance.

> Research into CEO pay shows that total shareholder return (TSR) is, by far, the most dominant performance metric. . . Yet, increased TSR often has little to do with CEO effort or actually growing a business for the long term. . . TSR is easily gamed through cost-cutting measures. . ., reducing R&D, stock buybacks, or financial engineering. In contrast, developing new products, training staff, and increasing sales take more creativity and may take years to bear fruit. Researchers found that economic performance explains only 12 percent of variance in CEO pay, whereas more than 60 percent is explained by company size, industry, and existing company pay policy. None of those other measures are performance driven.[38]   [Emphases mine]

Perhaps a better approach to measuring the performance of the CEO[39] would be to provide a "line of sight" to future value creation, with remuneration based on how well this is done. This forces the CEO and senior management to consider investing in process innovation, developing breakthrough new products, entering brand new markets, creating new business models, working in new industries and ecosystems, and investing new sources of capital (rather than buying back shares to improve the value of options).

This can be broken down into targeted levels of CEO performance for the board to evaluate in terms of creating current value (CV) and future value (FV).

CV creation consists of everyday "situational work" measuring improvement in revenue, margins, costs, TQM (total quality management), and manufacturing efficiencies on a quarterly and annual basis. CV creation also includes medium-term "systemic work" measuring improvements year-on-year from *existing customers* in revenue and margin growth, and profitability improvements achieved through strategic initiatives in innovation as part of the annual budgeting process (shown in Figure 12.1).

FV creation provides the metrics of long-term value creation, divided into three different time horizons:

a) ***Three–five years, where the CEO is assessed on progress made in "breakthrough work":*** This covers the portfolio of products and services and improvements in three–five-year revenue, margin, EBIT, and ROIC arising from new products, markets, technologies, and channels from *new customers*.

b) ***Five-year evaluation of the CEO's "transformational work" on the business model:*** This reviews the five-year growth in revenue, ROIC exceeding 8% and how relative P/E has performed, as a result of the long-range strategy and the implementation of innovation.

c) ***Seven-year perspective for "global transformation work" covering changes in the business portfolio,*** and their impact on portfolio revenue growth, ROIC, CV and FV growth in the light of industry and eco-system transformation.[40]

Figure 12.1 shows how CV and FV creation are linked by strategies and how the long-range goals cascade down to quarterly results to provide a short-term and long-term evaluation framework for the CEO, which still applies should the CEO depart unexpectedly.

Applying a framework of this type[41] to CEO remuneration would go a long way to reversing "predatory value extraction." As long as company law insists on shareholder primacy from directors, as it does in the US,[42] directors will find it difficult to implement the August 2019 US Business Roundtable Declaration, and move away from maximizing shareholder value. In the US they could be risking shareholder class actions unless Delaware law is changed.

Goal-setting
cascade linking
long-term plans
to quarterly
results

"Global transformational work" on business porfolio measuring:
7 year change in portfolio revenue growth, ROIC, P/E, CV/FV $ growth,
business portfolio, industry structure and ecosystem transformation

"Transformational work" on business model measuring:
Relative 5 year revenue growth, ROIC>8% and relative P/E through
business strategy and new business model measuring:

"Breakthrough work" on product/service portfolio measuring:
3–5 year revenue growth, EBIT, margin, NOPAT, ROIC growth from *new*
products, markets, technologies, channels and product portfolio strategy

"Systemic work" on core business processes measuring:
Year on year revenue growth, margin, NOPAT, economic profit through end-
to-end process innovation for *existing* products, markets and customers

"Situational work" on continuous improvement measuring:
Quarter on quarter and annual improvement in revenue, costs, margins
achieved through TQM, "lean" manufacturing, "kaizen", zero-based budgets

CEO
Work
Level 5

CEO
Work
Level 4

CEO
WORK
Level 3

CEO
Work
Level 2

CEO
Work
Level 1

FV creation

CV creation

**"Line of sight"
strategies
linking CV to
FV creation**

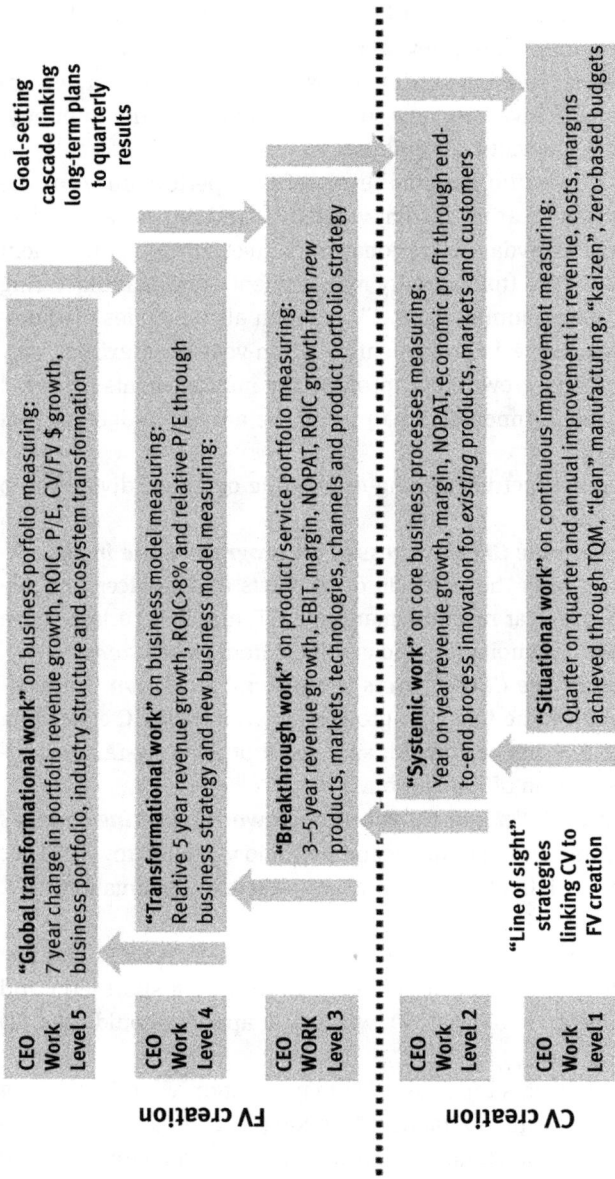

Figure 12.1: "Line of sight" linking CV and FV creation.

Improving Disclosure for Stakeholders

There are two ways companies must improve their disclosure to stakeholders according to Larry Fink. The first is to articulate clearly the long-term purpose and the contribution to society of the organization and the second is disclose what they are trying to do regarding sustainability.

1. ***Articulating the social purpose of the company:*** Larry Fink in his 2018 Letter to CEOs emphasizes the focus BlackRock places on understanding the social purpose and plans to achieve it of companies in whom they invest:

    Society is demanding that companies, both public and private, serve a social purpose. To prosper over time, every company must not only deliver financial performance, but also show how it makes a positive contribution to society. Companies must benefit all of their stakeholders, including shareholders, employees, customers, and the communities in which they operate.

    Without a sense of purpose, no company, either public or private, can achieve its full potential. It will ultimately lose the license to operate from key stakeholders. *It will succumb to short-term pressures to distribute earnings, and, in the process, sacrifice investments in employee development, innovation, and capital expenditures that are necessary for long-term growth. It will remain exposed to activist campaigns that articulate a clearer goal, even if that goal serves only the shortest and narrowest of objectives. And ultimately, that company will provide subpar returns to the investors who depend on it to finance their retirement, home purchases, or higher education. . .*

    Companies have been too focused on quarterly results; similarly, shareholder engagement has been too focused on annual meetings and proxy votes. If engagement is to be meaningful and productive. . .then engagement needs to be a *year-round conversation about improving long-term value. . .*

    In order to make engagement with shareholders as productive as possible, companies must be able to describe their strategy for long-term growth. *I want to reiterate our request, outlined in past letters, that you publicly articulate your company's strategic framework for long-term value creation and explicitly affirm that it has been reviewed by your board of directors. . .*

    The statement of long-term strategy is essential to understanding a company's actions and policies, its preparation for potential challenges, and the context of its shorter-term decisions. Your company's strategy must articulate a path to achieve financial performance. To sustain that performance, however, *you must also understand the societal impact of your business as well as the ways that broad, structural trends – from slow wage growth to rising automation to climate change – affect your potential for growth. . .*

    Boards meet only periodically, but their responsibility is continuous. *Directors whose knowledge is derived only from sporadic meetings are not fulfilling their duty to shareholders. Likewise, executives who view boards as a nuisance only undermine themselves and the company's prospects for long-term growth. . .*

    Companies must ask themselves: What role do we play in the community? How are we managing our impact on the environment? Are we working to create a diverse workforce? Are we adapting to technological change? Are we providing the retraining and opportunities that our employees and our business will need to adjust to an increasingly automated world? Are we using behavioral finance and other tools to prepare workers for retirement, so that they invest in a way that that will help them achieve their goals?

. . . Today, our clients – who are your company's owners – are asking you to demonstrate the leadership and clarity that will drive not only their own investment returns, but also the prosperity and security of their fellow citizens.[43]

2. ***Stakeholder disclosures regarding broad sustainability-related questions:*** Larry Fink in his 2020 Letter to CEOs explains the importance BlackRock places on improving disclosure for stakeholders; and that directors who do not address how they plan to achieve any of a broad array of business, social and environmental sustainability material issues, in their disclosures, should be held accountable:

> We believe that *all investors, along with regulators, insurers, and the public, need a clearer picture of how companies are managing sustainability-related questions.* This data should extend beyond climate to questions around how each company serves its full set of stakeholders, such as the diversity of its workforce, the sustainability of its supply chain, or how well it protects its customers' data. *Each company's prospects for growth are inextricable from its ability to operate sustainably and serve its full set of stakeholders.*
>
> *The importance of serving stakeholders and embracing purpose is becoming increasingly central to the way that companies understand their role in society. . .a* company cannot achieve long-term profits without embracing purpose and considering the needs of a broad range of stakeholders. . .By contrast, a strong sense of purpose and a commitment to stakeholders helps a company connect more deeply to its customers and adjust to the changing demands of society. *Ultimately, purpose is the engine of long-term profitability.*
>
> *Over time, companies and countries that do not respond to stakeholders and address sustainability risks will encounter growing skepticism from the markets, and in turn, a higher cost of capital. Companies and countries that champion transparency and demonstrate their responsiveness to stakeholders, by contrast, will attract investment more effectively, including higher-quality, more patient capital.*
>
> Important progress improving disclosure has already been made – and many companies already do an exemplary job of integrating and reporting on sustainability – but we need to achieve more widespread and standardized adoption. While no framework is perfect, BlackRock believes that the Sustainability Accounting Standards Board (SASB) provides a clear set of standards for reporting sustainability information across a wide range of issues, from labor practices to data privacy to business ethics. For evaluating and reporting climate-related risks, as well as the related governance issues that are essential to managing them, the TCFD [Task Force on Climate-related Financial Disclosures] provides a valuable framework. . .
>
> We will use these disclosures and our engagements to ascertain whether

companies are properly managing and overseeing these risks within their business and adequately planning for the future. In the absence of robust disclosures, investors, including BlackRock, will increasingly conclude that companies are not adequately managing risk.

We believe that when a company is not effectively addressing a material issue, its directors should be held accountable. . .[44]   [Emphases mine]

Summary

The findings of the 2020 Edelman Trust Barometer demonstrate a worrying collapse in public trust and belief in the current economic system. Majorities in rich countries worry about job losses; feel they have lost self-respect and dignity; fear that "fake news" will be use as weapon; and fear they are no longer in control of their destiny because of the pace of change. Trust has for the first time become decoupled from GDP growth because of rising inequality which has become the determining factor in trust in institutions.

The late Jack Bogle, Ray Dalio, and Larry Fink – three of the most successful capitalists since World War II – have expressed their serious worries about the sustainability of the economic system, given this level of public discontent with the way the system fails to deliver benefits to the many rather than the few. Reading what they have to say, it is clear that urgent reform of the economic system is needed to avert a social and "political tragedy of the commons."

Bogle focused on the problems created by a system where capitalism allowed managers to loot companies for their own benefit. Dalio worries that the existing system will increase inequality further, increase unemployment, and be bad for American workers' wages – and that this presents a danger to the system. Fink argues that climate change is real. The transition to sustainable energy will take decades and needs to be fair and just. Every company and government must develop sustainable climate change plans now, because climate risk is investment risk and once capital markets understand this, they bring the future forward, reallocating capital much faster than boards expect.

Meaningful reform can only be achieved if boards embrace a sustainable purpose by ending "predatory value extraction" and cease their "divest-and-distribute" practices, that benefit only short-term shareholders with a "rent-a-stock" mentality. Reversing "predatory value extraction" will only occur if open market purchases of stock are stopped as these reward unsustainable practices by management; if CEO remuneration is no longer primarily based on stock-based pay awards; and if company law is changed. Businesses must become part of the solution rather than continuing to be part of the problem by delaying policies designed to meet the four sustainability challenges. Boards will only do that if company law is changed to recognize the importance of reconciling stakeholder interests rather than just focusing on shareholder primacy.

Finally, as Larry Fink makes clear in his 2018 Letter to CEOs, disclosure for stakeholders must be improved with companies clearly articulating their social purpose and their sustainability targets, action plans, progress against those plans, and remedial action. BlackRock will hold boards accountable for proper disclosure and progress in achieving their declared objectives.

If, in addition, boards take the time and trouble to deal with VUCA proactively; develop new processes to meet the environmental, economic, employment, and social sustainability challenges; and value people properly; then CG may be able to avert a possible social and "political tragedy of the commons."

References

1 Reich, R. (2020), "Trump is on trial for abuse of power – the Davos elites should be in the dock too," *The Guardian,* January 19, 2020, https://www.theguardian.com/commentisfree/2020/jan/19/donald-trump-impeachment-trial-abuse-power-davos, accessed on January 19, 2020.
2 Nikkei Staff Writers (2020), " System glitches: Capitalism shows its age in the digital era," *Nikkei Asian Review,* January 1, 2020, https://asia.nikkei.com/Spotlight/Neo-Capitalism/System-glitches-Capitalism-shows-its-age-in-the-digital-era?utm_campaign=RN%20Free%20newsletter, accessed on January 1, 2020.
3 Edelman, R. (2020), "The Evolution of Trust," *2020 Edelman Trust Barometer,* Edelman Intelligence, p. 2, https://www.edelman.com/sites/g/files/aatuss191/files/2020-01/2020%20Edelman%20Trust%20Barometer%20Executive%20Summary_Single%20Spread%2, accessed on January 21, 2020.
4 Ferguson, N. (2019), "'Don't be the villain': Niall Ferguson looks forward and back at capitalism in crisis," *McKinsey Quarterly,* November 2019, https://www.mckinsey.com/featured-insights/long-term-capitalism/dont-be-the-villain-niall-ferguson-looks-forward-and-back-at-capitalism-in-crisis, accessed on January 21, 2020.
5 Bogle, J. (2003),"Owners Capitalism vs Managers Capitalism," Speech given to the 2003 National Investor Relations Conference, Orlando, Florida, June 11, 2003, *Bogle Financial Center,* https://www.vanguard.com/bogle_site/sp20030611.html, accessed on August 7, 2019
6 Dalio, R. (2019), "Why and How Capitalism Needs To Be Reformed," LinkedIn, April 5, 2019.
7 Ibid.
8 Fink, L. (2020), "A Fundamental Reshaping of Finance," *2019 Letter to CEOs,* BlackRock, January 16, 2020, https://www.blackrock.com/us/individual/larry-fink-ceo-letter, accessed on January 20, 2020.
9 McKibben, B. (2020), "Citing Climate Change, BlackRock Will Start Moving Away From Fossil Fuels," *The New Yorker,* January 16, 2020, https://www.newyorker.com/news/daily-comment/citing-climate-change-blackrock-will-start-moving-away-from-fossil-fuels, accessed on January 19, 2020.

10 Lazonick, W. and Shin, J.-S. (2019), *Predatory Value Extraction: How the Looting of the Business Corporation Became the Norm in the U.S. and How Sustainable Prosperity Can Be Restored* (Oxford: Oxford University Press).

11 Friedman, M. (1970), "The Social Responsibility of Business is to Increase Profits," *New York Times Magazine,* September 13, 1970, http://umich.edu/~thecore/doc/Friedman.pdf, accessed on August 8, 2019.

12 Armstrong, R. (2019), "Warren Buffett on why companies cannot be moral arbiters," *The Financial Times,* December 19, 2019, https://www.ft.com/content/ebbc9b46-1754-11ea-9ee4-11f260415385, accessed on January 7, 2020.

13 Lazonick, W. and Shin, J.-S. (2019), op. cit.

14 Booz Allen Hamilton (2004), *Too Much SOX Can Kill You: Resolving the Compliance Paradox,* cited in Zinkin, J. (2010), *Rebuilding Trust in Banks: The Role of Leadership and Governance* (Singapore: John Wiley & Sons), p. 131.

15 Johnson, R. W. (1943), "Our Credo," *Johnson & Johnson website,* https://www.jnj.com/credo/, accessed on December 8, 2019.

16 Ibid.

17 Bogle, J. (2003), op. cit.

18 Fiske, W. (2016), "Mark Warner says average holding time for stocks has fallen to four months," *Politifact,* July 6, 2016, https://www.politifact.com/virginia/statements/2016/jul/06/mark-warner/mark-warner-says-average-holding-time-stocks-has-f/, accessed on January 18, 2020.

19 Walsh, P. (2017), "Global securities lending hits $2 trillion mark," *Global Custodian,* March 13, 2017, https://www.globalcustodian.com/global-securities-lending-hits-2-trillion-mark/, accessed on January 19, 2020.

20 Lazonick, W. and Shin, J.-S. (2019), op. cit., pp. 2–3.

21 Greenwald, D. L. et al. (2019), "How the Wealth Was Won: Factor Shares as Market Fundamentals," NBER *Working Paper* No. 25769, May 2019 (Cambridge, Mass: National Bureau of Economic Research), https://www.nber.org/papers/w25769, accessed on January 19, 2020.

22 Reich, R. (2020), op. cit.

23 Orszag, P. (2020), "Milton Friedman's World Is Dead and Gone," *Bloomberg Opinion,* January 29, 2020, https://www.bloomberg.com/opinion/articles/2020-01-29/tell-davos-that-milton-friedman-s-world-is-dead-and-gone?utm_medium=email&utm_source=n, accessed on February 3, 2020.

24 Ibid.

25 Chandler III, W. (2010), *eBay Domestic Holdings, Inc. v. Newmark,* 16 A.3d 1, 34 (Del. Ch. 2010), quoted in Atkins, P. et al. (2019), op. cit.

26 Marsh, R. (2019), "Trump EPA set to officially roll back Obama clean water regulation," *CNN politics,* September 11, 2019, https://edition.cnn.com/2019/09/11/politics/epa-water-wotus/index.html, accessed on January 20, 2020.

27 Perkins, T. (2019), "The fight to stop Nestlé from taking America's water to sell in plastic bottles," *The Guardian,* October 29, 2019, https://www.theguardian.com/environment/2019/oct/29/the-fight-over-water-how-nestle-dries-up-us-creeks-to-sell-water-in-plastic-bottles, accessed on January 20, 2020.

28 "Restoring the Quality of Our Environment," report by the *American Association Advancement for the Advancement of Science,* quoted in Nuccitelli, D. (2015), "Scientists warned the US President about global warming 50 years ago today," https://www.businessinsider.com/scientists-warned-the-us-president-about-global-warming-50-years-ago-2015-11?IR=T, accessed on January 20, 2020.

29 Hall, S. (2015), "Exxon Knew about Climate Change almost forty years ago," *Scientific American,* October 26, 2015, https://www.scientificamerican.com/article/exxon-knew-about-climate-change-almost-40-years-ago/, accessed on January 20, 2020.
30 Mayer, J. (2019), "'Kochland' Examines The Koch Brothers' Early, Crucial Role In Climate-Change Denial," *The New Yorker,* August 13, 2019, https://www.newyorker.com/news/daily-comment/kochland-examines-how-the-koch-brothers-made-their-fortune-and-the-influence-it-bought, accessed on January 20, 2020.
31 Reich, R. (2020), op. cit.
32 Ibid.
33 Lazonick, W. and Shin, J-S. (2019), op. cit., pp. 193–206.
34 Schumpeter (2020), "The last GE Man," *The Economist,* January 11, 2020, https://www.economist.com/business/2020/01/11/the-last-ge-man, accessed on January 11, 2020.
35 Ibid., p. 192.
36 Ibid., p. 196.
37 Ibid., p. 197.
38 McRitchie, J. (2016), "The Individual's Role in Driving Corporate Governance," quoted in *The Handbook of Corporate Governance*, op. cit., p. 433.
39 Zinkin, J. (2019), *Better Governance Across the Board: Creating Value Through Reputation, People and Processes* (Boston/Berlin: Walter De Gruyter Inc.), pp. 229–235.
40 Van Clieaf, M. (2016), "Designing Performance for Long-Term Value," quoted in *The Handbook of Corporate Governance*, op. cit., p. 520, cited in Zinkin, J. (2019), op. cit., p. 234.
41 Based on ibid., p. 527, cited in Zinkin, J. (2019), op. cit., pp. 234–235.
42 Chandler III, W. (2010), *eBay Domestic Holdings, Inc. v. Newmark*, 16 A.3d 1, 34 (Del. Ch. 2010), quoted in Atkins, P. et al. (2019), "Social Responsibility and Enlightened Shareholder Primacy: Views From the Courtroom and Boardroom," *Skadden,* February 4, 2020.
43 Fink, L. (2018), "A Sense of Purpose," *2018 Letter to CEOs,* BlackRock, January 17, 2018, https://www.blackrock.com/corporate/investor-relations/2018-larry-fink-ceo-letter, accessed on January 20, 2020.
44 Fink, L. (2020), op. cit.

Appendix A: Setting KPIs and Targets Using a Ten-Step Process

Setting KPIs and targets is a critical responsibility of boards. The suggested ten-step process below may be helpful.[1]

Step 1 is for the board to determine its beneficiaries and stakeholders, what difference in their lives will our organization make, what value will they place on that difference, how much will it cost to deliver it, and how will we know we have succeeded?

Step 2 is to translate these beneficiary-stakeholder expectations into strategic objectives designed to meet each set of beneficiary-stakeholders.[i]

Step 3 is to develop a "success map":

> A success map is a visual tool that shows how lower level objectives link to higher level strategic objectives. It is a powerful communication tool that explains "what" is to be achieved and "why." It also shows where each part of the organisation contributes to achieving these goals.[2]

Figure A.1 illustrates a "success map." Starting from the top, it links the organization's mission and vision to its overriding business objectives via "purpose." This is where the first two steps of the process for setting KPIs and targets are taken care of.

The overriding business objective is then broken out into its component parts for each element of the value chain, to be translated into subordinate business objectives which support and reinforce the overriding business objective. The resulting mini-strategies are developed for each element of the value chain using the "Five P" framework's "principles," "power," "people," and "processes" to show what needs to be done and why and, as important, by whom and by when.

---

i This step is critical because, when done properly, it allows the board and management to determine whether a proposed project is within the boundaries set by the agreed strategies – allowing management to devote focused time and attention to doing what they are supposed to be doing rather than chasing after every attractive opportunity and ending up spreading their time and attention too thinly to be effective.

https://doi.org/10.1515/9783110670486-013

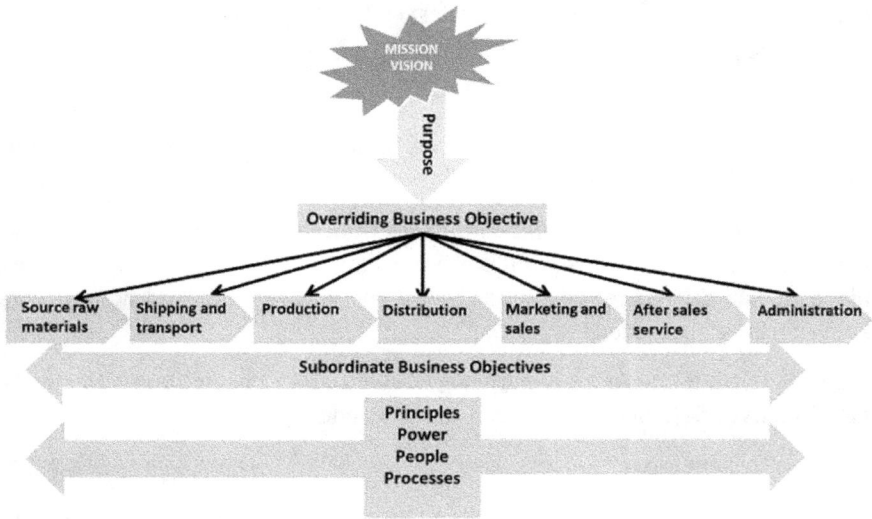

Figure A.1: Success map.[3]

Steps 4–10 are taken care of in processes created by using the four lenses of the "Five P" framework to define the priorities, allocate resources, and define with the people involved suitable milestones, due dates, and accountabilities.

Step 4 is where priorities are defined so employees can focus on what is most important. Too few priorities, and work becomes dull and routine; too many, and managers no longer know which priorities matter. The most appropriate number of priorities any one individual can handle effectively is supposed to be seven:[4]

Why seven? If people are given too few challenges, there won't be enough variety in their work to stimulate creativity. If people are given too many challenges, they quickly suffer from overload. Seven falls between these two extremes. And think of all the things in our lives that are configured in sevens: phone numbers, the days of the week, the musical scale. The number seems to contain just the right amount of information for people to remember and process effectively.[5]

Step 5 is when the KPIs are set to "operationalize" the processes:

This means designing appropriate performance measures. How you define the measure will drive behavior. So KPIs must reflect the organisation's goals and encourage the right behavior from those responsible for delivering the goals.[6]

Step 6 is the collection of timely and relevant data on which to base targets. This is often overlooked.

Step 7 is data analysis:

> You have to draw on your knowledge of the past and of the future to project what is going to happen. You also have to analyse the capability of your processes. Are the processes capable of delivering the forecast? *Most companies forecast, but fewer reassess their capabilities.*[7]   [Emphasis mine]

Step 8 is when targets are set.

Step 9 is developing the action plan with input from those who will have to deliver it, as opposed to handing it down from on high. This may require training/retraining of employees, new IT systems to track progress, and developing new ways of working with customers. In every instance, it is critical to have worked with the people who will make it happen to understand where the barriers are and whether they are obstacles, resolved by allocating resources accordingly; or they are objections, which require changing mindsets and persuading vested interests:

> Managers who must lead the implementation of observed best practices may resist practices that shift decision-making authority or greater autonomy into the hands of teams or lower level employees . . . "If we adopt this practice," they may tell themselves, "then I will become less important." Machiavelli may have said it best when he wrote that "The reformer has enemies in all those who profit from the old order," that is, current practices.[8]

Step 10 is continuous communication to all who are involved to remind them of the objectives and why they matter, to advise them of progress toward meeting those objectives and what still needs to be done, by whom, and by when.

References

1 Based on Cranfield School of Management (2012), "How to Set the Right Performance Targets: A Ten Step Target Setting Tool," published by Association of International Certified Professional Accountants, joint venture of American Institute of CPAs, New York and Chartered Institute of

Management Accountants, London, https://www.cgma.org/content/dam/cgma/resources/tools/ downloadabledocuments/target-setting-tool.pdf, accessed on September 23, 2018.

2 Ibid., p. 2.

3 Based on Zinkin, J. (2015), "Performance Driven Leadership," Star Newspaper Senior Management Program, Kuala Lumpur, September 1, 2015.

4 Miller, G. A. (1956), "The Magic Number Seven, Plus or Minus Two: Some Limits on Our Capacity for Processing Information," *The Psychological Review*, Vol. 63, No. 2, 1956, pp. 81–97, cited in Simons, R. and Davila, A. (1998), "How High is Your Return on Management?" *Harvard Business Review*, "Measuring Corporate Performance," p. 86.

5 Simons, R. and Davila, A. (1998), op. cit., pp. 86.

6 Cranfield School of Management (2012), op. cit., p. 2.

7 Ibid., p. 3.

8 Matheson, D. and Matheson, J. (1998), *The Smart Organization: Creating Value Through Strategic R&D*, (Boston, MA: Harvard Business School Press), p. 83.

Index

https://doi.org/10.1515/9783110670486-014

www.ingramcontent.com/pod-product-compliance
Lightning Source LLC
Chambersburg PA
CBHW060023030426
42334CB00019B/2161